THE AFRICAN HERITAGE OF LATINX AND CARIBBEAN LITERATURE

The African Heritage of Latinx and Caribbean Literature unearths a buried African archive within the most prominent writers of Latin American descent in the last fifty years. It challenges dominant narratives in World Literature and transatlantic studies that ignore Africa's impact on broader Latin American culture. Sarah M. Quesada argues that these canonical works evoke textual memorials of African memory. She shows how the African Atlantic haunts modern Latinx and Caribbean writing and examines the disavowal or distortion of the African subject in the constructions of national, racial, sexual, and spiritual Latin American identity. Quesada shows how themes such as the nineteenth-century "scramble for Africa," the Cold War-era decolonizing wars, Black internationalism, and the neoliberal turn are embedded in key narratives. Drawing on multilingual archives about West and Central Africa, she examines how the legacies of colonial French, Iberian, British, and US imperialisms in Africa have impacted the relationships between African and mainly Latinx identities. This is the first book-length project to address the African colonial and imperial inheritance of Latinx literature.

SARAH M. QUESADA is Assistant Professor of Romance Studies at Duke University.

CAMBRIDGE STUDIES IN WORLD LITERATURE

Editor
Debjani Ganguly, University of Virginia
Francesca Orsini, SOAS University of London

World Literature is a vital part of twenty-first-century critical studies. Globalization, and unprecedented levels of connectivity through communication technologies, force literary scholars to rethink the scale of literary production, and their own critical practices. As an exciting field that engages seriously with the place and function of literary studies in our global era, the study of World literature requires new approaches. Cambridge Studies in World Literature is founded on the assumption that World Literature is not all literatures of the world nor a canonical set of globally successful literary works. The series will highlight scholarship on literary works that focus on the logics of circulation drawn from multiple literary cultures and technologies of the textual. While not rejecting the nation as a site of analysis, the series will offer insights into new cartographies – the hemispheric, the oceanic, the transregional, the archipelagic, the multi-lingual local – that better reflect the multi-scalar and spatially dispersed nature of literary production. It will highlight the creative co-existence, flashpoints and intersections, of language worlds from both the global south and the global north, and multi-world models of literary production and literary criticism that these have generated. It will push against existing historical, methodological and cartographic boundaries, and showcase humanistic and literary endeavors in the face of world scale environmental and humanitarian catastrophes.

In This Series

Roanne L. Kantor
South Asian Writers, Latin American Literature, and the Rise of Global English

Sarah M. Quesada
The African Heritage of Latinx and Caribbean Literature

Levi Thompson
Re-Orienting Modernism: Mapping a Modernist Geography Across Arabic and Persian Poetry

THE AFRICAN HERITAGE OF LATINX AND CARIBBEAN LITERATURE

SARAH M. QUESADA
Duke University

Shaftesbury Road, Cambridge CB2 8EA, United Kingdom

One Liberty Plaza, 20th Floor, New York, NY 10006, USA

477 Williamstown Road, Port Melbourne, VIC 3207, Australia

314–321, 3rd Floor, Plot 3, Splendor Forum, Jasola District Centre, New Delhi – 110025, India

103 Penang Road, #05–06/07, Visioncrest Commercial, Singapore 238467

Cambridge University Press is part of Cambridge University Press & Assessment, a department of the University of Cambridge.

We share the University's mission to contribute to society through the pursuit of education, learning and research at the highest international levels of excellence.

www.cambridge.org
Information on this title: www.cambridge.org/9781009078139

DOI: 10.1017/9781009086806

© Sarah M. Quesada 2022

This publication is in copyright. Subject to statutory exception and to the provisions of relevant collective licensing agreements, no reproduction of any part may take place without the written permission of Cambridge University Press & Assessment.

First published 2022
First paperback edition 2025

A catalogue record for this publication is available from the British Library

ISBN 978-1-316-51435-1 Hardback
ISBN 978-1-009-07813-9 Paperback

Cambridge University Press & Assessment has no responsibility for the persistence or accuracy of URLs for external or third-party internet websites referred to in this publication and does not guarantee that any content on such websites is, or will remain, accurate or appropriate.

Contents

List of Illustrations	*page* vi
Acknowledgments	viii
Introduction: Textual Memorials of a Latin-African Literature	1
1 Fear: Junot Díaz's Zombies and *Les contorsions extraordinaires* in "Monstro"	33
2 Commodification: Black Internationalism and the African Safari of Achy Obejas's *Ruins*	76
3 Obliteration: Gabriel García Márquez and His Angolan Chronicles of a "Latin-African" Death Foretold	117
4 Archival Distortion: The Chicano Congo of Tomás Rivera and Rudolfo Anaya	160
Coda	205
Notes	221
Bibliography	252
Index	280

Illustrations

0.1	Gorée, Senegal's *Maison des esclaves* and "The Door of No Return." Photo: Sarah M. Quesada, 2012.	*page* 25
1.1	"Mémoire sur le Fort de Juda (Côte d'Áfrique)." Ministère des Colonies et de la marine et des colonies. 1763. Archives Nationales (DOM-TOM), Aix-en-Provence, France. Photo: Sarah M. Quesada, 2017.	51
1.2	"Port de Non-Retour." UNESCO, Ouidah, Republic of Benin. Photo: Sarah M. Quesada, 2012.	53
1.3	Ouidah's Slave Route memorial trail, Benin. Photo: Sarah M. Quesada, 2012.	58
1.4	Along Ouidah's route, guides stop at this shrub that commemorates the "Tree of Forgetfulness." Photo: Sarah M. Quesada, 2012.	60
2.1	The Slave Route heritage point at Badagry, Nigeria. Photo: Naija Rookie, 2012.	87
2.2	Masque Gorille Kwele, "Fleuve Congo." Musée du Quai Branly, Paris, France.	94
2.3	Pablo Picasso's *Les Demoiselles d'Avignon* (1907, 96 × 92 inches). Museum of Modern Art (MoMA), New York.	95
2.4	Wifredo Lam's *La jungla / The Jungle* (1943, 94 ¼ inches × 90 ½ inches). Museum of Modern Art (MoMA), New York.	98
3.1	Memorial to Christopher Columbus at Plaza de la aduana, adjacent to Bahía de las ánimas. Photo: Alejandra Pozas Luna, 2019.	118
3.2	Close-up of "Nouveau plan de Carthagène, Colombie, avec les dernières attaques des forts par l'amiral Vernon." 1741. Archives Nationales, Paris, France. Photo: Sarah M. Quesada, 2017.	130

3.3	First edition of García Márquez's "Operación Carlota." Courtesy of the Harry Ransom Center, the University of Texas at Austin.	136
3.4	"Relación histórica del viaje a la América Meridional," Madrid, 1748. Archivo Histórico del Guayas, Guayaquil (AHG), Ecuador.	154
3.5	Delta Airlines travel advertisement, "Colombia is Magical Realism." Photo: Sarah M. Quesada, 2016.	159
4.1	"Peixe-dourado" in Giovanni Antonio Cavazzi's *Descrição histórica dos três reinos do Congo, Matamba e Angola*.	194
4.2	"Pesce Donna" in Giovanni Antonio Cavazzi's *Descrição histórica dos três reinos do Congo, Matamba e Angola*.	196
4.3	Transcribed Proverb of Benin. Courtesy of Director Zphirin Daavo and l'Agence Nationale pour la Promotion des Patrimoines et de développement du tourisme au Bénin. Cotonou, Benin.	200
5.1	Local store in St-Louis, Senegal. Photo: Sarah M. Quesada, 2012.	218

Acknowledgments

As I look back on the decade-long labor that led to this book, I hope my writing honors the fields this work aims to bridge as well as the many lives it aims to memorialize. To that end, I am indebted to my editor, Ray Ryan, and remain in awe of his vision as I cannot think of a better series for my book. Likewise, I am grateful to Debjani Ganguly and Francesca Orsini, the co-editors of this extraordinary series, for championing this book from the beginning and expressing such enthusiasm for it. This book would not be what it is today if it had not been for the dedicated and insightful feedback of the anonymous readers. To Michelle Niemann, I have never met a better listener or a more careful reader. I owe my gratitude also to Edgar Mendez, Raghavi Govindane, and Helen Kitto, and the rest of the team at Cambridge University Press for keeping this project on track despite the challenges of an all-consuming pandemic.

This project grew out of formidable discussions within many intellectual communities across the globe that I was lucky to be a part of. At Stanford University, José David Saldívar, with his global scholarship and human kindness, has been pushing my project forward for more than ten years, exemplifying the kind of scholar one should aim to become. I treasure my conversations with Roland Greene, as they also left me feeling an empowerment that I look back on fondly. Elisabeth Boyi was a mentor and kindred spirit from the moment I stepped foot in her office. If this project takes African studies seriously it has been thanks to her guidance and that of Richard Roberts, whose course and encouragement to conduct fieldwork in Africa was a turning point in my career. Yvonne Yarbro-Bejarano introduced me to Achy Obejas's brilliant novel *Ruins*, planting the seed that would blossom into the chapter found here. I also thank Lisa Surwillo, who suggested visiting the UNESCO Slave Route, and Héctor Hoyos, who encouraged my particular comparativism. Jess Auerbach, Caroline Egan, Victoria Saramago, and Fatoumata Seck were wonderful commentors, reading drafts or discussing ideas, sometimes well into an evening or early in the morning. I was also fortunate to engage in meaningful conversation with Sepp Gumbrecht, Ramón Saldívar, Paula Moya, Dan Edelstein, Marília Librandi, and Ximena Briceño. And of course, I am also grateful to my mentors at the University of Georgia for early support. To Lorgia García Peña, who later joined my dissertation committee, I will always be grateful for her encouragement, both personal and professional.

In Benin and Senegal, I still remember as if it were yesterday the generosity of the people that made my fieldwork successful. While in Cotonou, I was privileged to have the guidance of Paulin Hountondji, who was also very kind to find the best interlocutors for me. In Abomey and Ouidah, Zphirin Daavo served as my guide and translator. I also want to thank Adrien Huannou, Adélaïde Fassinou, the students at the Université d'Abomey-Calavi, and my other informants in Ouidah, Cotonou, and Porto Novo. In St-Louis, Senegal, I want to especially thank Boubacar Boris Diop for his intellect and his generosity, as well as Nijah Cunningham, Mme. Diop, Rachel Petrocelli, Erin Pettigrew, Eloi Coly, Boubacar Fall, Ibrahima Seck, Ibrahim Wane, and the graduate students at the Université Cheikh Anta Diop in Dakar. I thank also the fellowship from the Center for African Studies at Stanford for funding this fieldwork.

The national archives in France—at Paris, Aix-en-Provence, Bordeaux, and Nantes—were stellar hosts during my research there during the summer of 2017, helping me interpret the hardest calligraphy and locate relevant materials. I was also supported by Marie-Christine and Jean-Christophe Brun in Nantes, who made sure my family felt at home while I spent long hours at the archive. In Paris, Charlotte Montin helped me translate some 18th century French when my eyes could not do it any longer. Many thanks to the Harry Ransom Center which provided access to Gabriel García Márquez's many documents during the pandemic.

My work in *The African Heritage of Latinx and Caribbean Literature* was also supported by the Andrew Mellon grant from the American Council of Learned Societies (ACLS). I am grateful to the fellowship committee for supporting this project in its early stages. The Postdoctoral Fellowship at the University of Illinois Urbana-Champaign in the Latina/Latino Studies Department provided me with the perfect platform to better shape the interdisciplinary focus of this book and discuss my work-in-progress. The seemingly unending library resources at UIUC also landed me in the possession of Cavazzi's documents as well as the British Parliament records, which established the foundation for my last chapter and strengthened my second. A particular thanks to my faculty mentor, Jonathan Xavier Inda.

Outside of the Latina/Latino Studies department, Dara Goldman and Susan Koshy were also extraordinary interlocutors.

I am very grateful to my former colleagues at the University of Notre Dame for leading and hosting discussions on chapters, providing feedback, or offering practical advice. I will never be able to adequately express my thanks to Kate Marshall and Mark Sanders for their wisdom and indefatigable support as faculty mentors. Special thanks to Marisel Moreno, Ricardo Ramírez, and Jason Ruiz for championing me. Tarryn Chun let me bounce many ideas off her and was a trusted confidant. To many of my colleagues in the English department but also in Gender Studies, Romance Languages, and American studies departments, thank you. The Institute for Latino Studies and its director, Luis Fraga, were steadfast supporters who provided resources for travel, hosted lectures that would benefit the book, and also afforded me with a second semester leave for writing. Many thanks also to my wonderful students for thinking out loud with me all these years and to my research assistant, Marie Shelton, for fetching permissions for images all over the world. My community in Chapin Park, South Bend, Indiana, provided me with the village that made this journey both supportive through tough times and joyful during the best of times.

I have presented parts of this book at many invited panels and talks, and thus benefitted greatly from these conversations. The second chapter of this book benefitted from discussions at the University of Chicago, where I was invited by Daniel Desormeaux; my sincere thanks to him and all participants for this generative discussion. This chapter also benefitted from invited panels at the Latin American Studies Association (by Carlos Decena and Elena Machado Sáez), and the American Comparative Literature Association (by Maia Gil'Adí). The last chapter of this book benefited enormously from discussing it at various other venues: the Colloquium for "Research on Latina/o Culture and Theory" at CUNY with Vanessa Pérez Rosario, Bill Orchard, Cristina Pérez Jiménez, Natalie Havlin, and Inmaculada Lara-Bonilla; the Modern Languages Association "New Diasporas" roundtable, organized by Sheri-Marie Harrison and Yogita Goyal; the Decolonial Research Group at Stanford; and the Arts and the Humanities Research Council in the UK. Chapter 3 benefitted from discussion at the fantastic *Post45*, organized by Kate Marshall. I am indebted to all organizers and participants for their generative questions and remarks. Likewise, my conversations with Roberto Fernández Retamar at Casa de las Américas in Havana and with the activist group protesting *La sentencia* during the ASWAD convention in Santo Domingo were foundational for my first chapter.

Over the years, I have benefitted greatly from conversations with many colleagues, too, including Leticia Alvarado, Frances Aparicio, Magalí Armillas-Tiseyra, Anke Birkenmaier, Sarah Brouillette, Debra A. Castillo, Maria Cotera, John Alba Cutler, Theresa Delgadillo, Naminata Diabate, Michael Dowdy, Kirsten Silva Gruesz, Monica Hanna, Rebeca Hey-Colón, Carmen Lamas, Antonio López, David Luis-Brown, Emily Maguire, Elizabeth Manley, Julie Minich, Urayoán Noel, Marion Christina Rohrleitner, Ralph Rodriguez, Ricky T. Rodríguez, Josie Saldaña-Portillo, Ilan Stavans, Lourdes Torres, Silvio Torres-Saillant, Lyonel Trouillot, and Roberto Zurbano. As co-chair of the Latino studies section for the Latin American Studies Association (LASA), I learned so much from Veronica Montes and Jennifer Harford Vargas.

Portions of Chapter 1 and 4 have appeared in different forms as "A Planetary Warning?: A Multilayered Caribbean Zombie in Junot Díaz's 'Monstro'" in *Junot Díaz and the Decolonial Imagination*, edited by Monica Hanna, Jennifer Harford Vargas, and José David Saldívar (Duke University Press, 2016, 291–318); and "The Congo in the Chicano Southwest: Atlantic Continuities in Tomás Rivera and Rudolfo Anaya" in *The Oxford Handbook of Latino Studies*, edited by Ilan Stavans (Oxford University Press, 2019, 104–124). I am grateful to the peer reviewers for their astute feedback that only strengthened later formulations of these ideas for the book.

I joined the Romance Studies department at Duke as this book was in its final stages and have found a formidable and caring intellectual community. Esther Gabara and Aarthi Vadde have been extraordinary cheerleaders, guiding this book into the finish line with all kinds of helpful and practical advice. Martin Eisner, Gustavo Furtado, Walter Mignolo, and Saskia Ziolkowski have welcomed us into their homes and have been such encouraging colleagues, as have been my other wonderful colleagues in Romance Studies and across the university and region.

Over the years, my close friends in Querétaro, the US and beyond, and my extended family have sustained me and have been championing me all the way, for which I cannot thank them enough. Thank you to Bekah Shyne for helping me select the image for the book's cover. I am eternally grateful to my parents, Sergio and Margaret Quesada, who raised me to be proud of my Mexican and American upbringing, free from the constraints of categorization and resilient against the exclusions of others. They nurtured instead the freedom to ask the kinds of questions about identity and belonging that this book is devoted to. Amanda and Sergio J., you also sustain me and care for me. Elsi Margaret was born when this project was a mere idea and Elio Kees, when it was a first draft. In fact, he was born just as my response to the reader reports were due, proving that life has a very particular sense of humor… We all survived as Kyle Williams carried us and the pandemic raged. He also read me (more times than I can recall), listened to me, offered suggestions, all while feeding us and cheering on my at times weary spirit. Les dedico pues este libro a mi familia, y es expresión de mi amor y mutuo sacrificio.

INTRODUCTION

Textual Memorials of a Latin-African Literature

The word "Africa" conjured "blurry images of wild animals, danger, and the end of the world," to the dismay of the Afro-Puerto Rican protagonist of Dahlma Llanos-Figueroa's novel *Daughters of the Stone* (2009). When Carisa announces her intentions to visit Nigeria, this protagonist reports that her neighbors responded with images of a "wild man swinging from tree to tree," "the jungle, cannibalism," and "people who didn't have enough to eat" (318). Throughout the intergenerational novel, Carisa's ancestors have dealt with variegated expressions of anti-Africanness in contexts ranging from early twentieth-century Puerto Rico to the 1970s New York in which Carisa comes of age, while the novel causally connects structural racism to racist discourses originating in Africa. Seeking to correct these tired tropes at their source, Carisa follows a heritage trail "to find a way back to older stories" in which her ancestor Fela was kidnapped on the banks of the Niger river in 1880 and forced into bondage on a Puerto Rican plantation. Becoming a site-reader of "the land where Fela was finally laid to rest" (92), Carisa retraces her steps: she seeks to "go back there and look for the river and walk through old villages and stand under the moon" (319). The novel anticipates Africa's UNESCO Slave Route, a project in which former slave trade sites were rehabilitated for heritage tourism. When Carisa "walks a path that is clearly marked" (323) as her Afro-Puerto Rican author Llanos-Figueroa did in Senegal during the advent of the Slave Route, the novel projects the physical memorials of this trail onto the page as a *textual memorial*. A gesture I term "visiting text while reading sites," this physical-turned-textual memorial in literature is an original feature of the novel – one that rehabilitates Carisa's evident "Latin-African" heritage, joining her US Latina and African identities despite the centuries-long excision of this transatlantic connection.

Llanos-Figueroa's novel exemplifies a geopolitical shift at the center of *The African Heritage of Latinx and Caribbean Literature*. This book performs a shift in transatlantic studies by privileging the African archive,

1

ignored until now, in some of the most globally influential literary writers of Latin American descent of the last fifty years. What Llanos-Figueroa has in common with recognized post-1970s authors, from Gabriel García Márquez to Rudolfo Anaya or Achy Obejas, is that their works involve *textual* memorials of the African slave trade that evoke the Slave Route initiative promoted by the United Nations Educational, Scientific, and Cultural Organization (UNESCO). But this gesture toward a re-cartography of the Atlantic through a Latin American-Africa axis, or what I term a "Latin-Africa," remains largely absent from Black Atlantic or South-South frameworks and, perhaps most strangely, from World Literature critique itself. I call this absence strange because these writers' "worldly" attentiveness to sites of African memory should not be unusual. After all, in the 1970s and 1980s, the Cold War shifted from the Americas to the African continent, as the Iberian colonization of Africa gave way to one of the most long-lasting decolonization movements in history, involving anti-apartheid struggles that in turn ignited resistance to racial violence and capitalist globalization across the Global South and even among US Latinx activists, as the historical works of George Mariscal and Lorena Oropeza have shown. Most pertinently, an ensuing neoliberal era witnessed African nation-states promoting heritage tourism of the UNESCO Slave Route, initiated through a partnership between Haiti and Benin in 1992 to recover from bankruptcy after decades of civil unrest in Africa. Using storytelling to narrate the slave trade and its aftereffects in Africa, the Slave Route recounts such tales along trails that lead pilgrims such as Carisa to former ports of diasporic departure. Thus, in the literary exegesis that preoccupies *The African Heritage of Latinx and Caribbean Literature*, the texts I have selected embed textual memorials of the Slave Route for the same purposes as the physical memorials themselves: to revisit the African point of view of the Slave Trade's aftereffects, from the colonial, to the imperial, decolonial and neoliberal eras. Yet, such textual memorials have gone undetected in part because an African-centric historiography has gone largely unexamined in the disciplines that study these authors. The textual memorials in these narratives contest this invisibility by using sites to revisit anti-African discourses that were produced in Africa *before* crossing over and plaguing the imaginaries of peoples of Latin American descent.

As I argue in *The African Heritage of Latinx and Caribbean Literature*, the praxis I term "visiting text while reading sites" provides a route along which a reader revisits sites of memory that recall a lost Latin-Africa. It is a feature in all of the narratives discussed here that enables the reader, as a "text-visitor," to interrogate crystalized colonial discourses about an imagined "Africa" in order to uproot said narratives in the present. The example of *Daughters of the Stone* interests me precisely because it features a praxis that intertwines textual narrative with Slave Route memorialization as a means to rehabilitate a Latin-Africa over the original spaces of anti-African discourses in colonial Atlantic treatises. Walking a heritage trail leading to Fela's resting place, Carisa terms this trail "the places of memory" and uses them as coordinates that locate the moment when African narratives became disconnected from her Afrolatina identity. The term recalls French historian Pierre Nora's celebrated "lieux de mémoire" or sites of memory that have "barely survived in a historical age."[1] Indeed the history contained in this site wills Carisa to its source "before it was all gone" (315). But while Nora's profoundly Gallocentric nationalism underscoring the concept of lieux de mémoire does not encompass France's imperialist enterprise – such as the French involvement in the slave trade – Carisa's places of memory do the opposite. Not only does Carisa textually memorialize stories told along routes that now constitute heritage tourism by walking such trails back to the historically charged site of Fela's kidnapping. The pilgrimage-made-text transcribes these imperial sites into fiction. In other words, Llanos Figueroa's sites of memory serve as conduits that, to borrow from Michel de Certeau, create a walking text in which we can imagine a "visitor" to the text returning to colonial or imperial fictions told over specific sites. This praxis of visiting text while reading sites enables the text-visitor to reexamine colonial discourses in which certain pronouncements about an imagined "Africa" not only crystalized into the sites of memory the reader walks upon – the very lieu de mémoire Nora celebrates – but were also reproduced, centuries later, by Carisa's neighbors. Discursively, Llanos-Figueroa's novel not only reveals a severed relation to Africa, but also reorients it through this textual memorial of a Latin-African connection by narrating Africa in its particularities. The oral African traditions the protagonist Carisa has inherited – "the stories of a time lost to flesh and bones" – have been transcribed as text in the novel but also "go back to the beginning" (315) in Africa. Most importantly, chiseled into her story is the "stone" of the novel's title, which revisits an archive produced *in* and *about* Africa.

Another key feature of *The African Heritage of Latinx and Caribbean Literature* is its consideration of African sources as epistemological sites that probe the ways in which an identification with Africa is overlooked at best or snubbed at worst in the formation of Latin American, US Latinx, and Caribbean identities. In the novel at hand, Carisa's *mandinga* "stone," guarded by five generations of women going all the way back to Fela, helps Carisa find a precise location of origin. As part of the Atlantic archive, Carisa's talisman originated in the Niger valley and was usually fitted into an "embroidered" "pouch" constituted of "old threads and bits of fabric" (68, 209). The stone recalls what were termed "Bolsas de mandinga" in eighteenth-century "Guinea" and "Mina" or Elmina, Ghana (Sweet *Recreating* 180–1), along the Niger river and on the West African coast respectively – that is, the place where Fela was captured and the place where she was put on a slave ship. Widely used across the Atlantic World, these *bolsas* consisted of "a cloth or leather" pouch and could contain roots or powders used for ritualistic healing. In the novel, the talisman also seems to "heal" each one of Fela's descendants from the pains of her time.[2] In Carisa's case, the stone heals her memory, enabling her to "remember" a past that took place in Africa as the novel itself becomes a memorial stone. But she must defend these memories from racist pressures to forsake her African heritage. The Eurocentric society in which she finds herself places Carisa's stories outside the "Age of Reason," in the same way that colonial agents treated African traditions as fantastical. From her grade-school teacher critiquing Carisa's myth of origin as "just plain superstition" (253) to her creative writing professors dismissing her African-based writing because it has "no place in belles lettres" (269), these incidents paint a painful picture of the rejection of anything "African." Carisa is forced to steep herself in "Western Thought" and only then "consider whether [she has] anything of worth to add to that exalted company" (269–70). Tellingly, the phrasing used to represent Carisa's stories as "clichéd ghosts and goblins" echoes that of the colonial African archive. After all, African religious praxis was subjected to a colonial gaze that understood healing mechanisms as witchcraft. As Achille Mbembe states, African traditions had to overcome the burden of colonial writings that depicted them as "charms, spells, and prodigies" within "an enchanted and mysterious universe" (*Postcolony* 4). The mandinga stone thus not only locates Llanos-Figueroa's novel in a Latin-African borderland, but also harks back to the African point of excision. Unsurprisingly, the rejection of a Latin-Africa represented in Llanos-Figueroa's textual memorial has significant implications for the global reach of Latinx literature. The African sources that illustrate the varied ways in which African traditions (and by extension, the othering of peoples of African extraction in terms of race) figure in Llanos-Figueroa's text are folded into the underside of modernity in Latinx literary studies – and to a lesser extent, Latin American literary critique – which neglects the truly transatlantic cosmopolitanism of Llanos-Figueroa's text.

While the Latin-African construct of Llanos-Figueroa's novel shatters readings that circumscribe it to local, regional, monolingual, or US contexts and overlook the novelist's cosmopolitan engagement with Africa, this transatlantic axis itself does not reduce her invisibility on the world stage. Llanos-Figueroa's work does not feature in any World Literature anthology and her novel was dropped by its original publisher, thus stymying its circulation. In fact, the paradigm of obscurity enveloping novels such as Llanos-Figueroa's indirectly drives the aims of this book – not because the present book engages with the politics of canonicity in World Literature, but rather because Llanos-Figueroa's exclusion reflects the fact that a Latin-African axis is absent from criticism of World Literature and from Latinx and Latin American literature, even though this axis profoundly shapes the works of some of the most lauded authors of modern times. I engage the Latin-African axis in canonical works as a way of opening the door to lesser-known global voices who share this framework with canonical authors. I do so not to suggest that these lesser-known voices cannot, on their own terms, dismantle Eurocentric or imperialistic structures of knowledge or create their own epistemologies. Rather, reading this Latin-African axis in the work of canonical writers revisits an always present but erased African spatiotemporality while undoing the Eurocentric understandings of their work that rendered it canonical in the first place. This first step is required before the canon of World Literature can be questioned and reconfigured.

The African Heritage of Latinx and Caribbean Literature unearths buried African influences in five of the most recognized Latinx and Caribbean writers of World Literature through their texts' active engagement in African historiography. This book examines Junot Díaz's short story "Monstro" (2012) and essay "Apocalypse: What Disasters Reveal" (2011), Achy Obejas's novel *Ruins* (2009), Gabriel García Márquez's journalism of the 1970s and 1980s about Angola and the US as well as *Chronicle of a Death Foretold* (1981), Tomás Rivera's poem "Searching at Leal Middle School" (1975), and Rudolfo Anaya's bildungsroman *Bless Me, Ultima* (1972). This selection of post-1970s Latinx and Latin American texts memorializes African memory and reorients traditional transatlantic studies. This book addresses the disavowal or distortion of the African subject, not only in terms of race but also with regard to historical constructions of identity. That is, the narratives examined here defiantly stretch the limits of a protean "Latin" identity, one that cannot be confined to specific parts of the Americas. These narratives and the Atlantic borderlands they construct geographically set the plot in an American continent or islands directly linked to the African continent or at times within the African continent itself. The invisibility of this Latin-African axis, however, is not exclusive to World Literature frameworks, but also characterizes approaches in American and Latin American studies, where a "transatlantic" focus, when present, largely evades Africa in favor of Western Europe. Rather than seeking to contest such occidentalisms, this book excavates a reconfigured transatlantic from the texts themselves. From Chicano writer Rivera's conjuring of imperialist Henry Stanley's Congo, to Cuban-American Obejas's exhumation of colonial slavery in Nigeria and Dominican-American Díaz's resurrection of zombies from their cradle in Benin, these canonical writers exhibit the symptoms of an African haunting projected textually into a Latin-African Atlantic setting. Drawing from multilingual archives about West and Central Africa and fieldwork at Slave Route sites, I elucidate how the legacies of Belgian, French, Iberian, and British colonialism, and, later, US imperialism have reproduced, *in Africa*, antiblack discourses that stymie African historiographical inclusion in literature. Central to this premise is that these virulent ontological decrees over the course of centuries weigh on these writers as they both question and enact discourses that render Africa *fearful, commodify* it, *obliterate* its history, or *distort* it – the four paradigms that constitute the chapters of this book. But as African sites become embedded in narratives, they function as specific spatiotemporal markers of African history that may also be revisited; mainly the era of the transatlantic slave trade in West and Central Africa, but also the "scramble for Africa" in nineteenth-century Congo, decolonizing wars involving Angola and South Africa, and the neoliberal era in which heritage sites in Nigeria, Senegal, and Benin proliferated. Bridging what Édouard Glissant terms a "relational" history of Latin America, the Caribbean, the US, and West and Central Africa, I develop in this book a new form of transatlantic study and rehabilitate a submerged Latin-African literary heritage in World Literature.

Latin-Africa in World Literature

The African Heritage of Latinx and Caribbean Literature maps the neglected Latin-African vector in the works of lauded Latinx and Caribbean writers and thereby reconfigures the critical frameworks for studying World Literature in transatlantic and Global South contexts. For all the authors examined here, this book unearths their works' discrete connections to Africa and unfolds them into a re-cartography of the Atlantic. I show that even if a Latin-American-African connection is discreet, the systematic location of this axis within such foundational writers constitutes a significant border space that should inform critical approaches, even though the diverse fields that study these authors – from South-South theory to Latin American studies, Latinx studies, and World Literature – have largely missed their connections to the African continent. First, in the configurations of South-South theory and transnational Black studies, Afrolatinos are critically absent despite the fact that they are members of the Global South living in the Global North. Second, in other Global South formulations such as US multiethnic or Latin American literature, Chicanos Rivera and Anaya and Colombian García Márquez are often read in homogenous ways – the former as representatives of ethnic Chicano expression having little to do with the Caribbean, and the latter as a representative of magical realism par excellence.[3] Moreover, none of them are usually read as identifying with Africa, despite the fact that they are both from regions with a plantocratic history. But reading Latinx, Caribbean, and Latin American literature comparatively and globally challenges ethnic and provincializing expectations about these authors, in whose works significant traces of a Latin-African axis are perceptible. For Rivera and Anaya, a Latin-Africa connects them to Caribbean epistemologies outside the ethnic expectations of Chicanidad, while for García Márquez, a focus on his Caribbean traces places emphasis on the African-centric legibility of his work, challenging a regionalist or essentialist perception of them that World Literature markets to a global reading public. Crucially, the Latin-African axis that this book unearths both underscores the inherent cosmopolitanism of these examples of World Literature and challenges World Literature's eurocentrism.

Since Johann Wolfgang Goethe coined the term *Weltliteratur*, World Literature has been conceptually occidentalist. Although, as Emily Apter explains, the field evolved into "a hosting ground to literary postcolonialism" in 1991 (1), it decidedly made a comeback in comparative literature with Pascale Casanova's path-breaking *Le république mondiale des lettres* (*The World Republic of Letters*, 1998), despite allegations that it preserved imperialist bias. Casanova's work and David Damrosch's *What Is World Literature?* (2003), among others, consolidated the field by either imagining literary works as circulating from a prominent center – such as Paris – or by casting translation and reception as key functions of globalized literary output. To deprovincialize its canon, however, World Literature has been rethought through connections to specific nation-states. Wai Chee Dimock, for instance, has positioned US American literature in a "wordly" apparatus not only to dislodge the insular notion of American studies but also to denaturalize global approaches to American literature itself – akin to what Ignacio Sánchez Prado or Eduardo Coutinho have done for Mexican and Brazilian literatures, respectively.[4] National literatures in this way defy their own political delimitations by stretching their cosmopolitan engagements, expanding paradigms of study in World Literature rather than defaulting to a homogeneous literary aesthetics. But as Apter and Sánchez Prado have both noted, these national or ethnically centered approaches still consolidate a niche-driven market that essentializes ethnic identities for a global system (2; "Hijos" 15–17) – a dynamic to which Latinx literature falls prey in terms of its odd essentialization.

Established in the 1960s, Latinx literature enters the world literary fray, first, as significantly underrepresented and essentialized, despite the promise of its initial global reception.[5] In Latin America, Elena Poniatowska's translation of Sandra Cisneros's *The House on Mango Street* in 1994 signified a clear turn toward a two-way transnational study of Latinx literature in the Latin American academy, also signaled by international conferences such as those of the Tepoztlán Institute and the Latin American Studies Association (LASA).[6] Meanwhile in Europe in the 1980s, the rise of border studies as a response to the impact of globalization and migration generated interest first in Chicano and then Latinx literature; in 1998, the Society for Multi-Ethnic Studies: Europe and the Americas (MESEA) was established and a polyphony of symposiums hosted all over the continent.[7] Renowned Africanist scholar Ato Quayson's tracing of US Latinx connections with Accra's salsa scene in Ghana or Elena Nakaznaya's survey of Trans-Baikal interest in US border writing, especially that of Anaya's *A Chicano in China* (1986), exemplify the impact of Latinx intersections across the globe. Of the Chicano and Latinx authors that feature here, Anaya and certainly Díaz are favorites of World Literature. While Anaya is the most anthologized Mexican-American author in World Literature globally, contrastingly fellow Quinto Sol prize-winning contemporary Rivera is usually marketed mostly in Latin America, where the edition of his work translated by Gustavo Buenrostro and Julio Ramos is prominent.[8] For his part, Díaz – a *New York Times* bestselling author whose work is canonized in Latin American and American literature anthologies alike – is a Latinx exemplar of World Literature. Not only has his work been translated into languages from Korean to Hungarian, but his short stories and scathing critical essays also circulate widely in *The New Yorker* and *The Boston Review*, and his accolades include the Pulitzer, Guggenheim, and McArthur Genius prizes. Featuring in outlets such as *World Literature Today*, Obejas's work has not only met transnational reception, but she also enters World Literature as a translator herself. After her translation work in the anthology *Havana Noir*, she translated Díaz's bildungsroman into a vernacular Antillean Spanish to much praise, which then set the stage for the inverse translation of the work of Cuban and Dominican writers – such as Ena Lucía Portela or Rita Indiana – for an Anglophone market.[9]

Despite the fact that World Literature remains a domain largely defined by its cross-cultural boundaries and critiques of literary systems of power, this field's marketing of Latinx writing has paradoxically played a role in essentializing Latinx literary output. For example, Anaya's work has been enthusiastically received in Europe and translated into Italian, Portuguese, and German, but this reception has pegged him as an "ethnic" and "magical realist" writer, likening him to García Márquez and exemplifying a trend that Frances Aparicio and Susana Chávez-Silverman term hegemonic "tropicalization" (8). In fact, Elena Machado Sáez and Raphael Dalleo bemoan how critics have categorized post-sixties Latinx literature as apolitical in general and applied a "universality" to Díaz's work or nativist approach to Obejas, in particular (2–4). More recently, Ralph Rodríguez has called for an undoing of the identity politics that hold Latinx or Chicano works hostage to ethnic descriptors. Despite this transformational work, World Literature's descriptors tend to exoticize Latinx works if we consider the characterizations of Cisneros's *Caramelo, or Puro Cuento* as "the bible of Chicano culture" in Spain (*El País* 2003) or Díaz's *Brief Wondrous Life of Oscar Wao* marketed as "Gabriel García Márquez on speed" in Germany (*Die Zeit* 2009). Some of these exoticizations have to do with the fact that ethnicity-based ways of reading these texts in the subfields concerned with them are later magnified in World Literature's approaches to them. For instance, Anaya and Rivera are often read as representatives of a Southwestern ethnography delimited by the US border. Anaya's revered folklorism is what World Literature emphasizes despite the fact that recent studies have engaged with the cosmopolitan implications of his work.[10] In the case of Rivera, as John Alba Cutler has stated, racial essentialism is usually ascribed to his canonical *...y no se lo tragó la tierra* (1971), despite the fact that it "represents something other than the narrow nationalism" that has been associated with its literary award, the *Quinto Sol* (71). Similarly, the Latin-African axis in the work of Díaz or Obejas is overlooked in favor of nationalistic or even US-centric approaches to hemispheric "Dominicanidad" or "Cubanidad," even if, as Lyn Di Iorio and Marisel Moreno have pointed in the case of Díaz, there is an ambivalence in his work toward a notion of "latinidad" ("The Latino Scapegoat") or even "Dominicanness" ("Debunking Myths"). This is not to say that transnational studies relating US Latinx writers to Afro-Caribbean ones have not been groundbreaking in their own right. Rather my point is that World Literature seems to ignore the transnational dimensions of Latinx criticism, opting instead for homogenizing ethnic readings that occlude the weighty claims of these transnational cosmopolitanisms.

While reading these canonical voices through the lens of Latin-African memorialization challenges the sociohistorical expectations and essentialization of Latinx letters within World Literature, an occidentalist approach to Latinx writing in turn renders this Latin-African vector invisible. Africa often remains an "imaginary" or teleological point of origin in transatlantic studies rather than a relevant archive probed historically, critically, and politically in scholarship on representative Latinx writers and even one of Latin America's most lauded authors. Colombian Nobel laureate García Márquez travelled to West and Central Africa during the Cuban-led decolonization program. In the 1970s, he published Angolan chronicles, the most detailed at the time, bolstering Cuba's Black international campaign before its failure as Ronald Reagan rose to power and sought to crush any socialist uprising in the Global South. But Latin American literary criticism and the field of World Literature mostly ignore the Latin-African political trajectory of one of the most influential writers in the world in the latter half of the twentieth century. Paradoxically, a tendency to read the Nobel laureate transatlantically disregards Africa, despite the fact that his journalism evinces his stark Angolan preoccupations during the height of the Cold War.

But García Márquez features in this book, which focuses largely on writers considered part of a Latinx tradition, because the Latin-African axis I unearth here has implications for the conceptualization of Latinx literary history and categorization itself. The writers in this study all embed a critical Latin-African connection in their work; indeed, all link their plots, which are set in Latin America, the Caribbean, or in the US Southwest, to Africa. García Márquez's Angolan experience, moreover, connects to a spatiotemporal marker crucial to the geopolitics of US Latinx studies. His Angolan journalism was spurred by the Cuban exodus to the US that he witnessed in New York and wrote about while employed by the renowned socialist Cuban press, *Prensa Latina*. Later, the Cuban-Angolan crucible of the 1970s that García Márquez guardedly praised becomes a site of retrospective disappointment in Achy Obejas's novel *Ruins*, set during

Cuba's economic depression in the 1990s. This stark preoccupation with Angola that the Boom writer and the Cuban-American one share underscores the trickiness involved in categorizing a protean "Latin" identity that crosses literary critical fields. In short, this book deprovincializes both Latin American literature and Latinx literary examples by drawing attention to their connections to the Global South Atlantic in Africa. I settle then on the category "Latin-Africa" as the term most apt to describe this field of World Literature; one that illuminates the transatlantic political trajectory of some of the most influential writers in the American hemisphere.

The global prominence of these authors offers an opportunity to read World Literature differently through a new approach to "transatlantic" studies. The notable African-centered praxis of these authors undergirds my identification of a Latin-African vector that gestures toward a "new" transatlantic for a literary world system that, most importantly, creates a world literature of its own, defying the western biases of the discipline itself. While transatlantic, Latin American, US American, and World Literatures overlook aspects of the porous literary worlds they probe, a Latin-African literature reclaims the connection between underrepresented peoples subsumed within the borders of countries with stronger economies such as Latinos in the US and the African continent. This "South"-South vector translates into a transatlantic and cosmopolitan axis, challenging the erasure of not only polities but also the western biases of our "wordly" discipline.[11] Thus, this book situates a more fluid "Americas" in a Global South literary frame, showing how the writers examined here emphasize their discursive transnationalism while also underscoring an unequivocal cosmopolitanism beyond the hemisphere. This book joins some transoceanic literary scholarship by influential scholars like José David Saldívar who unveils the trans-pacific influences informing the work of canonical Chicano writer Américo Paredes, María Josefina Saldaña-Portillo, who stretches the discourses of indigenous criminalization into the Middle East, or Alba Cutler and Ariana E. Vigil, who focus on Latinx artistic engagement with US foreign policy in the Middle East or Southeast Asia, respectively.[12] Anne Garland Mahler, who unveils how the leftist discourses of the Puerto Rican Young Lords and Nuyorican poets connects to the Tricontinental against apartheid South Africa, is one of the few scholars to date that devotes attention to how Latinx paradigms connect to modern African politics, including the decolonizing efforts of the Cold War era. Similarly, Yomaira C. Figueroa-Vázquez's recent study engages Afro-Diasporic Latinx texts with Equatorial Guinea. Vanessa Pérez Rosario's ground-breaking study on Puerto Rican Julia de Burgos identifies a subtle African internationalist vein in this canonical poet and other US Puerto Rican writers.[13] Finally, in a unique essay on US Puerto Rican poet Víctor Hernández Cruz and his incorporation of Northern Morocco, Moreno has also shown interest in theorizing this "South"-South axis.[14] *The African Heritage of Latinx and Caribbean Literature* builds on these foundational interventions, exploring Latin-African connections beyond Puerto Rico and its diaspora or beyond Spanish-speaking Africa. Similarly, the global reach of this Latin-African axis melts away ethnic expectations for Latinx literature as local, regional, or monolingual, replacing them with a framework that goes beyond a South-South approach while reducing Latinx literature's invisibility. As I mentioned earlier, my point beyond the politics of canonicity is less to question the exclusion of an author such as Llanos-Figueroa from anthologies of World Literature than to consider the structural preclusion of her Latin-African configuration from a world system of letters. After all, World Literature is not only a kind of timeless *littérature engagée* or a method for ethical commitment with literature beyond its local source; it is inevitably canonical by virtue of the field's attention to circulation.[15] Reading canonical figures through a Latin-African axis reconfigures the Eurocentric approaches that made them canonical in the first place, expanding the world literary network and laying the groundwork for continuously challenging its borders.

But while I am pointing out the absence of an important framework from the inclusive field of World Literature, this absence derives from colonialism and the excision of Africa both culturally and racially. Both African historiography and Afropolitanism have been excluded from the very concepts of Latin American identity within the US. To deconstruct the Eurocentric focus of the Atlantic World, which precludes a Latin-African borderland in World Literature or transatlantic studies, we must first examine the occidentalist bias permeating the "transnational."

The Question of "Latinidad," from Transnationalism to an African-Focused Transatlanticism

This book pushes into an Atlantic World that is African-centric. Thus, I do not expand on notions of Latin Americanness or Latinidad but rather move away from a variety of frameworks that position Latin American or Latinx expression as delimited by strict borders, whether national or regional, and missed within South-South dimensions. It is my contention that national and geographical expectations place the cosmopolitan assemblages of Latinx identity under erasure, in the same way that Afrolatinidad is often dismissed from conceptions of Latinidad itself. In fact, some of the most identifiable and characteristic cultural forms of Latin America and Latinos in the Caribbean and the US emerge from an intersectional relationship with Africa. What this signifies is that Latinx rejections of African tradition have everything to do with colonial discourses about West Africans, which were developed *in* Africa even prior to the Middle Passage.

This book's African-centered approach rests upon the notion that Africa's excision from the Latin American and Latinx literary imaginary involves historical and political considerations that go beyond race, even though the colonial establishment of racial hierarchies in the New World needs to be examined. For example, in the aspirational whiteness of Latinx identity, the hemispheric rejection of blackness can be partially traced to the ideological and ethno-racial hierarchies undergirding the Latin American colonial world. After all, a western need for labor powered the myth of an organic but "new racial identity" in the colonial Americas, building an alleged racial inferiority into the foundations of world capitalism (Quijano 538–9). A caste system reinforced by the likes of Bartolomé de las Casas or Juan Ginés de Sepúlveda bled into nineteenth-century decrees that make White supremacy evident, from Domingo Faustino Sarmiento's conception of indigenous people as backward to Simón Bolívar's use of Black slaves as cannon fodder.[16] Despite José Martí's much-anthologized and pivotal interventions on race, *modernista* discourses on blackness did not alter the prescient whiteness ideal in Latin America.[17] From the racist proclamations of José Antonio Saco or Juan Bautista Alberdi to slavery apologist or assimilationist novels such as Gertrudis Gomez de Avellaneda's *Sab* (1841) or Antonio Zambrana Vazquez's *El negro Francisco* (1873) – or even the Rousseau-esque use of African slavery as metaphor to characterize criollo men and women alike from José María Heredia to Maria Gowen Brooks – discourses on blackness still rested on the "scientific racism" that permeated constructions of a reviled *mestizaje*.[18] For mestizaje was perceived as an obstacle to modernity in the nineteenth century, even though this perception shifted in the twentieth century as it became a centerpiece of Latin American identity. An imagined racial democracy denied or elided racism by emphasizing an ideal mestizaje, as José Vasconcelos's *La raza cósmica* (*The Cosmic Race*, 1925) makes clear.[19] Discourses of Latin American identity, founded on a Eurocentric model of whiteness, dismissed its African components, as Llanos-Figueroa's Carisa was dissuaded from seeking a perspective originating in Africa. Ideologies of ethnoracial classification solidified into what Aníbal Quijano calls the "coloniality of power," where blackness, like indigeneity, was subordinated to Western hegemony via the discourses of creolization or mestizaje permeating the Latin American imaginary.

But mestizaje is further complicated by national identity, since republican states carved themselves out of the Spanish colonial landscape. As Jill Lane has traced in the case of Cuba, *teatro bufo* (comedy theater) serves as a site in which the blackface *negrito* (little Black) functions as a staple of an endearing Cuban nationalism – an "exotic criollo" that "felt especially Cuban" (14). Much like the colorblind society Martí hoped for, this representational "blackface negrito is 'more' than black, 'more' than white and instead combines these to produce the 'Cuban'" (16) – but it also dilutes and avoids the violence and trauma that produced the *real* "negrito" in the first place. This case is representative of Latin America's colonial trauma with blackness; in fact, this trauma is so great that humor must be used to deal with its legacy, laugh at its offspring, and thus forget the stain of slavery. In Spanish Latin America more broadly – encompassing South America, the Spanish Caribbean, and the US – there is both a discomfort with this legacy and an acceptance of resulting racial biases. This results, as Mark Sawyer succinctly explains, in blackness being placed at the "bottom of the racial hierarchy but Latin Americans and US Latinas/os have consistently denied problems of racism and the existence of blackness in their home countries" ("Racial Politics" 272).

As inheritors of these Latin American racial biases, US Latinx antiblack sentiment also hardens on the northern side of the Mexican-American border. "Central to afrolatinidad is the social difference that blackness makes in the United States," Antonio López explains, in that "an Anglo white supremacy determines the life chances of Afro-Latinas/os hailed as black" while "reproduc[ing] the colonial and postcolonial Latin American privileging of *blanco* over *negro* and *mulato* (mixed-race) identities" (4–5). This is especially clear among Latinx White-assimilationists, who elide Latinx racial guilt by faulting the US's Jim Crow system for racial derision and division and ignoring the pervasive antiblack attitudes plaguing Latin America, thus shrugging off any need for Latin-African alliance in the same ways mestizaje enthusiasts snubbed blackness.[20] But while the colonial Latin American caste system was reinforced in the US, these hierarchies were also inherited from the slave trade. As Christina Sharpe points out in her urgent study on the wake, "slavery's continued unfolding is constitutive of the contemporary conditions of spatial, legal, psychic, and material dimensions of Black non/being" (20). Whether or not slavery played a conscious role in Latinx conceptions of blackness, a rejection of blackness ensued. After all, in the Latinx imaginary, Africa – whether reproduced in Llanos-Figueroa's fiction or in society – remains "a dark continent situated at the margins of history and outside of civilization" (Laó-Montes 78–9). What results is an avoidance of blackness altogether lest the US Latinx population also falls prey to racialization; instead, this Latinx population gravitates toward what George Lipsitz terms "a possessive investment of whiteness" born of the slave trade (3; Sawyer 270; Torres-Saillant "Inventing Race" 124).

While the rejection of an imagined Africa might be legible in these terms, a sense of the perpetual oppression of the Black population in the US also precludes the healthy identification of most US Latinos – historically, racially, or ethnically – with the African continent. Antiracist decolonial movements in the Global South – particularly in South Africa – in part gave rise to the term "afrolatino" in the 1980s; adopted by its population in the 1990s.[21] But as Miriam Jiménez Román and Juan Flores point out, "the Afrolatin@ concept calls attention to the anti-Black racism within the Latin@ communities themselves," especially among recent immigrants to the US who inherit racial biases from Latin American countries (2–3). In fact, Black and Latinx tensions go back to the civil rights era, when class conflicts emerged. From the NAACP opposing extensions to the Voting Rights Act that benefited Latinos (Morales 500) to Latinx White-assimilationist discourses, the division between Blacks and Latinos ultimately comes from "the unresolved racism within Latina/o communities that has its origins in their respective countries of origin and by the frequently parochial way in which African Americans privilege the US-born Black experience and fail to recognize the struggles of immigrants" (Sawyer "Racial Politics" 265). A failure to recognize a nuanced sense of Black experience in the US, Dixa Ramírez argues, leaves those embracing their "afrolatinidad" an anomaly vis-à-vis other Latinx people who aim to present as White (169). While the scholarship of all those cited above demonstrates the centrality of the transnational dimension of Black racialization, Latinx rejections of a blackness connected to Africa have a lot to do with the categorization of Latinx-ness or "Latinidad" itself.

Like the history that shapes the excision of Africa from Latin American identity, the geopolitics involved in the conception of the term "Latinidad" eventually adopted by US Latinos also play a major role in the rejection of a Latin-Africa. From its original coinage for peoples of Latin American heritage living in the US, Latinidad has served as a complex umbrella term for the vastly different experiences of varied US Latinx groups. But the term Latinidad was, from the outset, based on an exclusionary principle adapted to Latin Americans of European extraction. As Walter Mignolo explains, Latinidad specifically draws on a French concept of "Latinité":

> "Latin" America was the name adopted to identify the restoration of European Meridional, Catholic, and Latin "civilization" in South America

and, simultaneously, to reproduce absences (Indians and Afros) that had already begun during the early colonial period. ... The idea of "Latin" America that came into view in the second half of the nineteenth century depended in varying degrees on an idea of "Latinidad" – "Latinity," "Latinitée" – that was being advanced by France. (57–8)

This etymology explains how much colonial weight an occidentalist ideal carries in the word "Latinidad," which erases the Indigenous and African presence in Latin America, especially *criollos*[22] and even *mestizos* and *afromestizos* (those of mixed indigenous, African, and European roots). But as a term adopted by the US imaginary, it has also flattened the heterogeneity of peoples of Latin American heritage living in the US.[23]

The term Latinidad has often assumed a panethnic unity, even if this imagined national-origin coalition has not actually materialized socially or structurally. This illusory sense of affiliation undermines racial, socioeconomic, and national identities, thus eliding, as Ylce Irizarry argues, the heterogeneity of Latinx experiences in the US (6). Moreover, as Marta Caminero-Santangelo's extensive work on the subject shows, Latinidad derives from a hegemonic US American order, where the literary market has for decades been "producing anthologies under the 'Latino/a literature' rubric" (*On Latinidad* 20). Indeed, I myself have contributed to anthologies that perpetuate categorical constructions of Latinidad as an US ethnic label. As this sense of generalization has to some degree bled into the Latinx literary canon, Caminero-Santangelo warns that "[e]ven narratives of panethnicity offered by Latinos themselves do not necessarily reflect a true sense of consensus or collectivity" (27). While Caminero-Santangelo concludes that categorizations are important for championing fields that have been sidelined institutionally, it is also true that the normalization of a panethnic literature has often overlooked Black and Indigenous writers.[24]

The advent of the transnational in Latinx studies helped conceptualize forms of racialization implicated in hegemonic structures on both sides of the Mexican-American border. In 1991, José David Saldívar's landmark study *Dialectics of Our America: Genealogy, Cultural Critique, and Literary History* broke with a sense of "Latinidad" as limited to the US and argued for an extranational space for US Latinx literary production. Drawing from Martí's transnational "Americas" ("Nuestra América") and Immanuel Wallerstein's world system analysis, Saldívar understood a South American dependency as a direct result of its contact with US capitalism and disengagement from monolingual and national frameworks. Some Latinx scholars shied away from the plurilingual accessibility of sources, despite the fact that this framework, as Saldaña-Portillo reminds us, "requires less fluency in multiple languages than a fluency of multiple Latin American histories as they intersect with the United States' bloodied quest for hegemony" ("From the Borderlands" 508). Notably, this paradigm shift aligned with forms of transnationalism in Latin American comparativism, or what was called inter-Americanist studies decades earlier, that "typically attempted to theorize [a Latin American] cultural identity in opposition to . . . the United States in the face of that country's aggressive hemispheric imperialism" (Bauer 234–5). Although the birth of Hemispheric studies – arguably with Enrique Rodó's *Ariel* (1900) – was at odds with Latin American inter-American studies and the "new" US-American Hemispheric studies,[25] this geographical shift away from what Marissa K. López terms "a critical evasion of US hegemony" (10) in Latinx studies pushes less for a panethnic label and more toward an inclusive bilateral framework. Indeed, the hemispheric approach that I take to Latin-Africa considers the transnational approach self-evident, in the same way that Kirsten Silva Gruesz's revisionist nineteenth-century literary project including discourses of blackness conceives of "a larger web of transamerican perceptions and contacts" (xii), via which belletrists were undeterred by national borders. Claudia Milian's competing notion of "Latinidad" breaks away from panethnic "latininity" as well, and opts instead to position Black and brown "economies" of writing as intersecting. And as I mentioned, Saldaña-Portillo's recent work focuses on the mutually constitutive and colonially rooted discourses of indigeneity on *both* sides of the Mexican-American border. These works all make varied shifts from a Latinidad panethnicity to mutually inclusive frameworks in which specific Latin American and Latinx identities are joined geo-historically and racio-politically. But the degree to which we owe up to un-decolonized biases in favor of Eurocentrism or even whiteness in Latin American or Latinx identities derives in part from paradigms that go beyond transnationalism. After all, the Atlantic system's effect *in Africa* – from the colonial imagery of the African subject to Africa's neoliberal commodification – has reproduced a racialized narrative of Africans, whom Latinos have predictably rejected as part of their kin. It is indeed in this vein that I approach the "transatlantic." *The African Heritage of Latinx and Caribbean Literature* builds on African Diaspora studies that includes African epistemology in order to nuance our understanding of the ways in which African historiography has been altered by a Latin American imaginary in which fictions about zombies, witches, curses, and African safaris abound to the detriment of a "South"-South alliance.

If a rejection of African history originates with colonialism and imperialism in the Americas and across the Atlantic, the continuation of this disenfranchisement in Latinx studies emerges from a disidentification with Africa that is also disciplinary. Notable is the exclusion of Latinos from Paul Gilroy's seminal *Black Atlantic: Modernity and Double Consciousness* (1993) as are most segments of the non-Anglophone South-South population from his African diasporic framework.[26] While I understand that Gilroy's omission speaks more to the purview of his field than to a conscious effort to exclude Latinos, my issue with "the Black Atlantic" is akin to Simon Gikandi's and Yogita Goyal's arguments that this framework paradoxically does not center on Africa, despite the fact that transatlantic studies usually place more emphasis on the first part of hyphenated cultural identifier.[27] Not only is an African-centered approach oddly absent from the Black Atlantic structure, this model runs the gamut in western modernity, as the reduction of Africa follows in the Hegelian tracks of Enlightenment. In Gikandi's words, "Gilroy can only engage with the continent either as the locus of tradition or as an amorphous arm in the chronotope of cultures created in the name of modernity" (148). Africa is often viewed as a force opposed to modernity, leading to rejection of a dialectical relationship with the continent. This Western construct hardly strengthens the idea of African history as relevant in studies on hybridity, which more often than not are confined to the Americas or circumscribed by a Britain-US-Anglo-Caribbean network, eliding those forms of creolization emerging from the entire African continent, as I have shown in another study.[28] To the contrary, the concept of the Black Atlantic "does little to reveal the impacts of African institutions and ideas on the making of the Americas" (Sweet *Domingos* 5) or ignores the fact that Afromodernity existed on its own plane (Green, "Fistful of Shells," "'Dubbing' Precolonial"). Thus, the fact that Black Atlantic studies paradoxically neglects an African-centered approach makes it not unlike the traditional Western imagination.[29] Most active in contesting Anglo-oriented versions of the transatlantic endemic to American studies, and the Europeanized frameworks of both American and Latin American studies, have been South-South or South Atlantic frameworks in comparative literature. David Kazanjian's multilingual framing of nineteenth-century discourses of emancipation among Liberian and Mayan rebels, Joseph Slaughter's work on human rights advocacy in Latin American and African examples of the bildungsroman, and Lanie Millar's study on the overlooked Cuban-Angolan Black internationalism in the wake of decolonial failure all feature South-South dimensions that are just as racio-political as geo-historical. As I mentioned, Mahler similarly traces this vector through the Tricontinental antiracist movement against the Jim Crow South and its spread throughout the Global South. In summary, what this scholarship has in common is a concerted effort to shift away from monolingual and Anglo-oriented scholarship in Black Atlantic studies.

The African Heritage of Latinx and Caribbean Literature endeavors to decolonize the euromodernist narrative by revealing a Latin-Africa constituted by African epistemologies. I do this by examining archival documents written about Africa as well as African oral histories and proverbs, and by offering occasional brief readings of African literary works. Like theories from the South, this decolonial framework seeks to "de-westernize" structures of knowledge.[30] I aim to destabilize the western scholarly status quo by centering African processes, for instance, of racialization. First, this African-centric archive requires epistemic access to multilingual sources (sources which, as Kazanjian has lamented, have often been neglected in Atlantic World scholarship) along with an interdisciplinary approach (Kazanjian "Two Paths"). In fact, Kazanjian argues, the centrality of monolingual approaches or the separation of North Atlantic from South Atlantic studies is to blame for "relegating Africa and Latin America to peripheral concerns" (*Brink* 5), akin to the exclusion I pointed out in World Literature. But, second, this multilingual work includes particular attention to records of criminalization – subsumed under hegemonic institutions such as the Archives Nationales d'outre mer in France or the British Parliament – via which I trace a through line from demonized African spiritual practices to racialized discourse on blackness in the Americas. These sources regarding religiosity are quite central, because even in the West, as Carlo Ginzburg has argued, Inquisition records show how thin the line separating the divine and the demonic really is (13). Yet, my approach to these archives differs from the Western construct of the historical. From Ginzburg to James Sweet, I contend that African history should never be reconstituted based on African criminalization drawn from archival fictions alone. Key to the interdisciplinary positioning of texts as sites of memory is the nature of sources to document obliterated histories. In Nora's theorization of the archive, he argues that "Lieux de memoire" are critical because "spontaneous memory" no longer exists (12). But as Africa's Slave Route shows, oral proverbs are invoked easily and often over the very sites of memory that Nora eurocentrically theorizes. As Jan Vansina has long argued, African history needs to be constructed based on oral African tradition and an assortment of sources that do not exist in written documents.[31] In this book, I undertake this shift in methodology and sources, not only drawing on archival materials in French, Portuguese, Spanish, and English, but, when relevant, also on West African oral histories that complement written records. Promoting de-westernization of Atlantic epistemology, the disciplinary turn I embrace implies a meaningful engagement with African oral history – such as proverbs – that have compelling connections to literary works of a Latin American tradition.

Lastly, the study of Latinx fiction has much to gain also from comparison not only with archives of African colonization but with the work of African writers. Though brief, my readings of these African works provide a glimpse into how the Latin-African connection moves in both directions. Thus, through all these methods, I explore the proposition that Latinos have also written a cultural history of Atlantic difference that pushes the limits of the archive in which we find ourselves confined. Taking a hint from the extra-hemispheric frameworks noted above, in *The African Heritage of Latinx and Caribbean Literature*, I argue that these allusions to African traditions in transatlantic studies are not only worth emphasizing but also worth pursuing from an Africanist perspective, in the same way we seek a Latin Americanist perspective in transnationalism.

"Textual Memorials": Context and Theorization

At the center of *The African Heritage of Latinx and Caribbean Literature* is a combination of empirical fieldwork and literary analysis. Returning to the original premise of this book, it is my contention that textual memorials in the work of the world literary authors selected here encode Latin-African memory – akin to the ways in which the UNESCO Slave Route memorializes an excision that originated in Africa.[32] For this purpose, my fieldwork along the Slave Route highlights the mutually constituting ways in which physical and textual memorials reconstruct a Latin American narrative in places we might not have looked initially. This book undertakes what Debra Castillo and Shalini Puri recently theorized as the praxis of fieldwork in the humanities, which makes use of a variety of archives, sources, and methods that reify the macro-explanations of literary scholars (10–11, 17). Their work points to a growing interest in the interconnectivity between the literary and the empirical. Saidiya Hartman's *Lose Your Mother: A Journey Along the Atlantic Slave Route* (2008) is the exercise in literary fieldwork most relevant to my study.[33] As she gathers sources from the Slave Route during her fieldwork in West Africa, Hartman seeks to make sense of the differing ways in which Africans and African Americans remember each other, if at all. While Hartman concludes with the moral complexity of West Africans' personal and emotional detachment from the experience of diasporic Africans despite their effusive stories at sites of memory, her narrative, recounted over a significant memory site, is of interest for *The African Heritage of Latinx and Caribbean Literature* as a literary site of revisionist experience. The subjective remembrance that pilgrims have in a particular site is not attained by, in Maurice Halbwachs terms, "reconstituting the image of the past event," but rather by establishing "emotional relationships" with a collective sense of self (28, 30). In addition to the African epistemologies that guide this book, empirical observation of sites of memory and of guides' stories imbue these "historical" sites with the emotional attachment that a collective memory signifies. This paradigm brings me back to the premise guiding this book: that Latin-African connections in literary works can function as *textual memorials* of a long-neglected African heritage, not unlike the UNESCO Slave Route itself.

In West and Central Africa, the Slave Route became a prominent destination for heritage tourism at the turn of the millennium, as an epicenter for revisiting African narratives of the African diaspora. During my fieldwork in two of these Slave Route sites, Ouidah and Gorée, I observed that guides' stories mediated emotional attachment to each site. Pilgrims' resulting affectual attachment to these sites speaks to the mutually constitutive power of symbolic spaces and fiction. After all, the textual memorials examined here *also* transport the reader to sites of African memory and affectively summon a centuries-old shunning of a Latin-African Atlantic heritage. Juxtaposing this empirical fieldwork with literary analysis connects the physical and textual objects of memory in important ways and ultimately reveals how, inversely, fictional narratives evoke physical sites to memorialize the past and, in this case, affirm the relevance of Latin-Africa. In this vein, I read the specific Slave Route sites of Ouidah in Benin, Badagry in Nigeria, Gorée island's House of Slaves in Senegal, the National Institute Museum in the Democratic Republic of Congo, and the Dr. David Livingstone Trail in Malawi alongside narratives that either refer to these sites directly or evoke their preoccupations. Such an approach shows that textual memorialization is a *function* of narrative itself.

The connection between physical memorialization and fiction in Latinx studies was first proposed in Mary Pat Brady's tracing of the modernization of the US Southwest. A de territorialized and abject landscape in Chicano memory, she proposes, is repossessed in Chicana fiction as a means to memorialize a past just out of reach. "[T]he memorial, or textual monument," she states, constitutes the archival work of so many Chicano texts for their contrapuntal reference to modernity's progress and to signs of the melancholic or mournful (24). While her work does not further develop this innovative term, it does locate the textual memorial alongside paradigms of ruins around which a political community of mourning forms as developed in the works of Susana Draper, Idelber Avelar, or even Judith Butler.[34] But if, in these works, the ruins of literature constitute an impossible or barely tenable reconstruction of history, *The African Heritage of Latinx and Caribbean Literature* argues that a literary genealogy is indeed perceptible in the faint memorial traces the texts in this study evoke. Textual memorials rehabilitate the Latin-African Atlantic by engaging with lieux de mémoire and reflecting on colonial myths of origin and their subsequent destabilization.

Derived from "memory," which involves both affect and factual recall, memorials and sites of memory are charged with solidifying one version of past events. According to its Greek usage, "memory" not only was characterized by affection and *pathos* but also signified "recall" or "recollection" (Ricoeur 4). The term "memory" as a concept became the center of nineteenth-century scholarly pursuits, from neuroscience to sociological inquiry (Fara and Patterson 3–4). In fact, Michel Foucault traces how hegemonic discourses used memorials to materialize history publicly: "[H]istory, in its traditional form, undertook to 'memorize' the monuments of the past, transform them into documents, and lend speech to those traces which, in themselves, are often not verbal ... in our time, history is that which transforms documents into monuments" (*Archeology* 7). Crucially, Foucault argues that documents-turned-memorials seem to project the unalterable truth of past events, leaving White supremacist discourses unquestioned, as statues of imperialists and proponents of slavery from Henry M. Stanley to Confederate General Robert E. Lee pose victorious in public view, materializing the ideologies recorded in the archive. Historian Ana Lucia Araujo in fact criticizes these memorials as "permanent forms" that can dangerously solidify public memory (*Politics of Memory* 1). Such monuments have in turn crystalized and even justified the colonial record. Accounts such as French "Mémoires," French *Rélations*, and Spanish *Relaciones* (from the verb "to relate" a story) fashioned, in writing, distortions of Africa and of blackness at a critical point of origin for such racializing discourses.

Because history remains somewhat static in memorialization, these structures offer a path along which we might deconstruct and revise their foundations. In the twentieth century, the "lieu de mémoire" was both "closed upon itself" and "open to the full range of its possible significations" (Nora 24). Such a site of memory connects with Brady's theorization of the "textual memorial" because focusing on people's production of space through memory – social relations in space, occupying space, or producing a signified space – allows texts to amplify that narrative moment and then dig deeper into its memorializing signifiers. To phrase it differently, the openness of a textual memorial within a narrative leaves room for a spatial engagement with symbolically charged sites, some of which have been perpetuating dominant historical narratives that can now be deconstructed. In the US, the ongoing dismantling of Confederate statues in the renewed Black Lives Matter era following the murder of George Floyd speaks to how attempts to deconstruct White supremacy target memorials that crystalize it as an ideology. Dismantling Confederate statues is part and parcel of a push to undo the solidified nature of White hegemonic memory. *The African Heritage of Latinx and Caribbean Literature* dismantles hegemonic memory by examining textual memorials that rehabilitate a severed connection with Africa through contested sites of memory.

This process of dismantling and reconstruction takes place through an interdisciplinary praxis I term "reading sites while visiting texts." While a work of fiction reproduces a site that in turn evokes a memory of colonialism, the act of visiting such a site in the text is a way to question and reexamine the events of history. In other words, a reader can visit sites textually through the physical places the text conjures up. This strategy of textual memorialization recalls Toni Morrison's explanation of "Sites of Memory": her "literary archeology" collects "some information and a little bit of guess-work" so that a reader can "journey to a site to see what remains were left behind and to reconstruct the world that these remains imply" (92). In revisionism of this kind, the visitor-reader of a textual memorial undertakes an emotional and speculative pilgrimage, or "an inquisitive nomadism" (Soja 82), not unlike visitors moving along the routes of a heritage trail. This movement and meditative attention to pauses along the trail provides moments for contemplation in which oppositional questioning can take place. Whether they emerge in the wake of decolonization in the 1970s or in post-1990s Slave Route neoliberal era, such textual memorials appropriate sites of memory to produce Atlantic countermemories of spaces lost.

I contend that fictional narratives can function as sites of memory, as their characters move along a path, trail, or route that brings them into contact with these individualized sites. This spatial movement in narrative is akin to a praxis in which one writes a text without reading it, to paraphrase Certeau's spatial theory (93). In this way, individuals unconsciously create a text with their physical movement, and thus space and language become interactive topoi. This emotive movement is not dissimilar, then, to characters' occupation of narrative space. As a tourist follows a historic circuit, she is sensitized by the relation she seeks with the heritage site, which is analogous to how readers follow the journey of a main character in a novel.[35] Thus, a novel, a short story, a scathing piece of journalism, or a poem can enable readers to imaginatively visualize walking through a system of routes, which in turn resonates with the ambulatory and sensory experience of walking down a marked heritage trail of memory. These texts' memorialization ultimately constitutes an elusive path that recounts sites resistant to hegemonic versions of memory.

This book also argues that physical and textual memorials are mutually constitutive of one another. In fact, walking the trails that lead to the memorials at Gorée, Senegal, and Ouidah, Benin as part of my fieldwork highlighted two ways in which literary and material memorials at times complement one another. First, sites of memory seek a reflective engagement and denounce hegemonic violence through more allegorical than historical means. In other words, stories told at these sites do not necessarily have to be "historically accurate" – in the Western epistemic sense – and instead take fictional liberties by which visitors to the site become more emotionally attached to contesting global capitalism. The *Maison des esclaves* (House of Slaves) on Gorée island in Senegal is a prime example because its main draw – its "Door of No Return" through which visitors gaze out on a symbolically charged Atlantic Ocean (see Figure I.1) – weaves a tale of colonial violence over a site that is arguably fictional. For example, guides there say that twelve million enslaved persons passed through its door, though that number is an estimate for the entire slave trade combined; moreover, debates abound about whether the Maison was used to embark slaves at all.[36] But such historical inaccuracies are not the point. My own fieldwork observations revealed that, as hegemonic violence is narrated at the site, visitors solemnly lingered at the Door of No Return the longest, as did President Barack Obama during his 2013 visit. So symbolic is this site that its Door of No Return becomes textual in the work of Nobel Laureate Wole Soyinka, who writes: "from Gorée through the slave forts of Ghana to Zanzibar – every fort and stockade, increasingly turned into museums, is filled with grim evocations of this passage of our history" (*Burden* 59). Historical inaccuracies are neither the point, for the slave

Figure 0.1 Gorée, Senegal's *Maison des esclaves* and "The Door of No Return." Photo: Sarah M. Quesada, 2012.

trade took place in the vicinity regardless, nor unique to UNESCO Slave Routes. In Latin America, Nobel Laureate Rigoberta Menchú's testimony registers a contested site of genocide. Despite the fact that numerous scholars discount Menchú's *testimonio* as "inaccurate," the text remains representationally powerful in its exposure of hegemonic violence. Textual and physical sites of Guatemalan or African genocide from Menchú to Gorée speak against regimes that annihilate human life in the name of modernity by using spaces of death to consider the mere possibility of survival, rather than seeking to be historical in the western sense. In fact, their symbolic power as spaces of hegemonic contestation echoes the formulation of a "potential history" that, as Ariella Azoulay explains, signifies a history that could have been if hegemonic powers had not precluded it (*Potential* 43–7). But the speculative is not taken seriously because, for Western tradition, eschatology was foremost an expression of the prescient and opposite of the unrealized possible (Koselleck *Futures Past* 22). From hindsight, history was constructed on Western domination, and thus the prescient became integral to Western tradition while the speculative was relegated to the realm of the dominated. In Reinhart Koselleck's explanation of Alexander's triumph over King Darius, for instance, Persians created a hierarchy of "desirable" realities based on "possible histories rather than about the actual history" (*Sediments* 142). But challenging this occidentalist myth of origin, sites of memory in this book denounce violence while imagining alternative ways of surviving that might have been successful if it had not been for the coloniality of power. This is precisely what draws visitors to the site: a chance to reflect on a desirable alternative, if only. Thus, the site of Gorée can be interpreted as an allegory (Nicholls 144). Through this literary device, Gorée's potential history at a physical memorial creates for the visitor a scene of the spectral and, in turn, a textual memorial of the captive. As Brady suggests, "[t]o allegorize it is to keep that alternative within memory's reach" (123).

As speculative spaces of possibility, sites of memory are emotionally charged because they announce the inevitability of death in both past and present. Thus, sites create an attachment to space via the foretold death that warns us of future iterations of capitalist violence. Ouidah's trail is a prominent example of this. Featuring a three-kilometer path on which enslaved people marched toward a slave ship, their eventual arrival at the Door of No Return (as Figure 1.3 in Chapter 1 shows) produces an emotional reaction to this prescient manifestation of oppression in a continuum of past and present. In fact, this temporal disjuncture troubles scholars such as Sharpe, who, in her discussion of memorialization's reparative role, questions how memorials negotiate a past that is still present: "how does one memorialize chattel slavery and its afterlives, which are unfolding still?" (20). For its part, the Slave Route aims to avoid the mistakes of the past in the future, though Sharpe might argue that this memorialization is insufficient. That is, the UNESCO Slave Route epitomizes an unalterable history, and its evocation in texts – whether allegorical or not – similarly wields an emotional power that transforms the past into a continuing event (Azoulay "Potential" 565). This is how textual memorials intervene. In fiction, and bound to signifiers, the reader-visitor is ultimately drawn emotionally to the site of memory because of the prescient ways in which it announces death both in the past and the eventuality. This is not unlike what Marianne Hirsch terms a "point of memory [that] punctures through layers of oblivion, interpellating those who seek to know about the past" (61). In this vein, textual memorials locate a layered history through which the pilgrim navigates while rehabilitating the past in the present. But rather than considering this an interrelated layered history, I offer that former colonial spaces of terror share a Glissantian relational South-South history, distinct from the historicization of modernity. For *The African Heritage of Latinx and Caribbean Literature*, the performative aspect of a site-as-text means that reading itself is an act of layered pilgrimage in the Global South. Physical and textual memorials function differently, of course. But as locators of the spatiotemporal, physical memorials recreated as textual ones offer a reckoning with a past called into the present and can reconstruct for Latin America, broadly construed, a forgotten racial geography linked to Africa.[37]

Four Eras of an African-Centric Approach and Chapter Summaries

The era of the slave trade provides an access point for considering the spatiotemporal beginning of a Latin-African literature since it was precisely the slave trade that linked the two continents. The UNESCO Slave Route evokes not only this colonial era but also its afterlives, shifting Africa into a central spatiotemporal marker for historicism. For indeed, as Mbembe suggests, during this depraved global capitalist exploitation of laboring bodies, "[t]he Atlantic gradually became the epicenter of a new concatenation of worlds, the locus of a new planetary consciousness" (*Critique* 13). The slave trade was not only the first prominent temporal marker in African modern history, but attention to it also shifts what we once termed "modernity" into an African-focused timeframe. For although "Africa" experienced a very different reality while Western modernity was unfolding, by centralizing the Atlantic as the "epicenter," Mbembe not only questions Western modernity as *the* spatiotemporal locus of origin, but also introduces the Atlantic World as a new epicenter for studies on Africa.

Because this book disrupts linear and teleological conceptions of historicism in order to rehabilitate an occluded Latin-African Atlantic memory, this book reads time backward. While all the chapters engage the spatiotemporal marker of the slave trade era, I read subsequent eras of African history in reverse, beginning with neoliberalism at the end of the Cold War. This second temporal marker ushers in narratives that dwell on the setbacks of a decolonial revolution across the Global South and that are deeply conversant with the rise of UNESCO-sponsored memorials of the Slave Route. Taking a cue from Paul Ricœur's "retrodiction" or reading from effect to cause (*Time and Narrative* I, 172), I start with this current era of African historiography and present-time circumstances in a revisionist attempt to change how our "past" retraces what we understand about our present, from the all-consuming effects of the slave trade to its aftermath.

Moving backward in time, the end of the Cold War and Western foreign aggression profoundly weakened both political and economic institutions in Africa as neoliberalization ran rampant. As examined in Chapters 1 and 2 on Díaz and Obejas, the neoliberal era was the result of uneven processes of democratization in the wake of interminable civil wars. African nations sought stability in economic institutions such as the IMF and the Organization for Economic Cooperation and Development (OECD), which prioritized short-term profits and eliminated the public interest (Bourdieu "The Essence of Neoliberalism"). By the 1990s, as Jean Comaroff states, "[c]olonial economies had been replaced by rapacious modes of extraction" that, she controversially notes, "make the racial capitalism of apartheid look almost gentle" (Comaroff, Mbembe, and Shipley 667–8). Bending to the demands of these institutions, many new African nation-states found themselves prey to this system, one from which the Slave Route emerges. As nation-states turned to heritage tourism, the Slave Route was partly financed by the IMF, the World Bank, and chiefly UNESCO, prompting criticism that this African trail "becomes just another commodity that brings financial profit or some kind of political or social reward."[38] Indeed, as I will show here, narratives that evoke these sites grapple with efforts to promote Black culture falling prey to a neocolonial mindset. This theme is evident in Díaz's short story, which satirizes the distortion of zombie culture – a byproduct of Vodun – as it remains obvious that society at large is completely unaware of its origin.

From the vantage point of the twenty-first century, Chapter 1, "Fear: Junot Díaz's Zombies and *Les contorsions extraordinaires* in 'Monstro'" traces Dominican anti-black discourses beyond the hemispheric and to the cradle of Vodun in what is today the UNESCO Slave Route site of Ouidah (formerly Dahomey, today the Republic of Benin). In Díaz's sci-fi eco-parable "Monstro" (*The New Yorker* 2012) about a futuristic epidemic that spreads on the Haitian-Dominican borderland, the racialized infected-turned-entranced allegorize a discourse of difference in Díaz's story. I read this discourse against the African archive about Vodun found in records like the French 1763 Relation du Royaume de Judas en Guinée, (in les Archives Nationales d'outre mer, Aix-en-Provence, France), but also oral proverbs preserved at memorial sites in Ouidah recovered during my fieldwork. This comparative reading sheds light on the ways Vodun and its product, the zombie, became distorted in Africa before becoming a symbol of fear that Díaz's story lampoons. Building from one of the first essays written on this story, "A Planetary Warning?: The Multilayered Caribbean Zombie in 'Monstro'" (2016),[39] I argue that Díaz's zombie figure not only draws from William Shakespeare's or Cuban intellectual Roberto Fernández Retamar's "Caliban," but also mimics the colonial distortions about Ouidah in the archive. In this renewed reading, Díaz's cautionary tale of race, class, and climate crisis connects with a UNESCO Slave Route site, as both physical and textual memorials redress the colonial and contemporary fear of Vodun's zombies and redraw a Latinx-African axis.

Obejas's novel *Ruins*, on the other hand, refers to the site of Badagry – a former port of embarkation on the Slave Route in Nigeria – as an African commodifier of Afrocuban forms. The second chapter, "Commodification: Black Internationalism and the African Safari of Achy Obejas's *Ruins*" looks back at the aftermath of Cuban decolonial intervention in Angola in the 1970s and 1980s, before Cuba's dire economic depression of the 1990s, termed "the Special Period in Times of Peace." In this earlier neoliberal era, *Ruins* is set during the period when Cuba opened its doors to tourism for the first time in fifty years. But amidst economic despair in Havana, the main protagonist, Usnavy, takes refuge in his imagined African utopia constructed from a glorification of the Angolan war, Ernest Hemingway's safari, imageries of modernism in Pablo Picasso and Wifredo Lam, and even from African heritage tourism. Yet this African safari often includes Badagry, Nigeria along the Slave Route. As I reveal the ways in which Nigerian writers such as Wole Soyinka and Pius Adesanmi bemoan Badagry's neoliberal developmentalism, so does Obejas in her novel, as *Ruins* sets up a comparison by which African commodification as much in Havana as in Badagry leads to Africa's excision from Cuban and Cuban-American identity. As the tourism industry threatens to turn the Revolutionary protagonist toward capitalism despite his nostalgia for Black internationalism, the novel suggests that a genuine Latin-African historicism might rehabilitate his commodified African safari.

The neoliberal era followed the failed socialist or socialist-leaning decolonization movements that global capitalism crushed. By 1945, while Latin American nations were solidifying their republics after almost a century of independence, the African continent was still divided up among European nations, a geography that would shift in less than two decades' time.[40] The decolonizing movements that broke the yoke of colonialism are at the heart of García Márquez's pointed 1970s journalism examined in Chapter 3. This third and overlooked temporal marker alludes to revolutionary independence movements that emerged well after World War II. But it is at a Cold War juncture with Portugal that a Latin-Africa takes shape in the twentieth century via US foreign policy's collision with Cuban Black internationalism.[41] In the wake of the overthrow of Portugal in June of 1975, Cuba dispatched thousands of troops in what would become "Operación Carlota," or the successful defense of Angola's MPLA party against CIA-supported parties and apartheid South Africa.[42] This victory was so significant that García Márquez memorialized it in his own report of the same name just a few years after he had criticized Cubans for fleeing to the US.

Chapter 3, "Obliteration: Gabriel García Márquez and His Angolan Chronicles of a 'Latin-African' Death Foretold," examines a hoped-for yet never realized Latin-Africa in García Márquez's essays on Angola during the Cold War period of 1971 to 1982. This Latin-African alliance was stymied by the Portuguese and, later, by US imperialism, which García Márquez covered in his journalism. Prompted by a sunken slave ship carrying Senegalese bodies in García Márquez's *Crónica de una muerte anunciada / Chronicle of a Death Foretold* (1981), I begin this chapter by tracing the allegory of a Latin-African death foretold in García Márquez's Angolan chronicles that precede the novel. Arguing that the Cuban exodus of the 1960s sharpened his deeply rooted criticism of US neocolonialism, this journalism led to an alignment with Fidel Castro culminating in the report "Operación Carlota," among others, on the Cuban mission in Angola, which was named for a woman who led a slave rebellion in Cuba, and the Cuban-Angolan initial victory over the US. In both García Márquez's narrative of the conflict and Fidel Castro's celebratory speech, the triumph was called "Latin-Africa" – a Black signifier applicable to a collective Global South struggling against centuries of antiblack oppression originating with slavery. For García Márquez, this victory upheld a Latin-African socialism opposed to the antiblack capitalism to which some Cubans fled.[43] Outlining Castro's proclamations about a "Latin-Africa" through allegories of slavery, I argue that traces of this African axis are embedded in both García Márquez's fiction and his journalism – a Latin-African hope reciprocated in Angolan writer Ondjaki's *Bom dia camaradas* (*Good Morning Comrades*, 2001). Returning to the ship of drowned Senegalese bodies in *Crónica de una muerte anunciada*, I connect it to Gorée's *Maison des esclaves* in Senegal to reflect on the mutually constituting ways in which textual and physical memorials lament the foretold death of an African heritage in Latin American literary tradition in particular, and in world literary critique in general.

Decolonization movements reacted to European pillaging during the nineteenth-century "scramble for Africa," evoked to differing degrees in the work of Anaya and Rivera that Chapter 4 examines. This prominent temporal maker resulted in takeovers of the continent, mainly by Belgium, Portugal, Spain, Britain, France, and, after World War II, the US. This imperialism extracted resources such as ivory, rubber, uranium, and other commodities; colonized religious, social, and political institutions; and adapted these to western standards (Nkrumah 18). While Latin America was under the discursive hegemony of antiblack rejections of mestizaje during its quests for independence, most of West and Central Africa remained under European rule. Thus, this temporal marker maps an imperialism of Africa, as the age of Enlightenment and its criticism of religiosity gave way to "a general spirit of adventure" (Mudimbe 46). This means that the missionary language in the proclamations of Capuchin or Jesuit missionaries – Cavazzi and Sandoval – cast African spirituality as opposed to Christianity, which in turn carried over into ethnographic writing by the likes of Stanley, Paul Brazza, and John Gregory Bourke. Their texts constituted a spatial epistemology in which, as V.Y. Mudimbe has explained, the traveler became simultaneously colonizer, anthropologist, and scientist, all while eerily perpetuating a missionary discourse that substantially altered African religious practice (44). As Mary Louise Pratt argues, this discovery discourse "consisted of a gesture of converting local knowledges (or discourses) into European national and continental knowledge associated with European forms and relations of power" (202) and also justified its takeover. Scarred by the Southwest's infamous Anglo-Protestant Manifest Destiny, the haunting legacy of imperial writing in Africa triggers deep memories of hegemonic antagonism that Anaya and Rivera reel from in an age of Chicano empowerment after the 1960s. As Chapter 4 argues, this period of imperialism was so relentless that Rivera and Anaya remarked on its intensity via their counter-discursive impersonation of infamous ethnographers Stanley and Bourke, enabling their texts to spell out a Global South relation between the Congo under imperial rule and the Southwest under US rule.

This last chapter, "Archival Distortion: The Chicano Congo of Tomás Rivera and Rudolfo Anaya," considers how the work of two canonical Chicano writers might be imagined as expanding the borders of a plantocratic regime into the US Southwest but via the colonial disfigurement of the Congo. In this chapter, I argue for further reflection on the rejection or excision of links to Africa in populations that are not obvious inheritors of the Atlantic World. After all, like the Caribbean, the US Southwest's significant plantation history informs moments in which slave trade or the imperial "scramble for Africa" distort the imaginary of the Congo in the work of Anaya and Rivera respectively. Against the backdrop of US extraction of natural resources in the Congo, I argue that Stanley's racist writings about colonizing "Darkest Africa" haunts the spatialization of Rivera's poem "Searching at Leal Middle School," in which Stanley's mission in the Congo is evoked. In Anaya's bildungsroman *Bless Me, Ultima*, by contrast, a young Catholic boy's confrontation of the fear of witchcraft and the pagan golden carp deity shores up Atlantic continuities of an understudied plantocracy in New Mexico that relate to Congolese writer Sony Labou Tansi's *Les sept solitudes de Lorsa Lopez* (*The Seven Solitudes of Lorsa Lopez*, 1985); both traced back to the colonial architects of distorted representations of West African spirituality. With these four chapters, I address the need for African epistemologies to contribute to the foundation of a Latin-African literary tradition that enhances the formulations of World Literature.

CHAPTER 1

Fear
Junot Díaz's Zombies and Les contorsions extraordinaires *in "Monstro"*

> No one dared to stop them, for they were corpses walking in the sunlight.
> W. B. Seabrook

It has been over a decade since Junot Díaz, the most anthologized Latinx writer to date, published his stand-alone and Pulitzer Prize-winning novel, *The Brief Wondrous Life of Oscar Wao* (2007). Since then, Díaz's varied publications – from a short story collection and critical essays, to a personal confession and even a children's book, *Lola* (2018) – have denied the public the continuation of a story that, at one time, Díaz promised to be the genesis of his second novel with a Black speculative bent.[1] Díaz's Caribbean sci-fi journey "Monstro" (*New Yorker*, 2012) is, in essence, a futuristic account of an unimaginably prosperous sugar island turned morbidly decadent. The transnational but also transatlantic narrative is set in the jarring misery of a futuristic Haiti on the cusp of a planetary disaster. In the Antillean dystopia of "Monstro," an unnamed Dominican-American Ivy League student socializes with his affluent college friend, Alex, in Santo Domingo, pursues a love interest, and recounts in analepsis how an environmental cataclysm erupted into an epidemic. But at the root of the story is Díaz's critical dialectic on race in his native Dominican Republic: the disease is a "negrura" ("blackness") that "makes Haitians darker," producing an acute rejection of blackness or any of the historical traditions tied to it. Later, in this predicted neoliberal future, where the precariat live in an environmentally degraded, socially unjust world, the infection turns its victims into a mainstay of popular culture: the living dead.

As the illness evolves, the most vulnerable "viktims" morph into a widely recognized and contemporary version of the zombie. Its symptoms include "low body temperature" fluctuating to "radiant blue," "roaming about the camp at odd hours," "never sleeping," unintelligibly "shriek[ing] together," and being described as "bewitched" ("Monstro"). As these seemingly entranced victims, whom authorities term "Possessed," begin "coming together" both literally and figuratively, they start attacking the noninfected. Widespread bloodshed follows; it is "so relentless" that the infected have to be "shot off" the bodies of their victims. They soon become so lethal that, to contain the violence, a Western "Joint Chief of Staff" drops a nuclear warhead that renders the world "white." The blast further reveals the ultimate transformation of the zombies into born-again Carib-cannibalistic-Caliban creatures (Quesada "Planetary" 310) who will forever threaten the delicate thread of "human" existence – a definition of humanity that Díaz's story questions.

In *Junot Díaz and the Decolonial Imagination* (2016), I explained that in Díaz's moralistic "Monstro," Haiti's final iteration of zombie dread in a post-neoliberal era tackles the Dominican Republic's crystallization of antiblackness fueled by colonialism and a US occupation, spanning the diaspora. But expanding on this reading, the ways the story addresses zombie symptoms are also reminiscent of archival sources describing Vodun-practitioners in a colonial West Africa, where the concept of the "zombie" originates. While I evince how "Monstro" satirically confronts colonial, nineteenth-century, and neoliberal era antiblack (and anti-Haitian) sentiment in the Dominican Republic and its diaspora, I also explain how Díaz's short story confronts this racial antipathy from its African source: a fearful discourse about zombies in Vodun in the former Dahomey kingdom, today the Republic of Benin. The disavowal of Vodun is traced back to Atlantic archives that include the anonymous French mémoire *Relation du Royaume de Judas en Guinée*, the ethnographic writings of Alonso de Sandoval and Thomas Phillips, and works on Haiti by Moreau de Saint-Méry, and especially the occultist, W. B. Seabrook. These discourses on the nonheteronormative practice of Vodun, so completely at odds with Judeo-Christianity, render its practitioners not only "monsters" but also symbols that comment on past transatlantic economies and current neoliberalization. To put it differently, in this chapter I will deconstruct Díaz's mimicry of fearful zombie discourse in "Monstro" by considering narratives told at the African heritage site where zombies emerged.

As a counterpoint to colonial discourses about Vodun in West Africa are the ways heritage tourism from where Vodun is celebrated responds to these discourses, both textually and physically. A focal point is, first, Díaz's essay "Apocalypse: What Disasters Reveal" (*The Boston Globe*, 2011) about the devastating 2010 earthquake in Haiti and a realist prequel to "Monstro." Two years before "Monstro" was published, Díaz's journalism and intimate experience with Dominican–Haitian racial conflict compelled him to write this philosophical meditation, where Díaz identified Haiti, the archetypal plantocracy, as a country oppressed by the coloniality of power and, in the neoliberal era, a microcosm or even telltale sign of the effects of global capital. But this piece also retraced both sites of memory and the discourses that led to Haiti's ruin. "Apocalypse" endeavored to perform "ruin-reading" and, as such, walks through the vestiges of a plantocratic history. As Díaz "peer[s] into the ruins," he treats this site of apocalypse as the heritage site of a once carib-populated island of "bounty," tracing the long history of its "rapacious" and capitalistic colonization.[2] Cuban writer Alejo Carpentier does the same in his revisionist novel of the Haitian revolution in *El reino de este mundo* (*The Kingdom of this World*, 1949). In the prologue, Carpentier describes his visit to Haiti, following a path of ruins that also leads to the site of Vodun from which an African rejection is conjured. The sites of memory rendered textual by both authors reflect back on the effects of a global capitalist system excising African epistemologies.

But while Vodun might be a site of African rejection in Haiti, the same cannot be said of its Atlantic counterpart in Benin. I thus read Díaz's (and Carpentier's) textual representation of heritage-trail reading against its physical site at Vodun's cradle: the rehabilitated UNESCO Slave Route site in Benin's port town of Ouidah. At this physical memorial in West Africa, pilgrims not only see vestiges of the slave trade at sites of departure from Africa but also discover a rehabilitated history of Vodun that questions contemporary conceptions of zombies. By placing Díaz's zombie haunting in "Monstro" and Ouidah's heritage site alongside each other, I ask what this diasporic memorial and its textual counterpart reveal about the ways a hemispheric Dominican identity rejects African ancestry on account of signifiers such as zombies and monsters reproduced even *prior* to a transatlantic crossing. Díaz's zombie in Haiti and Benin's Vodun on the Slave Route both negotiate with history and fiction to save reality. As this chapter will discuss, the signified space of Haiti becomes a memorial for Díaz and is textualized in his story. As such, the continual waves of devastation witnessed by the western part of the island formerly known as Hispaniola symbolize textually both interconnected global colonialities and anthropogenic catastrophes that not only affect Haiti but will affect a planetary community as a whole.

Ultimately, if the zombie apocalypse of Díaz's "Monstro" traces a colonial fear of Vodun and its distorted by-product into the future, its amplification during times of dystopian calamity sounds a warning. In a spectacular twist at the end of the story, Díaz's surreal zombies serve as allegorical signifiers of hope. After all, a Foucauldian reading of the "monster" notes that not only are these allegories strategic for tracing the genesis of difference in narrative, they also underscore the ultimate resilience of the monster due to its swift adaptation to change (*Order* 157). In Díaz's ecoparable, the zombie – from colonial Vodun in Benin to a plantocratic Haiti, to its neoliberal iteration in the Americas, to finally a resignified cannibal in the dystopian American future – underscores the zombie's myriad representations. Yet, its ability to survive implies an opportunity to halt a globalized capitalistic model that creates the variegated zombie in the first place and, in turn, ceases the ongoing anthropogenic extinction that will catch up to us all. If I had drawn from Foucault's *Les mots et les choses* (*The Order of Things*) (1966) and Cuban cultural critic Roberto Fernández Retamar's *Calibán; apuntes sobre la cultura en nuestra América* (*Caliban and Other Essays*) (1971) to examine how their theories of the "monster" are reused in the literary imaginary to convey the allegorical and futuristically cautionary symbol in Díaz's zombie, I expand from this reading to suggest that this zombie functions as a particular kind of memorial. By using Ouidah's functionality as a memorial to Vodun as a critical lens, this chapter shows how Díaz enables readers to unlearn the zombie as a figure defined by fear, resulting in a rehabilitation of a Latin-African heritage.

Like a memorial and through the signifier of the "Monstro," the story's title and the semantics of *monstruo* in Spanish, Díaz reflects on the word's Latin root, "monere," "to warn" and "to instruct" (*Oxford English Dictionary*). Although zombie apocalypse manias are commonplace, if we consider the monstrous as a derivative of the Foucauldian "se montrer" (or "to show oneself"), Díaz's giant "monster" also *demonstrates* to the reader that the real monstrosity is humanity's complicity in the making of what we know today as "monstrous." Situating the Dominican and diasporic Dominican rejection of Haitian blackness within a Latin-African framework, Díaz's confrontational sci-fi narrative not only destabilizes the ways in which Dominicans and Dominican-Americans alike more generally think about race, but also rehabilitates a subtle connection to an African heritage. After all, as inevitable products of contemporary consumerism and dread, the zombie "not only illustrates the idea of alienation," as Mabel Moraña points out, but also accentuates the "concept of the return of the repressed" (*Monster* 167). In this conceptualization, the zombie came into existence when an individual was "transformed purely into alienated labour power" and "made to serve as someone else's privatized means of production" (Comaroff and Comaroff 23). The oldest industrial means of production in the Atlantic World was slavery.³ But if zombies are telltale signs of disruptions caused by a capitalist system run amok, the ubiquitous nature of the figure seems, in this contemporary Latinx tale, symptomatic of the socioenvironmental degradation of past and future. The main claim I make is that the evolution of the zombie in "Monstro" tracks and therefore also memorializes the historical progression of capital-based societies back to colonial Africa. In the end, the transatlantic tale of "Monstro" not only cements Díaz's canonicity in World Literature, as this work circulates widely in *The New Yorker*, his story also breaks with a US-centric or even transnational understanding of the Dominican antipathy toward Haitian blackness; it includes Africa in the origins of this anti-blackness.

1.1 "La Negrura," Dominican Blackness, and Neoliberalism's New Zombie

The opening lines of "Monstro" announce a rejection of blackness as a racialized disease spreads in Haiti: "La *Negrura*, they called it. The Darkness." Emphatic and confrontational, "Monstro" traces anti-black sentiment to the era of slavery during the nineteenth century in what was a quintessential Caribbean plantation. It is worth recalling that, if the Caribbean was the empire of sugar production, the island formerly named Hispaniola was its capital. As a result, this "pearl of the Antilles" received more African slaves than anywhere else at the height of the slave trade in the eighteenth century, with the exception of Jamaica and Brazil.⁴ While Díaz's short story comments on the effects of the plantocracy on an persistent *blanqueamiento* ("whitening") of his native Dominican Republic, this sentiment Díaz knows personally then drives the fictionalization of disease. The nationalistic denial of an African heritage is represented in his story as the opposite of "racial whitening" that breaks out in "new infections each month in the camps and around Port-au-Prince." Díaz's invocation of "negrura" is audacious in framing "blackness" on the island as a "disease":

> At first Negroes thought it *funny*. A disease that could make a Haitian blacker? It was the joke of the year. Everybody in our sector accusing everybody else of having it. You couldn't display a blemish or catch some sun on the street without the jokes starting. Someone would point to a spot on your arm and say Diablo, haitiano, que te pasó?

With caustic humor, "Monstro" inscribes "negrura," the opposite of blanqueamiento, boldly onto the Haitian-Dominican landscape in order to reflect on anxieties about race. Mocking racialized anti-Haitian sentiment, Díaz compels the reader to confront Dominican White nationalism head-on and questions what is at the root of this racial derision. What, indeed, is funny about being accused of having a disease, of being "blacker," of being "haitiano"? Of course, Díaz principally uses negrura as a rhetorical device that signals the racial differentiation, and thus the difference in identity, between the Dominican and the Haitian in the derisive question, "Diablo, haitiano, que te pasó?" This racial distinction has left Dominicans and diasporic Dominicans reeling, given the history of the island as the birthplace of both a plantocracy-fueled rejection of blackness and an internalization of the "color complex"[5] that is not exclusive to Dominicans.

For Dominicans and their US diaspora, as Silvio Torres-Saillant points out, a "deracialized social consciousness" is in part explained by the era of the plantocracy, in which blanqueamiento differentiated Dominicans from their Haitian counterparts ("Tribulations" 1092). Initially, Dominican distancing from blackness had a lot to do with Haiti's inspiring Revolution as the first Black republic in the Americas to free itself from the yoke of colonialism, throwing off French rule between 1791 and 1804. But the Haitian Revolution did not sit well with all. Economically, the plantocratic US soon began to both snub the island and retaliate with embargoes while the French demanded a debt payment that brought the newly independent island to financial ruin.[6] Fears about the destabilization of the plantocratic system perpetuated the transatlantic myth that "black revolution led to wholesale carnage" (Sundquist *Wake* 31). Indeed, Victor Hugo's antiabolitionist novel, *Bug-Jargal* (1826), recounts the bloodshed of the Haitian uprising in gory detail, seemingly questioning whether it should be called a "revolution" at all. Thus, discursively, "Haiti came to be seen [as] the fearful precursor of black rebellion throughout the New World" (Sundquist *Wake* 32), so daring was the former slaves' defense of their freedom. As a result, the new leaders of Saint-Domingue and its citizenry were incessantly dreaded. Sara E. Johnson notes, "the 'French negroes' so feared and vilified throughout the Americas" were variously depicted as dominant and fierce, suggesting "anxieties about black rule" (49–50) that would help solidify White supremacy not only across the Americas but especially in Haiti's neighbor to the east.

For many Dominicans in particular, this public reaction to blackness also draws on *Antihaitianismo*, a contrapuntal relationship to or even visceral rejection of Haiti that was fueled by its occupation of the Dominican Republic in 1822.[7] The Haitian unification of the nineteenth century fanned the flames of nationalist discourse for Dominican intellectuals and artists alike, who linked Haitian blackness to uncivilized, barbaric, and even animalistic behavior (Moya Pons *Historia* 378–9; Johnson 68). Dominican elites, such as writer Emilio Rodríguez Demorizi, referred to the Haitian occupation as "'the blackest days of Ethiopian domination'" (Johnson 52). From 1916 to 1924, the occupation of the island by the Jim-Crow-era US further aggravated the racial divide and eventually promoted the rise of ruthless dictator Rafael Leónidas Trujillo. Preoccupied with eugenics, Trujillo launched a genocidal campaign against ethnic Haitians in 1937, murdering roughly 18,000 people and perversely solidifying the color line in Dominican nationalism.[8] In the dictatorship's propaganda, the *Trujillato* naturalized the genocide as "a simple frontier incident," while mounting an intense nationalist campaign that upheld Trujillo as "the savior of the nation" (Moya Pons *Dominican* 369). Moreover, a hostile Hispanophile takeover continued promoting this line of defense, with intellectuals such as Manuel Arturo Peña Batlle representing ethnic Haitians and Afro-Dominicans as frightful invaders and likening them to the Haitian military that had annexed the Dominican Republic in 1822. Succeeding Trujillo, the reign of a negrophobic intelligentsia continued with writer Joaquín Balaguer, who exalted a Dominican nationalism attributed to a romanticized Europe that was thought to constitute the opposite of blackness. As Lorgia García-Peña has argued, the post-Trujillato era was so sinister – doggedly pursuing ethnic cleansing in favor of Hispanism – that ethnic Haitian blackness, applied as much to Dominicans as to Haitians, became a stigmatized marker of Haitianism *tout court* and precluded upward social mobility (2). As a result, the Dominican Republic, whose population is at least 90 percent Black to some degree, often celebrates European and indigenous heritages "at the expense of an African past" and "have for the most part denied their blackness" (Howard 1; Torres-Saillant "Tribulations" 1086).

But contemporary Dominican politics and its racialization of Haitians has far from improved. In 2013, the administration of Danilo Medina waged a nativist campaign against Haitian immigrants that led to stripping Haitian Dominicans born to undocumented parents since 1929 of their Dominican citizenship and "repatriating" them to Haiti – a move widely condemned by the Dominican diaspora. As García-Peña has pointed out, the "TC 168-13" ruling, or what became known as *La Sentencia*, was a government response to the twenty-percent increase of undocumented Haitian immigration following the 2010 earthquake and was passed against the backdrop of a significant history of institutionalized racism.[9] The ruling was a recent iteration, García-Peña explains, of a long and "troublesome history of Hispanophile anti-Haitianism" that treats the black body as "foreign" (204). For his part, Díaz and Haitian-American writer Edwidge Danticat published a scathing critical response to this ruling. The Dominican Republic then revoked Díaz's Order of Merit, which the nation had bestowed upon him in 2009, after he won the Pulitzer Prize for *The Brief Wondrous Life of Oscar Wao*.[10] The government claimed that the rebuke was justified because Díaz was an "anti-Dominican" expat who could hardly understand Dominican politics. But this brief historical survey – from a public policy of anti-Haitianism during the Trujillato's ethnic cleansing to La Sentencia – shows that blackness continues to be a marker of Dominican difference vis-à-vis Haitians.

Anti-Haitianism, a lack of occasion for affirming Black Dominican pride like those Black empowerment movements provide in the US, and blackness as a marker of Haitian difference all work in tandem in Dominican literature, although these are not universal. Myriam J.A. Chancy in fact wonders if "reimagining the Haitian humanely" is even possible "in the face of a long history of cross-national antipathy" (48). Canonical Dominican-American writer Julia Alvarez's *How the García Girls Lost their Accents*, Chancy notes, presents a "consistent thread of anti-Haitianism": Alvarez depicts the Garcías' Haitian, Vodun-practicing maid sleeping in a coffin and haunting the girls in their sleep (69). Another example is the way Caribbean writers racialize and other working-class Haitians, as in Cuban–Puerto-Rican Mayra Montero's unfortunate novel *Del rojo de su sombra*. Featuring Zulé, a Vodun-practicing, bare-chested, sugar-cane harvester in the Dominican Republic, whose Dominican stepmother retorts "pareces una Haitiana" ("you look like a Haitian"), Montero draws a tiring distinction between civilization and barbarity. Zulé's reproachable habits seem encouraged by a Haiti that in Montero's other novel, *The Palm of Darkness*, is represented as "desolate," that "smells of death," and whose characters' "perspiration had turned rank" (22–35). These are just some antiblack examples in Dominican identity vis-à-vis Haitians, but as Dixa Ramírez affirms, Dominican cultural expressions with regard to its own representation "run the gamut from ultraconservative, anti-Haitian nationalist literature to present-day Afro-Latinx activism" (5). In the case of Díaz's "Monstro," while the beginning lines trace an undeniable Dominican–Haitian racial crucible, the story provides a different trajectory than most Dominican-American or Dominican works.

If Haitians signified blackness as Dominicans turned to blanqueamiento, Díaz's story traces this negrophobia, rooted in colonialism, back to the Atlantic World through the signifier of disease. An initial marker of blanqueamiento is

1.1 "La Negrura," Dominican Blackness, and Neoliberalism's   41

the object of the narrator's affection, Mysty, a character who modifies her skin color – she's "definitely on the receiving end of some skin crafting" – despite claiming "Lemba" origins in South East Africa. Mysty holds both her "impeccable French" and being "loved" by Frenchmen in high esteem ("Monstro"). While her acceptance of "Hispanic or mixed looks" and her claim of Lemba origins do not underscore a desire for universal whiteness, such assertions are common in Dominican femininity and still reject blackness. As Ginetta E.B. Candelario states in her influential study on transnational Dominican nationalism and its interconnectedness to the body, "white preference and pigmentocracy" work to devalue blackness (224, 234). With characteristic irony, Díaz confronts this rejection of blackness through the story's epidemic – and *epidermal* – disease (Quesada "Planetary" 297). As this new fictional disease along the Caribbean borderland points to an internalized "epidermis" complex, the endemic rejection of blackness suggests a pathological, pan-ethnic outbreak to which Dominicans and Dominican-Americans are not immune. It is precisely this "condition" of racism that Díaz allegorizes as "terrifying" (ibid. 297–8): a "Darkness" that eventually leads to "a black mold-fungus-blast" turning into an "enormous black pustule." While this disease, at first glance, seems to overtly reference the dichotomous Haitian–Dominican racial opposition I have been discussing, Díaz's racial disease is projected into a neoliberal era.

In Díaz's "Monstro," the further darkening of Haitians points to the historical alienation of Haiti and the perpetuation of Haitians' status as outcasts from even before the establishment of an independent Dominican Republic and into a neoliberal present. In Díaz's futuristic and fictional formulation, the racialized disease that makes an individual "blacker" also chooses "the poorest of the poor" ("Monstro"). As I have mentioned elsewhere, what then surfaces in the narration is a comment on how paradigms of race and socioeconomics merge into the global neoliberal apparatus: a system from which a new zombie emerges. In his essay "Apocalypse," Díaz points out that the earthquake in Haiti referenced earlier was devastating because of economic forces as much as natural ones. Starting with the plantation system, he explained, this economic frame would forewarn our present "zombie stage of capitalism" ("Apocalypse"), which is prototypically displayed in Haiti. In this modified economic system, a new signifier of the living dead came to the surface. Díaz's zombie thus reflects how slave-based economic structures developed into a free-market capitalism that borrows terms such as "zombie neoliberalism." Journalist Sarah Jaffe, for instance, defines "zombie neoliberalism" as "capitalism gone wild, bubbles inflating and popping, the takeover of government by capital." Similarly, in the absence of far-flung federal programs that could make up for the decline of the working and middle classes, Jaime Peck explains that, "'dead but dominant,' neoliberalism enters into a 'zombie phase.'"[11] Finally, as Moraña states in more global macroeconomic terms, "zombie economics" refers to reforms – such as privatization or trickle-down economics – that, despite their noted failure, continue reappearing over time and produce a zombie who, this time, is an exhausted, severely underpaid, exploited worker who lacks agency (*Monster* 172–5). In fiction, several zombie narratives directly precede "Monstro" and utilize these terms, such as the Cuban-Iberian film *Juan de los muertos*, Colson Whitehead's *Zone One* (2011), Puerto Rican writer Pedro Cabiya's novel *Malas hierbas* (*Wicked Weeds*) (2011), Argentine Esteban Castromán's *Pulsión* (2011), or Argentine-American Mike Wilson's novel *Zombie* (2010), to name a few. Staging zombie economics along the Haitian-Dominican borderland specifically, "Monstro" illustrates the disappearance of social benefits such as employment and healthcare, class disparity, migration, ecological disaster, and untreatable diseases; all which create the perfect circumstances for this "new zombie."

It is precisely through the spatiotemporality of an epidemic-infested future that Díaz's narrative links the zombie's history with the present. When the narrator in "Monstro" explains that he is joining his mother in the Dominican Republic, it is due to the dearth of summer employment in what is presumably the US: "I wouldn't have come to the Island that summer if I'd been able to nab a job or a summer internship, but the droughts that year and the General Economic Collapse meant nobody was nabbing shit." The use of capitalization in a play on words that echoes the Great Depression patently conveys that a period of economic stagnation, while treated with humor, seems to mirror the reader's reality. Actual fears of social benefits disappearing also connect Díaz's story, set in a distant future, with his contemporary readers' realistic concerns. When the narrator's mother is consumed with disease, she flees the "North" due to unaffordable health care costs:

> No chance she was going to be taken care of back North. Not with what you had to pay for medicines, or what the cheapest nurses charged . . . Say what you want, but family on the Island was still more reliable for heavy shit, like, say, dying than in the North. . . . Medicine was cheaper, too, with the flying territory in Haina, its Chinese factories pumping out pharma like it was romo, growing organ sheets by the mile, and for somebody as sick as my mother with only rental income to live off, that was what made sense. (2012)

Relying on his journalistic experience for the *Boston Review*, Díaz here recreates a situation similar to that of "medical tourism" in which patients travel abroad to have otherwise costly surgeries (Rosenthal "The Growing

1.1 "La Negrura," Dominican Blackness, and Neoliberalism's 43

Popularity of Having Surgery Overseas," Konrad "Going Abroad to Find Affordable Health Care").

But the shrinking of healthcare benefits is only one aspect of a neoliberal apparatus that strengthens the corporate domain, worsening class antagonisms in Díaz's "Monstro." In the Dominican Republic, the neoliberal system exacerbates class differences that have been racially charged since the colonial era. In "Monstro," the truly destitute are Haitians: "just poor Haitians types getting fucked up," "our poor west-coast neighbors, those who are also getting sick," "viktims who had nine kinds of ill already in them." But the characters in the Dominican Republic are not often racialized. The narrator, in fact, never identifies himself racially or ethnically. Rather, descriptions of the characters accentuate what Elda María Román terms "class identity performances" (12).

In contrast with the narrator's unfortunate economic status is his affluent Dominican and Brown University classmate, Alex. They may both be "Ivy Leaguers," but Alex, the narrator insists, is "a prince": "Alex was more than just a rico, he was royalty; a fucking V–, son of the wealthiest, most priv'ed up family on the Island."[12] As the narrator sees the stark difference between himself and Alex – "him prince, me prole" – in recounting how Alex was kidnapped in Mexico in an attempt at ransom, he reveals that Alex's father had an obviously profitable business that he moved overseas: "he used to live in Mexico, where the old man had a company." This passing comment could be read as an allusion to the aftermath of NAFTA. After this Free Trade agreement, Mexico came to host US corporations seeking inexpensive labor and the reduction of tariffs, enabling Alex's father's wealth, but also Alex's kidnapping in Mexico and his mother's flying to "Miami every week just to shop and fuck this Senegalese lawyer" ("Monstro").

While the story gestures toward globalization, the degradation of the environment is the backdrop for the emergence of a "new" zombie. Díaz's juxtaposition of natural and socioeconomic disasters – first in "Apocalypse," then in "Monstro" – both corrects the notion that Latinx cultures do not "identify as environmentalist" (Alaimo et al. 3) and indicts the human element as an imminent threat to the natural environment. As the unnatural stage for colonial indigenous genocide and the destruction caused by plantations, inhumane subjugation, and deforestation, the Caribbean now hosts multibillion-dollar corporations that further damage the ecosystem. The setting in "Monstro" evokes an eco-global continuity, as the narrator casually announces he will leave for the Dominican Republic to "take in some of that ole time climate change," alluding to the heat produced by global warming. The parallel story about the developing epidemics afflicting "the infected" also refers to environmental harm to marine life: "Coral reefs might have been adios in the ocean floor but they were alive and well on the arms and backs and heads of the infected." In the space of "Monstro," uncanny morphological diseases replace natural features.

The disappearance of coral reefs and extreme warming that produce "zoonotics by the pound" nevertheless allow for the emergence of Díaz's new zombie. As the sweltering heat generates erosion and alters the vegetation in "Everybody blamed the heat. Blamed the Calentazo. Shit, a hundred straight days over 105°" it provides a breeding ground for the new disease that is unfolding. Díaz's environmental critique becomes ever more pointed as the outbreak transforms the racialized zombie into an unquestionably bizarre creature: "A black mold-fungus-blast that came on like a splotch and then slowly just started taking you over, tunnelling right through you – though as it turned out it wasn't a mold-fungus-blast at all. It was something else. Something new." This ailment, like the narrator's mother's "rupture virus," points to a world so infected it cannot contain its epidemics and Mother Earth, "Monstro" seems to imply, can no longer heal itself.

Inevitably, the diseased will turn into zombies in a world not too far removed from our present circumstances. The story's futuristic setting ceaselessly points to the neoliberal policies that form the narration's context and that Díaz analyzed in "Apocalypse":

> In order to power the explosion of the super-rich and the ultra-rich, middle classes are being forced to fail, working classes are being re-proletarianized, and the poorest are being pushed beyond the grim limits of subsistence, into a kind of sepulchral half-life, perfect targets for any "natural disaster" that just happens to wander by. (Díaz "Apocalypse")

Díaz succinctly summarizes the elemental features that compose neoliberalism. Though disasters are called "natural" insofar as they are weather-related, Díaz postulates that the devastation of hurricane-prone nations is instead the result of the "explosion of the super-rich" at the expense of these states' poorest, such as Haiti's precariat. In "Monstro," the disease extends their infrahuman nature but only affects the poor *after* a significant amount of the Haitian population have been relocated to refugee camps. For instance, the story's reference to "a small boy in the refugee camps outside Port-au-Prince" calls to mind the thousands of real internally displaced people who lived in tents for years following Haiti's deadly earthquake. Díaz's "poorest" here, like the boy, live

1.1 "La Negrura," Dominican Blackness, and Neoliberalism's   45

a "sepulchral half-life" that echoes plantation life in the colonial era, as both the poor and the enslaved continue to be disregarded by state power. As the disease evolves in "Monstro," a stark socioeconomic imbalance surfaces when the outbreak does not preoccupy authorities: "In the end this one didn't cause too much panic because it seemed to hit only the sickest of the sick ... You literally had to be falling to pieces for it to grab you." Díaz's dark humor effectively pinpoints society's cruelest stances on race and class in the face of disaster. When it is evident that the disease only afflicts the poorest of Haitians, the narrator reports that there is "no real margin in that," as if recalling the indifference of the authorities after Hurricane Katrina that Díaz referenced in "Apocalypse." Despite its reputation as a beacon of Black resistance, neoliberal policies set in motion in Haiti over the last century, Díaz explains in "Apocalypse," have rendered the island the poorest nation-state in the western hemisphere. Moreover, foreign investments that fuel dictatorships have altered the agricultural self-sustenance of the citizenry, a sector that has visibly veered into ruin in Haiti's ill-fated democracy. In "Monstro," Henri Casimir, an infected patient who was once a minister, has been reduced to "carting sewage." Even the narrator's own unemployment leaves him meaninglessly wandering about the Dominican Republic – his class status and nationality the only way in which he differs from jobless Haitians.

"Monstro" seems to suggest a colonial continuity between the plantation and post-industrialist eras. As Díaz states in "Apocalypse," "[i]n the old days, a zombie was a figure whose life and work had been captured by magical means. Old zombies were expected to work around the clock with no relief. The new zombie cannot expect work of any kind – the new zombie just waits around to die." Indeed, if Haiti – with a 14.5 percent unemployment rate, more than 200,000 people in refugee camps, and with nearly 60 percent of the population living below the poverty line – represents real poverty (World Bank, 2020), then the emergence of the new zombie in "Monstro" is symbolic of coloniality's *global* continuities in a new age. After all, as Jean and John Comaroff claim, "zombie tales dramatize the strangeness of what has become real" (Comaroff and Comaroff 23). As a result of Haitian occupation, Díaz's zombie serves as a memory point that indexes both the past and its uncanny transplantation to a future that is not exclusive to the island. In the failed democratic, neoliberal but trans-global system conjured in "Monstro," the jobless and the poor sickened by disease not only persist in a decaying world as new neoliberal zombies, Díaz's ecoparable subverts the common perception of their very existence by tracing the zombie's origin to its cradle. Díaz's neoliberal zombie, in fact, echoes Achille Mbembe, who shows that this same phenomenon occurs across hemispheric lines: "[i]f yesterday's drama of the subject was exploitation by capital, the tragedy of the multitude today is that they are unable to be exploited at all" (*Critique* 3). Zombie crises, therefore, are not just fictional; they are inherited from global capitalistic systems of oppression just as modern as they are colonial, whether in the Americas as I have shown, or in the African continent where the discursive dread of the zombie originates.

1.2 Tracing Vodun across the Atlantic: A Historical Précis

As Díaz's playful albeit stern social commentary borrows from science fiction to portray a mainstay of popular culture, the short story's setting in Haiti underscores the zombie's origins in Vodun and the representation of its praxis at its point of origin in West Africa during the slave trade era. In what follows, I briefly trace the transatlantic history of the zombie to illustrate how the colonial system of slavery in Haiti produced both colonizers' fears of the otherness in Africa first, and resuscitated a Vodun belief that could both describe the conditions of slavery and push back against them. As will become clear, Haiti became known not only for an African-originating signifier of Vodun but also for the deity of the "loa" or serpent, which symbolizes evil in the Judeo-Christian tradition. As archival records elucidate, the signifier of the snake produced some of the most enthralling "extraordinary contortions" pertinent to the behaviors of Díaz's new zombies. Moreover, language reminiscent of the "hysterical" travels from Ouidah to Haiti and its New World plantation history, as "Monstro" satirizes the discourse of "extraordinary contortions." Of course, these conventional discourses do not color the denial of blackness, as I discussed earlier in the example of Mysty, as much as they inform the conception of Haitian blackness as contagion that torments Díaz's entire narrative. Antagonism toward Vodun and its zombie – which is tied to an anti-Haitianism in Díaz's futuristic allegory – traces a long lineage back to its African origin. Thus, the zombie in "Monstro" conjures a truly transatlantic haunting: this Afro-Caribbean or Haitian figure – Afro-Latinx by way of Haiti's relationship to the Dominican Republic – persists as a creature of dread. If colorism is prevalent in the Dominican Republic and its diaspora, Díaz's story invites us to trace the transatlantic origins of a denied African heritage back to the frightening distortions of Vodun. To better understand Vodun's mysteries as they are re-memorialized in Díaz's prophetic tale of doom, I examine the fearsome projections of "monstrosity" in the colonial African archive before engaging in interdisciplinary cultural and literary analysis of Díaz's decolonial "Monstro" and the UNESCO Slave Route of Ouidah.

As a point of contact among newly arrived slaves, the New World market also introduced slaves' syncretic resistance in the form of Vodun once practiced in Dahomey. Vodun was a spiritual buttress that found its home in Haiti, and the conception of the "zombie" arrived along with it as a derivative element. Slaves who had recently arrived in Saint-Domingue from Dahomey conceived of the "zombie" as an individual arrested while crossing from life to death. When slaves considered resisting plantation life, committing suicide meant a risk of being kidnapped by a spiritual presence and turned into a walking automaton, never to return to "Guinée" (the African homeland). But if devotees' hypnotic state also linked the term *zombie* with the walking dead, there has been a full-fledged scholarly debate about whether the zombie was transformed into a morbid signifier in Africa or after the Atlantic crossing.

African and African diasporic scholars state that zombie dread is derived from Haitian Vodun (Gehman 253; Dayan 37; Seabrook *Magic* 93, 97). Yet, as early as 1967, Melville Herskovits reported that such a signification was present in Dahomey,[13] and according to Atlantic historians, "all components of the zombie concept – name, duality of the soul, bodily and spirit zombis – are African in origin" (Ackermann and Gauthier 489). Recently both García-Peña and Sarah Lauro have suggested that the zombie distortion in popular culture and representations is colored by the US occupation of Haiti, arguing that the zombie might have been an intentional US American modification considering the Jim Crow US's opposition to Haiti as a Black American republic composed of freed slaves (81; 113). Indeed, while these different spatiotemporal moments reconfigure the notion of the zombie, the original frightening representations of it took shape prior to the Middle Passage, as both literary and physical memorials will show.

Importantly, zombie fear explodes during the plantocracy on *both* sides of the Atlantic, as authorities feared that slave-returnees exposed to French ideals of the Enlightenment would be further emboldened by this misunderstood spiritual practice and that the result would be an unrestrained revolution in the French colonies. This is because for the French hegemony, slaves' practice of Vodun "amounted to an escape" or "an aspect of the resistance" (Métraux 31–2), rendering slave traders and owners alike anxious about slaves' pushback against plantational life in the colonies in the eighteenth century. *Les Archives Nationales d'outre mer* in Aix-en-Provence feature a 1781 letter that a Mme. Paquet wrote from Paris to the French colonial authorities requesting that a domestic slave from Dahomey, née Lucille, be immediately sent back to an exploitative plantation in St-Domingue. In a case that spans almost fifty pages of correspondence, Mme. Paquet's sense of urgency in ridding herself of Lucille is underscored by the slave's admitted medicinal knowledge. The authorities feared that slave-returnees would spread metropolitan French ideals of liberty to a vulnerable colony, but the ministry of foreign affairs holds back upon learning that Mme. Paquet's initial intention in bringing Lucille from the colonies was to restore her child's health and that the "black slave was not corrected at all of her faults."[14] After all, the authorities also feared Lucille's Dahomenian "soin," meaning her Vodun medicinal knowledge, derived from her origin in "Juda" (Ouidah), the heart of the zombie imaginary.[15]

While Haitian scholars such as Patrick Bellegarde-Smith have credited Vodun with being the driving force behind Haitian independence in 1804,[16] Vodun had long been perceived as threatening to White hegemony, whether in France or the Dominican Republic (Métraux 41–2). After all, Catholicism versus Vodun is part of how Dominican elites have differentiated themselves from Haitians, especially as Vodun was seen to incite rebellion in various iterations. Historically, African slaves melded political agency and Vodun and projected it toward resistance against a White hegemony in Hispaniola.[17] As Johnson has also shown, for the White Dominican elite, not only race (the "former slaves-turned-Haitian generals") but also "religion (Catholicism as opposed to Vodou) stood as markers of difference from the 'brutes' to the west" (74). But Vodun also played a prominent political role in the literary arena.

Before featuring at the epicenter of Díaz's narrative, Vodun marginally appeared in Cuban writer Alejo Carpentier's arguably most famous work – the prologue to *The Kingdom of this World* – in which he coined the term "marvelous real." As I will argue, this philosophy that Latin America possesses a "marvelous" essence is profoundly Latin-African, a realization evinced through Carpentier's heritage tourism at Haiti's UNESCO site: the home of former Haitian emperor Henri Christophe. Carpentier coins "the marvelous real" – a prototype of American originality that is more marvelous than European literature – only after his 1943 pilgrimage to the ruins of Sans Souci citadel. Importantly, through heritage walking of these ruins, Carpentier invokes Vodun at a pivotal point in his Latin American version of the extraordinary.

1.2 Tracing Vodun across the Atlantic: A Historical Précis

> Having felt the indisputable charm of the Haitian landscape, having found magical portents in the red roads of the Central Plateau, and heard the drums of the Voodoo gods Petro and Rada, I was moved to compare the marvelous reality I had recently experienced with that exhausting attempt to invoke the marvelous which has characterized certain European literatures of the last thirty years. (Carpentier 5)

I focus on the "drums of the Voodoo gods" (the "loas" or serpents of Petro and Rada) because, although they are mentioned in passing, Carpentier's seeming exoticization of this praxis during his heritage tourism places a spirituality that originated in Dahomey at the forefront of what, to him, is Latin America's ethos. In other words, his visit to the ruins or his movement through Black historical space in Haiti reveal the roots of what, to him, is the "marvelous real" essence of Latin America, borne out of a distinct Latin-African connection, later echoed in Díaz. In fact, the notion that Díaz "expanded the marvelous realist tradition" (*Trans-Americanity* 103), as José David Saldívar notes, is exemplified in "Monstro" when Alex calls out to the protagonist, "welcome to the country of las maravillas." What is to be underscored here is that, although Carpentier's visit to Haiti and its descriptions of Vodun were "strategic" for writing his preface – as Emily Maguire has shown, Haiti was "seen as the site of the exotic primitive in the Americas par excellence" in the 1920s and 1930s – Carpentier's ruin-reading of Haiti and draw to Vodun (promoted by his "favorable review" of Seabrook's *The Magic Island*, as Maguire notes, *Racial* 86) shed light on the faint African influences of the marvelous real.

Despite Carpentier's damning representation of the Haitian revolution in the novel *The Kingdom of this World* that this prologue precedes, his mention of Vodun at Christophe's citadel emphasizes a deeply buried Latin-African spatial history. In his landmark study on the silence of the archive, Michel-Rolph Trouillot explains that Christophe named his favored fortress Sans Souci after the man Sans Souci, whom Christophe killed "a few yards away from – if not exactly – where he killed" this enigmatic enemy (64). While the name memorialized his triumph over his rival, or a "ritual to absorb his old enemy" (ibid. 65), the naming is not coincidental but explained in African oral history. In fact, the UNESCO heritage site of Sans Souci echoes a naming tradition tied to Christophe's African origins and the foundation of the Dahomey Republic itself. From oral sources, Trouillot recounts that Dahomey was named after its former ruler in Abomey: the ruler, "Da," was put to death by a cut to his belly ("homi") and the victor "placed his body under the foundation of a palace he built in Abomey, as a memorial of his victory; which he called Dahomy." This story interests me for two reasons; first, because Trouillot's historical anecdote informs how Christophe transplants his African history, spatially, to a site in the Americas; and second, because Carpentier's heritage tourism of the specific site where Christophe's memorialization chiseled Beninese history onto the citadel's foundation leads Carpentier to conclude that Latin America possesses a "marvelous" essence that is Latin-African.

Excavating a Latin-African heritage from this layered history also requires a third and final consideration that emerges from the African archive itself: that the Kingdom of Dahomey – which indirectly informs Carpentier's "marvelous real" – traces its origins back to these "Vodoo gods." For colonialists exploring the kingdom of Ouidah, which was later annexed to Dahomey, most bewildering were Vodun trances generated by none other than a "serpent" or "god of the nation." As one of the accounts in the *Relation du Royaume de Judas* shows (Figure 1.1), the "king of Judas was persuaded by his priests to depend on a serpent as god, to triumph over his enemies." Victory secured, the new king in turn venerated this deity by "offering sacrifices in honor of the serpent and after that he was generally recognized by his subjects as the titular God of the nation." As the population of Dahomey "recognize[d it] as the protector of their nation,"[18] serpent worship crystalized in contemporary proverbs told today at Ouidah.[19] But considered to be at the beginning of man's divine curse in the Judeo-Christian tradition, the snake, or rather the "'Iwa Damballah Ouedou' deity also known as the Grand-Zombi,"[20] led its adherents into what the archive terms frightening "extraordinary contortions." (As the French saying goes, "voilà le problème.")

As a signifier of sin even before Vodun had a chance to set foot in the "New World," the zombie as a macabre commercial figure traces its appearance to a fearsome snake-induced entrancement. In the *Relation du Royaume de Judas*, "vaudonou" praxis is particularly described: the ritual uses cages in which the entranced scream and "become possessed" during "ridiculous ceremonies" where they become "crazed."[21] This act was considered so barbaric that Sandoval also related its peculiarity: "all of the people together worship the snake" ("todos juntos adoran a culebras," 78) in a religion that is "false," "damned," and "demonic" (ibid. 71–8). Rescuing the snake from its colonial distortion, Guinean writer Camara Laye related in his memoir *L'enfant noir/The Dark Child* (1953) that the snake was the "god" that "guides [his] people," bringing good fortune as he once did to the ruler of Dahomey (5–6). Despite these

1.2 Tracing Vodun across the Atlantic: A Historical Précis

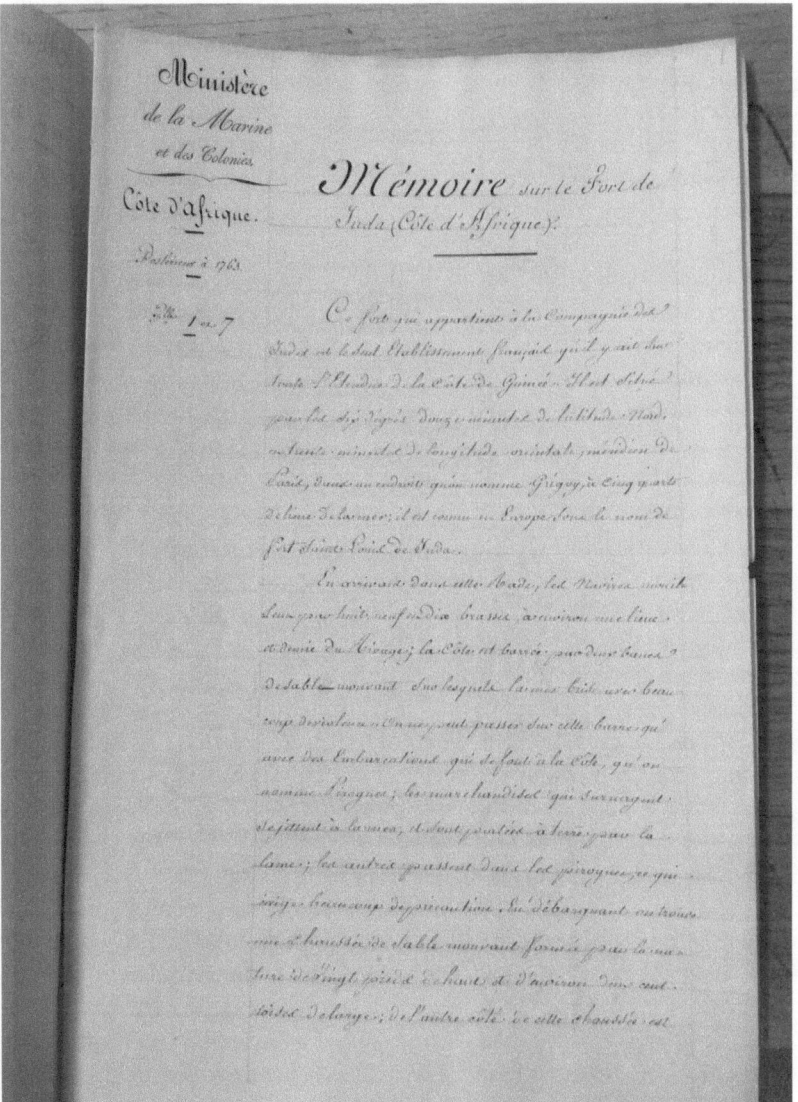

Figure 1.1 "Mémoire sur le Fort de Juda (Côte d'Áfrique)." Ministère des Colonies et de la marine et des colonies. 1763. Archives Nationales (DOM-TOM), Aix-en-Provence, France. Photo: Sarah M. Quesada, 2017.

postcolonial efforts, coloniality's centuries-old mythos of the snake, Vodun, and even the zombie would filter into the American psyche. For no other trope is more copiously reproduced than the zombie, however distorted its image may be. Although West African Vodun fashioned the caged and contorting automatons, the era of the slave trade ushered in a different kind of captive. Saidiya Hartman metaphorically argues that "the human pulse stops at the gate of the barracoon," alluding to the way that a zombie was code for a *slave* who, upon being deracinated, became an "earmark of the dead man" (*Lose* 158). In other words, blackness in colonial West Africa during the slave trade came to be perceived as synonymous with a person's "unnatural death." An enslaved African captive was not a citizen with agency, they were the opposite, and their skin color signaled their status.

In Díaz's "Monstro," then, the further darkening of Haitians points to the historical alienation of Haiti and the perpetuation of Haitians' status as outcasts through a discourse on a racialized disease polemically tied to spiritual praxis. Particularly damning are the descriptions of the disease morphing into "pustules" in the example of a young child: "his arm looked like an enormous black *pustule*, so huge it had turned the boy into an appendage of the arm. In the glypts he looked terrified" (emphasis added). This disease, the narrator explains, is different from "dengues or the poxes" and has a more "leprous spread" – it is "something else. Something new." I am struck not only by the newness of this disease in the context of Haiti's spatial history, but also by the bodily archive of disease as "pustules" flaring up on "black" bodies during the crystallization of color hierarchies in Africa's Atlantic World and fueled by a religion that was thought to encourage such metamorphosis. In other words, Díaz uses the "condition" of blackness as evocative of Vodun and its scary contortions memorialized in the colonial archive, to turn them on their head. This would not necessarily be new to Díaz, who in his bildungsroman *The Brief Wondrous Life of Oscar Wao*, replaces Joseph Conrad's "The horror, the horror!" in *Heart of Darkness* with "The beauty, the beauty!" Similarly, in "Monstro," a disease-infested Haiti intertextualizes the dehumanizing morphology of "Darkness" developed in nineteenth-century "ethnographic" accounts of Africa, such as those of Henry M. Stanley's *In Darkest Africa* (discussed in Chapter 4). In the context of expanded Hispanophile eugenics, "Monstro" considers how the West projects trepidation about the unknown onto overlapping accounts of the fearful that justify a much earlier colonization. In the dystopian catastrophe of "Monstro," the stigmatization of blackness can be traced back to colonial

1.2 Tracing Vodun across the Atlantic: A Historical Précis

myths in Africa of the "terrifying" disease endemic to Vodun-practicing rituals at one of the ports where disease was widespread. After all, traced over a diasporic continuum, Haiti emerges as the point of arrival of a new pustule disease in Díaz's story, and Ouidah – the site in former Dahomey, West Africa, from which most of the slaves who arrived in Saint-Domingue in the seventeenth century were sent – as its port of departure.

An infectious ocean-facing baracoon, Ouidah was one of the prominent ports of embarkation for the slave trade in what is today the Republic of Benin. Ouidah was often described as a pestilent source of epidemics where disease was ubiquitous because of the insalubrious conditions and length of time slaves were held there. Since this site has now been rehabilitated for heritage tourism by its renowned "Door of No Return" (see Figure 1.2), a magnificent arch erected over its seaboard, Ouidah invites us to revisit the specific language of disease that coursed through this portal. After all, Ouidah was first described in the French-Atlantic *Mémoires* as "the most unhealthy in the universe,"[22] where filth, disease, and famine manifested in joining pustules, as well as smallpox, hepatitis, dysentery, and intermittent

Figure 1.2 "Port de Non-Retour." UNESCO, Ouidah, Republic of Benin. Photo: Sarah M. Quesada, 2012.

fevers.[23] The spatiality manifested onto its enclosed subjects, as the colonial imaginary of eighteenth-century slave-trader Thomas Phillips referred to captives held in "Whidaw" as "creatures nastier than swine."[24] Thus, the perverse colonial discourse of this textual "Memory" presents an important reversal: disease was not a condition imposed on slaves by European colonial violence, but emerged innately from these so-called "creatures." Díaz's story goes beyond correcting this reversal in facetiously mimicking and exaggerating the *Mémoire*'s terminology. While it is not the first time that Díaz uses the language of disease to make a point about the effects of racialization, in this parody of "excess and chaos" (Arbino and Sabaté 1), Díaz widens the colonial to its extremes.[25] Díaz's political allegory relies on this traumatic site's distortion of captives' blackness to underline the unreliability and immoral illogicality of the colonial textual "memory" that undergirds Dominican racialization vis-à-vis the context of disease in the Vodun-practicing slave port of Ouidah.

In "Monstro," Díaz describes the newly discovered and rare disease as an "apocalypse" and "the nastiest thing you ever saw": the infected are "knotted together by horrible mold, their heads slurred into one." These descriptors conjure the ethnographic writings on Vodun that colonial and imperial records left behind. As Vodun attempted to cure disease from the sixteenth century onwards, the logocentric gaze of colonial records described Vodun practices as instead inflicting disease on a racialized Black population, an irony not unlike the US nativism against immigrants that, as prominent Chicano anthropologist Jonathan Xavier Inda writes, "attribute[s] social illness...to foreign bodies" (46). The contention here is not that these colonial discourses directly shape racial concepts across the board and crystalize into "Americanity."[26] Rather, misrepresentations of Vodun were central to later perpetuations of Black Atlantic colorism. The discourse of illness that Díaz's story invokes with terms such as "grotesque" and "pustule" not only allegorizes racism, but also connects with (mis)representations of Vodun in West Africa.

While the similarities of language between Díaz's story and descriptions of disease in colonial Vodun-practicing Ouidah precede those in Haiti, Eurocentric accounts of Vodun on both sides of the Atlantic share a fear of African-originating practitioners who were non-heteronormative female healers. In the West African Vodun records from which I draw, race was conflated with gender when Vodun's female leaders came into contact with Western belief systems. Although the colonial gender history of Vodun is absent from Díaz's short story, it is important to point out how this gendered contact zone in the African archive illuminates some of Díaz's most audacious claims about monstrosity in general. If anti-Haitianism

1.2 Tracing Vodun across the Atlantic: A Historical Précis

emerged in part from dread of a differing religious ideology, Vodun can be traced back to a supposedly disease-infested Ouidah, in which female practitioners abounded. Centuries before Vodun even established itself in Haiti, Alonso de Sandoval's *De instauranda Æthiopum salute* (1627) also interpreted the religious practice in the context of disease; here, monsters arise due to a myth uncannily evocative of a sinful Eve: "*It is a monster what is produced, according to that part in which its principle is differentiated, and thus it is said that women are somehow so as well*, because they do not have the perfection of their progenitor ... Although some have said that *this happens because women have a pact with the devil.*"[27] In this discourse, Sandoval implies that Vodun practices, which he finds demonic, have created the monstrous nature of its practitioners, and hence a diseased population. The Vodun-entranced women become these estranged and feared "monsters." As Sandoval pits entranced women against the hetero-patriarchal rule of colonial law in West Africa, their transgression becomes magnified in the eighteenth-century patriarchal *Relation du Royaume de Judas en Guinée*. As the slave trade progresses, Vodun in this text is rendered fearful precisely because of its spellbound victims. In the context of illness, "Le mal de maple" ("the evil of maple"), as it is termed, consists of "women healers" or "captains" ("femme qui soin" and "qui porte le nom de leur capitaines": *Relation* 43–50) who lead ceremonies where their infected victims become entranced (ibid. 49–50). For male missionaries who might have sneered at a spiritual belief system that was so completely at odds with their own, it must have added another layer of trepidation to witness female practitioners leading these ceremonies.

But key, too, in this mémoire is the description of *stupor*, since indeed, "those that were most forceful, were deemed the one that danced best" were seen undertaking such contortions (ibid. 49–50). At this archival juncture, the logocentric gaze of the French mémoire renders the practice savage and monstrous, describing how those "hated" because of the sins of the mother were killed in the mother's womb – a very probable misinterpretation – during an entranced, zombie-like ritual that renders them "fools."[28] Such stupor effectively brings women's "extraordinary contortions" ("contorsions extraordinaires") to life as it turns the spellbound and afflicted into a mainstay of European tropes of the zombified.

While most of the colonial records focusing on disease in Benin's coastal town emerge in the context of a western fascination with healing ailments, female contortions also function as the object of discursive and racialized fears that travel to Haiti, where Moreau de Saint-Méry describes those entranced as "turn[ing] round and round," "tear[ing] their clothes," and "even bit[ing] their own flesh" in a ritual that he finds both "disgusting" and "hideous."[29] In particular, the Lost Generation occultist William Seabrook, drawn to Haiti by the specter of disease, describes Vodun in an especially vilifying way in *The Magic Island* (1929). While his macabre text transformed Vodun ritual into the scary zombies of contemporary pop culture, the gender-nonconforming performance of that ritual is not lost on him either. Seabrook recalls how amidst an "altar of skulls," "three human figures, grotesque, yet indescribably *sinister*" and wearing "smoked goggles [that] seemed horrible" reveal Vodun's gender-nonconformity: "All three who stood there were women," but the central one held a cigar "grotesquely" in her mouth, had morphed into a "*male-female hermaphroditic* oracle of the dead," and was scandalously "*flanked on either side by two 'wives'*" (Seabrook *Magic* 84, emphasis added). Not only is the mere fact of female governance at odds with western religious doctrine, but "goggles" and a cigar seem so out of place on a woman that Seabrook calls her "grotesque." His description conveys how Vodun transgresses both gender norms and heteronormativity, as the practitioner is neither a man nor a woman and is "flanked" "by two wives." Those entranced by Vodun are thus rendered monstrous, as Seabrook uses signifiers such as "grotesque," "sinister," and "horrible" when describing a Vodun-related scene in which the entranced are "swaying, writhing, [and] moaning."[30] Ultimately, the colonial gaze prevails and vilifies what falls outside of patriarchal norms of gender and sexuality. It is, after all, colonization that introduced "complex gender norming" as María Lugones admits (750). But once again, this colonial gendering is not unique to Haiti.

Through colonial gender norming, Sandoval and Seabrook could easily demonize non-gender-conformity and non-heteronormativity by rendering Vodun-practitioners as capable of or even prone to distorted descriptions of "contortions." Especially since both assumed that the behavior Vodun seemed to inflict on its "victims" or participants was a sign of both mental and physical disease, even though twentieth-century ethnographies of West Africa, such as that of Melville Herskovits, revealed the contrary: admirable practitioners, dancing rather than contorting, and even described as devoted and saintly.[31] Similarly, in Haiti and decades after Seabrook's publication, anthropologist Alfred Métraux criticized his unpardonable "fantasy" of Vodun priests as a willful misreading shaped by American exoticism (54). Despite corrections offered in both Herskovits (with regard to Vodun in Africa) and Métraux (in Haiti), Vodun's distortion continued unabated. An ironic result of such discourses on both sides of the Atlantic is that, though Vodun seeks to heal epidemics initially produced by the slave trade, the practice of it is textually rendered frightening on the basis of its non-normative spiritual and gender structure by the very coloniality that inflicted disease in the first place.

1.3 Textual Memorials of Ouidah's Slave Route

Despite the prevailing discourse of fear enveloping Vodun and its zombie around the Atlantic, placing the fearful discourses of the archival over the physical – that is, *sites of memory* from which Vodun originates – exhibits how fictional texts, such as Díaz's, and stories told at Vodun's memorial site in Ouidah are mutually constitutive in unsettling the fearful projection of the zombie. This physical-textual connection is not simply allegorical, but functional, as both text and site recur to narrative as a means to rehabilitate the zombie fiction generated by Eurocentric "history." This is because, if the colonial mémoire distorted Vodun into a site of fear, Ouidah's Slave Route takes us back down a path where histories of Vodun abound. After all, Ouidah's 1994 UNESCO-sponsored "Route de l'Esclave" was established almost in tandem with the now-popular Vodun arts festival, *Ouidah 92: Retrouvalles Amérique-Afrique*,[32] and both became models emulated in other African nation-states I detail in this book. The Slave Route in Benin was not immune from criticism, however, as it was supported by neoliberal reform financed by the World Bank and the International Monetary Fund (IMF); it was however artistic in content, overseen by Beninese poet Noureini Tidjani-Serpos. The site single-handedly saved Benin from bankruptcy following the Soviet-backed Mathieu Kérékou dictatorship that ended in 1991 (Araujo *Public Memory* 154–5, 158). Currently, Ouidah's memorial route stretches three kilometers from the town's main square to the ocean front featuring the "Port de non-retour" ("the door of no return," finalized in 2004), on the spot from which slaves arguably embarked.[33] The walkable dirt road is dotted with twenty-one statues that recall customary life in the Dahomey kingdom (Figure 1.3), which dominated Ouidah from 1727 until French colonization in 1892. While visiting these sites, pilgrims may stop at up to six different stations commemorating slaves' Calvary,[34] but the main attractions for the Beninese are the sacred sites of Vodun.

If I have explained how Vodun has been demonized *textually* in the colonial and imperial record, it has also been suppressed *spatially* in West Africa until the advent of heritage tourism. The recovery of Vodun at its point of origin had to overcome the censorship of Benin's 1985 Marxist-Leninist regime, which aimed to "eradicate sorcery" (Ciarcia 692).

Figure 1.3 Ouidah's Slave Route memorial trail, Benin. Photo: Sarah M. Quesada, 2012.

Ironically, it was not until after the establishment of a sister-city relationship between Ouidah and Prichard, Alabama, that the beginning of a collective reflection regarding the history of slavery in Benin and the diaspora essentially liberated Vodun from prior censorship (692). Although this local example of diasporic memorialization reflects the heritage interests of a specific Black diaspora rather than a national US policy, what is crucial to point out is that a transatlantic relationship rehabilitated the perception of Vodun over the site of Ouidah. While scholars have noted Ouidah's "reinvention" as a *genre* – its rehabilitated spaces for tourism mourning the effects of the slave trade – its hybrid form also celebrates the endurance of Vodun, as practiced in both the Americas and Benin (Rush 149). In the case of Benin, as anthropologist Gaetano Ciarcia observes, the developmentalist initiatives spreading heritage tourism across the Ouidah routes went "hand-in-hand with the valorization of sacred sites and the manifestations expressing the vivaciousness and legitimacy, at times recovered, of beliefs and ancient practices."[35] As Ouidah's physical route rehabilitates Vodun from the colonial relation that rendered

1.3 Textual Memorials of Ouidah's Slave Route

it frightening, reading Díaz through this memorialization evinces how Díaz uses the category of the zombie as a signifier of difference that may also be rehabilitated. Placing together these physical and textual sites, the racialized zombies in "Monstro" read as a Latin-African textual memorial.

It is precisely the fictionality of physical memorials that encapsulates the mutually constituting effects that both genres of memorialization share. Comparing Díaz's afrofuturistic tale with Ouidah's afro-diasporic site of memory shows how both destabilize fear through storytelling. On the one hand, "Monstro" as a textual memorialization avails itself of sci-fi tropes to indeed draw in the memorial's readers. For Ouidah, on the other hand, Vodun is a site of fear that guides both mystify and decolonize through enthralling, fantastic storytelling. In other words, fiction is evoked precisely along Ouidah's heritage trail, as guides recount stories about slaves' captivity, crossing, and Vodun praxis. Although many practicing Vodun guides can earnestly speak of their own Vodun practice as authentic, thus minimizing tourists' dread of it,[36] the stories told as "historic" at these sites raise questions about how memory sites draw on historical fact and fiction.

One of the route's fictionalized sites is the "Tree of Forgetfulness." During my own visit, guides assured me that this "tree," or really a small shrub pictured in Figure 1.4, was used for slaves to circle several times in order to forget their origin.[37] The guides even insisted it was the same exact "tree" that grew there centuries ago even if the plaque refutes this claim (it reads: "In this place there was the tree of forgetfulness"). Moreover, the amnesic "zombification" said to take place at this site "has never been a named concept or process associated with Vodun in Benin" (Rush 144). Other stories regarding sites along the trail cannot be corroborated with written documents – Ouidah's "place des enchères" ("place of auction" in *Ouidah*, Law 132), the exact location of the Ouidah route, the number of slaves who traversed it, or the rituals slaves were forced to practice along the trail.[38] Even guides' stories may seem fantastic, created for the benefit of the tourist. But just as Díaz uses the recognized trope of the zombie as a fictional caricature to unveil a very real Latin-African axis, the memory site at Ouidah likewise accesses the entranced slaves circling around a tree to equally draw its spectators to a Latin-African memory.

While the zombification of slaves circling around the "Tree of Forgetfulness" might seem fictional, other stories told along the route are in fact based on African oral tradition. In other words, if storytelling's ability to deepen an emotional connection between site and visitor is notable both at Ouidah's memorial and in Díaz's textual memorial, this storytelling is not merely fictional. Just as the readaptation of a Latinx

Figure 1.4 Along Ouidah's route, guides stop at this shrub that commemorates the "Tree of Forgetfulness." Photo: Sarah M. Quesada, 2012.

zombie apocalypse in "Monstro" inspires people to confront colonial continuities head-on, Dana Rush states that, via Ouidah's "reinvention," guides' stories along the trail are "meant to appeal on an emotional level to foreign audiences" (135), and do so through African proverbs. For example, some guides at Ouidah recount a prescient Vodun proverb that foretells the doom that, from the vantage point of the present, awaits the slave who does not respect the snake: "Woe to he who grazes a minute snake," which means, he who disrespects a snake, ill fate will befall him.[39] Compellingly, quoting this proverb on Ouidah's Slave Route confers blame though prophecy; it implies that Vodun did not come to the aid of those who did not follow its praxis. Invoking this proverb seems to involve reevaluating the past, as if at a certain place and moment in time, slavery could have been avoided. Thus, the proverb seems to convey what Ariella Azoulay terms "potential history" (*Potential* 43–7): Ouidah becomes a prescient site that clues us in to what would have happened had constituent violence not triumphed. In other words, the site becomes less of a Vodun warning about respecting snakes and, rather, a reflection on regret during the slave trade or, to use Azoulay's terms, on "historical moments [that] reappear at junctions where other options could have been chosen" ("Potential History" 551). Like the prophetic environmental warning embedded in Díaz's ecoparable, the proverb uttered over Ouidah's site indeed prophesies both past and future: it presciently imagines what would have been if slavery had *not* been, and what could be if capitalistic forms of bondage persist. As a site perched on the verge of history, the proverbial storytelling enables Ouidah to move its pilgrims affectively by enabling the past to predict the future.

Beyond the thematic similarities between text and site, emotional attachment to a Slave Route memorial has to do, in great part, with its sites' ability to evoke for the visitor memories drawn from familiar or widely circulated histories of African diasporic trauma. This communal "cultural trauma" is part of "[p]ostmemory's connection to the past" which, as Marianne Hirsch argues, is "actually mediated not by recall but by imaginative investment, projection, and creation" from its original (5). While Ouidah's memorial sites in effect craft a story based on a collective trauma drawn from documentation (Araujo "Welcome" 165), Haitian-Venezuelan scholar Evelyne Laurent-Perrault corroborates these postmemory claims about Ouidah's emotional potency. During a professional sojourn in West Africa, she visited the Slave Route and writes that "[a]mong all of the experiences [in the African continent] perhaps one of the most powerful in terms of shaping my Afro-Latina awareness was visiting the port of Ouidah" (quoted in Jiménez Román and Flores 172–3). As Beninese proverbs invoked at particular sites imagine the trauma of slavery in the Americas, in Laurent-Perrault's account, the narrative of a Latin-Africa moves in the other direction, through physical space rather than a fictional story such as Díaz's. In fact, Ouidah's significance as a catalyst for Laurent-Perrault's Latin-African connection both corrects the fearful discourses about Haitian blackness that Díaz's critical story denounces, and rewrites the grand Eurocentric narrative that envelopes Vodun's zombie. Although the Slave Route point of Ouidah conjures the politics of memory I mentioned above, reading both textual and physical memorials together indeed nuance and deepen the Dominican rejection of blackness at its Atlantic source: walking the trail of Ouidah as an act of Vodun rehabilitation offers a key that unlocks the othering of "Monstro" as we consider the long-distorted trajectory of the Vodun-originated zombie. Thus, just as Carpentier's heritage tourism at Sans Souci prompted him to consider the centrality of "vaudou" for a literary Latin America, in Díaz's textual memorial, the site-reader of the short story revisits and contests the fear imbued in the zombie by reading Ouidah's heritage trail into Díaz's plot.

I trace the discourses that surround Vodun both in the story and at Ouidah's memorial site not only because Vodun happens to be one of the starting points of alienation between Dominicans and Haitians, but also to consider once again how texts and memorial sites mutually constitute each other and could together destabilize colonial discursive power. Discourses, after all, are "sayings and stories that organize *places* through the displacements they 'describe'" (Certeau *Practice* 116, emphasis added). In other words, the very discourse of "displacement" creates the distorted memory of "place" and, for Díaz's "Monstro," an Africa memorialized as frightening. And yet, these stories and the sites they either occupy or conjure are deeply imbricated in a far more dangerous way. As language forms the imaginary of space, to paraphrase de Certeau, the memory of that space can become manipulated by the very spatial discourse that describes it (Certeau *Practice* xx). Seabrook's reaction to Vodun in the epigraph, "No one dared to stop them, for they were corpses walking in the sunlight," for example proves how colonial discourses about particular places and racialized people can change those places and people. This powerful discourse of space recalls Fanon's interpretation of "*spaces of terror*," where the colonial imagination created fearsome creatures associated with a particular space, thereby negating any association between people and their place of origin.[40] And as Díaz's narrative illustrates, there is little appeal in morphing into the "infekted" zombie.

But while discourses that affect space can create fear, memory sites such as the ones in Ouidah resituate these fearful narratives not only in Díaz's story but also in African literary works. As an example of how a fictional work in Africa looks the other way toward the Americas, Beninese author Eric Adja's children's book, *Les trois héros de Ouidah* (1997), upends the colonial "spaces of terror" via a story in which three children seek to restore artifacts stolen from Ouidah's museum along the Slave Route. In a reversal of a Latin-Africa, rather than an American text looking toward Africa, here Beninese fiction, over the book's fictionalized Tree of Return, envisions the arrival of slaves in the Americas. "This tree," the narrative notes, is likewise one that slaves circled as a ritual that assured them that even "if [they] died in America, beyond the seas, [their] spirit would return to [their] native land," guided by Vodun's zombie. Notably, the tree, just as much as other sites along the trail, enables the students to evoke the lost slave – their "ancestor" as she is described.[41] In turn, they can bring her home, not through a dreaded zombie and its spaces of terror, but by the spiritual power of Ouidah.

For his part, Díaz's "Monstro" satirically amplifies these imaginary spaces of terror; the site of colonial fear that is Vodun and its zombie. Preceding the amplification of the zombie is that of the apocalypse. In his essay "Apocalypse," Díaz writes that "[a]pocalypses, like the Haitian earthquake, are not only catastrophes; they are also opportunities: chances for us to see ourselves, to take responsibility for what we see, to change." In "Monstro," enlarging and focalizing the zombie site of apocalypse is this opportunity to "see." For as Foucault states, "the monster provides an account, as though in caricature, of the genesis of differences" (*Order* 157) – and in the case of Díaz's ecoparable, these differences are tied to a Latin-African world. "Monstro" picks up on Foucault's nuanced reading of monstrosity and synthesizes the monster's link to slavery in the zombie. But the zombie's evolution in the neoliberal era produces consequences for the industrial complex of globalized capitalistic exploitation run rampant: the short story offers an allegory for humanity ignoring its own ongoing anthropogenic extinction as the misery the zombie had endured was tolerable no longer. In this literary piece, monsters are, as Foucault once claimed, a "necessity" for making poignant claims about history (*Order* 153). The poignant claim in "Monstro" is that a warning that was only too clear has been ignored for far too long. In the dystopian future of "Monstro," a refusal to heed this call of warning results in the final iteration of Díaz's zombie.

1.4 The Decolonial Zombie

In this final section, I argue that Díaz's "Monstro" subverts monstrosity to pinpoint its colonial projection onto the Vodun-practicing African subject. By extension, the story exhibits the rejection of African origins which are rehabilitated as a Latin-Africa by the end of the narrative. As "Monstro" exhibits the final transformations of the zombie – from going silent, to shrieking, morphing into one being, eating human flesh, and finally becoming a giant – the narrator describes the infected using colonial language reminiscent of the mémoires in Ouidah about Vodun-practicing peoples. In a reversal of monstrosity, "Monstro" exhibits how the cruel and emotionally detached language used by the noninfected to describe the infected belies any humanity vis-à-vis the suffering. Just as "Monstro" satirizes how slave traders projected their monstrous trading practice onto the enslaved earlier in the chapter, the story also underscores how the language of cannibalism is likewise projected onto the same Vodun-practicing peoples. When Díaz's story presents the transformation of zombies into cannibals, anthropophagy serves as a primal site of the rejection of African origins, pointing out the irony that Europe's taboo practice was projected onto the indigenous carib population – which was named the "Caribbean" – and, once they were exterminated, onto the African slave. As the story uses the trope of the cannibal-turned-Caliban to question the African roots of otherization found in the "monster," Díaz's ecoparable amplifies the zombie as it transforms into a colossal giant, which authorities attempt to contain through a bomb that "turned the entire world white." If notions of monstrosity were already being reversed in the story, here Díaz's narrative goes a step further by turning race on its head: the story denounces the violent effects of White colonial language attempting to preserve the status quo, but the zombie survives the apocalypse. Within this darkness, the original rejection of both Dominican blackness and African traditions is clear. The ending of "Monstro" alternatively suggests a rehabilitation of this blackness that was rendered fearful, by turning zombies into an allegory of survival and even hope.

In "Monstro," once the strange disease alters the morphology of its victims, as they relate to one another and draw together (recall the story's description of their "knott[ing] together"), they begin to display other characteristics that speak to their union. The infected become speechless, further othered because they literally all stop speaking. But their speechlessness, termed "the Silence," undergirds their subaltern position:

> Stranger shit was in the offing: eight months into the epidemic, all infected viktims, even the healthiest, abruptly stopped communicating. Just went silent. Nothing abnormal in their bloodwork or in their scans. They just stopped talking – friends, family, doctors, it didn't matter. No stimuli of any form could get them to speak. Watched everything and everyone, clearly understood commands and information – but refused to say anything. Anything *human*, that is.

The victims' "refusal" allegorizes a mute insubordination the narrator terms "unnerving," emphasizing their crucial solidarity in the face of dehumanization. But if the silence of Díaz's zombies is understood as a strategic subalternity that resists dominant hegemonies, this morphological adaptation to oppression transforms yet again, into the opposite: a "shriek" that further destabilizes the reality of the non-infected. After their period of devastating silence, "[t]he entire infected population simultaneously le[t] out a bizarre shriek – two, three times a day. Starting together, ending together." This "shriek" is so unbearable that "no uninfected could stand to hear it," but neither the narrator nor the doctors can explain how, without prior communication, the infected chant in unison. Out of fear, the narrator mocks the praxis, asserts that the infected are incapable of speaking a "human" language, and judgmentally interprets their communication patterns as "wailing" at best or producing an "eerie siren shit" at worst. The narrator's logocentric evaluations of an unfamiliar epistemology conjure a colonizing gaze, one that, as Ngũgĩ wa Thiong'o suggests, attempts to control a "people's culture" in order to, in turn, "control their tools of self-definition in relationship to others" (16). Fearing the unknown, the narrator dominates these colonized expressions through discourse. Yet, concealing his fear with sarcasm, in a distant tone he sardonically *names* the disease "the phenomenon that became known as the Chorus." As the narrator, in this act of naming, is mimicking European discourses, the story derides the narrator's rejection of the zombies' behavior and their admirable unity against all odds.

Perhaps the most obvious allegory for a colonial rejection of othered solidarity in "Monstro" emerges in the context of *physical* cohesiveness. First, the zombies in "Monstro" develop a stance on isolation vis-à-vis the healthy, as their "compulsion to stay together" becomes a metaphor for subaltern communities' resistant gathering – not unlike the *quilombos* and *palenques* that emerged at the height of the slave trade.[42] During the metamorphosis in "Monstro," the zombies develop a different frame of reference from the healthy, revealing an unbearable desire for clan-like closeness:

> Doctors began reporting a curious change in the behavior of infected patients: they wanted to be together, in close proximity, all the time. They no longer tolerated being separated from other infected, started coming together in the main quarantine zone, just outside Champ de Mars, the largest of the relocation camps. All the víktims seemed to succumb to the ingathering compulsion. ("Monstro")

In contrast with the narrator's distant tone, the fact that the infected – poor and diseased – cannot "tolerate" to be "separated" from other sufferers communicates their unity.

The colonial imaginary of the noninfected is underlined in "Monstro" when a doctor in Martinique attempts in vain to "isolate" one of his "infected" patients. This cruel scene suggests a reaction against separation that Glissant would term "Relation." The doctor's cruelty is explained as a response to a unity he cannot comprehend but also finds threatening to the status quo. After all, as Glissant explains in his theory of Relation, "violence is the response societies make to the immediacy of contacts"; a fearful response to change and contact (*Poetics* 141). This misjudgment of the zombies' relation jeopardizes the power of a ruling class, as this ruling class vies to isolate and control what they cannot understand. But when solitude and solidarity collide in "Monstro," they produce a scene in which "this frail septuagenarian had torn off her heavy restraints, broken through a mesh security window, and crawled halfway back to the quarantine zone before she was recovered." The site of brutality unveils not only coloniality's continuity but also an othered resistance, as the infected undertake a natural evolution.[43] As this evolution further unfolds, the ecoparable of "Monstro" deconstructs the discursive apparatus of difference through the zombie's ultimate transformation.

As if social behavior entails physical effects, the solidarity of the infected translates into physical mutation. The narrator reports that a "shaky glypt" presented "a pair of naked trembling Haitian brothers sharing a single stained cot, knotted together by horrible mold, their heads slurred into one" ("Monstro"). Mockingly, he judges that they "seemed to have a boner for fusion" and "respected no kind of boundaries." As they threaten to occupy space with their otherness, it is not so much that the infected isolate themselves vis-à-vis the "uninfected" as that the healthy create an inhuman and unsympathetic distance from the subaltern population. But importantly, Haiti's historical plantocracy has led to a faulty economy and plethora of diseases (World Bank, "Haiti"), expressed in "Monstro" as the infected tolerating "nine kinds of ill already." Far from eliciting compassion, this othered suffering instead renders the beholders' ethnographic gaze completely detached: the narrator states that his friend Alex was "[a]lmost delighted" when he witnessed the metamorphosis of the infected, adding that it was "[a]bout the nastiest thing you ever saw." The expression of rejection and disgust is not unlike that of slaver Phillips mentioned earlier describing the Vodun-practicing slaves he contemplated over the site of Ouidah. As this rhetoric of rejection conjures Ouidah, both Haiti and Ouidah become relatable sites of difference in the narrative of "Monstro," compelling its readers to consider where the colonial (and endemic) disavowal of othered solidarity originates.

Rather than seeing the evolution of othered creatures as a form of escapism, I propose that "Monstro" privileges them as Latin-African allegories exposing not the monstrosity of those infected, but rather the cruel detachment of the noninfected who project a colonial discourse onto the infected. Their extreme otherness underscores their purposefulness in the story vis-à-vis the narrator's rejection of them, a narrative strategy that, as Lugones proposes, reveals those who "occupy demeaning positions that make them disgusting to the social superiors" (751). In other words, their otherness reveals the prejudices of "social superiors" like the narrator. This is especially made obvious when the infected join together against adversity but the narrator describes this unison in both a gruesome and an amused tone. For instance, Alex is "delighted" by visceral suffering, or the dehumanization of descriptions such as "knot[ting] together" "horrible mold," and "nastiest thing you ever saw." These descriptors from the positionality of the narrator expose coloniality's reduction of people to subhuman categories that both Alex and the narrator deem inferior by nature. I suggest that it is precisely the coloniality of this discourse that Haiti's Atlantic racial history further elucidates. As the colonized persist despite coloniality's domination scheme, the narration focuses on the colonizers' own brutalization, which recalls Lisa Surwillo's explanation of how slave traders' "human essence" morphed into "barbarity" as they lost a sense of compassion and became "monsters by trade."[44] While the narrator of Díaz's parody belongs to an island where this historical process would have been familiar, he is nonetheless unmoved by the uncanny iterations of both the colonizers' brutalization and the barbarity of confining the colonized, distracted instead, as Maguire notes, by his pursuit of Mysty ("The Heart of a Zombie" 14). The narrator's discourse in the postplantation site of Hispaniola once again recalls the slave trader Phillips' assertion that the enslaved were "creatures nastier than swine" at Ouidah's port of departure. The mimicking of the narrator's derision of the infected traces the colonial discourse of difference back to its origin in West Africa, as "Monstro" parodies the irony by which, over this African site, the slaver projects his *moral* monstrosity onto the *physicality* of the slave.

The most significant bridge between the projection of monstrosity in "Monstro" and Ouidah's memorial site in Africa is the case of Casimir, a marginal character who appears to be diseased and entranced. When Casimir begins acting up, his wife claims he is "bewitched." The narrator further discloses "widespread rumors that the Infected were *devils*" (emphasis added); "reports" indicated that even "relatives attempt[ed] to set their infected family members on fire." The way in which a rumored zombie turns *demonic* once again conjures the Haitian plantocracy, where so-called "devil acts" were synonymous with slaves' Vodun practices. This praxis was called "black magic" and was punishable by the Inquisition's "witchcraft trials" in which the burning or lynching of those "bewitched" was commonplace from the sixteenth century onward (Sweet *Domingos* 51). Díaz's fiction relies on this history, since Casimir's "bewitchment" (his wife claims "Someone has witched him") involves him "tramping about without destination," reproducing well-known Vodun trances and contortions. In this state of mind, Casimir's removal from his kin results in him "exploding" and "bounding" "out the car." Crucially, his "twitching and twisting in his seat," "garbled" language, and his heeding of the "infernal chorus" of the infected camp all draw from the so-called extraordinary contortions in Ouidah. Given the story's allusions to clan-like gatherings, zombies, shrieking, lynching, and accusations of demonic acts, all set in former Hispaniola, the stigmatized group of the infected evokes the maligned Vodun hypnotism of former Dahomey.

Not only is the linkage of Vodun-reverie to "bewitchment" familiar from accounts of Haiti such as Seabrook's modernist one, but the discourse of dread and death surrounding the Vodun daze also dates back to the heterotemporality of "extraordinary contortions" in the colonial *Relation du Royaume de Judas*. According to this document, the origin of this trance is found in "howling women serpents" ("les femmes serpent hurlent"), "making the cries of priests" ("faisant les cris des prêtres") in an effort to pray for a good harvest.[45] Once "possessed" (*Relation* 61–2), they also "run" and "scream" ("ils voyaient ces femmes courir," "lorsque les femmes crient") and "will burrow into a hole to hide" ("se fourront dans un trou pour se cacher") – imagery that informs tropes of zombies as grave-seeking creatures. For Seabrook, on the other hand, it was not enough to distort Dahomenian Vodun transferred to Haiti; to complete the cycle of rejection, he had to make this distortion frightening by embedding stupor and grave craving into his explanation of Vodun:

> As they approached their graveyard they began to shuffle faster and faster and rushed among the graves, and each before his own empty grave began clawing at the stones and earth to enter again; and as their cold hands touched the earth of their own graves, they fell and lay there, rotting carrion. (Seabrook *Magic* 99)

Not only does the repetition of "grave" four times in one brief paragraph underline the fear of walking-dead automatons, the obsession with grave imagery is explained in the African colonial records. Once again in the

1.4 The Decolonial Zombie

Relation du Royaume de Judas, the colonial memorial states that "the negro is very inclined to flight, not one is bold enough to go and strip these corpses, for fear of being anxious after their death, and despaired of burials."[46] While in the French version of "le Negre soit très enclin au vol," the word "vol" has been interpreted as aerial flight – and consequently recalls *The Book of Negro Folklore* and its tale of "flying Africans" from plantations[47] – in the context of a description of Ouidah's Vodun, it clearly signifies the site of grave-raiding. Grave-robbing is specifically evoked here: the writer underlines that Judas's Vodun practitioners were *unlikely* to commit such an act for fear of afterlife retribution. Nevertheless, at some point during Vodun's transferal to the New World, the distortion of the grave-robbing trope becomes part of the zombie figure in Haiti, heightening the deathlike qualities of the zombie-figure. But a spiritual praxis presiding over a racial geography already considered "strange" further demarcated Vodun as the epitome of the "convulsive," where an imagined "Africa," Mbembe argues, is this figure par excellence of the frightful, "a headless figure threatened with madness" producing "*strange signs, convulsive movements*" (*Postcolony* 3, emphasis added). In "Monstro," Casimir's "strange signs" during his bewitchment – his "convulsive movements" – are, like those of others in the quarantine zone, categorized as markers of a "disease" in Haiti, just as they were deemed "madness" in former Dahomey. As the missionary value system amplifies fear to its extremes, the end of Díaz's story mimics this amplification but subverts the racialization, sexism, and religious chauvinism entrenched in this fear.[48] While "Monstro" does this through a sarcastic mimicry of colonial discourse it also does so, oddly, via one of the West's favorite tropes of otherness yet: cannibalism.

In *Junot Díaz and the Decolonial Imagination*, I explained how the futuristic setting of Díaz's apocalypse succumbs to cannibalism, registered through an odd polaroid that destruction leaves in its wake. "Monstro" ends with the multinational industrial war complex being turned against the lethal mass of the infected. As foreign governments attempt to contain the "diseased," they level Haiti during the so-called "Detonation Event" that, in seconds, "[t]riggered a quake that was felt all across the Island" and is reminiscent of Haiti's nonfictional earthquake. Rather than a mischievous satire at the expense of an impoverished nation, "Monstro" comes full circle and decolonizes a racialized zombie. After the explosion, the zenith of tension features the infected fully morphing into *man-eating*-zombies, as a Polaroid found amidst the debris exhibits those now termed the "Possessed" and a "Class 2" threat. Transformed into dangerous gigantic creatures, the infected turn against the healthy, not deterred by "point[ing] a gauss-gun at them," "stopped only when they [are] killed." They are described as "forty-foot-tall cannibal motherfuckers running loose on the Island." But the anthropophagic nature of the infected is coated in biblical meaning. On the back of the rescued photograph, there is a quote from scripture: "Numbers 11:18. *Who shall give us flesh to eat?*" ("Monstro"). Noticeably a dichotomy is drawn here. On the one hand, the cannibal emerges as if out of this biblical quote; on the other, this scripture conjures the very presence of Christian theology. The dichotomy established in the story criticizes religious scapegoating, foretold in Díaz's essay "Apocalypse," which presages that humanity will be "picked off by the hundreds of thousands by 'natural disasters'" justified as "acts of god.'" Thus, the photo not only "document[s] the fall of humanity," as Yomaira C. Figueroa-Vázquez argues (172). In the case of "Monstro," the fact that scripture appears on the opposite side of a photo of reemerging cannibals might imply a form of celestial punishment for deviating from Judeo-Christian ways and, in any case, a psychosomatic *transatlantic* trauma.

Anthropophagy, like race, was thus a discourse that was used to justify colonization of the Americas and was perpetuated as imagery to secure European nations' hold on their colonies. The reference to cannibalism in "Monstro" ironizes its European practice, in for instance eleventh-century Western Europe during unprecedented famines, while religiously being condemned as a biblical sign of the coming of Armageddon. Obviously Christian evangelization played a role in empire, and cannibalism was deemed barbaric. But it must further be noted that Díaz's Caribbean was named after "cannibalism." The term became attached to the Antilles when, lost in translation, the first explorers inferred that "caribs" – the inhabitants of Cuba and Saint-Domingue – meant "cannibal," projecting their own traumatic identities as former human-flesh-eating societies onto these inhabitants (Hulme 15). Moreover, while accounts of cannibalism in the Americas may have been refuted back in the sixteenth century, "carib" was not distinguished from "cannibal" until 1796, after the Caribbean had already been named. Like the zombie, the Caribbean itself was conceived through refracted European fears, similar to those perpetuated about West and Central Africa. If, as Cuban intellectual Roberto Fernández Retamar stated, the Caribbean provided a fertile ground for "the cannibal, the bestial man inevitably situated at the margin of civilization," this nemesis of colonial society was already rooted in a racialized Atlantic World. But once the carib disappeared, the cannibal to "be combated with *blood and fire*"[49] was not "the exterminated Indian," Fernández Retamar states, but none other than "the black man from Africa."[50]

1.4 The Decolonial Zombie

As if echoing Díaz's earlier *The Brief Wondrous Life of Oscar Wao*, whose colonial curse is embodied in "Africa," "screaming in the voices of the enslaved" (1), "Monstro" mocks coloniality's creation of both the myth of bestiality and its African origin. In Sandoval's account, the colonial perception is precisely that "extraordinary monsters are said to inhabit all the black kingdom" (22), from "women with beards on their breasts" to "ferocious" fish "covered in hair" and "long teeth" (22, 62). The colonizing gaze, the real disease, transforms this imaginary of bestiality into *actual* monstrosity, as Aimé Césaire masterfully pointed out: colonization is "a center of infection [that] begins to spread" decivilizing the colonizer beyond return as the "continent [Europe] proceeds toward savagery" (13). In Europe, Aristotelian reasoning understood the feared monstrosity as a sign of evil; monstrous subjects deserved their poor circumstances due to the *interior* divine curse of Ham. In Book I, when Sandoval lays eyes on the barbarity of the slave trade,[51] he explains "how to morally justify black slavery" (50), stating that "[s]ervitude" is "glorious" (ibid. 56). The textual memorial implies that suffering is justified as it restores depravity into whiteness or, in Africanist V. Y. Mudimbe's words, leads to "conversion from savagery and Satan's darkness to the light of civilization" (52). Of course, this civilizing mission helped justify exploiting those rendered infrahuman for capitalist gain, but paradigms of race and gender did not, on their own, make the African subject fearful enough to rationalize its enslavement. To use a spatial vocabulary from María Josefina Saldaña-Portillo, Black spiritual praxis and its subject were "coproduced in and by the confined spaces," in this case, of missionary discourse that distorted this practice over the landscape it was practiced upon (*Indian* 21), creating various otherizations of Vodun practitioners, from slave to neoliberal zombie.

As this particular Jesuit discourse about Africa perpetuated distinct otherness, it also left a textual trail from which to consider how a register originating in and about Africa shapes dialectics of blackness in Latinx stories such as Díaz's "Monstro." After all, as Mudimbe states, these missionary accounts "brought about serious doubt concerning the pertinence of western discourses on African societies" (44). Stigmatized terms such as "darkness," "deformity," "disease," "trances," and even "monstrosity," still demonized in the neoliberal era, serve as colonial reference points that stories like "Monstro" decolonize. Díaz's maneating zombies make a comeback, transformed from colonial subjects to colossal globalized creatures. However ludicrous this outcome may be, Díaz's new zombie forces a Foucauldian deconstruction of the very nature of monstrosity in order to question what causes fear in the other. Such a reading understands Díaz's supersized carib, not as a Rabelaisian carnivalesque freak, but more as "out of normalcy," in Montaigne's terms.[52] Monsters, according to Foucault, are "[m]ost apparently bizarre forms" and yet "metamorphoses of the prototype just as natural as the others" (*Order* 154–6). Disagreeing with Darwinian theories of evolution, Foucault believes monsters evolve accidentally; that is, they are formed by "a confused mingling of beings that seem to have been *brought together by chance*" (148, emphasis added). Even if the new zombies seem grotesque as they are physically "knotting together," with "heads slurred into one" ("Monstro"), Foucault would deem this monster a "solid expanse" or "merely the fragmentary result of a much more tightly knit, much finer *continuity*" (*Order* 154, emphasis added). It is indeed the continuity of this subject who is better equipped to survive that interests me here. For indeed, it is precisely Díaz's zombies who not only endure coloniality's continual repression, but also *survive* the devastation of planetary climate change. Foucault's monsters are the result of "natural revolutions" (153) or "geological catastrophes" (155), such as those described in Díaz's inhabitable setting. Yet, Díaz's allegorical figure traces the various configurations of a Renaissance Caliban, a continuity that undergirds this zombie's unique persistence.

Fernández Retamar's reimagining of Shakespeare's *The Tempest* (1611) projects Foucault's deconstruction of this discursive "monster" into an Antillean setting (Quesada "Planetary" 310). But building also on José Enrique Rodó's *Ariel* (1900), Fernández Retamar's *Calibán* (1971) envisions Foucault's perfected and *naturally* developed species as not only able to survive but also rooted in the culture of the marooned slave – specifically, Haiti's Toussaint Louverture and others before him who were less successful (Retamar 32). As in Foucault's deconstruction of the monster, Fernández Retamar likens the othered islander Caliban to the "mambí," a term for runaway slaves in the colonial era that was later used by colonial authorities to denigrate *criollo* uprisings in the age of nineteenth-century American revolutions. To this effect, Fernández Retamar adds that "they call[ed] us *mambí*, they call[ed] us negros, to offend us" (my translation, ibid. 37), implying that Cuban criollos would be offended not only by being called "slaves," but also by the *racial* designation linked to that term. The kind of transnational rejection of Latin American blackness that Fernández Retamar describes finds continuities in the present that Díaz critiques. That is, the same fearful disavowal of contemporary "negrura" that Díaz plays out at the beginning of "Monstro" resonates with the colonial use of the term "mambí." While the mambí signification might not be endemic in West Africa, the "monster" discourse memorialized in the colonial Mémoire discloses origins of the mambí-Caliban otherness in the Atlantic World. Like the terms "monster" and "zombie," "mambí" is used by colonial agents to spread signifiers of barbarism and marginality rooted in the fear of Black resistance.

Fernández Retamar and Díaz reclaim and rehabilitate terms like "mambí" and "monster" that entail these very continuities of institutional discourse. Recalling Cuba's nineteenth-century independence insurgency from Spain, Fernández Retamar states that the Cuban criollos like himself considered it an "honor" to be "considered descendants of *mambí*, descendants of revolted slaves, maroons, independents" (ibid. 37). Appealing to the discursive rejection of blackness, Fernández Retamar proposes that criollos envision themselves as Latin-African. Díaz, on the other hand, takes a different approach. As the story indicts the narrator's (and his friend Alex's) aloof and inhuman detachment from the infected vis-à-vis the zombies' survival in the face of calamity, the zombie undergoes a process of decolonization. For Díaz, terms that connote monstrosity – such as disease, pustules, trances, blackness, and socioeconomic disadvantage – do not incapacitate the zombie. Rather, these solidarity-practicing subjects survive despite hegemonic discourse and its distorted imaginary. Of further note is that, at the end of the story, the healthy are left out altogether, as the narrative focus shifts to the mambí-zombies deconstructing racial discourse. In other words, Díaz resignifies the etymological "monster," previously discursively crystalized in the colonial Atlantic memorial, and rehabilitates it as the sole survivor of a futuristic holocaust.

To nuance this decolonial reading of Díaz further, we must consider post-structuralism's blind spots and the materiality of discourses. Considering the will to extinguish the virus that spreads over the racial geography of former Hispaniola in "Monstro," the institutional assertion of hegemonic control over "disease" reinforces not only a practice of discursive state power that can be traced back to missionary language in West Africa, but also a violent and visceral reaction to a fear borne of said discourse. In Díaz's story, before total apocalypse, the frightening resilience of these new Calibanesque species leads to the deployment of a nuclear weapon against the previously "blackened" Haiti. As the assault "turned the entire world white" ("Monstro"), its intensity was so blinding that it "burned out the optic nerve [of scientist Dr. DeGraff's] right eye" as DeGraff attempted to watch what unfolded as the zombies were bombed. Recalling the beginning of the story, where the narrator confronts anti-blackness, the ending comes back to a dialectic of Black/White opposites.

In this case, whiteness as the counterpoint of its binary other is produced by such intense illumination that it does not reveal clarity. Rather, its brightness is blinding, both literally (for DeGraff) and figuratively, as it occludes real distinctions.

To return to the original Dominican rejection of Black Haitianism, and thus a cultural rejection of Africa, "Monstro" reverses the reinscription of the universal in light as it overturns the dichotomy of blanqueamiento and *negrura*. Díaz had already implied that *negrura* is an opportunity to see clearly, when in his essay "Apocalypse" he wrote, "Apocalypse is a darkness that gives us light." In "Monstro," the categories of light and white emphasize occlusion and blindness, whereas darkness and blackness are linked with revelation and truth. The usual understanding of these binary opposites, as defined by normative Eurocentric logic, is overturned, and within the story, new conceptions of both race and color are revealed. In this shift, blackness is rehabilitated through a spectacular reversal in which the colonially old memorialization of a "Dark Africa," or archival discourses representing Africans as subhuman is shattered in Díaz's textual memorial. From the plantation to the neoliberal era to an afrofuturist stage amidst ecological disaster, the etymological presence of blackness in "Monstro" reveals a resignifying of Latin-African sites of fear into sites of warning.

Perhaps most important is the decolonial shift that Díaz offers on both race and the fear attached to Africa's blackness. Far from terrifying, the symbolism that adheres to Díaz's zombie is just as much a force of life as the Vodun in Benin that inspired it. As the discourse of the zombie has changed, so too has blackness as it outlives the very hegemonic structures attempting to annihilate it. Foreshadowing Mbembe's concept of Black survivability, or a blackness that is "capable of living" new lives, expressing a "desire for life," and "engaged in the act of creation,"[53] Díaz's racialized zombies survive the apocalypse and more. Their "desire for life" fosters the means by which they might recreate themselves, better equipped to renew a world that coloniality disrupted. Before this happens, however, Díaz's zombie will end unjust humanity – figuratively or literally – just as scripture prophesied. Affecting the Caribbean initially, the monsters will become a true planetary transglobal concern, suggesting the interconnectivity of world history, from the Crusades, colonialism, and neoliberalism to, hopefully, afrofuturism.

The transatlantic plurality achieved in Díaz's story corrects the myopic perception of the geographical reach in his literary craft. If José David Saldívar implored us to explore "one kind of archive that gets lost in a world-system" to reconstitute a "literary history of the Global South" that Saldívar traces in the *Brief Wondrous Life of Oscar Wao* ("Conjectures" 121), this reading of "Monstro" seeks those traces across the Atlantic. Not only does the Latin-African axis in "Monstro" point out the shortcomings of a World Literature that conceives of Díaz as exclusively transnational, the short story calls for a parity in the ways the foundations of racialization and antiblackness are constructed. With regard to the former, this ecoparable offers an opportunity to conceive of a Latin-Africa constituted by African particularities, that are neither essentialized nor generalized but instead specific to a "South"-South Atlantic engagement (by "South" I mean the Dominican-Americans subsumed under the US). But regarding the latter, "Monstro" positions West African epistemology as an equal point of reference for determining the foundations of White hegemony and economic injustice at the root of Dominican and Dominican-American racialization. As a textual memorial, the zombie in Díaz's story, like Ouidah's Slave Route, negotiates with history and fiction to save a nonfictitious future, seeming to convey that we may revisit our histories over and over again, but catastrophe stories, such as slavery's evolution into zombification, are meant to change the degeneration of our times. As such, in both Ouidah and in "Monstro," the multivalent symbol of the zombie is rehabilitated and released from the colonial discourses in which it was held captive. Yet, its monstrosity mocked and denounced, the zombie plays a larger role in the decolonial world: like the Byronic antihero of a moralistic tale, this Foucauldian *monstro* is both a haunting Latin-African memorial of our past and a steadfast call for a renewed "South"-South solidarity in the face of a prescient global apocalypse.

CHAPTER 2

Commodification
Black Internationalism and the African Safari of Achy Obejas's Ruins

Cuban-American Achy Obejas's only novel set in Cuba, *Ruins* (2009), tackles the commodification of a Latin-Africa in the aftermath of Cuba's internationalist campaign in Angola at the end of the Cold War. The novel is anchored in Cuba's euphemistically named "Special Period in Times of Peace" of the 1990s, an era of unprecedented economic depression in the wake of both the 1989 collapse of the Soviet Union and the defeat of the Cuban-Angolan alliance. Beginning in the summer of 1994, as devastating poverty and hunger reigned, a *balsero* (rafter) flotilla of more than 70,000 Cubans fled to Florida, becoming the last significant wave of Cuban immigrants to the US. In *Ruins*, the protagonist Usnavy – a well-read revolutionary faithful – is haunted by this scene, which he witnesses from the port of Cojimar where Ernest Hemingway penned *The Old Man and the Sea* at La Terraza.[1] As *Ruins* critiques the tourists who seek traces of Hemingway's Antillean utopia and overlook the Cuban tragedy, the sight of rafters prompts Usnavy to muse that his kin were once "Africans – dragged [to Cuba] against their will" (151). Conflating modern and colonial trauma, Usnavy takes refuge in an "African safari." His exoticized imaginary clearly draws on different conventions – modernist safari scenes of Wifredo Lam, Pablo Picasso, or Hemingway that the novel alludes to, but also a Cuban collective memory of the Angolan war and a peculiar visualization of the UNESCO Slave Route site of Badagry, Nigeria. In this conflation of the era of slavery, modernist Havana, African decolonization, and the neoliberalism of the special period, Usnavy's Black utopian refuge begins to dissolve and give way to capitalism. Usnavy's commodified visions make manifest, the novel seems to imply, how forms of transatlantic capitalism structuring even heritage tourism and the arts preclude a visualization of Africa in its particularity.

As this chapter will show, the novel's representation of the balsero crisis memorializes not only the Cuban 1990s exodus, but a Latin-African period of commodification as Havana opened up to tourism. The novel connects this Cuban period to West Africa's inauguration of the UNESCO Slave Route. Indeed, while the special period sets up a nostalgic tourism circuit – where the tropical Havana of the 1930s and 1940s is superimposed on the "ruins" of the island's 1990s cityscape – Usnavy also gravitates toward Badagry; a former slave trade point of departure threatened by developmentalism. Meaningfully, both forms of heritage tourism in Havana and Badagry do not portend an acceptance of Africanness or a Black economic empowerment. When Cuban-Americans return to Cuba, this special period witnesses these returnees' disassociation with the working-class Afro-Cubans that never left. This disassociation runs contrary to Fidel Castro's pro-Latin-African (and pro-Non-Aligned Movement) rhetoric justifying Cuban participation in the African decolonization wars of the 1960s and 1970s, but aligns with his actions of ignoring and even censoring demands for racial equality on the island. Meanwhile, on the other side of the Atlantic, the neoliberal organisms financing Badagry as a Slave Route – such as the International Monetary Fund (IMF) – would hardly promote an empathy with the plight of those members of the African diaspora, despite this being their target audience.

While I begin by nuancing how blackness and antiblack discourses from Cuba's decolonization of Angola to the special period contextualize the transatlantic web of heritage tourism in Obejas's novel, I argue in this chapter that *Ruins* both exhibits how neoliberal models uproot a Latin-African history while the novel also mocks its glorification. If Chapter 1 discussed the ways in which the African imaginary is rendered fearful even after the advent of the Slave Route, in this chapter I consider the commodification of Africa during the Slave Route's apex. As I turn to literary analysis, I explain how Obejas's use of Badagry shores up a critique of the neoliberalization of an African imaginary, as Badagry's site is complicit in Africa's excision from the Latin American and Latinx imaginary more widely. Since institutions such as the IMF finance the UNESCO Slave Route, the reproduction of African imaginaries at these locations renders them crucial epistemological sites informing a Latin-African commodification at the original point of diasporic departure. In other words, Obejas's site of Badagry allows us to recognize the stakes involved in prioritizing a capitalist model over African epistemology when it comes to constructing diasporic identities.

Complicit with capitalism are the suspects of an African commodification identified in the novel as vanguard art or modernist co-optations of the "primitive" that make up part of the protagonist's "African" utopia. Usnavy's gravitation toward colonial capitalism outlines how both European and American modernist figurations of the primitive shape Usnavy's memory of "Africanness": particularly a Louis Tiffany lamp Usnavy owns – whose glass projects an "African safari" – Pablo Picasso, and Wifredo Lam, a Cuban painter inspired by surrealism and cubism. But while those fleeing Cuba dismiss Africa for the US – envisioned as a site of wealthy White futurity – Usnavy is able to cling to a romanticized Black utopia projected to Cuba through his internationalist archive. His African utopia is also shaped by modernist poets Langston Hughes and Nicolás Guillén, who uplift Africa, decolonial thinkers like Frantz Fanon and Wole Soyinka, but also, problematically, by Ernest Hemingway's depictions of an "African safari." Coupled with the modernist art I mentioned above, these additional textual memorials co-opt his African imaginary. The only way in which Usnavy might break from this commodification is through a memory of the Cuban-Angolan alliance that Usnavy often evokes. Midway through the novel, Usnavy attempts to see Africa in a non-essentialized way. But here too, Usnavy's African imaginary is essentialized through Castro's political discourses for African decolonization, in which Castro claims Cuba to be a "Latin-African" nation. Importantly, Castro evokes Cuba's plantocracy to liken Cubans to Africans, but despite the significant contribution of this rhetoric to a Latin-African history, here too, Usnavy seems himself a product of a failed Black internationalist project. When Usnavy turns to capitalism at the end of the novel – by selling pieces of Tiffany lamp he eventually realizes are profitable – this "selling" of his own commodified vision of Africa he had seen through this lamp implies a tragic turn from his internationalist solidarity. I argue that the novel makes manifest the unfortunate reversal of Castro's use of slavery, since for Usnavy, the slave trade will function as a memory of selling out to global capitalism. A systemic process of capital-based dependency emergent during the age of slavery that played out in the special period now threatens the island in its neoliberal era.

The Latin-African focus of a novel such as Obejas's *Ruins* highlights how this shifted transatlantic engagement questions the apparatus of World Literature of which Obejas is part; but not merely because the novel's Cuban setting and evocation of transatlantic geopolitics challenge readings of Obejas's work as exclusively transnational.[2] Rather, since her work figures as an example of World Literature by virtue of her literary *cubanidad*, Obejas's novel also reformulates the very notion of World Literature. Because this ambitious novel maps out distinct spatiotemporal trajectories and cosmopolitan assemblages, a "humanistic consonance" as Anita Duneer reads it (168), Obejas's *Ruins* questions the idea of US Latinidad and opts instead for a Latin-African concept that is more inclusive of Afrolatinidad. Ultimately, the novel challenges both Latin American and Latinx racist notions of the African continent, and by extension, Obejas emphasizes the projects that shape uncritical perceptions of Africa in the examples of World Literature that *Ruins* cites.

2.1 Blackness and Antiblackness in Cuba

In *Ruins*, the spatiotemporal site of the "special period in times of peace" serves to disambiguate the commodified relationship between Cuba and Africa. To overcome both the US embargo and the evaporation of Soviet subsidies, after decades of resisting capitalism, Cuba opened up to tourism in the 1990s. But urban renewal aimed to appeal to tourists rather than faithfully memorialize Cuban history. For instance, Antonio José Ponte points out that the Office of the Historian led by Eusebio Leal Spengler prioritizes memorials such as Lady Diana's garden or the statue of a folkloric mentally ill man sardonically called the "Gentleman of Paris" that have little do with the colonial history of the cityscape (253–4), and represent even less, I should add, the heritage of Havana's Black population. Most alarming is that the state provides resources for the renovation of museums and restaurants while Black Cuban residences threaten to collapse. In 1994, state indifference toward Afro-Cubans was exacerbated by the return of Cuban-American exiles, who bitterly reject blackness as they see Afro-Cubans occupying their former abodes. Meanwhile, when Castro had for decades glorified decolonization in Africa, many Cubans became disillusioned with his prioritization of Black internationalism over efforts to address racial inequality at home. Indeed, Castro denounced colonial slavery rather than contemporary structural racism on the island. This disappointment culminates in the last significant Cuban exodus to the US. Ironically, Cuban-Americans returning to the island as tourists also signal the Revolutionary government's retreat into neoliberal capitalism. While Obejas belongs to an earlier wave of Cuban exiles – one certainly more socioeconomically advantaged than the balseros – her work strongly distances itself from upper- or middle-class exilic Cuban-American narratives. With acerbic irony, *Ruins* pays special attention to the role that race, and more specifically the imaginary of Africa, plays in Cuban and Cuban-American memory and the ways in which it falls prey to commercialization along a complicated Cuban-US-African axis. While I start out by explaining how Obejas's literary trajectory distinguishes her from her contemporaries, this section also discusses the racial paradigms that affect imaginaries of Africa for both Cuban and Cuban-Americans.

Born in Cuba in 1956, renowned poet, translator, journalist, and writer Achy Obejas belongs to one of the first waves of Cuban migration of the twentieth century, whose aftermath is detailed in her collection of short stories, *We Came All the Way from Cuba So You Could Dress Like This?* (1994). Since the first wave of Cuban exiles to the US after the Cuban Revolution was made up of the affluent and the middle class, the title story of this collection, like *Ruins*, pulls from Obejas's parents' experiences to reflect on the socioeconomic disadvantages of the racialized Cuban exodus that followed. While Obejas's family benefitted from the Cuban Adjustment Act of 1966, granting this group of immigrants legal status in the US, the same privilege did not extend to exiles in the 1980s who tended to be non-white and of lower economic standing. The Mariel Boatlift crisis from April 15 to October 31, 1980 was set in motion by thousands of dissidents seeking asylum in and later storming the Peruvian embassy. Castro famously stated that those Cubans wanting to leave could do so, also releasing Cubans with criminal records. Thus, this mass exodus changed US authorities' perceptions of Cuban exiles. But, as Antonio López notes, "the presence of Afro-Cubans in the Mariel migration panicked the old-guard Cuban exile regarding its (purchase on) Cuban American whiteness" (16). In other words, the racial composition of the Marielitas, as they were known, was at odds with the perception of the former wave of White Cubans from the higher echelons of Cuban exilic society (de la Fuente 305). The US authorities reacted by denying them refugee status. Finally, in 1995, the US effectively closed its borders to Cuban balseros of the special period, ending the final wave of Cuban exodus that was also the most racially distinctive and socioeconomically disadvantaged.

That same year, Obejas went back to Cuba for the first time; a prototypical era of Cuban-American return. As the Cuban economy desperately sought revenue from tourism, many Cubans who had left after the revolution, from 1959 to 1962, answered the call. Their experiences were transcribed in a variety of narratives, emphasizing a spectrum of reactions to the island in the special period. For instance, Pablo Medina's *Exiled Memories: A Cuban Childhood* (1990) crystalized the now-commodified image of Havana as a ruined cityscape, while Alina Troyano's *Leche de amnesia* (*Milk of Amnesia*, 1994), Cristina García's *The Agüero Sisters* (1997), and Obejas's *Days of Awe* (2001) find redemption or rehabilitation of memory instead. Obejas's distinctive point of view, however, is informed by her midwestern distance from the Cuban-American community in Miami.

This distance, in part, distinguishes her from the likes of Carlos Eire or Gustavo Pérez-Firmat, some of whom viewed the island as what A. López

2.1 Blackness and Antiblackness in Cuba

terms an "Afro-Cuban occupied house" pitted against its privileged White Cuban-American former owners who returned in the 1990s (189–90). "[T]he afro-Cuban occupied house," he states, "is a signifier of the white Cuban-American condition, one in which Afro-Cuban servant women on the island figure centrally, underscoring how imaginings of race and gender together constitute the diaspora aesthetics of 1990s Cuban-American return" (188). This Black figure suggests detachment from and animosity toward those exiled despite Cuba's long and unique celebration of Afro-Cuban cultural and artistic traditions, from the ethnographic works of Lydia Cabrera and Fernando Ortiz to Afro-Cuban poets Guillén, Eusebia Cosme, and Georgina Herrera, and filmmakers Sara Gomez, Sergio Giral, and Gloria Rolando. But this estrangement arises because, for the Cuban-American returnee, Cuban blackness signifies a less-desired working-class status. Thus, Cuban Americans' nostalgic memories of the island, far from celebrating Afro-Cubans, instead see working-class Black people as rooted in Cuba and subservient to privileged, wealthy, mobile White people. The "unbecoming blackness"[3] that some White Cuban-American texts construct conveys animosity toward Latin-African heritage as well.

Unlike her Cuban-American compatriots, Obejas offers in *Ruins* a stark contrast. While her previous work manifested an obstinate refusal of her parent's generation to return to the island, *Ruins* questions an entrenched attachment to Cuba through Usnavy's obsession with a Latin-African past that only he seems to embrace. But it is not so much that Usnavy turns from a collective to an individualistic mindset that is doggedly revolutionary, as Odette Casamayor-Cisneros interprets Cuban narrative of the eighties (183–4). Rather, Usnavy still hopes for the Marxist brand of the 1959 Revolution which began equalizing the playing field for Black Cubans while curiously ignoring that this same government began censoring discussion of domestic racism in 1962. If accused of being an idealist, Usnavy clings to the Revolution's unprecedented support of Angolan decolonization of the 1970s. But as *Ruins* portrays how, despite his rootedness in Cuba, Usnavy imaginatively travels away from it in his daydreams of "Africa" – reflecting Castro's glorified Black internationalism – the novel mocks Usnavy's essentialist view of his Black utopia during the special period in an equally commodified Cuba. I will begin by first explaining the island's racial paradigm before turning to Cuba's transatlantic engagement.

Although the character Usnavy is based on a particular acquaintance of Obejas's who stayed in Cuba throughout the special period, *Ruins* was sparked by the racial crucible of September 11, 2011, and its aftermath – a distinctly xenophobic American attitude that prompted Obejas to settle temporarily in Cuba, where she found refuge in an old book she found in her home ("Author Tells of a 90s Cuba"). Hemingway's *The Old Man and the Sea* took her to the author's old haunt of Cojimar, the sea-facing town of the balsero diaspora that Obejas in turn would memorialize eight years later in *Ruins*. Hemingway's novel thus provided *Ruins* with the landscape of a heavily commodified port, one that offers no memorials to the nonwhite balseros lost at sea from the port of Cojimar. But *The Old Man and the Sea* also provided Obejas with a scaffolding for narrating the "silences" of Cubans when it comes to their repressed Black Atlantic history. In her interview with me, Obejas mentions that Hemingway's "tip of the iceberg" narrative strategy – which leaves much unsaid about the protagonist of a story and is well achieved in *The Old Man and the Sea* – echoes Cubans' silence on race:

> Post-revolution it became really difficult to talk about racism. Which is a very powerful silence when you think about the fact that Cuba is an African diasporic country and that almost everyone in Cuba has some racial mixture. But we stopped talking about racism because Fidel Castro stood up one day in 1962 and said, "We've eliminated racism," and so to talk about racism became counter-revolutionary. (Obejas and Quesada 133)

Obejas refers to Castro's statement to the Second National Assembly, in which he declared that Cuba had "suppressed discrimination on the basis of race and sex."[4] The hypocrisy that Obejas points out is that, if between 1959 and 1962 Cuba did make real efforts toward racial equality, after 1962, discussions on race were silenced even when racial equality was far from achieved.

Often alluding to the failure of an imperialist Republican Cuba to achieve the equality envisioned by José Martí in "Nuestra América" ("Our America" 1891), in the early years of postrevolutionary Cuba Castro vowed not to fail. His mandate was to "put an end to racial discrimination within the working sector with a new mandate: work opportunities for all Cubans, without discriminating on the basis of race or sex."[5] To this end, the revolution swiftly began desegregating public spaces such as schools, recreational facilities, parks, and beaches that were once reserved for international tourists and affluent White Cubans (de la Fuente 263–9). Most Black Cubans benefited from this redistribution of space, as the Revolution boasted of its difference from racist US (276–8). Moreover, Castro's anti-US rhetoric further linked Cuban-Americans to the imperialist US, pitting them against Cubans who stayed, White or non-White. Moreover, his assertions suggested that being racist also meant being "anticommunist" and especially "antinationalist" (de la Fuente 278). Thus, when in 1962 Castro's Revolution largely celebrated the end of racial discrimination, it became impossible to invoke, much less debate, any of the government's racial blind spots. In other words, "the push to unify the Cuban population around the cause of socialist revolution brought a premature end to the public dialogue on race" after 1962 (Morris xiv). As Obejas hinted, speaking of race would be incongruous at best or counterrevolutionary at worst.

A crackdown on manifestations of racial difference unfortunately ensued. As a secular state, Cuba deemed spiritual customs with African roots subversive (Matibag 1–3). Carlos Moore points outs that until 1975, Castro's Revolutionary committee did not think Black Cubans could represent Cuban civil society, influenced to a certain degree by residues of nineteenth-century US racist domination (Moore *Castro* 24–5; Guridy 10). He even went as far as to state that the Revolution had provoked a "relentless war against Afro-Cuban religions and also against autonomous ethno-cultural manifestations by Cuban Blacks" (Moore *Castro* 99). While this might not have been the case for all active Afro-Cuban groups, by the mid-1960s, Afro-Cuban clubs that had been influential in placing Black workers and intellectuals alike in positions of political authority had lost ground, both institutionally and through governmental control of the press, which Castro did not address until 1986 (de la Fuente 280; Pérez Sarduy and Stubbs 5). This irony came full circle when, in an attempt to stay afloat, Havana's tourism industry reemerged forcefully in 1994.

Previously desegregated beaches and hotels were made inaccessible to Cuban nationals. The attraction of the collapsing ruins themselves and a nostalgic return to 1950s Havana prompted the commodification that Obejas critiques in her novel. She also critiques the irony that those who supported the socialist Revolution were most harmed by Cuba's shift toward capitalism. For instance, Black people who migrated from the eastern provinces to the island's capital to seek access to tourists were discriminated against as a result of their urban relocation (Bobes 26). Having been subject to discrimination since before the Revolution, Black Cubans now found themselves precluded from entering spaces reserved for tourism and were, moreover, not allowed to question the Revolution's narrative that racial equality had been achieved. What emerges is a tourism-based revenue system that spurs racial inequality among those like Usnavy who remained faithful to the Revolution's anticapitalism. Ironically, as Obejas herself states, "tourism also teaches an acquiescence that is contrary to a lot of the national spirit and which is another way of sort of going back into a colonial mindset."[6]

Contrary to Cuba's marginalization of blackness at home was its glorification of Black internationalism. With its plantocratic past as the catalyst of its foreign policy, Castro celebrated Africanness in lieu of Afro-Cubanness. Historian Alejandro de la Fuente points out that this internationalist rhetoric "helped the revolutionary government advance its domestic agenda of national integration even if questions of race were not publicly debated after the early 1960s" (de la Fuente 307). If the justification for intervening in Africa was to confront the US and propagate a socialist system in formerly colonized regions, Castro linked the struggle to end nineteenth-century Cuban slavery with his decolonial efforts in order to cast Cuban socialism as a moral cause against the United States' racist ideologies and support for apartheid in South Africa (*Cuba y Angola* 3). For Usnavy, the most visible forms of Black international solidarity seem to emanate from Castro's 1975 speech during Angola's initial triumph. Addressing Havana's First Congress, Castro proclaimed that "African blood flows freely through *our* veins. Many of *our* ancestors came as slaves from Africa to this land.[...] We're brothers and sisters of the people of Africa and we're ready to fight on their behalf!"[7] The use of the possessive plural pronoun "our" emphasizes Cubans' Latin-African connection – and the betrayal of it by those who flee to the US. But if, as Anne Garland Mahler notes, "the level of engagement required of Cubans in Angola would necessitate a justification that appealed to nationalist mythology and prerevolutionary racial discourses" (179), the idealized, essentialized Africa that Usnavy sees exemplifies the effects of Castro's rhetoric. As Cuba began to intervene in decolonization efforts in the Global South, especially in the Angolan civil war, constant allusions linking Cuba's Black Atlantic with African decolonization begin to haunt Usnavy. As I will explain, Usnavy's projections of an essentialized Africanity indeed suggest that he ignores *domestic* antiblackness and instead embraces Castro's celebration of Africa and Cuba's role there as a "país latino-africano" (an "Latin-African" nation).[8]

But unlike Usnavy, at the end of the 1980s and early 1990s, many Cubans pivoted to placing the blame for the special period on Cuba's involvement in Africa. At the end of Obejas's novel, even a changed Usnavy refers to the 1990s exodus as haunted by Latin-African relations rather than the US embargo and likens Cuba's special period to "Africa and its curse" (202). *Ruins* thus works through the paradox that, despite these gains in egalitarianism, Cubans would remember this period as the beginning of the end, conflating Cuba's involvement in Angola with the special period. After all, in the wake of Angolan peace accords in 1988, many Cubans who had been deployed to Angola "return[ed] to an economic situation best described as critical" (Quiroga 6) or even "disappointing" as Lanie Millar describes in her study on both Cuban and Angolan narratives of the Latin-African Cold War alliance (xxxiii). Between 1988 and 1993, Cuba's per capita GDP indeed shifted from growing by 2.6 percent annually before the collapse of the USSR to shrinking by 15.3 percent annually.[9] In 1992, a loss of energy sources exacerbated problems in transportation and industrial production as people began to starve and residential buildings to deteriorate.

These ruins are projected onto the title of Obejas's novel, while the idealist Usnavy seems not to notice. Instead, his exoticized "Africa" provides respite from despair, but most puzzling in these imageries is the constant appearance of the site of Badagry. I turn then to explain how Obejas draws a comparison in the novel between Badagry and Havana, as the latter reflects the advent of a raging 1990s Cuban tourism industry. After all, Usnavy's Black utopia compels us to attend to West African heritage tourism as the novel repeatedly alludes to "Badagry." As I will argue, UNESCO's rehabilitation of Badagry prompts me to read Usnavy's American-made idealization of "Africa" alongside both African and Cuban instances of Black Atlantic heritage tourism. Usnavy's attraction to this site exhibits, after all, how the commodification of an African ideal is *transatlantic*, occurring as much in the Americas as in the African continent.

2.2 Badagry's Commodification and the Latin-African Memorial

The novel opens in 1994 Havana on a heartbreaking scene in which revolutionary zealot Usnavy replaces abject poverty with an idealized African safari or even heritage sites. Working as a clerk for a neglected *bodega* ("warehouse") that sells haphazard items, such as soap and peas, to supplement beans and even coffee collected with "ration books" (13), Usnavy considers the wellbeing of those less fortunate – "young mothers with kids like kittens clawing at their hems, frantic" – as the piercing scene implies hunger and desperation (14). Usnavy's own meager possessions further underscore this scarcity: "a windowless high-ceiling room, no bigger than one of those bloated American cars," decorated only with "[a] picture of a young Comandante," a "Soviet refrigerator," and a "threadbare but very clean towel" among Usnavy's books "about Africa, poetry books, books with ambiguous endings" (14–15). To escape this poverty, Usnavy could give in and turn to selling on the black market, but his idealism prevents him from interacting with the newly arrived hordes of tourists; at least initially. Instead, he elides this stifling quotidian poverty, replacing it with a utopian racial heaven. Usnavy imagines Egypt's "sculpted tomb found in Memphis," "lions" hidden in the imaginary urban savannah (160), a "market day in Dakar or Lagos" (156), and even Zambia's safari, the UNESCO world heritage site of Mosi-oa-Tunya (48). But while these locations and the word "Africa" permeate the novel, the site of Badagry, Nigeria, or "a trail of bones back to Badagry" (150) also emerges, appearing another ten times as the nickname Usnavy applies to an elderly Black neighbor.

Badagry is today a reconstructed UNESCO heritage site off the coast of Nigeria, but the first time the reference appears in the novel is when Usnavy discovers a Black woman with a Tiffany lamp. Like him, this woman attempts to hide this luxury item on an island immersed in precarity, despite Usnavy's efforts to peek into her abode, and better spot "a large auspicious shape above her shoulder" (58). While this woman will become important at the end of my analysis as Usnavy turns to capitalism and wrests away this lamp during the collapse of her building (and is unconcerned about her livelihood), the *naming* of this woman is central to my reading. A "mahogany-colored" woman with a "grandmother's face," the novel explains that "Usnavy imagined her ancestors tender and sweet, among the thousands of outwitted, unwilling seafarers at Badagry or Gorée more than a century ago" (57). Evoking two prominent UNESCO Slave Route sites in Senegal and Nigeria, respectively, Usnavy has never been to either, but it is significant that he names this woman after Badagry in particular. After all, Badagry is relevant to Cuba not because of decolonial history like that of Angola, but because like Angola, Cuba's *colonial* African diaspora originated, in part, from this port. Badagry, along with Lagos and Porto Novo, exported close to one million enslaved people to the Americas between 1650 and 1865 (quoted in Falola and Childs ed. 44). In the nineteenth century, Cuba received most of the enslaved from this region (Barcia 2). In fact, Badagry "in the mid-1820s," despite British abolition, was a "booming" and "busy" town for slave trafficking; as close to 53,347 slaves arrived in Cuba from Badagry between 1805 and 1845 alone, not including those smuggled in illegally (64).

While plantocratic history of Castro's discourse colors Usnavy's naming of his Black neighbor, I focus first on the ways in which the memorialization at this site – colonial and contemporary – shapes the idealizations of

2.2 Badagry's Commodification and the Latin-African Memorial

Usnavy's perceived Latin-African heritage. First, because oral proverbs evoked at this heritage point provide an explanation for a break with Africa. Second, the site's potential razing of its Atlantic history in favor of luxurious tourism provides important considerations regarding the global exportation of an African imaginary. Both examples nuance African essentialization fashioned within the continent itself.

The first form of African commodification involves a ritual found in the archive of oral tradition. Similar to Ouidah's site in Benin in Chapter 1, Badagry consists of a long memorial trail that, before reaching its end at the cathartic "Point of No Return" where slaves embarked for the Middle Passage, pilgrims must go by the "Well of Attenuation." This well (Figure 2.1) is arguably one of the most paradigmatic points along Badagry's trail not only because it happens to be one of the most well-preserved nineteenth-century artifacts of the slave trade but also because it is the original point of no return. As Soyinka explains, from oral tradition we know of the rituals performed at this "sunken water pot." Oral history in what is today Nigeria explains how slaves were stripped of their memories through "water laced with some kind of potion – or perhaps simply psychic potency!" (Soyinka *Of Africa* 61). Today, guides

Figure 2.1 The Slave Route heritage point at Badagry, Nigeria. Photo: Naija Rookie, 2012.

at the site will in fact revisit this belief, telling visitors that slaves allegedly were made to drink from the well's water so that they would drift into a permanent amnesia. In fact, according to these guides, traditional chiefs "put some herbs in this well that were believed to make the slaves lose their memory of the early days in the ship."[10] While some might dismiss the guides' stories as fictional, the well's somatic space is informed by "the experience or the environment [in Badagry] that yielded or birthed the proverb" (Obisakin 31). One common proverb is that of the Egun, which states that "[o]ne cannot get to the other side without transportation" ("Adan ma n yi tog tho" 31). The proverb's "get to the other side," oral historians suggest, reveals an anxiety about the slave trade's Atlantic Ocean, as the "other side" refers to "the sea separating them in Badagry" from Europe or even the Americas, and "transportation" to the slave ships.[11] In fact, Lawrence O. Obisakin states that "[i]f you think the Egun philosophers were thinking of streams or rivers, you are only too superficial. They should be thinking of the sea separating them in Badagry or West Africa from London – that is the river that you cannot cross without transportation!" (31). If oral history at Badagry's well has long reflected its spatial and cultural history (Harunah 162), this oral history looms large over Usnavy's inability to reverse a "trail of bones back to Badagry" (Obejas *Ruins* 150). In other words, despite Usnavy's fixation on Badagry – reflected in Usnavy's "mind still on the Badagry woman" (59–60) or his fixation with "the Badagry woman's home" (109, 161, 170) – oral tradition suggests that the effects of the "well of attenuation" preclude Usnavy's ability to know Badagry in its particularity.

The trauma created by the colonial period is thus expressed in Nigerian oral tradition, in which the slave trade era erased the individuality of those who were sold into slavery across the sea. Obejas's novel locates Cuban rejection of Africa at the diaspora's original site of departure for a reason. Usnavy's inability to understand his racial geography as constituted by African epistemologies is just as much a product of coloniality in Cuba as it is of erasure rituals practiced and recited in Nigerian proverbs prior to the Atlantic crossing. As Badagry teaches us, the fact that slaves were subjected to amnesia even prior to the Middle Passage through rituals at sites like the Well of Attenuation helps explain why Usnavy finds it so difficult to reclaim a Latin-African memory.

The second consideration informing Usnavy's exoticization of Africa is the commodification of Badagry itself, as the site's slave trade history faces razing. In 2009, the Jackson Five revealed a $3.5 billion-dollar

2.2 Badagry's Commodification and the Latin-African Memorial   89

development project turning Badagry into a "large-scale holiday resort development with a theme park" (Soyinka *Of Africa* 57). Although to this day, construction of the "Jackson Park" has been delayed, a project complete with "casinos, golf courses, cinemas, shopping malls, museums" has garnered as much praise as it has scorn.[12] But developments of this kind are not unlike the UNESCO World Heritage site of Old Havana, where Leal Spengler's Office of the City Historian has been under fire for renovating museums and monuments marketed as nostalgic infrastructure rather than the population's decaying residences (Ponte 263–4; Álvarez-Tabío Albo 164–8). Like Havana, Soyinka writes sarcastically that Badagry is indeed "an appropriate setting for the tourist industry, as it is a place of tears and bitter memory" (*Of Africa* 57–8). Development of Badagry would eliminate from view slavery's modest remnants, replacing them with what Nigerian writer Pius Adesanmi terms "casino capitalism" (62).

The commodification of this site would further substitute images of a Black Atlantic memory with those of African grandeur. In fact, in her renowned literary travelogue along the Slave Route, *Lose Your Mother*, Saidiya Hartman laments how African memories of slaves are replaced with tales of African royalty and might. During her own visit of the Slave Route to Elmina's former Portuguese fort in Ghana, Hartman explains that the history of slavery seemed to be remembered as one of "fugitives and warriors, not masters and slaves" (233). Indeed, in my own fieldwork in Ouidah, Benin, I recall a driver boasting that he descended from a long line of chiefs that had been involved in the transaction of slaves. I do not share this story or Hartman's to imply that this is a general disposition of West Africans living at memory sites, but rather that Usnavy's admiration of African grandeur is shared by real individuals on the other side of the Atlantic, too. Mbembe echoes such a conclusion, regretting that despite twenty-first-century commemoration of the slave trade in Africa, this spatiotemporality "has been essentially forgotten by Africans" ("The Subject" 21), recalling Hartman's observation that locals "didn't imagine that [slavery] had any lingering effects" (*Lose* 73). And indeed, these sites of slavery reflect back on African responsibility of the trade, fueling perhaps locals' detachment. But the ability of a heritage site like Badagry to conjure a meaningful memory of the African diaspora is just as hindered by the afterlives of slavery as by the demands of neoliberal policies.

With the rise of the IMF and World Bank programs in West Africa, several nation-states have bent to the demands of these institutions, hoping to spur economic growth and foreign investment and to revitalize markets. Instead,

James Ferguson argues however, that these reforms have forced the "collapse of basic institutions (including major industries as well as social infrastructure such as schools and health care)" in much of the continent (35). As a result, locally built organizations with African-centric approaches have been supplanted by Eurocentric and capitalist concerns. Funded by these international organizations is the UNESCO Slave Route, and the effects of this neoliberal overreach on Badagry specifically are development plans that overlook the history of slavery and replace it with essentialized versions of Africa. A heritage site of this kind can indeed constitute "an ideological act and a destructive activity, since it erases memories of the violence and removes physical evidence" to appeal to the general public (Kalman 538). Reading the real site of Badagry and its textual evocation in Obejas's novel, it becomes clear that Usnavy's imagined Africa is also constituted by both Badagry's colonial history of amnesia represented by the "magical" well and the site's capitalist commodification, which plagued African nation-states at the turn of the millennium.

Thus, by embedding Badagry's site in *Ruins*, Obejas suggests Cuba become vigilant in its preservation of collective memory after it failed to do so during the vulnerable special period of the 1990s. In relating a cultural alliance with Cuba's former socialist allies, the novel's textual memorialization of Badagry seems to consider possible futures for an island long dependent on allies and overlords like Spain, the US, the Soviet bloc, China, and Venezuela. Obejas hints at spatiotemporalities that would bequeath Cuba with a newfound sense of identity, if only it could remain strengthened by the memory of its Global South alliances, not hampered by it. But for Usnavy, his memories of Africa are imagined and never drawn from personal experience but rather a sense of Cuban Atlantic history. Unfortunately for Usnavy, imperialist conventions also shape this history. In a continuation of this textual analysis, I unfold the ways in which Usnavy's utopic Latin-Africa is also informed by both collective and individual memory that dismiss African epistemologies from their source.

2.3 Traveling to Africa through Tiffany, Picasso, and Lam

In this section, I focus on the conventions shaping African essentialization, even in the arts that Usnavy assumes are for and about Africa. In other words, although Usnavy finds release in this imagined Black utopia, he does not recall an actual personal memory, but a collective memory shaped by the pervasive and in some ways concealed system of global capitalism. This system is even implied in his very name: pronounced "according to

2.3 Traveling to Africa through Tiffany, Picasso, and Lam   91

Spanish grammar rules – *Uss-nah-veee*," Usnavy – who is mockingly called "El Yanqui" – was named after the "emblazoned," majestic "US navy" ships at Guantánamo Bay in pre-revolutionary Cuba (Obejas *Ruins* 17, 25). His name not only hints at the spoils of the 1898 war – namely, for Obejas, Cuban territories under US jurisdiction – but underlines a prominent US presence that at one time literally labelled its colonized subjects. Not only is the label of empire carved into Usnavy's name, but the novel also seems to imply that what Usnavy sees is filtered through an obvious relic of US imperialism. Usnavy's only material possession of value is a Louis Comfort Tiffany lamp by the late nineteenth-century US entrepreneur of stained glass.

This object of excess dangles hopelessly from the ceiling of his bedroom, juxtaposed with dismal poverty. A lens through which utopian space is projected, it creates a respite for its beholder: "In the damp and acrid tenement, the lamp was a vibrant African moon in a room that was by nature spectral" (19). But as the ruins of the special period hark back to the imperialist tropical paradise of 1940s Havana, the African projections of Usnavy's art nouveau lamp promise a lost Eden:

> [t]o relieve the gloom, the family's room – a breadbox, a shoebox – was illuminated by a most extraordinary lamp. Were it not for the sheer size of it, Usnavy could have built a second floor – a barbacoa – like many of his neighbors. Made of multicolored stained glass, like an oversized dome, the lamp was wild. Almost two meters across, the cupola dropped down with a mild green vine-and-leaf motif that flowered into luscious yellow and red blossoms, then became a crimson jungle with huge feline eyes. (In truth they were peacock feathers, but Usnavy… imagined them as lions or, at least, cats.) The armature consisted of branches at the top, black and fat to resemble the density of tree bark. The borders were shaped with the unevenness of leaves and eyelids, petals and orbs, in a riotous yet precise design. (16–17)

The lamp's sheer size implies, among other things, that its light shines throughout his impoverished "shoebox" of a room. More broadly, the object paints the city's achromatic melancholy with the colors of a seemingly precolonial and unsullied Africa he shares with his daughter, Nena, who

> engaged in a never-ending staring contest with the lamp's feline eyes. Sometimes, especially when she was younger, his daughter Nena would curl into the curve of his arm and join him, imagining all the possibilities within the lamp's vast offerings. That, she'd say, aiming a finger at a green slice of light, was the fertile Nile traversing the continent, and that, he'd point out in the opaqueness of tiny triangle, the whirling sands on the beaches of Madagascar. (20)

Usnavy's nostalgia for exotic African shapes speaks to both *representation* and *collective memory*, and recalls both twentieth-century Cuban art and history.

Cuba's nationalistic collective memory seems tied to imaginary renderings of, say, an exoticized Nile. As Paul Ricœur notes, "collective memory" is that which "evoke[s a] sort of hauntedness" but also "constitutes the soil in which historiography is rooted" (54, 69). Cuban historiography is rooted in the Atlantic World, and Usnavy's most proximate spatiotemporal marker of that world is the Black internationalism justified by Castro's proclamations of Latin-African connection. As Obejas herself argues, "one thing that the Cuban revolution has done, ... is that it's pivoted our history from the Spanish empire to Africa as points of great influence and almost in a way as a point of origin" (134). At the Fifteenth UN General Assembly in 1960, Castro's support for African self-determination and his stay in Black Harlem's Hotel Theresa – not to mention his public shift to the Non-Aligned Movement – was unprecedented in Latin America. Castro in fact used the UN's General Assembly in New York as a global platform for solidarity among the marginalized and racialized within the belly of the beast. Castro's grandstanding from this moment forward led to the "African Decade" of the 1970s, when there was "a steady flow of visiting African, Caribbean, and Black American leaders, delegations, and cultural groups."[13] That decade was preceded by Cuba's hosting of the 1966 Tricontinental Conference for Non-Aligned states, attended by leaders such as Amílcar Cabral and honoring Patrice Lumumba among other revolutionaries. All these markers of history are melancholic, yet serve as memorial sites of a collectivity. In recalling the cultural significance of Castro's stay in the Hotel Theresa in particular, José Quiroga views the site as one of "symbolic memory," stating that it remains a site of memory even if people have not visited it (34). Like the Hotel Theresa, sites such as the Nile, Madagascar, Dakar, or Lagos recall a sense of Cuban greatness for Usnavy because they are symbolic sites of memory that he sees projected onto the "Africanization" of Cuba, seen for Usnavy, through his lamp. As Usnavy boasts later to a friend who wants to leave Cuba, "We have, first and foremost, set an example" (114), as Cuba took charge to promote African independence movements and anti-capitalism in the Global South more generally. Usnavy's comment underscores the revolutionary hopefulness that comes from affirming Africa, both during the rise of Black internationalism in the 1970s and in his present times of despair.

But while Usnavy's concept of safari-like utopia draws on this collective memory, its form derives from an entirely different spatiotemporality. The

2.3 Traveling to Africa through Tiffany, Picasso, and Lam

exotic composition of "multicolored stained glass" that constitutes Usnavy's Black utopia – its exotic "wild" and "riotous" representation of a "crimson jungle" – in fact recalls pre-revolutionary 1940s Havana; the same era that the 1990s tourism industry seeks to evoke. Echoing the structures that have become ruins in a 1990s Havana, the images that Usnavy allegedly "remembers" conjure modernism. The ruins that Usnavy sees are actually imagined – at age fifty-four, Usnavy would have just been born in 1940. But, as Marianne Hirsch reminds us, the resurrection of an unlived but collectively-transmitted past tends to create memories from the "superimposition of images" drawn across temporalities (159), and thus what idealistic revolutionary Usnavy "remembers" during the special period speaks less to memory and more to the influence of a nostalgic modernist primitivism.

A salient trace of this modernism emerges when Usnavy witnesses the traumatic departure of his kin from Cojimar beach. As Usnavy approaches the shoreline, he watches as "people hammered away at their rafts, tying ropes around pieces of rubber, metal kegs, and plastic jugs for buoyancy," in sharp contrast with the detached tourists lounging at the "protected confines of elegant Las Terrazas" (42). As he attempts to shut out his brethren's dramatic leap onto unseaworthy rafts, "in his mind" he replaces what he judges as their philistine betrayal with "Katanga or Shaba" or "an impenetrable forest full of wild geese and ostriches, buffalo, and lions" (42). Rather than seeing the rafters for what they are, Usnavy visualizes "fields of coffee and cotton." Conjuring the Cuban colonial plantocracy, these fields materialize as a plantation projected onto Africa – a place where, instead of slaves laboring in the fields, wild geese, ostriches, buffalo, and lions roam freely through an unperturbed myth of the African safari. Most importantly, as an angry Usnavy continues to shield his mind from the rafters and their reality, one morning back at his home he sees his neighbors' faces as "distorted," their mouths shaped like "red ovals, eyes shaped in the same feline fashion as the magnificent lamp" (97); that is, he sees their faces through the modernist lens of the Tiffany lamp. He closes his eyes to imagine "his neighbors' faces as Kwele Gon masks, their wearers anonymous and immune." But when he returns to the material world, he does not see himself "in an idyllic Ginen, but here, where it was just another day in a traumatized Havana" (98). As the departing rafters at Cojimar had conjured a plantational past, this time the distortion of diaspora – literalized as distorted faces – recalls the modernist representation of an "idyllic" Ginen.

Usnavy replaces his traumatic present with a memorialization of Ginen's precolonial past through a vision of a Kwele Gon mask.[14] Despite a restitution agreement to return these artifacts to the former

Figure 2.2 Masque Gorille Kwele, "Fleuve Congo." Musée du Quai Branly, Paris, France.

French colonies of Guinea and Benin, the Kwele Gon masks are – at the time of this writing – exhibited in Paris's *Musée du Quai Branly* (Figure 2.2). The fact that such masks are only accessible through a Western gaze echoes Usnavy's own commodification of the artifact. As "a system of appropriation and alienation" Felwine Sarr and Bénédicte Savoy write on the subject, Western museums "unwillingly have become the public archives" (2). These Eurocentric institutions mold the romanticized gaze of the object (Diagne et al. "Artwork"); the effects playing out in Usnavy's imagination when the Guinean mask transports him to "an *idyllic*" location that contrasts strongly with his less-than-ideal reality (emphasis added). Crucially, when Usnavy enacts a mythic "return to Africa" within Cuba, modernist representations of the continent overshadow both the recent history of Latin-African decolonization efforts and the more distant one of Antillean slavery. In other words, Usnavy sees both the recent and distant past through the lens of modernist representations of Africa, as he gravitates toward a vision of Ginen appropriated by the West, not only because the masks are displayed in a French museum, but also because one of the most famous European modernist paintings draws on them.

Usnavy does not visualize the Kwele Gon mask through his own memory of the original object, but rather through Pablo Picasso's controversial *Les Demoiselles d'Avignon/The Young Ladies of Avignon*. The painting, featuring nude multiethnic sex workers in a brothel, inspired cultural primitivism meant to rejuvenate the West and emblematizes colorful precolonial African imagery in the reproduced African masks. The introduction of a colorful and primitive blackness into modernism, as Edward Said has long pointed out, further fetishized non-Western conventions (17). This painting also resonates with Usnavy's lamp because of its violent juxtaposition of angles that create the impression that the figures are "too sharp to touch" (see Figure 2.3).[15] MoMa Curator Ann Temkin even explains that Picasso's contours "look like shattered glass."

Figure 2.3 Pablo Picasso's *Les Demoiselles d'Avignon* (1907, 96 × 92 inches). Museum of Modern Art (MoMA), New York.

Indeed, this modernist painting recalls the stained glass in Usnavy's Tiffany lamp and its projection of a similar modernist primitivism. Obejas's insertion of Picasso through the Kwele Gon mask featured in *Les Demoiselles d'Avignon* clearly references the dislocation of the object from its African origins and instead dissolves it into an African exotica that Usnavy sees in modernist glass. While French Marxist theorist Henri Lefebvre has read this painting as "cruelly" distorting the nonwhite body and dislocating their exact location (*Production* 302), the masks forced into Western cubism prevent Usnavy from regaining contact with an unfiltered Africa. In other words, by framing Usnavy's visions through modernist exoticizations of stolen objects, Obejas shows how even his revolutionary idealization of Africa contributes to dislocating it from modernity.

Modernist dislocations of Africa further unfold in the novel when Usnavy's best friend, Obdulio, threatens to become a rafter. When Usnavy attempts to stop Obdulio from fleeing to Miami at Cojimar, his angry friend confronts him about his nationalistic zeal:

> …when you look at that crazy lamp of yours – do you realize it's the only thing you have of value, my friend? Don't you see anything in all that light and color besides clouds and giraffes and Africa? Africa – I mean, Usnavy, how perverse is that? Who dreams of Africa when you can dream of Miami? (46)

On the one hand, Obdulio's claim again underscores Usnavy's idealistic impracticality in ignoring the possibility of a better life in the US. On the other hand, the scene also refers to the global dynamics of imperial usurpation through Obdulio's attachment, not to Picasso's Europe, but to Miami. Although Miami is referenced in the novel because it is the renowned port of Cuban exilic arrival, Miami can also be read here as a metaphoric site of aspirational – White – capitalism. Miami happens to be Tiffany's former dwelling, where he built his mansion on Brickell Avenue in Miami's historic Millionaire Row. Now surrounded by 1990s condominiums, the Tiffany home stands for future possibilities and capitalist accumulation in the US, while Africa and the legacies of Cuban slavery – Obdulio imagines – are tied to the past. Obdulio's flight to Miami, *Ruins* seems to imply, is in some ways motivated by race and indeed denies the centrality of Black internationalism, thus replacing Cuba's Latin-African decade with Obdulio's overestimation of the US.

Moreover, the Tiffany lamp's nonmonetary value eludes Obdulio, who thinks Usnavy's Latin-African vision is "perverse." When he asks, "don't you see anything in all that light and color besides clouds and giraffes and Africa?" he refers to the lamp's monetary value, but hauntingly implies a dramatic refusal borne of hierarchies of race: who would want to remember Africa and the racialization that memory entails? Rather than envisioning an African safari, Obdulio collapses slavery's subjectivity and ensuing poverty into an image of "Africa" that places it on the losing end of the victor-loser spectrum of racial capital. Obdulio's underestimation of the continent even seems to confirm Mbembe's argument that it is "impossible to articulate a discourse about Africa that does not reflect this paradigm of victimization" ("The Subject" 21, 26). Regardless of the racial background of either Obdulio or Usnavy, Obdulio, by sneering at Usnavy's "perverse" obsession, markedly denies himself a Latin-African borderland. Instead, Obdulio's racial unconscious yearns for the imagined space of Miami, which signifies economic deliverance and White wealth.

If Picasso and Tiffany created global forms that commodify Africa, Cuban modernist artist Wifredo Lam brought them home to roost. In a remarkable scene in which Usnavy laments that "the world was sepia, warm but colorless," he hungers for color in the tales of his neighbor Jacinto, a veteran of the Angolan war: "Usnavy remembered when Jacinto first returned from Africa, how he was full of stories about wild animals and the *flushed palette of the jungle*" (105, emphasis added). Given that the novel mocks modernist renderings of "Africa," the term "flushed palette of the jungle" is a provocative one that alludes to Lam's most famous painting, *La jungla/The Jungle*. Moreover, at another point in *Ruins*, when Usnavy and one of his best friends, Diosdado, argue about Cuba being ripped off in terms of innovation, Usnavy suggests that Picasso "rip[ped] off Lam" (115). When Usnavy imagines "the flushed palette of the jungle," he again seeks a colorful "Africa" in the midst of despair and finds it in modernist art.

Lam's *The Jungle* has a very particular global appeal that is central to the commodification of Africa not only in Cuba but also around the world. Composed in 1943 in gouache on paper and canvas, *The Jungle* stands as an example of global modernism, but it also gave Cubans a local way of experiencing cubism, as *Ruins* teasingly hints in the question, "What if Lam had been Picasso?" (115). When Usnavy mentions Lam, Diosdado becomes exasperated with Usnavy's blind idealism, retorting, "what have [Cubans] ever done that is so great?" (114). As Obejas uses Diosdado's question to highlight amnesia about the revolution, aesthetically *Ruins* seems to convey admiration of the painter who placed Cuban modernism on the world stage. But the novel also problematizes the ways in which Usnavy recalls Latin-Africa through Lam's famous painting.

98   Commodification

Lam's surrealist and cubist take on African and Afro-Cuban forms in *The Jungle* (Figure 2.4) has itself become institutionalized as a way of perceiving a utopian "Africa." The painting's size creates an all-encompassing and dream-like effect, with odd hybrid creatures that seem both human and animal making up the Cuban landscape. And yet, the oversized limbs, breasts, and buttocks of the figures as well as their masks – the same ones Picasso must have taken Lam to see at Trocadero's *Musée de l'homme* after the two met in 1938 – represent its subjects as both exotic and magical. Noted Cuban intellectual Alejo Carpentier even hailed Lam as a practitioner of his termed "the marvelous real," an artist in whose work

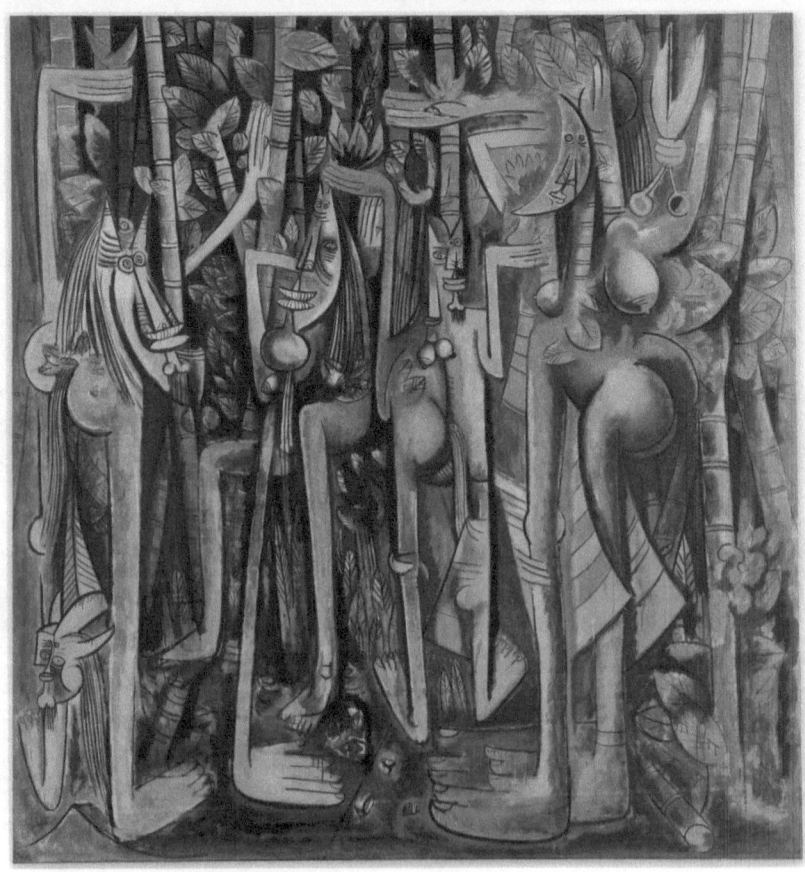

Figure 2.4 Wifredo Lam's *La jungla / The Jungle* (1943, 94 ¼ inches × 90 ½ inches). Museum of Modern Art (MoMA), New York.

"the magic of tropical vegetation" comes to life.[16] Indeed, the ruins of Usnavy's 1990s reality project a nostalgic memory of modernist Havana's Lam-like "tropical flavor."

But it is precisely such "magical" representations of Latin America that problematize Usnavy's visualization of an African safari, as these are filtered through Western artistic conventions. As art historian Bárbaro Martínez-Ruiz notes, Lam sought to "simultaneously exoticize, marginalize and conflate not only [Cuban avant-garde] contributions to wider Cuban society, but also the diversity and richness of their component cultures" (24). Even as Afro-Cuban rituals and their plight in prerevolutionary Cuban society motivated Lam's art, his artistic production seems disjointed both from the Afro-Cuban identity he seeks to represent and the African origin from which his forms are borrowed (quoted in Max-Pol Fouchet 188–9). Thus, Lam's modernist representations paint for Usnavy an exoticized imaginary of what he imagines is a truthful portrayal of African reality. The caveat is that Lam did not elaborate the Afro-Cuban dimensions of his art through active observation on the ground, but rather through the conventions of Western modernism. Lam's African mask figure, argues Natalie Melas, "bears the traces of his encounter with Picasso and Cubism," which in turn defined "his visual signature and which we have come to associate with a particularly Caribbean modernism" (106). Unbeknownst to pseudo-literati Usnavy, his desired attachment to "Africa" – as he imagines the Nile or Madagascar – is hindered not only by the mediation of a Tiffany lamp tied to US imperialism, but also, as it turns out, by Lam's investment in the European avant-garde.

Even as his friend Obdulio readily dismisses Africa in favor of Miami, Usnavy clings to an African utopia that is just as political as it is racial. But the memory sites on which this Latin-Africa rests are dubious because they are filtered through modernism, did not originate in Africa, and are entangled with commodification. As Brent Edwards points out, the main issue with the brand of in-vogue culture known as *art nègre* was "the acquisition-minded European fascination with black performance and artifacts" (44). This avant-garde engendered a primitivist "epistemology of blackness": the "obsession" with all things Black was an exportable and importable product that adhered to hegemonic cultural norms. Usnavy's memories of Africa commodify an Atlantic past through his modernist lamp and Lam's celebrated Afro-Cuban forms. But this imaginary is also circumscribed by his literary archive. While I have explained how US economics and earlier imperialist ventures have commodified Africa's ontology, in what follows, I unpack how Usnavy's visualizations of

Africa – made into textual memorials in the novel – are also informed by a literary "safari" he reads.

2.4 The African Safari: Hughes, Guillén, and Hemingway

If Tiffany, Lam, and Picasso shape the collective memory of "Africa" from which Usnavy draws, his literary reading constitutes his individual memory of the Black Atlantic. As a beneficiary of a historic literacy campaign in Cuba, Usnavy is a proud and avid reader of "books about Africa" and "poetry," including Afro-Cubanista poet Guillén, Harlem Renaissance poet Hughes, postcolonialists Fanon and Soyinka, and even Hemingway (15, 144–5). But these writers' portrayals of "Africa" do not align with each other. In fact, Hemingway, renowned for big game hunting in Kenya and Tanzania as well as for enjoying commercialized Havana from the 1930s through the 1950s, projects a hegemonic discourse of African appropriation. His African safari contrasts with Hughes's and Guillén's more complex relationship to the continent and their heightening of the motherland trope. Meanwhile, Fanon and Soyinka, as staunch supporters of decolonization in Algeria and Nigeria respectively, align with Castro's Black internationalist rhetoric but are wary of essentializing African cultures. In what follows, I examine how Usnavy's African imaginary is complicated, not only by the textual memorials that he visits through his Black internationalist archive, but also by his "memory" of African decolonization via the novel's references to Cuba's thirteen-year engagement in Angola. This historical excursion will reveal the lessons that both Cubans and Cuban-Americans learn from a much-neglected stage of Latin-African history that, the novel seems to imply, has been replaced by safaris.

Usnavy's literary archive emerges at the same time as the novel reveals a shift in his revolutionary fervor. As he learns about the monetary value of Tiffany glass, Usnavy begins to collect it from collapsed buildings in Havana, turning to capitalism and selling pieces of lamps to a technician named Virgilio. Usnavy's eventual selling of the coveted panels of glass on the black market metaphorically implies the "selling out" of his socialist ideals. His initial encounter with Virgilio marks this ideological change as Usnavy unknowingly cites Saint Thomas Aquinas to seize Virgilio's attention:

> "The reality of things is their light," ... [Usnavy said]. Virgilio finally looked up ... "You don't read Thomas Aquinas," he said, not as a question or

2.4 The African Safari: Hughes, Guillén, and Hemingway

accusation, but a simple statement of fact ... "I read Fanon, I read Soyinka," Usnavy responded, flustered ... "And Hemingway, of course." "But not Guillén and Langston Hughes?" ... Usnavy sighed, "Of course Guillén and Langston Hughes. I meant *beyond* that." "But you're not interested in light, not really," said Virgilio. "You're interested in glass." (144–5, emphasis added)

According to Thomism, an object's form can be discerned through its radiance or clarity (Eco 160). Due to "the radiance of that marvelous lamp," Usnavy used to be able to see a "vibrant African moon" (19) through the object's radiance, but for the neo-Thomist Virgilio, Usnavy is now losing this ability to *see*. The illocutionary act in Aquinas' statement, "The reality of things is their light," marks the end of Usnavy's entrapment in the aesthetic. Virgilio's assertion that "you're not interested in light ... you're interested in glass" reveals Usnavy's disinterest in the lamp's everyday use and implies that he has just discovered the materialistic value of "glass" over "light" or enlightenment. As Usnavy's thoughts of viewing Havana in "sepia, warm but colorless" (105) allegorize this shift, the novel hints that Usnavy's ability to see the post-1959 Revolution as a colorful beacon of hope and intellectualism is fading.

But Virgilio's accusation that Usnavy is eschewing Hughes and Guillén also suggests that the revolutionary idealist is trading in a Caribbean racial ideology for an uncritical Black internationalism. In other words, Virgilio mocks Usnavy as stuck in political isolation, seeking to *travel* through the literary sites of Hemingway or Soyinka rather than the more geographically proximate ones of Guillén or Hughes. This is not unlike Castro's glorification of African liberation and simultaneous snubbing of Afro-Cuban equality. After all, "Virgilio" evokes counterrevolutionary poet Virgilio Piñera, who claimed that Cubans are "haunted by history, and condemned to live within their geographic fatality" (Quiroga 26) – an allusion that serves to critique Usnavy's ideological entrapment. Virgilio's rebuke is especially stinging when he implies that Usnavy reveres his own made-up Jamaican ancestry though he is actually a descendant of US Jews (*Ruins* 172–3). Virgilio's charge that he does not read Hughes also specifically implies that Usnavy is uncritical of his identity, for Hughes – albeit polemically – linked "segregated Negroes" to the "ghettoized Jews in Europe," in his *Fine Clothes to the Jew* (1927), a work that would help Usnavy understand his own identity in a more nuanced way, but which he snubs (Sundquist *Strangers* 212).

The translation of Hughes' work appeared first in Cuba in a literary supplement titled "Los negros en USA," in the journal *Revolución* in 1960 (Quiroga 40) to much acclaim. But if Usnavy gravitates toward Hughes, the latter's autobiography, *The Big Sea*, about visiting the African continent, connects most to Usnavy's safari idealizations. Like Castro's Angolan rhetoric, *The Big Sea* exalts a blackness found in an African-safari space: for instance, "And when finally I saw the dust-green hills in the sunlight, something took hold of me inside," or "My Africa, Motherland of the Negro peoples! And me a Negro! The real thing, to be touched and seen, not merely read about in a book" (10–11). While this valorization of African roots "challenged inherited formations of an absolutist American blackness" (Kun 144), Virgilio seems to surmise that Usnavy's idealization of Africa could just as well be derived from diasporic poets in this hemisphere as from the others he cites. Virgilio implies that Hughes's Black cosmopolitanism escapes Usnavy.

While primitivism was helpful in enabling South-South alliances, Usnavy's ideas about self-determination and self-representation are warped by a selective view of modernism. As Usnavy does admit to reading some Hughes and his contemporary Afro-Cuban poet Guillén, his selective attention results in a superficial understanding of a primitive African landscape. When Usnavy perceives that "his circulation" was "flowing free like the Nile" (Obejas *Ruins* 108),[17] this feeling echoes Hughes's "I've known rivers as ancient as the world and older than the flow of human blood in human veins" (*Collected Works* 36). Similarly, Guillén appeals to the fourth-largest African river in "Madrigal" in the line "sign of your forest, ... swimming in the Zambeze of your eyes,"[18] resonating with Hughes's "My soul has grown deep like the rivers/ I bathed in the Euphrates when dawns were young/ I built my hut near the Congo and it lulled me to sleep/ I looked upon the Nile" (*Collected Works* 36). Usnavy senses the ebb and flow of African waterways in his circulatory system via these poets. As Usnavy reads this river onto his lamp, his index finger following the trace of a "fertile Nile traversing the continent" (*Ruins* 20), he internalizes the poets' celebration of blackness through their exploration of the continent. Despite the fact that the exaltation of Africa served to resist neocolonialism – indeed, as David Luis-Brown notes, it functioned to "contest and affirm nationalist discourses of modernization and progress via the racialized figure of the primitive" (198) – Hughes's and Guillén's transnationalism is marked and plagued by a political rhetoric that does little to enable Usnavy to *know* Africa. After all, Castro's color rhetoric was not always conceived of as racial per se but as an effort to bring exploited peoples together to fight against class struggle in an imperialist nation-state. In this way, modernist rivers guide Usnavy's ideological pan-Africanism out of modernism and into decoloniality.

2.4 The African Safari: Hughes, Guillén, and Hemingway

Usnavy's turn away from Hughes and Guillén is explained by Cuba's shift from hemispheric to transatlantic Black internationalism. Castro's Black solidarity rhetoric justifies decolonization in Africa but does little to transform racial inequality on the island. In the 1960s and 1970s, this irony prompted condemnation from African-Americans who were previously enthusiastic supporters of the Cuban Revolution, such as Stokely Carmichael, Eldridge Cleaver, and Robert F. Williams. Despite the fact that African-American political engagement was key to Castro's politics at the beginning of the Revolution – as his visit to the Hotel Theresa attests – African-American and Afro-Cuban activists alike broke with this alliance as the Cuban government shifted its focus from the US South to apartheid South Africa, which threatened Cuban interests in Angola and elsewhere (Mahler 16). Thus, this African-American and Afro-Cuban critique of Cuban racial censorship runs counter to Usnavy's revolutionary fervor and exhausts him. His turn to Fanon and Soyinka is only too obvious of an allegorical shift toward internationalism. Indeed, Fanon's and Soyinka's Marxist stances joined the fight against global capitalism with the struggle for racial justice. Because he is so invested in Castro's Latin-African rhetoric, Usnavy takes signifiers of race in modernism and Hemingway to claim an idealistic utopia that he mistakenly reads into Fanon and Soyinka.[19] That is, even as Usnavy praises Fanon and Soyinka for advocating African decolonization, he seems to overlook the fact that their decolonial politics were neither racially deterministic nor idealistically utopian.

In what follows I argue that Obejas uses Fanon and Soyinka in the novel to critique stereotypical images of Africa that Guillén, Hughes, and Usnavy are invested in. This all begins in 1955, when Fanon's participation in the Algerian National Liberation Front marks his work as a reliable textual site of African memory. While initially, Fanon seems to echo Hughes's and Guillén's primitivism (he notes that the Black man "discovered himself to be a transplanted son of slaves; he felt the *vibrations of Africa in the very depths of his body*," Toward the African Revolution 27, emphasis added), in the same essay, he critiques primitivism, suspecting that romanticized African journeys have perhaps unwittingly promoted a subjectivity of blackness within modernism (Grohs 544). As Fanon describes, "[t]he metropolitan civil servant, returning from Africa, has accustomed us to stereotypes: sorcerers, makers of fetishes, tom-toms, guilelessness, faithfulness, respect for the white man, backwardness" (*African Revolution* 19–20). Fanon refers to stereotypical images representing an idealized precolonial Africa – "tom-toms" not unlike Guillén's "tambores" ("drums") in his poem "Balada de los dos abuelos" (*Sóngoro Cosongo* 66–7), and also not unlike Usnavy's Tiffany lamp reminds him of a similar version of African utopia. But what is central here is that the imaginary of Africa structures a dichotomy within the racial geography of blackness that so obsesses Usnavy; one that imperialism has co-opted, as the novel's reference to Fanon vis-à-vis Hughes and Guillén seems to imply.

While Fanon critiques these symbols that for Guillén and Hughes empower blackness – and which Usnavy uncritically absorbs – Usnavy's reading of Nigerian Nobel laureate Soyinka suggests a willingness to inquire into the "African" literary point of view of these modernist renderings. Soyinka, who in 2001 was bestowed with an Honorary Doctorate in Cuba, indeed is not particularly partisan to Caribbean renderings of a primitive Africa, believing they hinder pan-African empowerment. In his denunciation of Négritude[20] – arguably the Francophone counterpart of Afrocubanismo – he argues that the lyrical movement is unable to go beyond nativist identity, stating that its aesthetics were steeped in a "pre-set system of Eurocentric intellectual analysis" (*Myth* 129, 136). Despite his reading of decolonialists, Usnavy fetishizes a selective Africa, seeking "lions" (160) or Zambia's safari of Mosi-oa-Tunya (48). This imaginary is at odds with Soyinka's critique of discourses in which Africa remains "obscured by villainous dragons in festering swamps," as he puts it (*Of Africa* 38). The imaginary of Africa has long been distorted but in Usnavy's transnational reality of the 1990s, a folkloric African subject and landscape takes precedence.

Despite Usnavy's reading of decolonial sites, his commodification remains paramount to him because of Hemingway's African safari. After all, the novel not only references Hemingway's twenty-year residency in Cuba, but also the author's travelogues about hunting in Kenya and Tanzania. In the scene most exemplary of his susceptibility to Hemingway's representations of Africa, Usnavy dreams of hunting while attempting to recover his daughter Nena's missing ID card. Usnavy tries and fails to find his daughter's number in "room full of books with yellowed pages" amid idling nurses in an inefficient bureaucratic hospital (148–9). Upon finding the right tome but an indecipherable number, Usnavy's chimerical reverie ensues: "'There are no wild animals in Cuba,' Usnavy thought as *he hunted*, none. 'No wild animals here,' he muttered to himself, 'only anteaters, transparent frogs, and tiny, tiny birds. No bears, no lions, no tigers, not even a sighting, a description of one'" (151, emphasis added). Confronted with disillusionment, Usnavy's mind takes refuge once again in an African imaginary; his "hunting" alludes not only to his unsuccessful search but also to the lauded US expat.

The connection between Hemingway's work and Usnavy's idealization of an African safari is central to *Ruins*. Avid readers like Usnavy associate the continent with iconic safaris and exploitation of exotic animals, from *Roosevelt in Africa: Wild Animals of the World* (1909) to Hemingway's *Green Hills of Africa* (1935), where stalwart hunters pose next to their monumental kill. But following World War II, Hemingway's textually memorialized safaris popularized the White male sport (Kerasote 82–3). In Cuba, displays about Hemingway's trophy hunting are exhibited prominently over the walls of his former dwelling, Finca Vijía. In fact, in Usnavy's youth, representations of big game hunting were commonplace and a centerpiece of US imperial power on the island. The novel references how a young Usnavy used to listen to men boasting of "rhino noses, lion pelts, and elephant tusks" at the Brooklyn building (18). Within the imperial space of the Brooklyn, the men drawn to "prizes taken from the Serengeti, the stolen home of the Maasai" (151) in mystical "African safaris" (18), not only nostalgically invoking 1940s Cuba, but also glorifying Hemingway's masculinized trophies at Finca Vigía. But at Finca Vigía, no marker acknowledges the exploitative nature of these African trophies, nor is it even mentioned that Hemingway's abode was a former plantation. As a memorial to Hemingway, Finca Vigía is fifteen miles inland in the region of San Francisco de Paula, and is one of Havana's most visited former plantation lookouts as its name "finca" ("plantation") implies, but its plantocratic surrounding is certainly not emphasized during the tourist's visit.[21]

Despite its role in the slave trade, the site of Cojimar does not host a single memorial to its Black Atlantic history either, but it is the site where, as I explained, Usnavy superimposes the bodies of African slaves on those of non-White rafters fleeing to the US.[22] Moreover, while the unfortunate rafters conjure up the slave trade for Usnavy, this spatiotemporal site could not be more removed from the minds of tourists. At La Terraza in Cojimar[23] – one of the island's main attractions because Hemingway penned *The Old Man and the Sea* there – the rafters are mere spectacle. Indeed, Obejas writes, the "elegant *Las Terrazas*– one of Ernest Hemingway's old haunts," features "foreign tourists, their giggles bubbling in the air, and journalists too" whose camera lights are "washing the landscape" watching balseros' flight from the comfort of their "protected confines" (*Ruins* 42). Adding insult to injury, "TV camera lights" detachedly attempt to capture the rafters' flight, objectifying their bodies. At the beach, some rafts successfully float, while the "chancy-looking homemade dinghy" (42–3) forecasts the tragic fate of those aboard. While this scene all but preoccupies the giddy tourists at La Terraza, in the restaurant, Hemingway's old captain, Gregorio Fuentes, who is "propped up to play checkers or dominos for the tourists' delight" (42), provides a distraction from the tragic and likely death of rafters dotting the sealine.

Undoubtably, Usnavy's shift to Hemingway-esque game hunting allegorizes his turn toward capitalism: as the novel explains, he turns to "hunt" for Tiffany glass he can sell. But while Usnavy becomes entrapped in the wilderness of Hemingway's textual journey through "Nubia, Napata, Kush" (Obejas *Ruins* 99), he shapeshifts from imperialist hunter into exotic hunted, revealing surviving traces of his Cuban revolutionary fervor. Even though his vision of Africa is filtered through imperialism and capitalism, he still "imagined himself not as a hunter or a stateless native," as would Hemingway, "but one with the beautiful beasts, feral and unbound" (18). He imagines himself in Namibia, where he'd be a "fierce hunting dog among sleek Herero heroes relaxing in the hot springs between the mountains and Windhoek" (134) opposite the Herero's German colonizers. Among Hemingway's typecast hunters, Usnavy envisions himself instead as the safari animal: one that is beautiful and seemingly unbound by the imperialist demands of hunting for sport.[24] While I have explained the imperialist mold that shapes Usnavy's understanding of Africa, the political ideology in the sutures of this safari reveal how the troubled Usnavy still seeks a Latin-Africa along the lines of Castro's proclamations that Cuba is a "Latin-African" country or that colonized Africa *is* Cuba. If, as Obejas explained, Hemingway and Castro were two opposites of the same coin in "Hemingway writes about Africa a lot, and Cuba under the revolution has idealized Africa too" (Obejas "Achy" 134), for Usnavy, Hemingway begins to resemble the hegemony whereas his textual safari becomes the idealized Global South family of which Usnavy will become a part. So while Usnavy might harbor a constructed memory of Africa through the filter of the West (and with no epistemological reality of Africa), Usnavy's possibilities for an unfiltered Latin-African memory are still attainable through Cuba's historic involvement in Angola.

2.5 Memorializing the Angolan War with Transatlantic Slavery

The decolonization effort of interest in *Ruins* is the post-1975 period of an unfinished war in Angola. Especially because the aftermath of Cuba's defiance of the US in Africa was Cuba's special period, which drove Cubans into the diaspora in the US in the 1990s. As Cubans flee for Miami, the intersection between the US's antiblack intervention in

2.5 Memorializing the Angolan War with Transatlantic Slavery 107

Angola and Castro's antiracist support for African decolonization is important to Usnavy's exotic projections. After all, those fleeing snub the glory days of Third World internationalism, and even Usnavy, who conflates the Angolan war with the slave trade, perceives Latin-African history as a "curse." This conflation, however, is key to understanding the commodification of Usnavy's Africa and its possible rehabilitation. While Castro's endorsement of African liberation contrasts ironically with the repression of Cuban blackness at home, colonial slavery in Cuba justifies Cuban transatlantic engagement. In this way, Usnavy's overlaying of slavery onto the memory of the Cuban-Angolan alliance is not only reminiscent of Cold War-era geopolitics, but also presents opportunities for him to visit sites of memory that nuance a Latin-African connection from an African point of view.

When the Cuban-supported People's Movement for the Liberation of Angola (*Movimento Popular de Libertação de Angola* or MPLA party) celebrated independence from four centuries of Portuguese rule in 1975, it underscored the strength of Black Cuban-Angolan alliance. And indeed, Cuba poured more resources into Angola than into any other of its interventions on the continent, and sent more than 375,000 members of the Cuban Revolutionary Army there. This victory against an antiblack regime seemed to signal that the US would not be able to preserve White ruling classes in African countries. But in 1978, an attack by US-supported South African forces eviscerated that hope.[25] With Ronald Reagan's rise, not only did the US fail to sanction South Africa for its relentless destruction of Angola, but his administration also funneled $250 million in military assistance to the National Union for the Total Independence of Angola (*União Nacional para a Independência Total de Angola* or UNITA Schmidt 133, 135). Even though Cuban-led efforts in South Africa and Angola would once again succeed with the Tripartite Agreement in 1988 and the UN-monitored 1992 elections (Schmidt 132), the US-supported UNITA party rejected the results of the MPLA election, plunging Angola back into a relentless war that continued until 2002. The fall of the Soviet Union, and with it the disappearance of its subsidies to Cuba, was the final blow to hopes for this Latin-African victory. As Cuban veterans of the Angolan mission returned in the wake of the Soviet collapse to find that their island had been plunged into economic despair, it would have been easy to blame the Angolan war rather than a US strangulation of trade.

One of the most notable moments in which the memory of Africa all but conceals a disappointment for decolonial failure is when Usnavy projects

African slavery onto the Cuban-Angolan crucible right before his friend Diosdado becomes a balsero:

> "Do you ever think about Africa?" Usnavy asked suddenly.
> "Africa?"
> "Yeah, Africa."
> Diosdado shook his head. "Can't say that I do."
> "I do," confessed Usnavy, "all the time."
> "You mean Angola?"
> "No, no" said Usnavy, who had wanted to volunteer for that struggle but was kept from doing so because of his flat feet and back pain.
> "I mean Africa – its vastness. Maybe it's because I'm part Jamaican, I don't know. I think about its destiny."
> Diosdado said nothing.
> "It's a curse, really," Usnavy continued. "Maybe the plagues, the famines – sometimes I wonder whether all that isn't the price of having once participated in selling its own sons and daughters." (125)

Cuba's intervention in Angola lasted 21 years, involved a world-renowned literacy campaign, and resulted in 14,000 scholarships for study in Cuba. It was indeed a time of unprecedented internationalist hope. Nevertheless, Diosdado's specification of this geopolitical moment still privileges a barely tenable Latin-African consciousness. Importantly, when Usnavy brushes aside the particularity of Angola and collapses all his fantasies about different regions of the continent into "Africa – its vastness," the gesture seems to both sustain a co-opted African imaginary and recast Castro's Latin-African rhetoric through the imagery of slavery. It is hard to tell whether Usnavy's embittered reference to "plagues and famines" refers to Africa itself or a mirror he projects from Africa onto his island; I argue that it is a confluence of the two. If, on the one hand, the "cursed" continent remains relevant to Diosdado only geopolitically, on the other – and in a tragic reversal of Castro's use of slavery to forge the Cuban-Angolan alliance – the slave trade functions for Usnavy as a memory of selling out to the unassailable powers of capital and empire. It suggests that the special period repeats a systemic process of capital-based dependency that existed as much during the age of slavery as during the decolonizing era. While the novel superimposes Angola onto slavery in a way that is reminiscent of Castro's political discourse, I argue that this conflation actually rehabilitates Usnavy's Latin-Africa, wresting it away from commodification or at least signaling how a commodified Africa is constructed on both sides of the Atlantic.

Perhaps one of the best examples in which the Angolan war forces Usnavy to nuance his idealized vision of "Africa" is Usnavy's queer encounter with his neighbor, Jacinto, a veteran of the Angolan civil war. Importantly, Jacinto's nostalgic stories of Angola shore up paradigms of gender and sexuality connected not only to Cuba's postrevolutionary period but also to colonial African history, conflating both eras. Specifically, when Usnavy reports that Jacinto was full of tales about "wild animals" and the colorful "palette of the jungle," Jacinto gropes Usnavy's knee and runs his hand upward. While Usnavy turns down his advances, Jacinto justifies his come-on by recounting that "long ago in ancient times, Shaka, the Zulu king, encouraged his soldiers to have what they called *uku-hlobonga* – thigh sex – in order to keep them strong" (105). Jacinto further reveals that while he was serving, he had "energy-surging intercourse with a South African transvestite" (105). Both Jacinto's experience with this "transvestite" and his attempt to seduce Usnavy contrast strongly with Cuba's recent history of persecuting queer people.

Jacinto conjures up Havana's Military Units to Aid Production (UMAP) camps from 1964. These camps forced queer people, political dissidents, and religious minorities into sugarcane fields, subjecting them to hard labor and physical and emotional abuses, tragically echoing Cuba's long plantocratic regime. As Obejas has stated in an interview, Jacinto's gender flexibility is as much an affirmation of the Afro-Cuban pantheon of Santería from the days of slavery – "where gods change sex every six months," Obejas states – as a condemnation of the post-revolutionary labor and re-education camps that produced "a very damaged generation of queer people."[26] In the novel, both Jacinto's queer gesture but more importantly his invocation of Shaka's position on gender noticeably complicates Cuban narratives of Angola: it gestures toward the continuity in Cuba's repression of nonbinary gender expression from the colonial era through that of decolonization. In particular, however, Jacinto's queer sexuality and gender nonconformity are reinforced by a transatlantic experience that originates in Africa.

While Jacinto's queer narrative refers vaguely to "ancient times," his equally romanticizing memory of Shaka locates the site of colonial repression in southwestern Africa. The cross-dresser in question, the war hero argues, might not have considered themselves a "transvestite" at all: "[S]he wasn't like the locas here," Jacinto argues, "[s]he had lived like that her whole life. Where she came from, in her tribe, if she acted like a woman, if she believed she was a woman, well … she was … except for … you know" (105). The story that Jacinto recounts suggests an African positionality on gender performance. In other words, as Jacinto speaks of the West and Central African regions that he visited in the twentieth century, his story of Shaka "in ancient times" essentially subverts westernized constructs of gender. The novel's juxtaposition of this ancient story, Jacinto's "transvestite," and "the locas here" encourages us to examine transatlantic connections among constructs of gender and sexuality.

Jacinto's "loca" locates African epistemology in the records of the Inquisition, tracing a direct line of suppression between Lusophone Africa and Cuba's UMAP camps. In the tribunals of Lisbon, there is evidence of "flexible gender categories in various parts of Africa."[27] Specifically, Atlantic historian James Sweet reveals the case of a slave from Benin who arrived on Ilha Terceira in 1556 and "assumed the uncertain gender identity" that they maintained from their homeland (*Recreating* 53). When questioned by the Inquisition for charges of sodomy, the slave Antônio claimed that they had a "buraco" – Portuguese for a "woman's orifice" – and that many of their community members in Benin had one as well. The records show that in Antônio's place of origin, this third gender category was common construct, spreading in the Portuguese colonies to the point that, when Cuba sent its convoy to Angola, it was still common currency. What is telling of Jacinto's resistance to attempts to confine a person to "western standards of sexual gender and family categories" (54) is that he finds a way to transplant this African memory to Cuba. While Cuba's plantocracy may have shaped Jacinto's gender nonconformity, it also seems to have been reinforced by Jacinto's 1970s mission in Angola. In other words, the queer behavior of King Shaka's troops, despite being criminalized in the sixteenth century and diluted in the postcolonial period, not only endures well into contemporary times but also breaks down essentialist versions of Africa for Usnavy.

Jacinto's nostalgia for his days in Angola and Usnavy's earlier disappointment with a failed Latin-African connection, however, is not unique to *Ruins*. In fact, *Ruins* converses with Angolan and Cuban post–Cold War narratives that trace a trajectory of simultaneous disenchantment and nostalgia. Angolan works dialoguing with *Ruins* are Pepetela's *A Geração da Utopia* (*A Generation of Utopia*, 1992) and Boaventura Cardoso's *Maio, Mês de Maria* (*May the Month of Mary*, 1997), with the Angolan film *O herói* (*The Hero*, 2004) directed by Zézé Gamboa representing the most pertinent example, as I will explain. On the Cuban side, Eliseo Alberto's stern critique in *Caracol Beach* (1998) is also of the most relevance to Obejas's critique of a neoliberal model that uproots a Latin-African history while simultaneously celebrating its essentialization. Beginning with the Angolan example, *O herói* displays both a glorified postmemory of the Angolan war and Black internationalism's failure to produce Black solidarity. During a scene in a pawn shop in which a young boy orphaned by the war, Manu, seeks to trade in a stolen radio amidst devastating poverty, he inquires if the clerk has a gun from the war. The clerk then mentions that if the boy wants a war relic, he can take a veteran's stolen prosthetic leg. The scene not only underscores the boy's disregard for the war's violence, but placed next to *Ruins*, the scene also emphasizes how profoundly disjointed Usnavy's idealization of the Angolan conflict is. Moreover, the prosthesis serves as an allegory for the dismemberment of the Cuban-Angolan alliance. The sacrifices of veterans – such as that of Vitório, the former owner of the stolen prosthesis – are lost. Instead, Angolan people must necessarily focus on survival in the aftermath of civil war, even if it means that veterans must sell their prosthetic limbs, as the film resonates with the dire circumstances of Havana's special period.

On the Cuban side of this paradigm is Alberto's novel *Caracol Beach*, in which the Angolan conflict haunts the protagonist Beto Milanés, who is a Cuban veteran suffering from posttraumatic stress disorder as the sole survivor of a conflict that killed the rest of his squad. *Caracol Beach* "fails to reproduce the conventions of a heroic war epic" (Millar 59) that Usnavy initially wills onto the pages of *Ruins*. In fact, Alberto's novel, Millar explains, renders the Angolan war "as merely senseless and too long-lasting" from the Cuban point of view (59). In an interesting counterpoint to Usnavy's daydreams of exotic African animals, Alberto uses the same fauna to convey detachment and trauma. When the omniscient narrator in *Caracol Beach* relates how Beto first saw a tiger in Angola that later haunts him in Miami, the tiger prophesizes the character's end: "The first time he faced the tiger was on the afternoon he lost his mind in Ibondá de Akú" (Alberto 6). While lions characterize a paradisiacal safari tamed by men like Hemingway in Usnavy's imagined memory of Angola, in Beto's real memory, the fauna's violence stands out: "He would remember little of those days except for the African leopard that emerged suddenly from the underbrush and began to slash open the black man's torso" (7). The story is in line with the accounts that historian Christine Hatzky finds regarding Cuban veterans' feelings of "fear and trauma" caused by a sense of rejection while in Angola (216). Thus, Black internationalism in Alberto's literary example, like in the Angolan one above, contrasts greatly with Usnavy's idealized postmemory of Africa. Moreover, they also express the ways in which Gamboa's film reverses Latin-African connections. But while these narratives express pessimism about the internationalist alliance in line with a dystopia in renown Cuban writers such as Reinaldo Arenas or Pedro Juan Gutiérrez as Casamayor-Cisneros explains in her own study (189–211), the narratives described here also underscore the incongruence between Black Atlantic alliances and the social inequalities in both Angola and Cuba. *Ruins* dialogues with these paradigms as it also seeks to recover a buried Latin-African history despite this disappointment, from both sides of the Atlantic.

To conclude, I turn to a final example in which an African epistemology embedded in the novel critiques Usnavy's dogged essentialization of Africa and thus rehabilitates, or at least explains, a commodified Latin-African memory. In one of the arguably most upsetting moments of the novel, the departure of Usnavy's own daughter Nena conjures up a significant site of African slavery. When Usnavy sees "an adolescent: slender, long-limbed, with charcoal eyebrows and skin like wax" board a raft (181), he impotently realizes this balsera is his daughter: "*Nena? Nenita?*" (181). The acute moment of anxiety underscores Usnavy's extreme ideological paralysis and thus his inability to save her from the diaspora. In other words, Usnavy's rootedness has frustrated his daughter and, seeing that there is no hope that he might change and find a better life for them, Nena flees. This break immediately prompts Usnavy's imaginary diaspora. As Nena takes off, Usnavy visualizes another neighbor he calls "the Badagry woman": in acute despair, Usnavy muses to himself, "Okay then, he thought: Badagry" (193). Usnavy's palpable resolution refers to a Tiffany lamp he believes this woman owns and that he is determined to wrest away from her. While this moment is a clear sign that he has given in to capitalism, Usnavy's interest in her origin – Badagry, Nigeria – serves as a metaphor for repossessing a Latin-Africa.

Recalling the neoliberal developmental project planned for Badagry, I return to the imperial history of Badagry that adds to the site's controversial commodification. The British parliamentary documents reveal Badagry as a site where a heinous crime committed against a young slave girl was intercepted but is not memorialized anywhere on Badagry's heritage trail. If Usnavy's contemporary Badagry woman emphasizes the *imaginary* site of an "African safari," the Badagry woman in the colonial archive contributed to the immortalization of Nigeria's *physical* site. As the parliamentary documents reveal, this nineteenth-century "Badagry" woman was fourteen when she was murdered in one of the most barbaric ways imaginable. Her murder brought attention to the fact that slavery remained customary within the confines of the British empire. This case, spanning over seventy pages of correspondence in the British archive, was

2.5 Memorializing the Angolan War with Transatlantic Slavery 113

crucial to reinvigorated policing of Britain's slave coast; the case emphasized that Nigeria's far eastern provinces continued to fuel slave traffic and deportation, enriching Britain's competitors. I term her the "Badagry" woman because even though her murder occurred in Onitsha, 400 kilometers east of the "slave coast," Badagry was the place where her story was intercepted and laws amended to halt slave trafficking.

In the archival correspondence mentioned above, a document from March 29, 1888, reveals that a British inspector from the Gold Coast, a M. Cuscaden, arrived in Badagry in 1877 to inquire into the murder of Amé, a young enslaved girl who attempted to escape.[28] He finds an interpreter for the missionaries, W. F. John, guilty of the crime. The manner in which he carried out the punishment for running away was so barbaric that I will not recount its ruthlessness here. Badagry features prominently in the British archive not only because it was a critical outpost of the slave trade, but also because, in the later nineteenth century, the site served as a reminder of Britain's failure to halt the terror of the slave trade (Geary 171–2). As the continuing, illicit traffic in slaves troubled British officials, they created boundaries to prevent crossing of the Atlantic. In the correspondence after the verdict, British authorities implemented "a new Order in Council for regulating consular jurisdiction on the West Coast of Africa" (No. 62, 51), which would enable the policing of "natives of Sierra Leone" to be "tried in Lagos or the Gold Coast and vice versa." For the British authorities, the abhorrent case justified not sympathy for victims of antiblack violence, but rather increased border patrols targeting freed Black bodies at the very site where these bodies had once been policed as slaves. Moreover, while Britain raised borders, other imperial authorities continued to transgress them, facilitating the continuation of the Cuban plantocracy.

Nearly a century later, Usnavy finds himself hemmed in by the oceanic borders that created the balseros in the twentieth century. If Usnavy's traumatic witnessing of his kin fleeing to the US on rafts at Cojimar evokes a diaspora that drives him to name his neighbor the "Badagry woman," his imaginary of Badagry conflates the diaspora of the slave trade with that of 1990s Cuba. As the site of Cojimar prompts lament for a global capitalist model that drives both the transatlantic and transnational diasporas, detachment from the fate of these coerced travelers – which the novel aptly critiques via the tourists at La Terraza – now envelops Usnavy. In arguably one of the most damning moments in the novel, Usnavy fails to save the Badagry woman and chooses her lamp instead. As the Badagry woman's building collapses – presumably on top of her – Usnavy digs for the lamp "underneath the wreckage" (197). In the process, he "did not think of Badagry, or where she was, or her sisters or whether they were alive," instead, he just "dug and dug and dug." Despite Usnavy's reading of decolonialists Fanon and Soyinka, Usnavy performs a damming detachment, underscored in the phrase "he did not think" of Badagry. His neighbor, like the archival Badagry girl has fallen out of history. This moment of detachment during the special period's desperate times seems to signify that memory of Badagry is akin to that of the countless "dead girls" of the transatlantic slave trade archive that, as Saidiya Hartman states, "exist only within the confines of [archival] words." These "dead girls" who Hartman exhumes from the archive are nevertheless "buried under [the] prose" of colonial narratives (Hartman "Venus" 6) and now under the prose of Obejas's allegorical ruins in the wake of collapse.

If we were to read Usnavy this way, we would conclude that any rehabilitation of Latin-African connection is doomed: not only because Usnavy, despite his reading of decolonial theorists, fails to help his fellow subaltern, but also because the commodification of Africa – represented by the selling of the lamp – takes material precedence over his Black comrade. If Usnavy fails to save the Badagry woman, his decision to save an exoticized Africa in the form of her lamp suggests not only that he seeks financial reward, but also that he is metaphorically trying to possess a location. Usnavy seeks to trace the Badagry woman's origin, as he muses to seek a "trail of bones back to Badagry." But Usnavy does not achieve it.

When the Badagry woman's lamp fades into rubble after the storm and Usnavy attempts to recover the shards of glass as they pierce his hands, he digs deeper and pulls up "roots and earth, black and fertile and wet" (199). The fact that Usnavy pulls up roots after following an imaginative route toward Badagry recalls cultural historian James Clifford's contrast between "roots and routes," or when an individual finds collective strength outside of the nation while rooted in the nation.[29] As new neoliberal reform begins to plague his island, Usnavy, by uprooting himself ideologically, travels along an Atlantic borderland despite his rootedness in a commodified Latin-Africa. At the end of the narrative, a wounded Usnavy sleeps beside his wife, and the omniscient narrator informs us that if he were conscious, "he would have imagined Jacinto like the slaves who brought rice to the New World, grains hidden in his hair" (201). Awakened, he turns to his wife and utters, "[i]t's like with Africa ... Africa and its curse" (202). In this utterance, the temporalities of slavery, Angola, and the special period – like the shattered panes of Tiffany glass – all merge into a memorial for a Latin-Africa that the

2.5 Memorializing the Angolan War with Transatlantic Slavery 115

novel mourns. In his essay regarding the memory of slavery for West Africans, Mbembe suggests that this memory is characterized "by diffraction," by a "set of fragments of metaphors" ("The Subject" 25); such is also the case for Usnavy on the other side of the Atlantic. But at least in the end, this memory is no longer subjected to utopian fantasies. Indeed, as Usnavy, his wife, and a neighbor leave to find medical attention, a tourist snaps a picture of the ruins of Usnavy's lamp, obviously unconcerned with the wounded (202–3). Recalling British indifference toward Black female bodies or Badagry's neoliberal erasure, *Ruins* stages what global capitalist indifference in the face of twenty-first-century heritage tourism looks like. Usnavy "cringes" when he hears a tourist armed with a camera scream excitedly, "A light in the ruins!" as he leaves behind his once-exoticized African safari in the textual memorial of *Ruins*.

Allegorically, the shattered lamp reflects a rehabilitation of memory that also shatters African commodification. Indeed, Usnavy's sense of memory is *doubled* as the plot in *Ruins* stretches across an Atlantic. This doubling is not only transnational, but transatlantic, supranational, and multilingual. Usnavy's grasp on a globalized world outside of his rooted ideology and nomadic nationality is not confined to the racial geography of Cuba, nor is it tied to a post–Cold War US empire. Rather, Usnavy rewrites the trails of Badagry over the city of Havana and seeks to inhabit a Latin-Africa beyond blackness, or at least via a blackness that is not circumscribed by the hemispheric. In other words, Usnavy exchanges Afro-Cubanness for a Latin-Africa that originates in the African continent and is continuously crossing over and back. Through Obdulio's overestimation of the west, Jacinto's commodified Angolan war, and finally Usnavy's own exoticization of and desire for the Badagry woman's lamp, the novel outlines a trail along which Usnavy realizes that his memory of a Latin-Africa is ultimately commodified.

In the end, one could undoubtedly conclude that physical and textual sites of memory, while mutually constitutive in expanding Atlantic memory, do not necessarily portend solidarity across the Black Atlantic. After all, both Usnavy and the site at Badagry commodify African heritage. However, even if a Latin-Africa seems irretrievable, in *Ruins* Atlantic memorialization still promotes Global South solidarity. By using Badagry as a site that meditates on African transatlantic history within her novel *Ruins*, Obejas seeks to connect a Latin-Africa to paradigms of African representation in the work of world-renowned authors from Soyinka to Hemingway. Yet Obejas expresses a notion akin to that of a younger generation of Nigerian expat writers, who as Caren Irr explains, break away from a "nostalgia for the presumed purity of village tradition" (127). Contemporary writers, like Obejas thus seek more global connections to critique the effects of global capitalism haunting the Latin-African imaginary. As Soyinka critiques Badagry's UNESCO site, Obejas in turn textualizes Badagry in *Ruins* to critique a neoliberal Cuba. Not only does the novel carve out a space to consider Latinx writing in a South-South framework or South Atlantic studies in World Literature, it creates a World Literature of its own. As a result, the Latin-African space that *Ruins* creates speaks less to allegorical connections among histories of coloniality – like those espoused by Castro, for instance – and more to a Black political solidarity across the Global South that can undo the machinations of commodity capital.

CHAPTER 3

Obliteration
Gabriel García Márquez and His Angolan Chronicles of a "Latin-African" Death Foretold

In an easily overlooked moment in Gabriel García Márquez's world-renowned novel, *Crónica de una muerte anunciada/Chronicle of a Death Foretold* (1981) memorializes Senegalese slavery over the site of Cartagena's Bahía de las ánimas (Bay of Souls). A story about protagonist Santiago Nasar's stabbing for his alleged sexual abuse of recently wedded Angela Vicario is suddenly interrupted. While Angela's new husband, wealthy immigrant Bayardo San Román, discovers that she is no longer a virgin, Santiago takes his friends to a pier after the wedding festivities and points to something shining on the horizon over the Atlantic Ocean. He remarks that the Colombian bay is named after the souls ("ánimas") of Senegalese slaves who were lost in the wreck of an unnamed slave ship. But the novel's main plotline buries this seemingly incidental mention of the sunken slave ship just as swiftly as the actual Atlantic buried the Senegalese bodies. The story moves on: Bayardo shamefully returns a jilted Angela to her family shortly after their consummated marriage, setting in motion the events that lead to Santiago's death. And yet, while the memorialization of Bahía de las ánimas might seem insignificant in the novel, the journalism that García Márquez published the same year makes clear its centrality. In the Colombian journal *El Espectador*, García Márquez wrote that "el rincón más nostálgico de Cartagena de las Indias es el muelle de la Bahía de las Ánimas" ("the most nostalgic corner in Cartagena is the Bay of Souls").[1] With Cervantine irony about the Bay of Souls, a renowned slave depot in the Atlantic World,[2] the author mocks the kind of "nostalgic" yearning evident in Cartagena's memorial to Christopher Columbus seen in Figure 3.1. In another journalistic piece that year, "Como ánimas en pena," García Márquez reflects this time on the mourning souls of *literature* in "las ánimas en pena de la literatura," using the exact same phrase ("las ánimas en pena") as the passage in *Crónica de una muerte anunciada* quoted above (*Notas de prensa* 1991, 102). This piece, moreover, holds that the mourning souls of literature "adhere more to the heart than to

Figure 3.1 Memorial to Christopher Columbus at Plaza de la aduana, adjacent to Bahía de las ánimas. Photo: Alejandra Pozas Luna, 2019.

memory," setting up a peculiar relationship not only between journalism and fiction, but also between the way in which the name of the Bay of Souls recalls its Atlantic history and literature's role in memorializing that history. The echoes among "mournful souls," "the Bay of Souls," and the slave ship in these three pieces triangulate a Black Atlantic heritage not unfamiliar to Caribbean Colombia but certainly not at the center of literary criticism on García Marquez's oeuvre. Thus, in placing together García Márquez's journalism and literature, this Black Atlantic past contrasts with Cartagena's physical obliteration of a Latin-Africa, which replaces the memory of slavery with a fantasy of colonial discovery symbolized by the Bay of Soul's statue of Columbus.

It is not a coincidence that Black Atlantic politics of memorialization surface in the Nobel laureate's fiction and nonfiction. *Crónica de una muerte anunciada*, the Latin American Boom writer's most famous novel at the time of its publication, conjures a slave trade port after García Márquez had, for years, been steeped in the Atlantic World as a journalist; specifically, in Angola. His decade of transatlantic journalism was first prompted by his work covering the US invasion of Cuba's Bay of Pigs of the 1960s while García Márquez was living in New York and reporting for the Cuban-run *Prensa Latina*. This geopolitical tension sharpened his stern criticism of US neocolonialism, and even strengthened his friendship with Fidel Castro as other Boom writers broke with the Cuban Revolution following the Padilla Affair in 1971.[3] Crucially, during this time, Castro began using proclamations about the history of slavery to justify Cuban involvement in the burgeoning African decolonization movements I described in the previous chapter, in particular against both Portugal and the US in Angola. When Castro's military mission in Angola "Operación Carlota" ("Operation Carlota") defeated these forces in 1975, Castro prematurely invoked a victorious "Latin-Africa;" one that would be asphyxiated years later by US intervention. Prior to this outcome, García Márquez traveled to Angola himself to report on the 1975 victory, making his chronicle "Operación Carlota" (using the same title of Castro's mission), one of the most detailed accounts of Cuban Black internationalism between 1975 and 1978. Curiously, his report on this mission is filled with subjective remarks from a first-person point of view; its style borders on that of fiction. Notably, as García Márquez used fictional techniques in his reporting, his Angolan "chronicles" relate to *Crónica de una muerte anunciada*, the novel he finished after his return from Angola and in which he conjured a factual slave ship from Senegal found in the French "outer seas" archives (*Les Archives nationales d'outre-mer*). Finally, by focalizing on the centrality of García Márquez's Angolan writing, other traces of an evident Latin-Africa in the novel emerge, such as Bayardo San Román's blackness and subsequent racialization, his repossession of a Catalan mansion as a memorial, and a conjuring of spaces of slavery and the slave trade within a plot that is far more cosmopolitan than appears at first glance.

I begin this chapter by examining how the figure of the ship sunk in the Bay of Souls functions as a point of access to Latin-Africa in the journalism of one of World Literature's most venerated writers. Later, in examining his intrepid journalistic coverage of the Cuban intervention in Angola, I argue that Angola becomes a means of reading García Márquez's once hopeful but ultimately failed and forgotten Latin-Africa. After all, in an interview García Márquez states:

> El periodista tiene ese raro destino de dar opiniones y tratar de reflejar realidades que a veces le son completamente extrañas. En el caso de Angola particularmente, la pregunta me interesa mucho porque yo soy de la costa caribe de Colombia, que es la región de América Latina, con Brasil, donde hay mayor influencia africana. Mi viaje a Angola ... me partió la vida por la mitad porque precisamente yo fui a Angola *convencido de encontrarme un mundo totalmente extraño* y desde el momento que desembarqué ... me encontré otra vez con toda mi infancia y me encontré con costumbres que ya había *olvidado por completo*. ("Llegué a creer que Franco" 171, emphasis added)

> The journalist has that rare destiny to give opinions and try to reflect realities that sometimes are completely strange to them. In the case of Angola in particular, the question interests me greatly because I am from the Caribbean coast of Colombia, which is the Latin American region, along with Brazil, that was most influenced by Africa. My trip to Angola ... broke my life in half precisely because I went to Angola *expecting to find a completely foreign world* and the moment I arrived ... I found myself with my youth, and found customs that I had *completely forgotten*.

In García Márquez's account of his experience as a journalist, Angola figures prominently, not only because it reminded him of how his roots went back to Colombia's participation in the Atlantic World system of slavery, but also because it "broke his life in two," thus marking his realization of his Latin-African identity. So much did Angola preoccupy him, he reported having nightmares after his return and even stated that his reports on the decolonial war were his most passionate journalistic pieces.[4] Moreover, his view is not unlike those expressed in some Angolan and Cuban narratives of the war that I will briefly mention, which share with García Márquez's a nostalgia for the promise that a Latin-Africa once held. And yet, a thread of lament is also latent in García Márquez's assertion that Latin-African history "had been completely forgotten" – both narratively and physically – akin to the sunken ship whose brief mention is also easy for literary critics to completely overlook.

What emerges through a contextual reading of García Márquez's understudied journalism is a mournful textual memorial to the death of a Latin-Africa foretold. In this chapter, I argue that García Márquez's overlooked journalism about Angola from 1971 to 1982 envisioned a hopeful yet never realized Latin-Africa which was stymied by imperial US intervention as the

Cold War shifted to Africa. In establishing the important relationship between his fiction and journalism, I explain how his Angolan enterprise offers an access to García Márquez's Latin-African memorialization in both fiction and nonfiction. I analyze not only "Operación Carlota" but his many chronicles regarding US foreign affairs to show how the cultural forms of Latin America emerge from an intersectional relationship with Angola that has been overlooked in literary criticism. Recalling Cartagena's glorification of Columbus, García Márquez's journalism makes up for a lack of public acknowledgment of slave trade history in Cartagena by way of Cuba's Black internationalism memorialized textually in "Operación Carlota" and other chronicles. The mourning souls of a failed Cuban-Angolan alliance are the textual memorials that inform the African origins of the Bahía de las ánimas name that García Márquez conveys fictionally in *Crónica de una muerte anunciada*. Indeed, after examining the textual memorialization of the Angolan conflict in García Márquez's journalism, I return to this novel to reveal other moments that evoke subtle but critical textual memorials to slavery and the slave trade, in addition to the drowned ship from Senegal. But if "Operación Carlota" as a site of memory in Angola is projected onto the novel's fictionalized Senegalese slaves, the mutually constitutive nature of fiction and journalism brings me to consider how Senegalese slaves depicted in the novel are brought to bear on the UNESCO Slave Route in Senegal; especially since the memory site's application of both fact and fiction convey a similar story of lament for slaves' lost memory. The end of this chapter reflects on the ways in which García Márquez's brief mention of Senegalese souls at Cartagena's pier complements Senegal's memorial at Gorée island: the renowned *Maison des esclaves/House of Slaves* facing the Atlantic Ocean and memorializing the slave ships' captives. The memorializing principle in García Márquez's work conveys, like most Slave Route memorials, a lament for an obliterated African heritage that Latin Americans rarely claim as part of their own.

I end by evincing how his Angolan chronicles should make critics question universalist readings of *Crónica de una muerte anunciada* in World Literature and pay attention to García Márquez's transatlantic ventures in Angola more broadly rather than burdening his oeuvre with magical realist expectations. Of interest to transnational literary history is that García Márquez's writing reveals how a historical transatlantic axis crosscuts a transnational one, expanding the geographical but also thematic aims of his work beyond magical realism. After all, as Mariano Siskind cogently critiques, magical realism gone global has adhered to a "pluralistic aesthetic that satisfies a demand for *local color* from marginal cultures in the global field of world literature" (59). While Siskind explains that magical realism morphs into an extension of the postcolonial for World Literature (for which it is later appropriated and commodified, 60), García Márquez's Latin-African journalism provides a far more exemplar picture of the postcolonial. In other words, the Nobel writer's Angolan-Cuban axis exemplifies the cosmopolitanism of regionality without having to fall prey to essentialization.

3.1 *Crónica de una muerte anunciada* as Point of Access to Latin-Africa

Crónica de una muerte anunciada is based on two real-life accounts made fictional: the assassination of García Márquez's family friend, medical student Cayetano Gentile Chimento, in Sucre, Colombia, and the story of an unfortunate couple who reunite in old age and are the epicenter of *El amor en los tiempos del cólera/Love in the Time of Cholera* (1985).[5] In *Crónica de una muerte anunciada*, the two stories merge in a nameless Caribbean town facing Cartagena as the drama of an honor killing unfolds. It begins with the arrival of an affluent outsider, Bayardo San Román, a Caribbean man of dark complexion, who marries Angela Vicario but discovers after their vows that she is no longer a virgin. When Bayardo returns Angela to her abusive mother and disappears for decades, Angela faults a wealthy Arab-Colombian Santiago as "[su] autor" ("my perpetrator" 113, 100), which leads Angela's reluctant yet determined brothers, Pedro and Pablo Vicario, to publicly swear revenge and vow to butcher Santiago. Despite the fact that Santiago's murder is thus "foretold" or announced, not a single member of the community impedes it. Meanwhile Angela later discovers her passionate love for Bayardo only after he has already left town, driving her to madly scribble love letters to him daily – letters that remain unopened but that he brings along when he eventually returns to her decades later. While Bayardo's Caribbean background is important in my analysis, as I will later explain, the sinister nature of both Santiago's foretold but impossibly fateful death and the communal guilt engulfing the town leads the unnamed narrator to return to the scene of the crime to negotiate with the town's guilty conscience. The novel pieces together his detective work in interviewing eye-witnesses who even report such things as smells and interpretations of dreams, resulting in the postmodern chronicle that we are reading.[6] The denunciation of the murder as a crime in *Crónica de una muerte anunciada* derives from Latin America's

3.1 Crónica de una muerte anunciada *as Point of Access*

long history of *crónicas* ("chronicles"), but the faintly class-conscious and ultimately political thread palpable in the novel as well as its universalist trope of impending doom was partially informed by García Márquez's transnational but also transatlantic journalistic experience.

Both *Crónica de una muerte anunciada* and García Márquez's journalistic crónicas trace their ancestry to nineteenth-century Latin American chronicles, which in turn had departed from their colonial conquistador origins to become a central form for belle-lettrists. Exemplified by the work of José Martí, Rubén Darío, and Enrique Gómez Carrillo, among others, such literary chronicles also drew on a French concept introduced into Spanish American journalism by Mexican Manuel Gutiérrez Nájera as early as 1873. In time, its popularity as the main genre for Latin American Modernistas consisted in the intersection of the periodical and the political with a "self-consciously literary style" (González "Modernist Prose" 73); such chronicles were otherwise described as "poetic-philosophical-humoristic-literary notes."[7] But well into the twentieth century, the chronicle would transform yet again into a brisk journalistic style. As Carlos Monsiváis notes, the chronicle is best defined as the "literary reconstruction of events or figures, a genre in which an attention to form dominates over pressing information."[8] Still, the chronicle would preserve the intersectional quality that had made it a preferred genre for Modernists. As Susana Rotker famously noted, "fiction and journalism are tied by the umbilical cord of the chronicle."[9] Further, the chronicle's wide circulation in the privileged space of the press offers authors an authoritative voice on issues of social concern. In this vein, the language used to describe the chronicle evolved again, as it became constituted within "narrative journalism" (Darrigrandi 124), spurring debates about whether a chronicler was a writer or a journalist. Intellectuals at the renowned Latin American cultural center in Havana, *Casa de las Américas*, such as Alejo Carpentier, responded that there was no distinction between the two (124).

This debate about the rank of a journalist vis-à-vis a writer, which lays bare social-class hierarchies, also took place in the US New Journalism of the 1960s. As Tom Wolfe explains in his 1972 genealogy of the form in *Esquire*, journalists were considered the "lumpenproles" of literary culture, while critics made up the middle ranks and novelists traced their upper-class status to the elites of the nineteenth century ("Why They Aren't"). Perhaps this debate intrigued the playful writer in García Márquez, who, after his success with *Cien años de soledad*, turned to his journalism and created a "chronicle" that would revive such debates. While much has been written regarding the complex genre of García Márquez's famous short novel, no account has, to my knowledge, considered the journalistic quality of *Crónica de una muerte anunciada* as a clue that García Márquez's experiences in Angola, which immediately preceded the completion of a novel thirty years in the making, were central to it.

García Márquez's reporting on Angola was the culmination of a long friendship with Castro that harkened back to the 1959 triumph of the Cuban Revolution. García Márquez would eventually be appointed as a journalist for the then-burgeoning Cuban press *Prensa Latina*. An initiative of Ernesto "Che" Guevara and founded by Argentine Jorge Ricardo Masetti, *Prensa Latina* recruited the best Latin American journalists of the time (among them, leftists Plinio Apuleyo Mendoza, Juan Carlos Onetti, García Márquez, and his close friend, Rodolfo Walsh), seeking to counterbalance US press coverage of Cuba with notoriously worldwide reach.[10] While anti-imperial views are palpable in García Márquez's initial work as a journalist for Cartagena's *El Universal* in 1953 and subsequent work for *Momento* in Venezuela from 1957 to 1958 – when he was exposed to the US's attempt, and failure, to prop up dictator General Marcos Pérez Jiménez (*Por la libre* 118–21) – his work for *Prensa Latina* notably sharpened his anti-US sentiment. Importantly, García Márquez's first deployment as a journalist for Castro began as assistant bureau chief in the press's New York satellite office in the wake of souring relations between Cuba and the US. García Márquez personally witnessed and later wrote "El drama de las dos Cubas" ("The Drama of Two Cubas," 1979), which both referenced the failed Bay of Pigs invasion on April 19, 1961 and condemned the death threats he received from Cuban emigres; a significant catalyst for his Angolan journalism which in turn predates and informs one of World Literature's renowned books of fiction.[11] *Crónica de una muerte anunciada* not only distinguishes itself from both the Latin American chronicle and New Journalism's experimental ways of denouncing a crime, but also registers a geopolitical and transatlantic context in its trope of foretold doom.

While *Crónica de una muerte anunciada* mimics news reportage in form, the unreliability of the events narrated led many critics to oppose a reading of the novel as journalistic. Not only are the unknown narrator, vague setting and temporality, and uncertainty about the "author" of Angela's ruin unlike the components of a traditional news story, but also, as Jorge Olivares notes, "[*Crónica*'s] achronology violate[s] the norms of the [chronicle] genre; in addition, the account neglects to establish the facts" (483). Olivares refers to the conventional rules of the *crónica*, which follow "a global and schematic order" in which the story moves chronologically

3.1 Crónica de una muerte anunciada *as Point of Access*

from "exposition, development, resolution, and epilogue."[12] But like his Angolan reports, the blending of nonfiction and fiction in the novel's title is just as elusive as the historical Atlantic context that conceptually informs *Crónica de una muerte anunciada*. Just how historical is this novel, if it is merely fiction attempting to conceal "facts"? Others argue that the novel is just as historical as its title implies. For not only has García Márquez "called it a chronicle and not a novel to present the historical reality of the events it narrates,"[13] the novel's postmodern parallels with historical events are so close to García Márquez's life experiences that Ángel Rama sees the novel as a fusion of journalism and detective story ("García Márquez" 7). Aníbal González more concretely reads the novel as an examination of "journalism's links with literature" due to García Márquez's own "century-long association" with the profession ("The Ends of the Text" 62, 66). To this point, the similarity of García Márquez's later *Crónica de una muerte anunciada* to Walsh's reporting is important stylistically. The novel's disjunctive form lends itself to being read in relation to the "historical reality" of a journalism, though critics often overlook the Angolan context. The Latin-Africa I trace against more Eurocentric approaches is based on the assessments that literary critique has snubbed the Angolan journalism of García Márquez as marginal to his story, or incorrectly apply it to works where slavery featured more prominently in the plot. For instance, Hugo Méndez Ramírez's reading of *Crónica* as the one novel that most resembles the Spanish Golden Age in García Márquez's works (937) or Raymond L. Williams's both eliding Angolan regional specificity in "Africa" (135) – tying García Márquez's trip to the more obvious *Del amor y otros demonios* in which the protagonist lives among slaves – and reading a medieval Spain into *Crónica de una muerte anunciada* (120). This Eurocentric transatlantic lens denies both considerations of García Márquez's journalism between 1975 and 1982 and misses the Latin-African vector.

But what emerges in this prolepsis of the novel becomes typical of García Márquez's disappointment in humanity. Indeed, traditionally most critics had read the foretold death in García Márquez's *Crónica de una muerte anunciada* this way, as Méndez Ramírez stated in 1990: "On the one hand, there are those who interpret the novel in terms of fatality, a *persistent* trope in García Márquez's oeuvre ... on the other, there are those who interpret it as a function of collective violence (guilt)."[14] With important origins in "El drama de las dos Cubas," García Márquez's prolepsis comes to serve the sense of fatality that, by 1990, was considered a "persistent" feature of his writing. The universalist trope of impending doom in *Crónica de una muerte anunciada*, which makes it of such interest in World Literature, also prompts my reading of the novel as a textual memorial to García Márquez's Latin-Africa. A novel he published one year prior to winning the Nobel Prize, *Crónica de una muerte anunciada* and its universalist tropes render it "a classical story of world literature"[15] that has been echoed around the globe by works from Congolese Sony Labou Tansi's rewriting of it in *Seven Solitudes of Lorsa Lopez* (1985) to director Manjari Kaul's theatrical adaptation of it in New Delhi, India. Notably, the novel's magical realism, albeit not as prominent as in *Cien años de soledad*, also commercializes it quite well with regard to the style's "globalization" (Siskind 57, 95.) Additionally, *Crónica de una muerte anunciada* is not only one of the author's most taught and anthologized texts, but was also more widely read than any of his other works at the time of its publication because it was simultaneously printed by prestigious publishing houses in three Latin American countries and Spain.[16] Thus, the novel's undisputable indexing in World Literature has more to do with a political Latin-Africa that García Márquez's journalism charts, than an abstract motif of human doom. While the novel's brief mention of the slave ship evokes a Latin-African imaginary, as García Márquez only completed the challenging novel after his return from Angola, the impending foretold death in the novel resonates with the witnessed doom of Black internationalism.

Of special interest in García Márquez's reportage on Angola is "Operación Carlota" named after the Cuban mission there, which was in turn named for the leader of a nineteenth-century slave rebellion in Matanzas, Cuba. Although this investigative piece is hopeful, García Márquez also evokes the ominous sense of doom in *Crónica de una muerte anunciada* in his writing about Cuban-Angolan decolonial failure. As a Latin-Africa is subsumed under the colossal powers of capital, García Márquez seems to project the Angolan defeat onto the novel's obliterated Senegalese bodies through Castro's Latin-African trope of slavery when he declared Cuban people descendants of African slaves during the US invasion of the Bay of Pigs (35). García Márquez interpellates a Latin-African memory as a result of his transatlantic journalism. In fact, as R. Williams states, "García Márquez's journalism and its intimate relationship to his fiction make his journalistic writings essential to a complete study of his work" (134), even if critics of his work, including Williams himself, have not consistently practiced this. But it is precisely what García Márquez perceived as imperialist aggression that propelled his own Latin-African imaginary; he took a definitive hiatus from fiction in 1973 to protest US imperialism and focus on what Gene H. Bell-Villada terms "advocacy" journalism.[17] In

1974, he began to cover Angola's struggle for independence against Portugal and its ally, the United States, traveling there in 1978 to write his Angolan reportage.

García Márquez's textual memorialization of Carlota prior to the publication of *Crónica de una muerte anunciada* is significant, for it conjures Cuba's colonial plantocratic heritage as a racial bridge between Cuba and Africa against US White supremacy. While García Márquez called out the US as an ally of racist republics, especially apartheid South Africa,[18] Castro related how slavery tied Cuba to Africa, and as I explained in the previous chapter, conceived of Cuba as a "Latin-African" nation. This term, "Latin-Africa," continued to be used for years as Cuba forged its decolonial alliances in Africa and beyond in the Global South. In hindsight, while García Márquez admitted that he was unable to finish the novel because there was "a leg that was missing" ("la pata que faltaba"), his reports on the hope for a Latin-Africa provide *Crónica de una muerte anunciada* with this missing limb.[19]

Nevertheless, most readings centered on *Crónica de una muerte anunciada* or even García Márquez's journalism do not attend to this Latin-African language nor to the Cold War's shift into the African continent. With few exceptions, notably those of Vera Kutzinski and Steve Hunsaker, the Atlantic World inherent in García Márquez's narrative has been mostly overlooked.[20] García Márquez's biographer, Gerald Martin, admits that the author came to an awareness of "black blood" in the Caribbean "slow[ly]" and that he "makes up for this omission" in *El general en su laberinto/The General in His Labyrinth* ("The General" 107). William Megenney, on the other hand, claims that García Márquez "never realized that his world ... possesses live elements of a former sub-Saharan tradition."[21] But this apparent obliteration of diasporic Africans is perhaps informed by the fact that *Crónica de una muerte anunciada* has most commonly been read through western tropes. For instance, the novel has been lauded for its parodying of Greek or classical myths, its echoes of Spain's Generación del '98, and chiefly its proximity to *Oedipus Rex*.[22] Even if Antonio Cornejo Polar uses *Crónica de una muerte anunciada* to claim the distinctiveness of the postmodern Latin American novel, he too likens it to western tragedies (141–2). While Cornejo Polar is not wrong and even if western tropes are privileged – and the most obvious – they are only one approach to the many perspectives García Márquez's novel offers.[23]

While García Márquez never denied his admiration for the western canon, he repeatedly exalted world literary authors from the Global

South or marginalized within the Global North, from Constantine Cavafy, to Pablo Neruda, to Muhammad Ali's biography.[24] Moreover, and contrary to Megenney's claim, García Márquez was profoundly aware of the creolized roots that constitute his Caribbean hybrid identity, as reflected in his oeuvre, from the realities of Latin American dictatorship, to Afro-Cuban music, to Angola as an example of socialist success, all of which defined his 1970s interest in merging fictional narrative with political reality.[25] During an interview in 1976, when asked what he is working on, he states that he is writing a "reportaje" but that it is more "like a novel" ("como una novela") that leaves nothing to the imagination, echoing the narrative *technique* – but not reality – in *Crónica de una muerte anunciada* (134). With regard to merging poetry, reality, and Angola, this is revealed during the same interview, in which – in answer to the same question – García Márquez admits to both his formation as poet and also comments on the need to defend the Cuban revolution, citing Angola as a clear example of success ("Es un crimen" 137). He also mentions that his trip to Angola helped him better understand Latin American culture: "In my trip to Angola, I found that aesthetic manifestations that we have in the Caribbean region are very similar to many African popular art forms."[26] García Márquez insists on his Angolan experience in particular, and in 1978, even marks this as "one of the most fascinating experiences that I've had."[27] Echoing Castro's prophetic Latin-Africa, García Márquez's "fascinating" memory of Angola, which reminded him of his childhood, visualizes a clear Latin-Africa that is at best ignored and at worst sneered at.

It was precisely during this trip to Angola that García Márquez remembered the impact of slavery. In an interview, he said that the "unbound imagination" he draws from when writing about the Caribbean originates, in part, from African slaves.[28] Latin America's plantocratic regime would continue to take up more and more narrative space in his subsequent novels, culminating in *Del amor y otros demonios* / *Of Love and Other Demons* (1994). But while slavery certainly appears in more obvious ways in these later texts, one of the issues this chapter seeks to resolve is the metaphoric significance of the slave ship in *Crónica de una muerte anunciada*. The "ship" as a metaphor – one that actually emerges in some of García Márquez's most important journalistic narratives as well – often symbolizes the relationship between the state and Black survival and is necessarily tied to the slave trade and thus the Latin-African connection this book traces. In her brilliant reading of "the ship," Christina Sharpe elucidates a trajectory in which the slave ship marks and haunts Black life, from the violent throwing of Africans overboard during the Middle

3.1 Crónica de una muerte anunciada *as Point of Access* 129

Passage to repeated re-manifestations of this callousness throughout the long history of the Black Atlantic. In her own terms, Sharpe views the ship as "state's national and imperial projects" driven by the engine of racism (3). The ship's effects on Black lives, as she explains, is a way of speaking of the afterlife of slavery. While I am not suggesting that García Márquez's brief mention of the slave ship in *Crónica de una muerte anunciada* offers the level of revisionist commitment that Sharpe brings to the ship metaphor, this fleeting allusion to Atlantic history opens onto journalistic narratives that connect to García Márquez's Angola specifically and to Latin-Africa at large.

While the drama of Bayardo and Angela's consummated marriage unfolds in *Crónica de una muerte anunciada*, Santiago Nasar heads to the pier with his friends Luis Enrique and Cristo Bedoya when something shining over the Bay of Souls seizes his attention:

> Santiago Nasar señaló una lumbre intermitente en el mar, y nos dijo que era el ánima en pena de un barco negrero que se había hundido con un cargamento de esclavos del Senegal frente a la boca grande de Cartagena de Indias. (77)

> Santiago pointed to an intermittent light at sea and told us that it was the soul in torment of a slave ship that had sunk with a cargo of blacks from Senegal across from the main harbor mouth at Cartagena de Indias. (Rabassa 67)[29]

Because Santiago refers to "souls" at Cartagena, "across from the main harbor mouth," geographically he alludes to Cartagena's Bay of Souls. Moreover, this reference is historically accurate in that Cartagena's famed bay began receiving slaves as early as 1510 (Palacios Preciado 24). But it is less certain exactly which shipwreck Santiago is referring to.

Santiago's shipwreck most immediately evokes the recovered Spanish warship that was sunk in 1741 at Cartagena Bay during the War of Jenkins' Ear – a conflict between Britain and Spain over control of the Caribbean. This battle has long been a historical reference point in Colombia, as it involved one of its most celebrated admirals after Columbus – Basque-born, one-legged Don Blas de Lezo. One memorial to him, which faces the Bay of Souls directly, also aligns with the statue of Columbus; the two are separated by colonial fortifications. One of Cartagena's busiest avenues, Avenida Blas de Lezo, also follows the right-hand side of the Bay. Lezo, who was familiar with both Spanish and French navies, faced off against the mighty British Navy and became mythical. Lezo's famous defeat of Admiral Vernon's fleet was engraved on maps, such as an eighteenth-century French map of

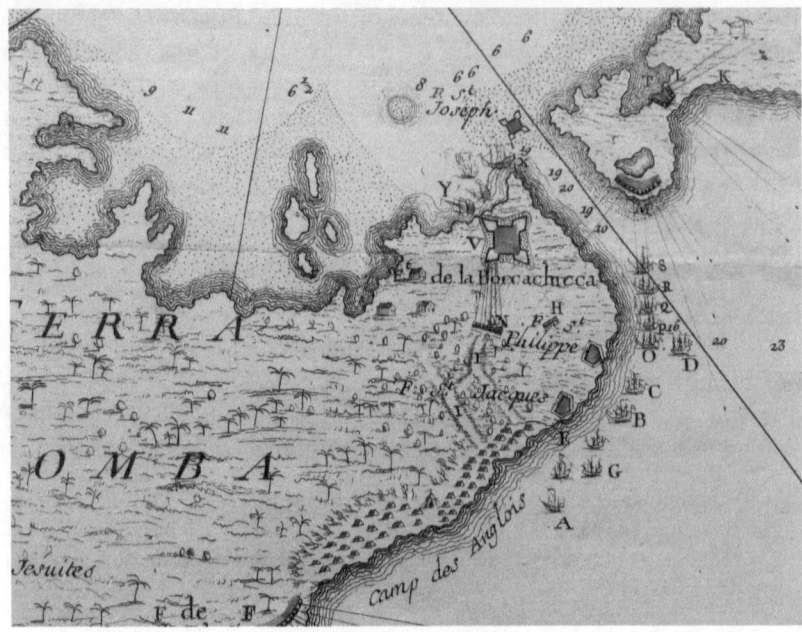

Figure 3.2 Close-up of "Nouveau plan de Carthagène, Colombie, avec les dernières attaques des forts par l'amiral Vernon." 1741. Archives Nationales, Paris, France. Photo: Sarah M. Quesada, 2017.

Cartagena in Figure 3.2. Here, the map features the English flotilla with the title "Camp des Anglois" ("English Camp"), facing the Atlantic, and the shipwreck on the other side of the peninsula just off of Boca Chica (spelled "Boccachicca" on the map), visible across the slight opening of the Bay of Souls to the right. This battle is so memorialized that a statue of Blas de Lezo also adorns the Castillo de San Felipe, commemorating his daring defense of Cartagena for the Iberian empire.

These memorials of a shipwreck at the Bay of Souls, a little over a kilometer from García Márquez's former residence, would seem to obviously resonate with Santiago's allusion, but the archives on this sunken Spanish warship do not include a direct connection with Senegalese slavery. However, the French ship *L'Hermione*, which was shipwrecked in 1707 at Cartagena's bay, does. Almost contemporary to the Jenkins battle, a letter dated from August 3, 1707 features a commissioner writing to the French King and requesting an unnamed "sieur marin" ("Monsieur mariner") to neglect *L'Hermione*'s losses at Cartagena and return to France. Although the "losses" are not identified, the correspondence about this

3.1 Crónica de una muerte anunciada *as Point of Access*

shipwreck traces *L'Hermione*'s trajectory from Senegal through Cayenne and St-Domingue, prominent French plantations. The letters also mention the ratio of "one white per every 10 blacks" on deck, which was imposed by law, and name "the fortification of the Ile de St-Louis in Senegal," a notable French slave depot of the sixteenth century.[30] At the time, France was an important ally of the Spanish against the British,[31] and this fleet would have enabled the French to transport slaves to Cartagena through a Spanish *asiento* – a contract issued by the Spanish crown that granted a monopoly on a certain trade route from West Africa to the Americas. In fact, in the same trail of correspondence preceding this shipwreck, a letter dated July 14, 1706, to M. de Chauillars features a payment for slaves through "Assientos" to Philip V of Spain.[32] While it is possible that Santiago's comment on lost Senegalese slaves conflates the mythical 1741 battle of Cartagena with the earlier *L'Hermione*'s slaves, his mention of Senegal emphasizes the colonial obliteration of subaltern bodies.

Beyond its historical significance, the shipwreck in *Crónica de una muerte anunciada* metaphorizes an emphasis on property value over Black life. The shipwreck off the Colombian coast symbolizes – both literally in *Crónica de una muerte anunciada* and historically as I have shown – the erasure of Black bodies that traces its origins to the slave trade and has repercussions into modernity and beyond. The drowned Senegalese bodies of the novel's slave ship recalls Sharpe's analysis of the *Zong*, in which she contends that this memorable shipwreck was brought to the attention of the public through the ship's owners' insurance claims over the 132 Africans they threw overboard to save the ship (35). It was "a case of property loss and not murder" (36–7), Sharpe clarifies, one that in her study resonates with the detached treatment of Haitian boat people, or the indifference of state authorities to the deaths of Black migrants trying to reach European soil in the present. In other words, the slave ship serves as a metaphor for the ways in which the subaltern bodies entrapped in it become peculiarly erased – not only because of the way they enter the logs of mariners as "property," but also because throwing them overboard into the wake of the ship manifests, elusively at times, the valorization of capital over life or what Achille Mbembe terms "necropolitics." The lack of memorialization of these Senegalese bodies at the Bahía de las ánimas certainly reflects this necropolitcs and also contrasts with García Márquez's textual memorialization of their absence in the novel. While the statues of Columbus or Blas de Lezo certainly chisel what García Márquez considers an ironic "nostalgia" of colonial times, it is indeed this global Marxist ideology that García Márquez fully endorses as the Cuban Revolution triumphs. The spatiotemporal marker serves as the catalyst for his stern anti-imperial journalism to come.

3.2 Angolan Journalism and the Hope of a Latin-Africa (1974–1982)

As a distant backdrop to *Crónica de una muerte anunciada* is the Cuban-US conflict at the Bay of Pigs. The event propelled García Márquez back into journalism, a genre in which he would be immersed almost exclusively, bringing along his command of fictional techniques, by the 1970s, as the Cold War shifted into the African arena. In 1975, Castro sent García Márquez to cover the Angolan decolonization movement, which fascinated García Márquez due to what he perceived as Cuba's audacity in confronting a giant empire and probably a somewhat fantastical situation. But in any case, it is precisely in this Angolan war that García Márquez reads the continuity of colonial slavery in an imperial takeover of Africa that Cuba attempts to impede. It is worth noting, then, that the Cuban exiles' attitude toward the Cuban Revolution actually served as the harbinger for García Márquez's Latin-African expression – a kind of transatlantic *becoming* materialized in his Angolan writings.

Having been blacklisted from entering the US in 1961, García Márquez's first open and stern nonfiction account of imperialism, "Chile, el golpe y los gringos" ("Chile, the coup and the gringos" in *Por la libre* 1974), foretells the demise of a once-hopeful socialist democracy in the southern cone in the 1973 due to the military coup against Salvador Allende. From this day forward, García Márquez vowed to set fiction aside – with the exception of *El otoño del patriarca/The Autumn of the Patriarch* (1975) – as his journalistic critique turned transatlantic. Between 1975 and 1977, three notable chronicles described what he saw on the ground in Angola and became some of the most detailed chronicles on 1970s Black internationalism at the time. These are "Portugal, territorio libre de Europa" ("Portugal, free territory of Europe" *Por la libre* 1975), "Angola, un año después" ("Angola, a year later"), and "Operación Carlota," all of which condemn Portuguese colonization and later antiblack US capitalism and its coziness with apartheid South Africa. Notably, García Márquez's Angolan chronicles mark an evolution from his earlier work as a journalist. Not only do the New Journalism and the testimonio genre forcefully inform these 1970s transatlantic chronicles, but they also become a political Latin-African genre of their own. And yet in "Operación Carlota," García Márquez resorts to a metaphor of slavery that recalls colonial Atlantic history. By memorializing a female slave rebellion leader, Carlota, in the title of his piece, García Márquez not only links Cuba's plantocratic past to Angola, but also connects the daring slave revolt to Cuba's equally daring liberation of Angola after centuries of Portuguese colonialism.

The Portuguese presence in Angola began in 1483 and lasted until 1975. The most profitable of all of Portugal's African colonies – endowed with land, oil, water resources, minerals, and diamonds – Angola was also the most exploited. It was crucial to the slave trade as early as 1540, and the racial hierarchies that the trade established relegated Angolans to the margins of society, where, by the 1960s, a meager 1 percent were able to reach the desired status of educated and assimilated (Malaquias 28, Cooper 139). Angolan scholar Assis Malaquias has termed this marginalization of indigenous populations a "Portuguese apartheid" (29) that curtailed advancement, exacerbated segregation, and even constituted modern enslavement (30). These conditions precipitated Angolan independence with Cuban support. In late June of 1975, Cuba's Operación Carlota dispatched thousands of troops to the former Portuguese stronghold in what would become a postcolonial scramble for Angola in the wake of decolonization. But Portugal was not alone in fighting a leftist-leaning Angolan independence, as NATO allies had been subsidizing the colonial enterprise since the 1960s out of fear of Soviet influence in Africa. The US specifically provided military assistance, warships, ammunition, and millions of dollars to anti-communist political parties in Angola, even though the Senate had precluded further involvement in 1976.[33] Portugal, weakened by an internal military coup and incessant wars in its colonies, eventually declared it would liberate them, beginning with Guinea Bissau and Cape Verde, where Portugal ceded power to the Cuban-affiliated party of Amílcar Cabral. Angola followed in November 1975, with power up for grabs by whichever party could control the turmoil of civil war that Portuguese colonization left behind.

This time period is important for Cuba, because it was in great part thanks to Operación Carlota that the Cuban-allied People's Movement for the Liberation of Angola (MPLA) won the war for independence and also initially the civil war among Angolan political factions. Symbolically, moreover, the Cuban operation was a global refutation of mighty empires. García Márquez uplifts both Cuban and Angolan efforts by emphasizing how much groundwork this alliance had to do following Portugal's near-total destruction of its former colony. In "Portugal, territorio libre de Europa," García Márquez condemns a "dictadura [que] había saneado la economía y reducido al mínimo la deuda exterior, en primer término por la explotación desalmada de las colonias en el África" ("the dictatorship [that] had sanitized the economy, and reduced the minimum external debt, primarily with the heartless exploitation of the colonies in Africa" 42). As a result of 400,000 Portuguese fleeing the "territorio vasto, rico, y ajeno" ("the vast, rich and alien territory" 164), and taking with them all the economic resources, technical skill, and means of transportation, the new government faced a "país de escombros," illiterate, sick, and hungry. In this freed Angola, public service vehicles such as buses and ships were thus unavailable to transport staples and supplies to the capital since they had been stolen, destroyed, or sunk in the ocean (166). The local economy was made to fail ("en cosa de horas devastaron el comercio local" 166) and, García Márquez adds, the Portuguese childishly "demolieron los lavamanos y los inodoros de las casas que abandonaban, descompusieron los ascensores de los edificios, los controles de la luz y teléfono, y rompieron los focos, los cables eléctricos, las cerraduras de las puertas y los tubos de agua" ("demolished sinks and toilets of the homes they abandoned, broke elevators of buildings, light switches and phone lines, lightbulbs, electric cables, door locks, and water tubes" 166). As Africanist historians insist, the "tasks facing the MPLA" were "immense" (Somerville 47). And indeed, the local economy was torn to pieces, essentially because the Portuguese had monopolized "skilled and managerial manpower" (47), and the results were shortages and a wrecked distribution system. Laying the groundwork for Cuban-Angolan relations, García Márquez's Angolan chronicles were initially hopeful about what was to come.

Operación Carlota's euphoric triumph in wresting power away from both Portugal and the US would not last. When the Cuban-supported MPLA party took possession of Angola on November 11, 1975, the embers of the Angolan civil war, destined to last decades, were already smoldering. Portuguese rule had left a legacy of deeply embedded color lines that "further divided Angolan society" (Malaquias 31), a tribalism exacerbated by Western-backed political rivals vying for control in the wake of independence (Marcum 19). But because Cuba supported communist-leaning Agostinho Neto and his MPLA party, the US – fearing Soviet influence in Africa and threats to US interests in the region – funded Holden Roberto's National Liberation Front of Angola (FNLA) in the 1960s and later, during the Reagan administration, the violent but supposedly anti-communist Jonas Malheiro Savimbi and his party, the National Union for the Total Independence of Angola (UNITA). US influence through the CIA was so relentless it finally destabilized the Marxist-Leninist MPLA and all the advances that Operación Carlota had secured. Thus, if Portugal had succeeded in establishing a color hierarchy that heightened ethnic rivalries, US imperialism during the Cold War – driven by economic interests and racist ideology – ensured that this anti-colonial war evolved into one of the bloodiest and most drawn-out civil wars in African history.

When García Márquez wrote about the initial defeat of White supremacy in Angola in 1975 in the Mexican journal *Proceso*, none of this was yet foretold. Rather, his version of Operación Carlota (see Figure 3.3) highlighted how Cuban troops were victorious in securing the MPLA's rule in Angola despite incessant attacks by the CIA and South African forces (Gleijeses 259). As an apartheid state, one of South Africa's main motivations for attacking independent Angola was to destabilize its government, as it did any government that "sought to undermine white-minority rule" (Schmidt 127). The US, on the other hand, not only supported this ideology, but also pressed South Africa to intervene militarily (94–5), fearing Soviet military expansion despite the fact that the latter was not financially involved in Angola at this juncture.[34] As South Africa and Rhodesia continued to elicit European and US support by raising fears of communism,[35] Nixon's infamous "Study in Response to National Security Study Memorandum 39" revealed the White supremacy of US policy. It considered the following as one of the premises for apartheid support: "the whites are here to stay and the only way that constructive change can come about is through them. There is no hope for the blacks to gain the political rights they seek through violence, which will only lead to chaos and increased opportunities for communists."[36] García Márquez's Angolan journalism in general, and "Operación Carlota" in particular, responded to this White supremacist attack on Black socialist democracies. For not only did the Cuban operation enable an initial victory for Angola's MPLA, García Márquez's narratively compelling chronicle memorialized both the victorious battle and this alliance of Latin-African partners.

Although García Márquez's Angolan journalism reports facts, he employs the same attributes of storytelling that, as I have mentioned, memorials use to narrativize space. That is, he makes a factual account sound like a subjective, almost literary story. His strategies are not unlike those used in the testimonio genre or even the US New Journalism, but with some notable differences. New forms of literary journalism in Latin America and the US shared many aesthetic commonalities – "all resorted to similar techniques and devices of the kind we associate with literary journalism" (Calvi 63) – but were ideologically disparate. While New Journalism sought to make journalism literary and thus resonated with Angel Rama's

Figure 3.3 First edition of García Márquez's "Operación Carlota." Courtesy of the Harry Ransom Center, the University of Texas at Austin.

3.2 Angolan Journalism and the Hope of a Latin-Africa (1974–1982)

formulation of an elite readership in *La ciudad letrada*, Latin American literary journalism and later testimonio had more popular, socially engaged principles.[37] As I have mentioned, testimonio journalism was steeped in the ideologies of the Cuban Revolution. In fact, both García Márquez and his *Prensa Latina* colleague Rodolfo Walsh had a hand in shaping the genre. García Márquez's earlier *Relato de un náufrago* (1955) or even his fellow colleague at *Prensa Latina* Rodolfo Walsh's *Operación Masacre* (*Operation Massacre*, 1957) – the testimony of *Caldas* shipwreck sailor denouncing Colombian dictator Gustavo Rojas Pinilla's elicit contraband and the violent coup that ousted democratically elected Juan Perón in Argentina, respectively – are exemplary of a style of investigative political work that uses "specularisation," or the value of the spectacular in fiction (Sims 149), and lays the groundwork for political testimonio.[38] New Journalism, on the other hand, could not be "classified as personalist, activist or advocacy journalism" of the social revolutions taking place in the 1960s, but did seek revolutionary ways of accurately narrating a story through literary devices (Murphy 24). In García Márquez's later work, these two literary genres collide and the result characterizes his Angolan chronicles. To start with New Journalism, García Márquez employs many techniques used by writers such as Wolfe, Joan Didion, and Truman Capote, such as taking on a "participant-observatory role" or diluting the "I" in a third-person account that still sounds subjective. But in postcolonial Angola, the landscape felt *known* and politically personal. With regard to testimonio, García Márquez details this familiar place not so much through a bird's-eye view as through the subjectivity of a narrator whose ideological participation in decolonization informs his chronicle. Indeed, Angola reminded him of his youth because of African influences on the Caribbean, and García Márquez reveled in Angola's "muy notable" "influencia negra" ("very notable" "black influence"), celebrating that "todo el país está saturado de música caliente de Cabo Verde y Angola" ("the whole country is saturated with hot music from Cape Verde and Angola," in "Portugal, territorio libre de Europa" in *Por la libre*, 37). Details of the Angolan landscape and strategies for overcoming centuries of colonialism felt hauntingly familiar to the Latin American experience, and thus García Márquez's chronicle also reveals his progressive determinism.

García Márquez's Angolan chronicle, "Operación Carlota," not only memorializes a socially engaged Latin-African connection through the prototypical attributes of his fiction – humorous exaggeration, absurdity, and of course fantastical prolepsis – but also employs the techniques of narrative journalism. For instance, he injects both humorous and terrifying exaggeration into the serious matter of war by recounting how soldiers en route to Luanda slept in a warehouse that had "tantos mosquitos que las sábanas de los catres quedaron ensangrentadas" ("had so many mosquitos that the cot sheets were all bloodied" *Por la Libre* 130). A similar example is his ironic mocking of Cubans' innately festive nature, which resulted in "prodigios de pirotécnia" ("pyrotechnic prodigies") that could have pulverized the arsenals nearby (126). Both these exaggerations mark the odds against a fantasy-like Angolan victory. But the ironic inflection here is such a signature of García Márquez's now-famous narrative style that even though he does not use the first person, the chronicle reads as if his subjectivity were narrating the facts. For instance, in a scene that dramatizes the significant odds against liberation, García Márquez drenches the scenario in the absurdity of colonization itself, commenting that Portugal had been "feliz durante quinientos años" ("happy for five hundred years" 126), as the ironic "happiness" punctuates the length of colonial suffering. While the comment recalls the fact that Portuguese colonization had been ongoing since 1483, the sarcasm in "feliz" identifies the narrator's subjectivity despite the piece's third-person narration. García Márquez employs a technique also used by Capote and Norman Mailer, in which the narrator's presence is felt despite the absence of first-person narration (Weber 50). In fact, such traces of commentary abound in García Márquez's condemnation of colonialism. For instance, García Márquez notes that this long colonial period led to the absurd "condiciones de miseria y retraso cultural que dejó en Angola medio milenio de colonialismo sin alma" ("The conditions of misery and cultural backwardness that were left in Angola by a soulless colonialism of half a millennium" 133), where the word "soulless" obviously marks the subjectivity of the observer-journalist. Thus, not only is the contrast between *foreign* "happiness" and *local* "misery" absurd, but García Márquez also grimly notes that this "soulless" apparatus ironically contributed to the impossible odds against Angolan decolonization, to which the narrator is committed, as these techniques make clear. Lastly, García Márquez's Angolan chronicles use a personal voice and the strategies of fiction (Murphy 7) that echo New Journalism, except that the Colombian author's text is tinged with political ideology. For instance, terming CIA-supported Jonas Savimbi an "aventurero sin principios" ("an unethical adventurer") or the US's methods "los recursos más rapaces y devastadores del imperialismo" ("the most rapacious and devastating resources wielded by imperialism" 132) is not unlike the participant-observatory narrative strategies employed in Wolfe's *The Electric Kool-Aid Acid Test* (1968) about the Merry Pranksters and their psychedelic journeys. Yet, García Márquez's chronicles diverge from

3.2 Angolan Journalism and the Hope of a Latin-Africa (1974–1982)

Wolfe's in that they reflect the political ideologies of testimonio as underwriting an "unambiguous political undertone" and "journalistic urgency" (Calvi 73). In other words, his Angolan chronicles merge New Journalism's techniques with testimonio's ideology to create an unequivocal textual memorial in support of a hopeful Latin-Africa.

To further emphasize this hopeful Latin-African borderland, García Márquez uses one of his favorite fictional strategies. In what would otherwise be a dry, objective military account appears a playful turn of serendipity bordering on the fantastic. Depicting Cuban solidarity with Black internationalism as boundless, García Márquez recounts how a young boy defiantly left for Angola without permission from his parents. While in Angola, however, the boy bumped into his own father who had also left, admittedly "a escondidas de la familia" ("in hiding from his family" 141). This almost unbelievable incident underscores fervent Cuban internationalism guided by el Che's famous philosophy of revolutionary love. Despite such eager volunteering for Angola, Cubans could not have foretold their impact, as García Márquez describes: "Es probable que ni los mismos Cubanos hubieran previsto que la ayuda solidaria al pueblo de Angola había de alcanzar semejantes proporciones" ("It's probable that not even the Cubans would have foreseen that their help and solidarity with the Angolan people would reach such proportions" 128). He contrasts this modesty with the arrogance of the enemy's blind belief that they will win. With dark humor, García Márquez recalls how a missile that hit a group of mercenaries revealed the absurd contents of a female victim's suitcase – a gala outfit and an invitation to US-supported Holden Roberto's victory party (132) – as their overconfidence was numinously punished. Nevertheless, this revelation begins to foretell a recognizably fantastic Cuban-Angolan victory.

After Operación Carlota, South African troops retreated on April 27, 1975, granting Cuban ally MPLA an unimaginable victory. As García Márquez mournfully reflects on the losses of Latin American socialism and the assassinations of Salvador Allende and Che Guevara, the extermination of Latin American guerillas, and the US embargo in Cuba (156), these US-supported precedents punctuate his account of the fantastical and hopeful socialist victory that Angola signifies for African nations. Recalling "El drama de las dos Cubas" in which García Márquez denounced the US's Bay of Pigs fiasco, García Márquez's textual "Operación Carlota" bookends an antiblack, capitalist, and imperial US failure after that of Vietnam. With "Operación Carlota," the Boom writer celebrates the Latin-African victory as "la gratificación de la victoria grande que tanto estaban necesitando" ("Angola gave them at last the gratification of a significant victory that they so badly needed" 156), memorializing textually an outcome that once seemed like an impossible fantasy.

3.3 "Operation Carlota" and Castro's Latin-Africa

While I have detailed some of the ways in which García Márquez used tools from his writing of fiction to report on the events he witnessed in Angola, I turn now to how his work comes to conflate his Angolan experience, or the fight for twentieth-century "African" freedom, with freedom from colonial slavery – a marker that later constitutes the memorialization of Senegalese slavery in *Crónica de una muerte anunciada*. If García Márquez's shipwreck memorializes a transatlantic relationship between the Caribbean and the West African coast – whether the transatlantic commerce of slavery from Senegal to Colombia in *Crónica de una muerte anunciada* or the Cuban Black internationalism of García Márquez's journalism – the title of García Márquez's "Operación Carlota" directly memorializes slavery through the figure of the revolt leader Carlota.

Although she was used as the codename for Cuba's Angolan operation, Carlota is strangely buried, both in the pages of history and the archival record, where she is portrayed as murderous, and in public life, somewhat ignored as the Cuban nation-state turned away from matters of race. But it is precisely Carlota as a picaresque nineteenth-century Cuban slave along with the subsequent colonial obliteration of her bravery that makes the naming of an equally obliterated Cuban intervention after her so fitting. Carlota Lukumí, also known as la negra Carlota, was an African-born slave leader of the 1844 La Escalera slave rebellion on the Triumvirate plantation in Matanzas, Cuba. While there is scant information on her leadership, her role as a conspirator in the uprising against plantation masters was an uncommon one for female slaves. Yet Carlota emerges in the archive as a daring, rogue figure who attacked her overseer's daughter, María de la Regla Pérez, according to witnesses interrogated by the Inquisition.[39] Although these testimonies decried her actions, historian Aisha Finch reads Carlota's alleged aggressions as "a textual archive of black female insurgency" (148). This insurgency, now much neglected in Cuban public memory, was revisited on the eve of Castro's deployment of troops to Angola. On August 27, 1974, the Oficina de la Ciudad de la Habana's historian José Luciano Franco led a conference on "La gesta heróica del Triunvirato" ("The heroic deed of Triumvirate") – an homage to the Cuban slave rebellion that underscored Carlota's role in it. This event

3.3 "Operation Carlota" and Castro's Latin-Africa

helped promote a postrevolutionary image of Carlota as daring, powerful, and heroic.

While Carlota's daring might have been the catalyst behind the naming of the Angolan mission, the conference in Havana contrasts strongly with the obliteration of archival memory of Carlota. In discussing Carlota's critical leadership in the successful uprising despite her own death, historian Michele Reid-Vazquez notes that "[t]he general participation of women of African descent, however, has been otherwise obscured within both the contemporaneous and historiographical literature" (158). As Carlota's involvement was vilified, Finch reminds us that colonial records are precisely mechanisms for obliteration – "part of a colonial knowledge project that sought to discipline and punish" (150). Dying a day after the uprising, Carlota's punishment was to be not only obliterated beyond the confines of the body, but also remembered through the testimonies of those who justified her execution due to the danger she posed. While erased in the colonial text, she lives on, albeit precariously, in post-1970s physical and textual memory. As Aline Helg recalls, the UNESCO-sponsored Museo de la Ruta del Esclavo (Museum of the Route of the Slave) memorializes this battle (221). Since 2015, Matanza's Rebel Slave Museum on the grounds of the former Triumvirate plantation has featured a memorial statue of Carlota, though the museum is not easily accessible and under-visited. Textually, Carlota lives on in Cuban military history, mythicized in García Márquez's "Operación Carlota." It goes without saying, however, that neither of these interventions – physical or textual – circulate widely, not even in the case of a writer of the caliber of García Márquez.

But the use of Carlota's name for a successful Cuban intervention in Angola interests me for reasons other than her obliteration from historical memory. It is precisely her identity as a daring slave and the marker of slavery that this mission employed that need to be examined in the context of African decolonization. Though multiple shipwrecks appear in García Márquez's work, these were not racialized until *Crónica de una muerte anunciada*, a novel finalized only after García Márquez's return from Angola in 1978. Not only does his nonfictional "Operación Carlota" trace the continuities of coloniality from slavery to imperialism on the African continent, but its title also sets up a dichotomy in which Cuba is on one side of a racial continuum for Black freedom and the US and its recent Cuban political refugees on the other.

"Operación Carlota" immortalizes a female Cuban slave through a renowned Latin American voice, addresses the unending problem of racism in postrevolutionary Cuba, and justifies Cuban intervention in Angola vis-à-vis relentless US involvement.[40] If Cuba struggled locally to eliminate structural and systemic racial inequality, Cuba's Black internationalism bolstered African diasporic unity while simultaneously countering the antiblack policies of the US. Reading García Márquez's "Operación Carlota" through a Latin-African lens thus implies a critique of the Cuban exodus to the US. After all, as Alejandro de la Fuente notes, "[i]dentification with Africa and its descendants in the diaspora also gave the Cuban government the opportunity to construct a notion of Cubanness that was in stark contrast with that of its archenemy: the exile community in Miami" (303). But the victory of Operación Carlota not only memorializes Cuban internationalism, it marks Castro's "Latin-Africa" as the opposite of the antiblackness of its imperialist antagonist and Cubans who allied themselves with the US, even as Castro pursued an equally imperialist project in Angola.

A Latin-Africa begins to crystalize when Castro projects the Angolan landscape as not only related to that of Cuba, but actually *Cuban*. Castro had become so obsessed with Angola, García Márquez remarks, that he could cite any point on an Angolan map "as if it were Cuba" (150–1). Remarkably, "hablaba de sus ciudades, de sus costumbres y sus gentes como si hubiera vivido allí toda la vida" ("he spoke of its cities, of its customs and its people as if he had lived there his whole life" 151). García Márquez's comment emphasizes how it is through the mapping of Angolan space that Castro constructs a seamless Latin-Africa that is equated with the Cuban landscape. While not the same as US imperialism, the appropriation of Angolan space as Cuban is nevertheless imperialist. After all, Castro's effort to wrest Angola from imperialism (and colonialism) drives this spatial and transatlantic rapprochement, but this assertion of geographical sameness enables another kind of authoritarian takeover. Perhaps García Márquez misses this, steeped as he was in admiration for Castro. Instead, García Márquez focuses on a benign sense of Latin-African rapprochement. As he notes, "En realidad, los cubanos encontraron el mismo clima, la misma vegetación, los mismos aguaceros" ("In reality, the Cubans found the same climate, the same vegetation, the same torrential rains" 146). Thus, as Castro's revolution sought to identify "with the poor and blacks," the whiteness of those who fled to Miami represented the opposite of his revolution's mandate: "class exploitation, foreign dependency, and racism" (de la Fuente 303), which US policy did little to discourage.

In a statement that had a reverberating effect on García Márquez's Atlantic, Castro cited hostile antiblack US policy against Africa and

3.3 "Operation Carlota" and Castro's Latin-Africa

Cuba, blamed US racial amnesia, and said that the "Yankees" forget that Cubans are Latin-African (*Cuba y Angola* 31). In a telling metaphor, this figure of speech likens Cuban blackness to African liberation from a White supremacist US. In Lanie Millar's words, this rhetoric, for the first time in Latin American history, is "articulated through notions of Africa-diaspora siblinghood as well as through anti-imperialist leftist solidarity" (xx). In what becomes one of the first genuine projections of Latin Americans as "Africans," Castro's proclamations do not end there. At the commemoration of the US's failed Bay of Pigs attack, Castro likens playa Girón to Africa: "En Girón se derramó sangre Africana, la de los abnegados descendientes de un pueblo que fue esclavo" ("At Girón, African blood was shed, that of the selfless descendants of a people who were slaves," *Cuba y Angola* 35). In the same speech, he visualizes Cuba as reluctantly receiving slaves and then fighting back against colonialism by "liberating Africa" (36). Conflating colonial slavery with US empire's obliteration of Black bodies, Castro makes a case for pan-Africanism. In a separate speech, on May 3, 1972, in Guinea, he similarly notes that against imperialism, "siento que hay algo en nuestros corazones que nos acerca mucho a ustedes" ("I feel that there is something in our hearts that endears us to you," in "Discurso en el estadio" 17). Castro's speech in Cuba emphasizes a blood lineage through slavery, whereas his speech in Guinea justifies Cuban intervention on an ideological basis and seeks an international solidarity with the Global South (Mahler 178). This inversion occurred in Cuba because, as Anne Garland Mahler explains, such a "level of engagement" in Angola required sharpening the "mythology and prerevolutionary racial discourses at the core of Cuban national identity" (179). The inversion of these speeches certainly marks an uneven distribution of slave trade memory on the two sides of the Atlantic. In the absence of *actual* slave trade memory, the Angola conflict served as placeholder for the origins of slavery, in Latin America in general and in Cuba specifically.

Like the slave ship that stands for the erasure of bodies – and bodies of knowledge – an Atlantic history that began in Africa undergirds a metaphor that sets up a hopeful and even utopic Latin-African borderland; a metaphor that worked to a certain extent across the Global South. If Castro previously connected Cuban intervention with African liberation by lamenting slavery, his African allies requited the gesture. The use of metaphors that deem Cubans "brothers in terms of culture, but also in terms of blood-links" (Moore *Castro* 291), as Guinea's president Ahmed Sékou Touré declared, echo Castro's remarks. Sékou Touré even requested that Black Cubans be dispatched to operate under the US's radar, implying that Afro-Cubans were the most culturally similar to the Guineans (Gleijeses 189–90). Similarly, Guinea Bissau's leader Amílcar Cabral only wanted Cuban soldiers to intervene, because he remembered when "Fidel told [him] that Cuba is also Africa" and that "the souls of our forefathers who were taken away to America to be slaves are rejoicing today to see their children reunited and working together to help us be independent and free" (199). Even fervent Castro critic Carlos Moore interpreted Castro's first visit to the African continent as him "cross[ing] the middle passage, the infamous sea lane that had linked Cuba to the Gulf of Guinea throughout more than three centuries of slave trade" (*Castro* 288). Thus, the history of the slave trade came to inspire a hopeful Latin-African decoloniality on both sides of the Atlantic. And García Márquez was no stranger to this symbolism.

3.4 The Death of a Latin-Africa Foretold

But despite Cuba's initial success in Angola in 1975, which García Márquez witnessed – and as the previous chapter on Obejas attests – imperialist powers extinguished both the socialist victory in Angola and its history. As García Márquez's later Black internationalist chronicles make clear, while Portugal's four centuries of African colonization will collapse under a hopeful Marxist-Leninist outlook, US imperialism outlasted Portuguese dominance and foretold an end to his political hopes for a Latin-Africa.[41] Compared to "Operación Carlota," where a socialist Cuban-Angolan takeover seems tenable, most of the journalism that García Márquez published from 1975 to 1982 was not only anti-capitalist but also profoundly sorrowful. "Cuba de cabo a rabo" ("Cuba from cape to tail," 1975 in *Por la libre*), "Los meses de tinieblas — el Che en el Congo" ("The dark months, Che in the Congo," 1977 in *Por la libre*), "Los cubanos frente al bloqueo" ("Cubans facing the blockade" 1978 in *Por la libre*), "EEUU y la política de las suposiciones" ("The US and politics of assumptions," 1982 (in *Notas de prensa*, 1991), and "USA mejor cerrado que abierto" ("The USA better closed than open," 1982) (in *Notas de prensa*, 1991), are just a few examples of García Márquez's fervent criticism of imperialist US foreign policy. From this list only the one centered on Che Guevara, "Operación Carlota," and "Angola, un año después" focus on US intervention in Africa, but all of these chronicles foretell the demise of socialist hope in the Global South.[42]

Although Portugal could not prevent the rise of a socialist Black republic, García Márquez feared the US could. A litany of derisive remarks ensues: he calls the US media "periódicos tramposos del capitalismo"

3.4 The Death of a Latin-Africa Foretold

("cheating newspapers of capitalism," "Cuba de cabo" in *Por la libre* 85), decries US control of telecommunications through "servicios secretos de los Estados Unidos" ("Los cubanos" 232), and, in perhaps one of his most scathing remarks, mocks "los gringos pendejos que se jodieron ellos mismos tratando de jodernos" ("asshole gringos who fucked themselves trying to fuck us," 71), referring to the US embargo. In an attempt to denounce a Manifest Destiny expanded to the Global South, García Márquez calls out what he considers American brutishness cloaked in false sophistication. As if prophesizing Venezuelan leader Hugo Chavez calling George W. Bush a devil reeking of sulfur, García Márquez writes that Dwight Eisenhower "solía disimular el olor a pólvora de su corazón con los vestidos más caros de Bond Street" ("he used to hide the smell of gunpowder from his heart with the most expensive suits from Bond Street," "No se me ocurre" in *Por la libre* 117), and contrasts the cultured literary *tertulias* by Cubans on the island with "marineros gringos [que] se orinaban en las estatuas de los héroes" ("gringo sailors who urinate on statues of heroes" 115). Both quotes pit American boorishness and warmongering against the sophistication of a multiracial civil society. In his 1982 articles, "EEUU y la política de las suposiciones" and "El pez rojo" ("The red fish"), he again criticizes US destabilization of the Global South, lamenting how the US's "creative genius" wastes its "sterile money" on wars.[43]

García Márquez's most sorrowful hints are reserved for the destabilization of Black internationalism and the obliteration of memory of it. First, García Márquez criticizes US corporations such as Gulf Oil, which both controls and exploits oil reserves in Angola but then punishes the state for the destabilization that the US created in the first place.[44] This was not the first time the US would punish the audacity of African states that stood up to it. As Kwame Nkrumah states, when the US deemed African critiques of its institutions "anti-American in tone," the US resorted to cutting off aid or food supplies to vulnerable villages (310, 312), just as it had supplied Portugal with weapons. The fact that the US destabilizes regions via allies like Portugal, or corporations such as Gulf Oil, means its executive branch cannot be blamed directly, and US intervention is easily forgotten. But one of the most damning forms of memory obliteration resulted in former Secretary of State Henry Kissinger's Nobel Peace Prize. Not only had Kissinger intended to, and to some extent succeeded in, obliterating socialism in the Global South, he was also the architect of Angolan destabilization in particular. An indignant García Márquez writes that Kissinger was receiving the most prestigious award for ending wars that he had ironically caused (*Notas* 1996, 116–17). Even though Kissinger was controversially granted the Nobel for a failed ceasefire in Vietnam, giving him a "peace" award of this magnitude obliterates the destabilization of Angola from public memory.

In the 1980s, Reagan's presidency ended any hopes for the Latin-African state that García Márquez had envisioned. Not only would his administration veto a bill to cease intervention in Angola, it provided one of the most significant forms of military aid and equipment to UNITA, destabilizing the country until 2002, as Reagan sought to obliterate socialism in all of the Global South. In "El Kissinger de Reagan," a sign of defeatism emerges in García Márquez's eternal prolepsis: "Tampoco nos equivocamos en la profecía fácil de que el esfuerzo había de comenzar por América Latina" ("We were also not wrong in our easy prophesies that the efforts would have had to begin in Latin America" *Notas de prensa* 1996, 80). In just thirty days, García Márquez explains how this "effort" refers to Reagan's focus on obliterating Latin America's socialist uprisings. García Márquez unleashes a series of accusations,[45] from his comparison of the failed war in Vietnam with the fiasco in Central America ("EEUU" in *Notas de prensa* 1996, 302) to Reagan's manipulation of distorted quotes by José Martí and Benito Juárez to justify invasion ("El fantasma" in *Notas de prensa* 1991, 232). But one of his most contemptuous critiques of the US is arguably his most defeatist. In admitting that the US's foreign policy is based on "suposiciones" and hoping that public opinion sways the government, he ends by doubting its citizenry will make any significant change this time.[46] After all, he states, "la política de suposiciones está fundada en un sistema de pensamiento que se alimenta a sí mismo" ("the politics of assumptions is founded on a system of thought that feeds on itself" 305). Using Vietnam as a famed reference for failed and unnecessary wars, García Márquez's frank journalism reveals the unending terms of imperialism.

And yet along this Latin-African trail, García Márquez is not alone in memorializing the foretold death of a Latin-Africa. As Millar points out, on the Cuban side of the Angolan-Cuban axis, several films upheld this alliance as both hopeful and nostalgic, including *Kangamba* (2008) by Rogelio París, *Angola, victoria de la esperanza* (*Angola, Victory of Hope*, 1976) by José Massip, and *La guerra de Angola* (*The War in Angola*, 1976) by Miguel Fleitas, which employs anonymous interviews that implicate the US in aiding UNITA (29, 32). A comparable albeit more recent African example is Ondjaki's seminal *Bom dia camaradas* (*Good Morning Comrades*, 2001), a coming-of-age novel in which an innocent young boy, Ndalu, recounts his school days with Cuban teachers in an Angola at war. Drawing on his own experience of the Angolan conflict from the beginning of the

3.4 The Death of a Latin-Africa Foretold

civil war in 1975 to the Cuban military withdrawal in 1991, Ondjaki gives a sense not only of admiration for Cuban volunteers but also of impending doom. Like García Márquez's "Operación Carlota" or "Angola, un año después," Ondjaki looks back fondly at the Cuban revolutionary mission. Although the novel remains coolly cynical about the failed decolonization project in Angolan politics from the vantage point of the present, Ondjaki frames the Cuban presence as inspiring.[47] In a scene where Ndalu and his fellow classmate Romina discuss their Cuban teachers, Cuban internationalism is memorialized via their admiration: "'I think they're brave . . .' 'just think what it's like to come to a country that's not theirs, to come and give classes that may or may not work out, and then there are the ones who go and fight in the front lines . . . how many Angolans do you know who went to fight in a Cuban war?'" (60). While slavery may well be the link that connects Cuba and Angola, in Ondjaki's novel a much more recent Cuban-Angolan affiliation memorializes an undying Latin-Africa that survives despite the failed decolonial mission that awaits the children in the novel. Thus, while the novel indeed criticizes decolonial failure – as, for instance, when Ndulu tells his aunt, an exile in Portugal, that fountains only exist in Angola when pipes burst (49) – Ondjaki's memorialization of an Atlantic borderland is infused with a nostalgic Latin-Africa that might have been.

Long after García Márquez had returned to fiction, Cuban internationalism would not suffice to liberate Angola and would promptly fade into historical oblivion. In fact, Castro's Cuba would be criticized for its role in Angola and framed as just another colonial power "fuel[ing] the civil war" and "benefit[ing] from Angola's natural resources," eliding US intervention (Franqui 84; Kaun 35; Cooper 235). In 1993, the United Nations special representative Margaret Anstee termed the unending war a "Forgotten Tragedy" as Reagan's anti-decolonial aid was in the form of "covert" operations (Minter 135). Shortly after, debates would ensue as to whether the US had been involved at all.[48] A 2018 article in *The Atlantic* that examines Paul Manafort's role in the Angolan war even condemns US amnesia about this intervention: "Americans' forgetting of the conflict is a testament to the ways in which the effects of Washington's petty dealings ripple out across others' lives, uncared for by the agents in pursuit of pay or power" ("How an American Lobbyist Stoked War"). It is precisely this "soulless" foreign policy that García Márquez critiques in so much of his journalism prior to *Crónica de una muerte anunciada* – a policy which, whether overtly or underhandedly, destabilized a potential Latin-African stronghold. But most damningly of all, García Márquez laments that the US elides this involvement in the same way that coloniality concealed the memory of Carlota's resistance. His novel communicates a similar sense of doom: As Castro once used the legacies of slavery to connect Cuba with West and Central Africa, *Crónica de una muerte anunciada*, through the sunken ship of Senegalese slaves, links the obliteration of Cartagena's colonial past to US imperialism's impact on the foreclosure of a Latin-African dream. In the section that follows, I close with a final literary analysis, showing how the dying Latin-Africa of García Márquez's post-Angolan lamentations provides access to the novel's Atlantic spaces of slavery, which in turn make perceptible the failure of a subaltern takeover that permeates the doom of *Crónica de una muerte anunciada*.

3.5 *Crónica de una muerte anunciada* after Angola and Senegal's House of Slaves

Most critics look away from the plantational Latin America that so obviously haunted García Márquez in the 1970s and beyond. In contrast, I argue that *Crónica de una muerte anunciada* discloses a fading Latin-Africa that the novel both laments and foretells via one of the novel's most mysterious characters, Bayardo San Román. Through this Caribbean outsider, who not only marries Angela but also comes to own the town's most elegant mansion (which belonged to a wealthy Catalan creole widower, Xius), I turn to the ways in which Angola influenced *Crónica de una muerte anunciada* conceptually, through an Atlantic World frame. Bayardo is a dark foreigner, and problematic references to his African origin other him further. But beyond the town's racialization of Bayardo, it is significant that this othered subject reappropriates the only colonial mansion or *quinta* in the novel. A spatial analysis reveals other plantational coordinates that surround this allegorical master's house replete with colonial objects that Bayardo is interested in acquiring. Bayardo's symbolic repossession also disorients memorialization itself: the quinta comes to represent the memory of a subaltern such as Bayardo rather than a nostalgic relic of colonialism akin to Cartagena's statue of Columbus. But Bayardo's takeover does not last, as his quinta falls into ruin. If the obliterated slave ship carrying Senegalese bodies is a point of access into García Márquez's Angolan spaces of lament, Angolan failure in turn illuminates the metaphorical lament in *Crónica de una muerte anunciada*, by which ebbs and flows of hope and disappointment mark Bayardo's story. Returning to the evocation of the disappeared Senegalese slaves, I conclude this chapter by tracing the mutually constituting conditions by which the textual

3.5 Crónica de una muerte anunciada *after Angola and Senegal's* 149

memorial of Bahía de las ánimas in *Crónica de una muerte anunciada* connects to Senegal's Gorée island, where the *Maison des esclaves* (*House of Slaves*) mourns disappeared African lives over Senegal's quintessential Slave Route memorial.

A foreigner who comes to settle in the town and marry Angela, Bayardo is immediately perceived as an outsider by virtue of his wealth and physical appearance. The townspeople refer to him as a "marica" ("a fairy" 31, 26) for wearing tight trousers and calfskin gloves (31, 25), and even the narrator's mother states he is "un hombre muy raro" ("a very strange man" 32, 26). Some of the most insightful interpretations of Santiago's difference explain that he is a Christ-like figure (Alvarez-Borland 278, A. González "The Ends of the Text" 69, but especially Penuel 192–205), a symbolic feature to destabilize a hermeneutic "structure" (Alvarez-Borland 278–85), a bad reader of omens (Pope 188–9), or part of the symbolism inherent in Latin American sense of destiny (Cornejo Polar 140–2). Building on these interpretations, Bayardo is also distinct vis-à-vis race; he is described as having "piel cocinada a fuego lento por el salitre" ("skin slowly roasted by saltpeter," 31, 25) and as the son of a mulata woman from Curaçao.[49] When a mournful Angela seeks to reconnect with him, she reportedly yearns for his "verga africana" ("African tool" or "dick" as the translation of the colloquial term should read, 107, 94), suggesting a problematic stereotyping of Black virility. The narrator recounts how Bayardo's "golden eyes had caused the shudder of fear" in his mother because he "reminded [her] of the devil" (28, "sus ojos de oro le habían causado un estremecimiento de espanto," "se me pareció al diablo" 33–4). The narrator himself characterizes Bayardo as "just as strange as they had said," and "with a hidden tension that was barely conceived" (28, 34). So mysterious is he that he is imagined as the reincarnation of a French (and White) Victor Hughes who "wiped out villages" in French Guiana and escaped from Devil's Island (39, 33). Because this eighteenth-century French governor reinstated slavery in the Antilles, the novel's conjuring of Hughes is traumatic. On the metanarrative level, however, this intertextuality underscores García Márquez's admiration of Cuba, since Cuban writer Carpentier's historical novel *El siglo de las luces / Explosion in a Cathedral* (1962) immortalizes Hughes.[50] Although Bayardo is from the Caribbean, unlike Hughes, he is perceived, ironically, as just as foreign to the town as ice was to Macondo in *Cien años de soledad*.

Because of Bayardo's racialization and foreignness, it is possible to read his decision to acquire the only mansion in town – the Catalan quinta – as a symbolic repossession of the colonial.[51] I read this deterritorialization as an allegory for repossessing the Master's house, not only because descriptions of it demonstrate its coloniality but also because, historically, the slave trade generated considerable Catalan wealth in the Spanish colonies, as Lisa Surwillo's study of Iberian creole wealth details.[52] *Crónica de una muerte anunciada*'s mansion reflects this legacy: it is "la más bonita del pueblo," sits over a "colina barrida por los vientos," with a view of "el paraíso sin límite de las ciénagas," "el horizonte nítido del Caribe, y los transatlánticos de turistas de Cartagena de Indias" ("a windswept hill," "the limitless paradise of the marshes," "the neat horizon of the Caribbean, and the tourist ships from Cartagena de Indias," 42, 35). Moreover, the mansion's view of a "limitless" paradise not only echoes Spanish colonialism's layering of utopic imagery of Genesis over a mythical El Dorado, but also would have enabled its Catalan colonist-owner to observe the arrival of slave "cargo," not unlike the vision Santiago conjures at the pier. But unlike Santiago, Xius, the mansion's current owner, ignores this historical marker and replaces it with a view of the "touristic ships" at Cartagena's bay, echoing its contemporary commodification.

As tourism in the example above neglects the memorialization of slavery, so too does Xius. Initially refusing to sell his colonial relic, he says to Bayardo, "ustedes los jóvenes no entienden los motivos del corazón" ("you young people don't understand the motives of the heart" 43, 36). Xius's reasoning, however, read through a colonial lens, is both perverse and typical of García Márquez's irony. Xius wants to preserve the Master's house for its colonial sentimentality ("motives of the heart") rather than acknowledging the ties between the building and the slave trade. But Bayardo's insistence on appropriating the mansion with all of its contents, sentimental or not, speaks to a repurposing of the Master's house. Resolute, Bayardo persists:

> – Viudo – le dijo – : le compro la casa
> – No está a la venta – dijo el viudo.
> – Se la compro *con todo lo que tiene dentro*.
> El viudo de Xius le explicó con una buena educación a la antigua que los objetos de la casa habían sido comprados por la esposa en toda una vida de sacrificios, y que para él seguían siendo como parte de ella.
>
> (42, emphasis added)

"Widower," he told him, "I'll buy your house."
"It's not for sale," the widower said.

3.5 Crónica de una muerte anunciada *after Angola and Senegal's*   151

> "I'll buy it along *with everything inside.*"
> The widower Xius explained to him with the good breeding of olden days that the objects in the house had been bought by his wife over a whole lifetime of sacrifice and that for him they were still a part of her.
>
> (Rabassa 35–6, emphasis added)

Although Xius relents, lured by a sum of money "he cannot refuse" (44) and signaling that everything – including memory – has a price, Bayardo's interest in buying the widower's "objects" is telling in terms of the museification of colonial legacies.

This is especially important considering the Catalan role in transatlantic trade. As Surwillo notes, not only were Catalans particularly involved in the slave trade that consumed Cuba's Black Atlantic in the nineteenth century, their presence also left a nostalgic material memory of colonial power in the Caribbean (167, 172). In this context, Bayardo's takeover of the mansion with all its relics "inside" both evokes Castro's appropriation of wealth for socialist redistribution and has colonial roots. As Yi-Fu Tuan states, "space can be variously experienced as the relative location of objects" (12). When Bayardo, as a racialized Caribbean man, repossesses the house's contents, he destabilizes the experience of these objects as celebrating colonialism. In other words, Bayardo's reappropriated objects shatter the nostalgic memorialization of colonialism that García Márquez also criticized in his journalism when he referred to Bahía de las ánimas's "nostalgic" colonial history.

Most telling of this deterritorialization of memory is how the mansion is remembered by the townspeople after Bayardo leaves town. When a forlorn Xius returns to the Big House years later, he invokes the memory of his wife to the town's mayor. The mention of the mansion makes the mayor remember, not Xius – much less his deceased wife – but that "poor man" Bayardo:

> Sin embargo, nadie se había acordado de [Bayardo] hasta después del eclipse de luna, el sábado siguiente, cuando el viudo Xius le contó al alcalde que había visto un pájaro fosforescente aleteando sobre su antigua casa, y pensaba que era el ánima de su esposa que andaba reclamando lo suyo. El alcalde se dio en la frente una palmada que no tenía nada que ver con la visión del viudo. – ¡Carajo! – gritó – ¡Se me había olvidado ese pobre hombre!" (96)
>
> Still, no one had thought of him [Bayardo] until after the eclipse of the moon the following Saturday, when the widower Xius told the mayor that

he'd seen a phosphorescent bird fluttering over his former home, and he thought it was the soul of his wife, who was going about demanding what was hers. The mayor slapped his brow, but it had nothing to do with the widower's vision. "Shit!" he shouted. "I'd completely forgotten about that poor man!" (Rabassa 84)

Even though Xius's comments seek to reclaim the mansion through his wife's spirit ("was going about demanding what was hers"), the indirect symbol of colonial Catalan wealth recalls Bayardo instead. The deterritorialized former master's house has now come to memorialize those who built it in the first place. Far from suggesting that Bayardo erases plantational history, *Crónica de una muerte anunciada* gestures to a history that has receded underground. If we consider Xius's dwelling to symbolize the master's house, marginal characters like Bayardo point to the submerged presence of this history and, as Elizabeth Russ argues, "return to that center of the patriarchal power, the Big House, in order to transform it" (18). At meta-narrative level, this takeover of the Master's house by its former subjects parallels García Márquez's Angolan chronicles that memorialize a Latin-African connection.

Moreover, via a spatial analysis, the surroundings of Xius's former mansion can be read as plantational. Bayardo's Big House faces the river, which leads to "tambos de pobres que empezaban a encenderse en el puerto antiguo" ("the poor people's eating places that were beginning to light up by the old harbor" 77, 67). But the English translation of "tambos" immediately erases the spatial significance of Xius's mansion since Gregory Rabassa translates "barrels" as "eating *places*" (emphasis added).[53] "Tambos" or barrels, often used by afromestizos as drums, are a prototypical African trope that García Márquez even mentions, as "tambores de comunicación" and "tam tam" in his work on Angola ("Operación" 149). This notably transatlantic term loses its meaning in English translation, but in Spanish, its African resonances connect it to plantational spaces: a decadent "cementerio" ("cemetery"), a "sembrado de plátanos azules bajo la luna" ("grove of blue banana trees in the moonlight"), a "ciénaga triste" ("sad swamp" 66), and the Atlantic represented in "línea fosforescente del Caribe" ("the phosphorescent line of the Caribbean" 76, 66) where the shipwreck occurred.

While the Atlantic Ocean as a horizon of arrival and the "sembrado de plátanos" both allude to slave ports and slave planting respectively, the "ciénaga" (swamp) and the cemetery were crucial points of reference in Cartagena's colonial mapping. The slave cemeteries were often close to "depósitos," or "cárceles" (depots or jails) where slaves were

3.5 *Crónica de una muerte anunciada after Angola and Senegal's*

held captive before sale (Vidal and Elias 27) because, as colonial records show, many of them died due to the terrible conditions of their captivity (Gutiérrez Azopardo 201). As an eighteenth-century map of Cartagena shows (Figure 3.4), the item numbered 11 is the depot, located precisely near the port of arrival, and misspelled "carzel" in Spanish. As for the ciénagas, these were another source of death and disease; a cesspool of germs from which yellow fever epidemics arose. Ironically, epidemic illnesses that emerged from swamps were attributed to Africa – or in Cartagena's case, to Angola specifically – as yellow fever was named "el mal de Luanda" after Angola's capital ("the Luanda disease," Vidal and Elias 26). In other words, the Big House's surroundings evoke the novel's metanarrative and transatlantic context.

An anticipated critique of this reading, especially as it concerns Bayardo's repossession of Xius's quinta, might suggest that the novel's landscape is designed simply to convey the Antillean spatiotemporality of its plot. Yet, a spatial reading of *Crónica de una muerte anunciada* demonstrates García Márquez's intermixing the historical or journalistic with the fictional, revealing a recurrent Latin-African space in the novel as well. In this vein, Henri Lefebvre usefully reminds us that the notion of "space as innocent" or "free of traps" is incorrect. Critiquing the idea that "an encrypted reality" is intelligible through a character's actions rather than space, or that landscape is subservient to narrative, Lefebvre warns that this conception is categorically Eurocentric (*Production* 28). Narratives from the margins, such as one that depicts a small town on the periphery of Cartagena, Colombia, write against this tradition, conveying how plot and space are mutually intelligible through histories lost to time. In fact, as the spatial analysis of Stanka Radović points out, "Caribbean literary engagements with space often break the binary logic of space-as-real and space-as-metaphor by carving out, through narrative, a 'third space,' where the imaginary and material aspects of spatiality are treated as inextricable and complementary facets of our daily spatial practice" (3). To treat the landscape in *Crónica de una muerte anunciada* this way implies seeing the real or journalistic and the fictional or figurative as inextricable from the plot, especially when it comes to Caribbean history, whose legacies of genocide, forced migration, and exploitation are unique.[54]

As García Márquez's journalism lamented a foretold US annihilation of socialism in the Global South, a similar defeatism saturates *Crónica de una muerte anunciada* when Bayardo's quinta falls into ruin. Once Bayardo leaves town, the ensuing wailing of Bayardo's family is so fierce that the narrator remarks that they "hide other, greater shames" (85). But when the

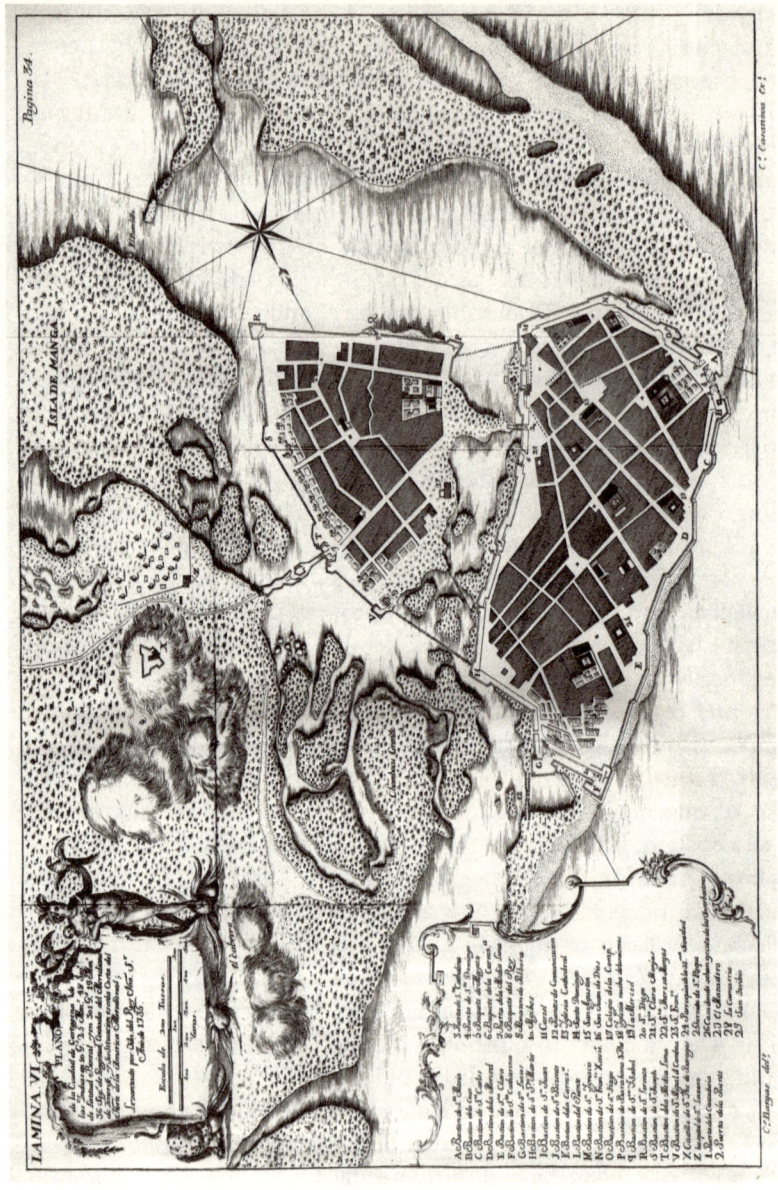

Figure 3.4 "Relación histórica del viaje a la América Meridional," Madrid, 1748. Archivo Histórico del Guayas, Guayaquil (AHG), Ecuador.

3.5 Crónica de una muerte anunciada *after Angola and Senegal's*

quinta does fall into decay, the mayor remarks that "[t]hings looked like they were under water" (84). The statement recalls Glissant's theorization of the Caribbean's slave trade history as submerged – a history "marked by these balls and chains gone green," the shackles of slavery buried under the sea and in public memory (*Poetics* 6). As if mimicking the submergence of Cartagena's violent Atlantic history, the Big House deteriorates, and the contents that locate its historicity become displaced.[55] When Xius witnesses this outcome, he cheers, suggesting that this displacement signals his wife's mystical return as a "spiritual séance" confirms that Yolanda Xius's spirit was recovering these objects for her "casa de la muerte" ("house of death," 99, 87). As the territorial battle continues even in death, the mansion's ruins both obliterate Bayardo's initial triumph and serve as a spatial reminder of the all-powerful colonial order.

The quinta's repossession and then ruin mirror the hopefulness and ensuing disappointment of García Márquez's journalism in the 1970s and 1980s. But this and other fictional instances in the novel reflect an ultimate disappointment conveyed in the journalistic site of Angola, even if the novel's traces of it are subtle. For if the Angolan chronicles used fictional techniques to present a failed Latin-African victory, *Crónica de una muerte anunciada* memorializes the nonfictional and disappointing site of a failed Latin-Africa through fiction. Recalling the essay mentioned at the beginning of this chapter, in "Como ánimas en pena" ("Like souls in mourning" 1981, in *Notas de prensa* 1991), written the same year as *Crónica de una muerte anunciada*, García Márquez suggests that tragic life is best represented through the literary. An essay on countless examples of absurdity bordering on the fictional – including a man who regrets his suicide as he marvels at the life he witnesses on each floor as he falls – García Márquez states that these are "fascinating stories – written or told – that adhere forever, more in the heart than in memory" ("historias fascinantes – escritas o habladas – que se le quedan a uno para siempre, más en el corazón que en la memoria" 101). He concludes that absurd real-life stories are "perhaps the mourning souls of literature" ("Tal vez sean las ánimas en pena de la literatura" *Notas de prensa* 1991, 102). Echoing the novel's "mourning souls" of Senegalese slaves who inspired the name Bahía de las ánimas but go unacknowledged publicly, in this essay the mourning souls of literature are akin to the absurdity of Cartagena's lack of Black Atlantic memorialization. But placing his Angolan chronicles and *Cróncia de una muerte anunciada* together, the metaphor of mourning intercedes to memorialize the nonfictional account of slavery and slavery's role in naming Bahía de las ánimas. The mourning souls of a failed Cuban-Angolan mission are reflected in García Márquez's conception of a Latin-African death foretold in his journalism and then projected onto the Bay of Souls of *Crónica de una muerte anunciada*. The novel's Senegalese slave ship could be read not only as García Márquez's memorialization of Castro's rhetoric of slavery over the Bay of Souls, but also as registering a leftist defeatism permeating the testimonio genre in the 1970s and 1980s. His journalism covering Angola's decolonization seems to convey conceptually what *Crónica de una muerte anunciada* and its Bay of Souls evokes thematically: the death of a Latin-Africa foretold.

I conclude this chapter by comparing García Márquez's textual memorial to the death of a Latin-Africa with a physical memorial addressing lament along Senegal's UNESCO Slave Route. As García Márquez's journalistic lament for Angola informs the figure of Senegalese obliteration in *Crónica de una muerte anunciada*, so too does Senegal's *Maison des esclaves* enable the expression of grief for unnamed and departed slaves. In fact, narratives told at these sites are reminiscent of debates about literary journalism, especially as the memorials of the Slave Route are imagined as historical. The relationship between physical and textual memorials also enables us to distinguish the memorialization of Senegalese slaves in García Márquez's oeuvre, post–*Crónica de una muerte anunciada*, and thus ultimately consider the weight of Latin-Africa in a key representative of World Literature.

The *Maison des esclaves* brings Senegalese slaves, inevitably lost to the ocean, back from oblivion through the former trading depot's memorialized site – its "House of Slaves" – but also via certain stories that historians argue are fictional. Gorée's Maison allegedly held slaves captive prior to their embarkation on ships bound for the Middle Passage, but as records show, the site of memory was not central to the Slave Trade as much as the site would have us believe (Ralph 102). Although Gorée did not deport slaves in record numbers, as did ports such as those on the coast of Angola ("Maison des esclaves" 18), the Maison has been turned into the quintessential memorial of the Black Atlantic. The site's popularity has a lot to do with both its legendary "Door of No Return" that faces an endless Atlantic Ocean and its late curator Joseph N'Diaye (Araujo *Public Memory* 85). Not only does the Door of No Return face the Atlantic, which symbolizes slaves' break with Africa and into lives of bondage,[56] N'Diaye has also performed as a witness, recounting in hindsight the inevitable events that reportedly took place at the site on which visitors stand (62). These stories are underscored by an incorrect number that amplifies the site as a point of

3.5 Crónica de una muerte anunciada *after Angola and Senegal's* 157

departure; the memorial's brochures say that between ten to fifteen million enslaved Africans passed through the tiny opening of the "Door of No Return." While his language uses tones of the foretold, the numbers are equally fictional for this estimate is higher than that of the entire slave trade combined, which estimates approximate 12,521,337 (Eltis *Slave Voyages*). While Gorée is insignificant to the slave trade historically, as Santiago's slave ship is to the novel's plot, N'Diaye uses fiction to memorialize slavery as García Márquez used literary devices to memorialize Angola.[57]

These narratives interspersed with spatial memory at Gorée seek to, quoting García Márquez, "adhere more to the heart than to memory." If N'Diaye "was able to narrate past events in a place where these events were said to have taken place," as Ana Lucia Araujo notes, the narrative also "allow[ed] visitors to actually feel for themselves the experiences of the enslaved men and women" (*Public* 62). And indeed, Gorée's House of Slaves has unequivocally been thought as a "shrine of emotion," even if UNESCO's objective was to transcend "the emotions, feelings of guilt and shame" through the project's analytical aims (quoted in Seck "Senegal" 545). The memorial site's fictions, loosely based on the historical, hope to create an affectual experience for the site-reader or pilgrim through the primary metaphor of inevitable loss in the "Door of No Return." García Márquez's *Crónica de una muerte anunciada*, inversely, uses the symbolic space of the Bay of Souls to make up for Cartagena's obliteration of the slaves who came from Senegal. Most importantly, the connection the novel makes between Gorée and Cartagena echoes Castro's linkage of African liberation and colonial slavery, which resonates with García Márquez's journalism.

Moreover, *Crónica de una muerte anunciada* arguably sets the stage for more significant textual memorialization of a Latin-Africa. Four years after this novel, *El amor en los tiempos del cólera* featured the literal scars of the plantation on former slaves. This physical reminder of slavery, however, is swept under the rug of the novel's melodramatic genre. Almost a decade later, *Del amor y otros demonios* anchors its plot in Cartagena's colonial seventeenth-century plantocracy, where references to slave ownership, the slave trade, and slave customs appear.[58] The drowned Senegalese souls who name the famous Colombian bay re-emerge as living medicinal healers who tend to protagonist Sierva María, a young girl who lives among slaves and was bitten by a rabid dog. The novel seems like it will dwell on the perfunctory treatment of Sierva María to relieve her of her "African ways," but instead this Atlantic paradigm recedes to privilege the feverish passion of a Jesuit priest for the young girl. Moreover, this novel faded into oblivion as it "drew relatively little fanfare when it first appeared" (238–9), underscoring Latin American criticism's reluctance to address these tropes in the wake of globalization, as Bell-Villada implies.[59]

As I have been arguing in this book, placing textual sites of Atlantic memory alongside the physical sites of the Slave Route offers an opportunity to ask how representatives of World Literature frame the memorialization of a Latin-Africa that World Literature itself has neglected. García Márquez's memorialization of the Atlantic connections between Angola, Senegal, and Latin America challenges the ways in which World Literature snubs such Latin-African connections in favor of the more marketable trope of magical realism. In fact, in the wake of the Cold War, contemporary Latin American writers vehemently protested this commodified staple of regionalism, gesturing toward urban cosmopolitanism's "interconnected centers" and their express desire for modernization, as Héctor Hoyos has pointed out (7). But despite the post-Boom rejection of this trademark, World Literature continues to be invested in it, projecting its imaginary as an unequivocal representation of Latin America in general and of García Márquez in particular. Not only did magical realism become literary gospel, meeting the regional or folkloric requirements of a Latin America imagined as peripheral, *Cien años de soledad*, as Siskind explains, "came to represent and express what a large portion of the world's literary public assumed to be the essence of Latin American culture and social history" (54, 59). Indeed, one has only to look, for instance, at Delta Airline's tourist advertising campaign "Colombia is Magical Realism," which depicts a smiling couple deciphering a map with the word "magic" infusing the colorful Cartagena background (Figure 3.5). The image's foregrounding of magical realism and its invitation to "walk amongst the magic that inspired the Nobel Prize winning literature" casts a shadow over Cartagena's submerged slave trade history. Moreover, it reinforces tendencies to read García Márquez primarily in terms of magical realism – the approach that World Literature chiefly markets – rather than through the spatiotemporalities in his work this chapter has been tracing.

Resisting the urge of World Literature to transform Latin America into a magical realist playground, the Latin-Africa of García Márquez challenges this marketing practice. After all, García Márquez's post-1981 fictions consistently turned Antillean regionality toward the global in ways other than the stereotypically magical and folkloric ones. From his Angolan chronicles and other political essays to aspects of *Crónica de una muerte anunciada*, a snubbed rurality can also be read as cosmopolitan

3.5 *Crónica de una muerte anunciada* after Angola and Senegal's   159

Figure 3.5 Delta Airlines travel advertisement, "Colombia is Magical Realism."
Photo: Sarah M. Quesada, 2016.

because of its own interconnectivity with global centers. In other words, from the 1970s on, García Márquez's work built a bridge between World Literature and Global South writing in ways beyond a magical realist reading of Latin America for World Literature's publics. The Cuban exodus and the failures of the political left embedded in García Márquez's 1970s and 1980s oeuvre memorialize instead the loss of an ideologically Marxist Latin-Africa that was weakened by a global shift to neoliberalism. Through journalism and fiction, García Márquez drove home a Latin-Africa that was unfortunately forgotten, metaphorized in the erased slaves that both Gorée and *Crónica de una muerte anunciada* memorialize. If García Márquez's experiments in journalism and fiction sought to redefine a cosmopolitan *littérature engagée* as the Cold War became anchored in the African continent, the result was the imaginary of a successful Latin-Africa never to be.

CHAPTER 4

Archival Distortion
The Chicano Congo of Tomás Rivera and Rudolfo Anaya

> In a colony, one function of language is to distort everything.
> Achille Mbembe

The transatlantic African slave trade is usually not at the center of the Chicano imaginary, much less a paramount spatiotemporality in Chicano literature or critique of it.[1] Unfamiliar though it may be, however, prominent Chicano writers Tomás Rivera and Rudolfo Anaya each memorialized the Congo through the direct specter of nineteenth-century imperialism and the indirect conjuring of colonial slavery, respectively, with a major caveat. While both texts selected for discussion here focus on Chicano youth who seem to venerate a darkened complexion, this racial celebration is associated with problematic evocations of African racialization and exploitation. Rivera seems to adulate infamous Welsh mercenary Henry M. Stanley for his exploration of the Congo, while traces of African spirituality during the often-overlooked era of the slave trade in the US Southwest are repeatedly marked as evil witchery in Anaya's bildungsroman, *Bless Me, Ultima*. Despite such traces of a noticeable Latin-African haunting in two of the most lauded Chicano male writers, this paradigm has been elided in literary criticism about their work.

Turning first to Rivera, his posthumous poem "Searching at Leal Middle School" (1975, 1991) maps the "scramble for Africa" onto his own Chicano imaginary. The semi-autobiographical poem narrates Rivera's visit to a school, where the sight of playing children takes him back to his youth and he imagines himself engrossed in boundless exploration. Inciting this nostalgic reverie are children whose black hair the poem describes as "brillante" ("shining"), their faces both "smiling" and "playful" as they learn "love for others" and "for ourselves." Following these descriptions of brown love and racial solidarity, the poem perplexingly shifts to quite the opposite: the poetic voice inhabits the body of Stanley, who shackles non-White features to a "darkness" he described infamously in his nineteenth-century ethnographic work *In Darkest Africa* (1890). The connections between the schoolchildren and Stanley further converge on an African axis when Rivera-as-Stanley focuses on an important discovery in the schoolyard's dumpster: books about the "exploration of Africa." I reproduce part of the poem here:

> At first I saw only
> the backs of black hair heads
> Cabezas de pelo negro, negro era
> Cabezas de pelo negro
> brillante, de brillo, brillo era
> . . .
>
> I saw their limitless eyes
> ojos sin límites
> ojos oscuros
> ojos sonrientes,
> juguetones
> . . .
>
> We talked of thinking
>   of inventing ourselves
>   of love for others
>   of love to be
>   of searching
> for ourselves
> . . .
>
> Away in the dump yards
> where smoke curled and
> with long sticks we turned and turned and
> found half-rotten fruit
> to be washed and eaten
> and books –
> Livingston's exploration of Africa
> the maps,
> the blacks,
> I became Henry L. in the forest –

However innocent the poem might seem as its narrator embarks on an expedition to rescue Scottish abolitionist David Livingstone in the line "Livingston's exploration of Africa,"[2] this personification of Stanley is indeed puzzling. For the speaker's disconcerting embodiment of Stanley in the line "I became Henry L. in the forest" hardly recalls an innocent safari adventure, but rather evokes the ghosts of modernity's colonization, enslavement, and oppression of Africans. As an infamous appointee of Belgian King Leopold, who was responsible for ten million Congolese deaths and the plundering of $1.1 billion of the Congo's natural resources, Stanley played a central role both in the genocide that surged in the aftermath of Belgian colonization and in setting in motion the Congo's current debt-laden governance. Moreover, even though he absolved himself of guilt by affiliating himself with Livingstone the abolitionist – indeed, Stanley is most famous for uttering the phrase, "Dr. Livingstone, I presume?" when rescuing him in Tanzania – Stanley was a merciless slave driver. Nevertheless, in an interview with Juan Bruce-Novoa in 1980, Rivera admits that this book, a two-volume collection about "Stanley's expedition into Africa in search for Dr. Livingstone" that he had found in a library dump, had "especially impressed [him]" in his youth – a fascination now embedded in his poem.

A similar complexity extends to a writer affectionately known as the "godfather of Chicano letters," Rudolfo Anaya, who was honored with the National Endowment for the Humanities Medal by President Barack Obama in 2015. But in his canonical coming-of-age novel *Bless Me, Ultima* (1972), Anaya at times uncritically others categories inherited from New Mexico's understudied plantocracy. When the young boy protagonist, Antonio Márez Luna, comes under the tutelage of a *curandera* ("healer"), Ultima, he is accused of practicing "voodoo." For her part – and despite the fact that she is usually read as indigenous – Ultima's spiritual-praxis-cum-witchcraft involves cures that seem to originate from an alternate racial geography: she owns clay dolls, leads trances, and is accused, though not explicitly, of dealing in Vodun. Moreover, during his time with Ultima, Antonio also discovers the repressed golden carp, a deity that dialectically opposes his Catholic upbringing. Importantly, however, the novel marks both Ultima's remedies and Antonio's newfound pagan zoolatry as profoundly othered; its explicit racialization of this spiritual praxis curiously evokes the US Southwest's overlooked but significant plantocratic regime. Further unsettling are the ways in which these othered spiritualities find echoes in similarly denunciatory descriptions of them in much older texts – especially Antonio Cavazzi's seventeenth-century ethnography about animistic belief systems in the Congo region, which arguably made its way to the US Southwest during the era of the slave trade. While this chapter uses these treatises on colonial Africa's difference as source material for identifying the African roots of Anaya's tale – thus challenging exclusively indigenous or even hemispheric interpretations of Anaya's US Southwest – the similarity between the language of these colonial texts and that of Anaya's contemporary one is initially disconcerting.

If Chicano literary criticism shies away from attending to this African paradigm in two highly esteemed authors, it ought not to. For these works offer an opportunity to rehabilitate a severed Latin-African connection. As this chapter will initially explain, these works are part of a complex network of colonial and imperial distortions of Africa. Revisiting this network exposes the various ways in which Africa has been distorted from within and *also* explains why Rivera and Anaya perceive Africa this way. In other words, Rivera's and Anaya's problematic literary representations that subtly conjure sites in the Congo, through Stanley on the one hand and a maleficent darkness on the other, both reveal discreet connections to an African Atlantic World that affected the US Southwest. But they also fall within a long history of disfiguring representations of Africa that goes back to works by colonial and imperial ethnographers *in* Africa. Of course, the problematic evocations of "Africa" in Anaya's and Rivera's Chicano imaginary, direct or indirect, were shaped in the Americas by sources ranging from Mexican conceptions of "Africa" to the American imperialist John Gregory Bourke's "The American Congo," whose projected transatlantic frontier colors the Chicano writers' Mexico-US borderland.

Such textual memorialization of the Congo is only part of a larger whole, however. For instance, Rivera's *textual* memory of Stanley's "Africa" is complicated by Stanley's *physical* memorialization in the Atlantic World. In 1971, the Democratic Republic of the Congo attempted to erase Stanley's memory by toppling a statue of him in its capital. By contrast, Stanley's nostalgic hometown of Denbigh, Wales, defiantly celebrated his legacy by erecting a controversial £31,000 bronze statue of him in 2011. While this chapter examines the overlooked and undervalued role of African historiography in Chicano literature that informs Rivera's reflection on Stanley's *textual* "exploration of Africa," in this chapter, I will also link Rivera's and Anaya's textual memorials of the Congo to myriad examples of physical memorialization, including statues of Stanley and a UNESCO Slave Route site in Malawi that conjures Livingstone, to name a few, to convey the mutually constituting force of Latin-African memory. Reading Rivera and Anaya through this historiography, as routes that revisit a Latin-African history, suggests that these works' textual trails repossess imperialist language, repurposing the signifier of "darkness" to decolonize racial imaginaries from the confinement of the imperial gaze. As a result, these sites seem to help both authors understand the shared coloniality of the Congo and their native US Southwest.

In this chapter, I intervene in the muffled and inconvenient truth of an Atlantic haunting in Rivera's poem and Anaya's groundbreaking novel to reveal how imperial and colonial histories of Africa enter Chicano literary perception. While such an intervention suggests a meaningful imperialist ghosting of transatlantic proportions, distorted representations of Africa in these two Chicano writers indeed complicate what Amy Kaplan explains is the centrality of the Congo as a "frontier tale" over which "American studies is conceived" (3, 9) – not least because these subtle allusions to Africa by multiethnic US writers change the way the Congo is remembered as a "wilderness" in the American experience. As I will first explain, these Chicano authors participate in a complex transatlantic network memorializing the Congo that, when revisited, explains the anti-African biases undergirding the Chicano imaginary. But by reading Rivera's and Anaya's texts through the lens of distorted representations and memorializations of Africa, I show how these literary works contribute to a reassessment of such racialized distortion and move toward rehabilitating it. Thus, second, this chapter will detail how two prominent 1970s Chicano writers, much like the Caribbean authors noted in this book, both borrow differently from colonial and imperial travelogues about Africa to reveal a Latin-African connection that expands a Chicano identity into the Atlantic World. Far from suggesting that these texts rewrite imperial or colonial scripts, I argue that they can be read as sites that chart out a *relation* to a racialized spatiality in order to repossess such distortions and enlarge Chicanos' hemispheric imaginary within an imperialistic US borderland. In other words, while Rivera's embodiment of Stanley or Anaya's infrequent othering of "voodoo," for example, might seem to simply perpetuate this tradition of transatlantic distortions of Africa – and even explain literary scholarship's neglect of such apparent slippages – these textual sites of African memory can also be read as counter-discursive. Rivera's poem functions as the space over which blackness shifts from a negative category of distorted identity confined *In Darkest Africa* to an open and playful freedom of possibility and solidarity. For Anaya, something similar happens with Bourke's distorted representation of African spirituality, which I trace back to two important seventeenth-century European missionaries in Africa, Antonio Cavazzi and Alonso de Sandoval.

Finally, I explain the ways in which both examples of a Latin-African connection have important implications for the apparatus of World Literature. After all, Rivera's and Anaya's memorializations of the Congo that I trace in this chapter revise the hemispheric boundaries that have usually defined their work, stretching the literary US Southwest into

Caribbean parameters. In previous criticism, Rivera's transnational purview involves mainly the relationship between Mexico and the US. For Anaya, recent anthologies have celebrated his transatlantic connections, but delimitated this network along an occidentalist axis with Europe. World Literature, especially, has tended to market Rivera and Anaya as representative of Mexican traditions constituted mainly by indigenous and Spanish heritage, eschewing traces of Africa or the African diaspora that their corpus presents. In this vein, the hints of an Atlantic World in these US-Mexican borderland writers suggest that Rivera and Anaya belong to a cosmopolitan category previously considered applicable only to the Caribbean authors in this book due to their plantational heritage. But as I will explain, despite Rivera's distorted "memory" of Africa constructed via Stanley's account, the poem subtly locates the Congo alongside traditional Chicano cultural paradigms of bilingualism and race epistemologies to weave Manifest Destiny in the US Southwest and the nineteenth-century "scramble for Africa" together as examples of global coloniality. By contrast, Anaya's text, whose spiritual elements are usually considered indigenous cultural retentions, shows traces of the US Southwest's plantocracy during the slave trade era. While this book has mostly focused on regional Caribbean writers, previously unidentified traces of African influence in these classic Latinx writers underscore a Latin-African relationality that has gone unexplored until now. This chapter thus places canonical examples of US multiethnic literature beyond the borders of American studies and beyond the insular, traditional, and regional classifications to which they are often confined. To word it differently, I think of these texts, not as organic to the US-Mexico borderland, but as "diasporic" and part of the Atlantic World that frees them from the kinds of ethnographic regionalisms that World Literature has used to market them.

4.1 Stanley and the Distortion of the "American Congo"

When Rivera embodied Stanley in his poem, the former farmworker-turned-Quinto-Sol-Prize-winner had already made a name for himself. By 1981, Rivera was a literary representative of Chicano awakening, serving on various national boards and committees in higher education, including the presidential commission (Leal and Stavans 226). But his canonicity is also reflected in the transnationality of his groundbreaking *...y no se lo tragó la tierra* (1971), which was translated into English by Herminio Ríos, published in Argentina by Corregidor Press, and reprinted by México's *Fondo de Cultura Económica*. With a transnational focus himself, Rivera has praised Gabriel García Márquez for having "established the American continents as humanistic metaphor as never before" and publicly recognized the accomplishments of Jorge Luis Borges, Héctor Murena, and Octavio Paz, among others, suggesting that he incorporated their cosmopolitan engagements into his own worldview (Rivera "Y no se lo tragó la tierra" 218–62). Rivera's partiality to Mexico and Argentina and the often bilingual circulation of his books in Latin America place him in a peculiar World Literature framework because, at the same time, he is read as a mostly regional borderlands author, with interpretations of his rhetorical strategies rarely looking beyond the US Southwest.[3] Thus, to understand how Rivera's poetic voice might embody Stanley, it is necessary to turn to the politics of Atlantic memorialization. I do so to point out not only the myriad ways in which Rivera's poem is part of a complicated web that memorializes African historiography – and specifically the Congo – but also how, in revisiting this memorialization of Africa and the architects of its distortion, we can begin to see how the poem rehabilitates a Latin-African memory.

In this section, I begin by focusing on disjunctures in memorialization of Stanley around the Atlantic, not only to contextualize the imperialist conjuring in Rivera's poem, but also to underscore how central a role memorialization plays in the process of distorting Africa both textually and physically. To memorialize the Atlantic World, Rivera's poem takes paths that traverse both Stanley's eurocentrism and personal introspection. I thus retrace the path of imperialism in the Congo to understand the uneven distribution of memory about both Stanley in the context of the nineteenth-century scramble for Africa and the Congo as a haunting literary figure. Recalling the physical memorialization of Stanley in both Africa and Europe I mentioned above, I consider how Africa becomes a site for exploration when Rivera admits that Stanley's text was a complex prototype for his cosmopolitan engagements. Ultimately, I show how one of the most canonical Latinx figures in American literature participates in a much wider memorialization web of the Congo. This memorialization is at the root of a complicated Latinx relationship with Africa and racialization, enabling us to unearth a Latin-African connection that challenges perceptions of Rivera's work as regional.

Rivera later admitted that there was more to his memory of Stanley than just the mention of him in "Searching at Leal Middle School." In 1980, when asked what book had had the greatest impact on him, Rivera answered,

4.1 Stanley and the Distortion of the "American Congo" 167

[t]here is one which especially impressed me: *In Darkest Africa* by Henry M. Stanley. I found it myself in the dump, you see; a two-volume collection of Stanley's expedition into Africa in search for Dr. Livingstone. Of course, I didn't know anything about history at the time, or the exploration of Africa but with the books came maps of the terrain which Stanley had to travel ... It fascinated me. It was better than going to a Tarzan movie. *It carried over into my own life*, because I started making maps of the terrain we traveled, and my brothers and I would explore and draw maps. It became a living thing. I haven't read them for a long time, but that title *stuck in my memory* because of the exploratory aspect. Later, when I ran into other similar things, I was able to understand the exploration of America and Latin America because I could understand this one man's exploration of the Dark Continent. (*Complete Works* 143, emphasis added)

What is striking here is how Rivera personally related to the sensational account of a Victorian explorer. Stanley's "Victorian invention" fostered sagas that unsurprisingly resonate in Joseph Conrad's 1899 *The Heart of Darkness* (Brantlinger 198). Not only are its descriptions of blackness troubling, but Stanley's *In Darkest Africa* details "a sadistic, genocidal drama," as Mary Louise Pratt emphasizes (210), seen through the imperial eyes of a nineteenth-century bicultural man. But if most biographers contend that Stanley's work was almost fictional and that he made up most of his account – his own name and birthplace as well as the number of people he killed during his expeditions – perhaps Stanley's self-representation as an epic warrior attracted Rivera, who admittedly admired Américo Paredes' *With His Pistol in His Hand* (1958).

Thus, the Stanley that Rivera textually memorialized was, above all, a master of fabricated stories. Penniless at his origins, Stanley came into the spotlight in 1871 when he rescued Livingstone from Ujiji in present-day Tanzania. Reporting on this adventure, he drew in audiences with his prototypical "new sensationalist, voyeuristic style" of writing that emphasized suspenseful and violent battles against ruthless and exotic civilizations (Berenson 27). Stanley's own writing memorialized him as the "Napoleon of African travellers" in his lifetime (*Scottish Geographical Magazine* 284); contemporaries hailed him as a conqueror and internationally bestselling author (Amodeo 34; Headley "Wilds," 102, 136, 150, 341). But for Africanist scholars such as Makau Mutua, Stanley's *In Darkest Africa* is an archetypal distortion of Africa. In his condemnation of Tim Jeal's recent biography of Stanley, Mutua states that Jeal's apologetic memorialization highlights "that which is wrong with Western *perception* of Africa" (172, emphasis added). This "perception" relies on an Atlantic politics of memory that emphasize Stanley's exciting adventures – the same ones mentioned in

Rivera's interview — but ignore Stanley's real imperialistic enterprise: his murder and torture of Congolese people, his "racial hatred, and ignominy." Stanley's intimate "connivance" with the slave trade is either woefully forgotten or willfully overlooked.

Most significantly, Stanley's involvement in the slave trade had been elided through the textual and physical memorialization of his rescue of an abolitionist. But the fact that Livingstone was an abolitionist was merely incidental and was at odds with Stanley's ventures in Central Africa. In fact, Stanley repeatedly disclosed fortunes to be made in ivory and slaves, even though these details are absent from contemporaneous accounts (Edgerton 93; McLynn 5–6; Pratt 204–6). And there is a reason for this: in his writing, Stanley deflects blame by juxtaposing Arab slave traders with innocent whites. These overwhelming signposts vilifying Arab traders vis-à-vis imperial White men were symptomatic of fierce British pro-abolition sentiment at the end of the nineteenth century. In this way, Stanley uses his rescue of Livingstone to deny any involvement in slavery. Anti-slavery campaigns of the kind in which Livingstone was involved encouraged a "civilizing mission" that provided the scramble for Africa with the "moral justification" of abolishing the Arab slave trade (Driver 156–7). Stanley likened his enterprise to this kind of "mission" and in 1878, when accused of "selling of labourers into slavery," he justified his ventures by stating his defense of natives and not unlike the way Livingstone "the saint of the British anti-slavery movement" opposed Arab slave trading (Driver 160). To add to this irony, in 1885 he published his infamous account of the establishment of the Congo Free State in the *Anti-Slavery Reporter*, of all places, while simultaneously prolonging the slave trade. Despite all this, one of the most enduring legacies of Stanley's physical memorialization is the catchy inscription "Dr. Livingston, I presume?" which implies his friendship with the noted abolitionist. Thus, even though late nineteenth-century exhibitions about Stanley's adventures often uncritically featured slavery,[4] they emphasized a nostalgic version of history that, to paraphrase James Clifford, perpetuated a hegemonic narrative in line with national and class interests (216). In the twenty-first century, this nationalistic functionality is exemplified in Denbigh's bronze statue, which emphasizes Stanley's and Livingstone's friendship while eliding the conflict between Livingstone's anti-slavery stance and Stanley's slave-trading practices. This memorial of a Stanley-Livingstone alliance absolves Stanley-as-hero of slave driving, while importantly casting slavery as Africa's problem on one hand and as what has rendered the Congo "darkest Africa" on the other.

4.1 Stanley and the Distortion of the "American Congo"

This disjunctive memorialization of slavery in Africa does not so much constitute a historical influence on Rivera's poem as a process of distortion by which racialized peoples and their landscapes are transplanted to Rivera's US Southwest, of all places. In other words, Stanley's representation of the Congo as a site of "darkness" and slavery becomes a reference point for describing non-White populations along the border in the nineteenth century. The processes by which Stanley's quests were mythicized globally are essential to "Searching at Leal Middle School." Stanley provides a bridge for understanding the origins of a Chicano rejection of the Congo: the Congo was invoked to other an equally distorted Mexican population along the Río Grande in one of the most foundational texts for understanding the imperialist project in the US Southwest in American studies: Bourke's infamous "The American Congo" (1894). A Gilded Age frontiersman and West Point lieutenant commissioned to New Mexico, Bourke was indeed obsessed not only with stalking and hunting New Mexican Pueblo Indians and Mexicans, but also with committing their traditions to writing in an ethnography that legitimated genocide. If the Congo became the epitomic site of difference in the nineteenth century, Bourke's all too well-known account, what José David Saldívar terms "the American heart of darkness" (*Border Matters* 164), likened an African frontier to ethnic Mexicans along the border:

> Through the center of this unknown region, fully as large as New England, courses the Rio Grande, which can more correctly be compared to the Congo than to the Nile the moment that the degraded, turbulent, ignorant, and superstitious character of its population comes under examination. (Bourke "The American Congo" 594)

Bourke's cavalier projection of the Congo, which he had never visited, onto the ethnic population on the Mexico-Texas border not only restores colonial racial hierarchies, but also recalls how the othering of the Mexican borderland in the nineteenth century was constructed within the Congo. As Maria Cotera astutely notes, such a "reference to the Congo is not unusual given the popularity of textual explorations of the 'dark continent'" during Bourke's lifetime, especially that of Stanley's, which in turn "bolster[ed] Victorian notions of cultural superiority" and "generate[d] popular support for the colonialist project" (80). Bourke's preconceived notions of "degraded, turbulent, ignorant, and superstitious" people were not only inherited from this imperialism but the synecdoche of an unknown Central African frontier offered the following relation: it justified US empire and its conquest of Mexican peoples inhabiting the

Southwest in the same way Stanley's text encouraged the scramble for Africa. Thus, if Saldívar claims that Bourke's account "effaced the local inhabitants of both continents" (*Border* 167), tracing a transatlantic "Congo" more specifically underscores how these two segments of the Global South were put in relation to one another in order to justify settler colonialism.

The scramble for Africa indirectly shaped Rivera's youth, not only because he read *In Darkest Africa* but also because he uncannily did so as US imperialism in the Congo was being modeled in part on Belgian and British mercenary enterprises.[5] From Stanley to Bourke, or from Belgium and Britain to the US, Rivera's conjuring of African exploration speaks to the festering inextricability of this eerie transatlantic imperialism. Stanley functions as a symbolic proxy for this global takeover, which was metaphorized in Prime Minister Patrice Lumumba's capture in Stanleyville by dictator Joseph Mobutu's CIA-assisted mission. Lumumba was physically and metaphorically erased beyond the limits of the body, as his death involved beatings, flogging, and torture before he was wrecked with a "hail of bullets" and then erased by way of "sulfur acid" eating up his skull (Namikas 3). The Congo then fell under US-supported Mobutu and his anticommunist regime has destabilized the region to this date. Not only did Stanleyville serve as a reminder of British and Belgian imperialism – as Stanley's name branded the city until 1966 – it also served as the precise coordinate where social democracy ceased when Lumumba was seized, denying the Congo its democracy as the name "Stanleyville" promised the continuation of colonialism. The scars of this Africa-centered imperialism would fuel multiculturalism in the US when, prior to the emergence of 1970s neoliberalism, Angela Y. Davis, then a graduate student and participant in the Che-Lumumba Club, publicly endorsed Chicano awakening by demanding a "Lumumba-Zapata" college as Rivera drafted his poetry (S. Ferguson 28–9). At the same time, this period also saw the rise of Anglophone African novels denouncing neocolonization, by authors from Nobel Laureates Wole Soyinka, J. M. Coetzee, and Nadine Gordimer to Chinua Achebe and Ngugi wa Thiong'o, which circulated widely in the US (Irr 121–2). Yet, despite social resistance and literary representation, issues persist as African writers are to this day criticized for catering to Western audiences, who are themselves drawn to "stories about 'darkest Africa'" (Brouillette "African Literary") available under the rubric of World Literature.[6]

A logical conclusion would be that the heritage I have traced explains the uncritical literary representations of Africa in Rivera's poem, but this

4.1 Stanley and the Distortion of the "American Congo" 171

deduction overlooks unambiguous biases about Africa on the *Mexican* side of Rivera's Mexican-American identity, which are especially important given his assertion that *In Darkest Africa* helped him better understand his travels to "America and Latin America" (143). After all, representations of Africa on the southern side of the US border not only involve similar racial and economic prejudices but also contend with much lower circulation of African literary referents. In fact, as Ignacio Sánchez Prado points out, Mexican writer Enrique Serna's short story, "Tesoro viviente" (in *El orgasmógrafo*, 2001) – which cynically depicts a fictional African state producing a national literature that consists of blank pages – places in relief an absent African referent in Mexican culture. This example indeed reinforces a South-South framework in the works of Chicanos and Mexicans alike but not necessarily highlighted or even acknowledged in World Literature's representation of these canons.[7]

Pertinent to Rivera's self-reflexive "Searching at Leal Middle School" is Mexican writer Maria Luisa Puga's semi-autobiographical novel *Las posibilidades del odio/The Possibilities of Hate* (1978), in which an African referent serves as a relational counterpart to lived experience. While Rivera claimed that *reading* about travels to "the dark continent" helped him understand his spatial borderland, Puga admits that her *real* travels to Kenya helped her see her native Mexico:

> Venía con mi novela sobre México a medias, pero eso no fue lo que *hizo que encontrara a México en Nairobi*. . . . Fue otra cosa. Algo que me permitió ver México por primera vez. Las contradicciones, los racismos, los colonialismos de México. La gente con sus mil identidades, los disfraces, las mentiras. El maquillaje tramposo, en una palabra. . . . *Nairobi podía ser descrita en términos mexicanos*: el desastre del turismo, la pobreza, la corrupción, los hoteles gringos, la Ford anunciando en el aeropuerto: Ford invierte en Kenya. (Puga *De cuerpo entero* 47–8)

> I came with my novel about Mexico half-finished, but that is not what *made me find Mexico in Nairobi* . . . It was something else. Something that allowed me to see Mexico for the first time. The contradictions, the racisms, the colonialisms of Mexico. People with their thousands of identities, their disguises, their lies. Their deceiving makeup, in a word. . . . *Nairobi could be described in Mexican terms*: the disaster of tourism, poverty, corruption, American hotels, Ford announcing at the airport: Ford is investing in Kenya.

Kenya for Puga, like Angola for García Márquez in the previous chapter, is eerily recognizable because of the coloniality it shares with the writer's homeland. Thus, in Puga's novel, the racial and economic inequalities of Mombasa, a popular beach destination, remind a Mexican student protagonist of Acapulco's coast, establishing a relation by which Mexican readers can be both repulsed by neoliberalization in Africa and shocked by how familiar it is within their own borders. But despite this promising African-Mexican literary connection in the 1970s, this cross-Atlantic relationship did not evolve and African referents in Mexican literature continue to be limited.

It is key, then, to think of Africa as a ground of relation, not because distorted representations of its "darkness" in the Chicano tradition – or more widely, in Latinx literature – deserve to be criticized, but rather because, as Puga's novel suggests, these different populations in the Global South from East Africa, Mexico, or the Chicano US Southwest, have all been deceived and ruined by modernity's capitalism and greed. The relationship between Mexico and Kenya, or between the Congo and Rivera's US Southwest, enables an essential meditation on how biases implicit in Rivera's poem emerge from a long genealogy of disfiguring representations of subalterns that were devised in Africa *first*, even before crossing the Atlantic, with the Congo as their source. My purpose, then, has been to point out how Rivera's poem is part of a much wider literary memorialization of Africa in general and the Congo specifically. Literature is culpable in this process of distorting Africa and diasporic Africans, as it indeed shapes narratives of empire, whether in textual or physical memorials, that affect the memory of a Latin-African connection. But in what follows, I explain the ways in which Rivera's "Searching at Leal Middle School," far from racializing a US Southwestern space through the specter of Stanley, rather utilizes Stanley's Congo route to familiarize the reader with a racial darkness that reverses Stanley's "darkest Africa."

4.2 Textual Routes in Rivera's "Searching at Leal Middle School" and Slave Route Sites

Rivera's poem "Searching at Leal Middle School" exemplifies the effects of a far-reaching imperialism. In "Searching at Leal Middle School," which was penned in 1975 but only published posthumously in 1990, bilingual descriptions of the "blackness" of the schoolchildren's hair ("black heads"/ "pelo negro") locate the Mexican-American imaginary within an Atlantic spatiotemporality, but focus more specifically on the Congo, materialized in the mentions of "Livingston," "exploration of Africa," and "I became Henry L." Rather than simply expanding a racialized landscape, Rivera's

4.2 Textual Routes in Rivera's "Searching at Leal Middle School" 173

poem seems to use these imperial sites to familiarize the reader with a brownness and blackness that texts like Stanley's *In Darkest Africa* principally othered. This reconception of Stanley-esque "darkness" not only critiques the boundless range of imperialist domination, but also suggests the formation of a Latin-African memory by tracing routes from the present backwards, much like the organizing principle structuring this book.

The imagery of a trail in "Searching at Leal Middle School" recalls the physical paths of heritage trails. The poem starts out by announcing the day's exploration as a journal entry that notes the weather conditions – "foggy," "rainy," and "good for searching" (231). But as such features draw parallels with Stanley's journals, the poetic voice maps the "long / roads, / dusty roads" ahead (232). While the "long / roads" evoke an extended journey of heritage recovery, the imagery of these paths reconstructs a heritage trail over which signposts announce the appearance of Atlantic memory. Walking these trails leads to powerful imagery, both repressed and emergent, as the Chicano searcher sees himself reflected so improbably in an imperial explorer of Africa: "I became Henry L. in the forest" (233). As the ethnopoet relates himself to Stanley, he also translocates "Livingston's exploration of Africa" (232) onto the southwestern middle school. Then, before he inhabits Stanley's body in the Congo, the speaker sees a remarkable array of visions inspired by Stanley's account. The recurring motifs dotting the playground, such as a "dump yard," "smoke," "long sticks," and "half-rotten fruit," are all common in Stanley's memoir.[8] But when the explorer notably comes across Stanley's book in the "dump" (232), the poem also locates a discarded African historiography in the refuse pile of Chicano memory. While approaching the dumpster of marginalized history, the poet-explorer relates that these discarded books detail "Livingston's exploration of Africa" with "maps / blacks." The book's content further tells of "disease" that is seemingly racialized in "red, blue, brown and purple" – a disease that inevitably leads to the book's castoff destiny. Relegated to oblivion by a "rich" hegemony that the poetic voice finds "strange," the book's spatiality further contributes to its neglect in the "dumpster." Over a space "where smoke curled," littered with "half-rotten fruit," Rivera seems to paint a landscape that is as much marginalized as haunted by the trauma of Stanley's distorted equatorial Africa in the emphatically juxtaposed "maps, / blacks" (232–3). While Rivera seems to mimic nineteenth-century discourses about blackness and Africa, they can be read as overturned by his juxtaposition of them with localized and positive descriptors of black hair. In the poetic searching that ensues, the bilingual anaphora "black" and "negro" in the lines "black hair heads/ Cabezas de pelo negro, negro era / Cabezas de pelo negro" ("Heads of black hair, black it was / Heads of black hair," 231) insists on a black mapping of the school's space. Not only is this image of black heads formally echoed in the lines "heads / at the back of heads" in Rivera's poetic summa "Searchers" (225), but the constant references to blackness in "Searching at Leal Middle School" make it familiar and endearing, unlike those in *In Darkest Africa*. For Stanley, blackness was clearly opposed to a White hegemony and thus rendered foreign. Stanley's maritime epic was in fact familiar to European audiences; similarly, in Latin America at the time, treatises such as Domingo Sarmiento's *Facundo* (1845) or Andrés Bello's epic *El Arauco* categorized nonwhite populations, whether it was in the colonized space of the Argentine llanos or the Chilean sierras, as naturally "barbaric." *In Darkest Africa* narrated familiar tropes amidst the African plains and jungles precisely because of the dichotomy between a known "civilization" on the one hand and a blackness figured as "darkness" on the other. While there are important differences between blackness and darkness, Stanley conflates them on the basis of a danger to the nation-state not unlike the nationalist rhetoric against the pejorative term "cabecitas negras" in Argentina against a pro-Perón population descended from indigenous people and working-class immigrants. As was commonplace in texts of exploration, the Congo and its population were deemed both frighteningly foreign and a "burden" to European civilization. And so *In Darkest Africa* describes a contested imperial civilization in the Congo by virtue of the deemed-reprovable actions of "black men." The result is a juxtaposition of White versus other that defamiliarizes a foreign landscape by describing aliens such as "cannibals, incorrigible savages, dwarfs, gorillas" in the most despicably racialized ways and setting them against pious, God-fearing White men (124, 174, 456). It is precisely at this site of difference – the Congo as seen through the imperialist "exploration of Africa" – that Rivera's poetry captures the imagery of blackness but reconstitutes it as affectively familiar.

At the site of the middle school, where the speaker finds "Livingston's exploration of Africa," the poem rehabilitates bodies who currently occupy space and undoes Stanley's racial defamiliarization. At the end of the poem, the speaker promises to seek out this blackness or darkness, stating: "And now, in the future, / I will search for it also / and for a few / cabezas de pelo negro / de ojos oscuros." Underlined in the final lines of his poem is the enjambment of dark eyes and heads ("cabezas de pelo negro / de ojos oscuros," 233) as well as the repetition of smiling dark eyes ("ojos oscuros /

4.2 Textual Routes in Rivera's "Searching at Leal Middle School" 175

ojos sonrientes"), which contrast strongly with Stanley's racialized landscape. Further, against the dialectic of "limit" that Stanley invokes to demarcate both colonial territory and Central Africa's captivity in "the limit of [a] territory,"[9] Rivera's poem reworks the use of that term in its final "limitlessness." Through a borderlessness projected onto the diacope of "ojos sin límites / ojos oscuros / ojos sonrientes, / juguetones" ("eyes without limits / dark eyes / smiling eyes/ playful," 231), the poem recalls its opening lines in which racial identification expands globally within Leal Middle School. Most importantly, as Rivera entangles the schoolchildren's black hair and eyes with a transatlantic exploration, his final repetition metaphorically mimics the *retracing* of Stanley's text. Instead of mimicking a discursive praxis in this retracing, however, Rivera's poetic repetition insists on recentering a blackness no longer shackled to Stanley's racialized descriptors around smiling and playful faces. Decolonizing a Stanley-esque spatiality, Rivera's positive darkness smiles in the face of a positivist "darkest Africa," as the "darkness" of smiling children becomes desired and comforting. In this way, Rivera-as-Stanley inhabits Stanley's imperial eyes to underscore how to view a historical Congo differently. In doing so, he moves blackness from a category of obscured and negated identity to an open and playful freedom of possibility.

Beyond this familiarization of blackness through the endearing features of the schoolchildren, the repetition of the children's black hair emphasizes a relation to "the exploration of Africa" that reinforces the poem's transglobal graphing. If *In Darkest Africa* defamiliarized blackness and darkness and represented both as frightful, Rivera's reconfiguration of these operating terms suggests an expansion of their meaning in the twenty-first century. The poem's resignification recalls Achille Mbembe's notion that, rather than seeing blackness as a term denoting exploitation of African labor in the capitalist era, it ought to be resignified and read in a "fungible" way across the world (*Critique* 6). The repetition of the Spanish word "negro" – which means "black" but is quite unlike the same US American term in its connotations – does indeed revisit Stanley's reviled Africa at Leal Middle School, but does so through an antiphrasis of the term "black" that turns racialization on its head. Resignified and cherished through the innocence of children, an endearing darkness is also projected onto the schoolchildren's guardian, Doña Cuquita. As the poem's speaker looks up at her, he reflects on her "cobwebbed eyelashes" that "could not hide her dark eyes / ojos oscuros *que fascinan*" ("dark eyes *that fascinate*," 233, emphasis added). In other words, a caring Doña Cuquita renders blackness at once endearing and wondrous, as it marks a desire for *relation*.

Thus far, I have explained how the poem works against Stanley even as it retraces his exploration. But what is still so telling in terms of the poem's textual memorialization is how Leal Middle School functions as a site of memory in which the Congo is distorted. The only memory the poetic speaker has of this disfigured Congo is through a text he finds in the schoolyard's dump. By visiting this discharged *text* and reading its *sites*, the speaker adds another journal entry. Channeling Stanley again, he writes: "Monday 11," "Thursday, foggy day / a good day for finding at / Leal Middle School" (233). The searcher then faces Doña Cuquita once again and, reflective, wonders, "Did she know about Livingston? / Through the smoke" (233). Here, memorialization of a Black Atlantic remains somewhat distorted, as if viewed through fumes. But the question is even more significant for the distortion of Africa in Chicano literary memory. The speaker's desire for a relation with a Black Atlantic hangs on this eternal if ambiguous question: Did she know about Africa? Curiously, the darkness marking Cuquita's eyes – like the cabezas negras dotting the schoolyard – locate Livingstone's exploration and insert this relation into the Chicano imaginary. Yet the poem's speaker not only doubts the existence of collective Atlantic memory, but gazes upon it "through" the cloudiness of "smoke." Acknowledging that an imperialist apparatus conspired to render Latin-African memory ambivalent at best or irrelevant at worst, the speaker insists throughout the poem on the impossibility of its complete recovery. With the repetition of blackness at the beginning and the final diaphora of "Livingston" as bookends, along with a middle part that refers to "the exploration of Africa," the poem structurally memorializes Africa albeit through a veil of smoke. While the speaker traces a racialized path that leads to some historical recovery, a rejected imperialist book about Africa remains in the refuse pile – where it arguably should – as does a Chicano sense of relation with a distorted history of the Congo. This Atlantic site of memory haunts the lines of the poem, as if insisting that a Latin-African solidarity be restored despite the Stanley-esque distortions that render the Chicano connection with the Congo murky, as though seen through smoke.

If I have argued that "Searching at Leal Middle School" can commemorate a rehabilitated darkness through a long process of Central African memorialization, I end my analysis of Rivera by explaining how said conjuring behaves as a textual memorial via spatial analysis of Stanley's and Livingstone's memorialization in Africa. The disjuncture between statues of Stanley in Kinshasa and Denbigh affects our reading of Rivera's poem because of the festering public presence of imperialism in

4.2 Textual Routes in Rivera's "Searching at Leal Middle School" 177

the Global South. After Mobutu's reign spurred anti-colonialists to topple all relics of empire in the Democratic Republic of the Congo, Stanley's bronze feet were cut off, as the statue fell awkwardly to the ground. His detached feet have been interpreted as symbolizing punishment for severing the limbs of Congolese people during the terrifying Belgian reign, and are eerily reminiscent of a similar vandalizing act in which the feet of a statue of conquistador Juan de Oñate in Alcande, New Mexico, were also cut off (his Basque name means "at the foot of the mountain pass").[10] But, despite this form of decolonial forgetting, Stanley's memorial was rehabilitated for Kinshasa's Institute of National Museums, which incidentally stands over what was formerly known as Mount Stanley. As with debates concerning the revival of Leopold's memory in Belgium,[11] Stanley's memory in the Congo inflames opinions on opposite ends of the spectrum.

On the one hand, Stanley represents "the chilling life of a man many Africans would rather *forget*" (Mutua 172–3, emphasis added). This decolonial sentiment underscores the need for a clean slate so that African nation-states can move on from the pains of imperial memory and suggests that allusions to Stanley, such as those in Rivera's poem, should also be forgotten. The fear of placing a statue of him in such a prominent cultural role – in a museum in the country's capital – is linked to the effects of uncritical memorialization. Especially since memorials tend to cleanse and crystallize Eurocentric history or, in Kirk Savage's terms, "purify the past of any continuing conflict that might disturb the carefully constructed national narrative" perpetuated "by white male elite[s]" (2). The most compelling objection to rehabilitating colonizers and imperialists for heritage projects is that it seems to vindicate their hegemonic purpose somewhat. On the other hand, rehabilitating the memory of an imperialist offers an opportunity to "fight to reduce the scars," as the director of Kinshasa's National museum, Joseph Ibongo, affirms. After all, a memorial to colonization is only as apologetic as its focus allows. A prominent African example is the Malawi UNESCO-sponsored trail that memorializes Livingstone but focuses on the slave trade. In fact, UNESCO's aims with the "Malawi Slave Routes and Dr. David Livingstone Trail" is both to underscore an underemphasized segment of the slave trade in East Africa (as opposed to the more noticeable ones in West and Central Africa), and to accentuate British involvement in its abolition. Even though this trail perpetuates a White savior complex – underscoring Livingstone's valiant efforts to halt the slave trade and a British Commissioner, Sir Harry Johnston, as the ultimate hero that triumphed[12] – it is the structure of this trail that interests its pairing with Rivera's poem.

I argue that the poem uses the neoliberal structures against itself to create a Latin-African space of its own. This is because Malawi's Livingstone trail consists of numerous paths that were used to capture and enslave people in the nineteenth century, but today, pilgrims walk these dusty roads to see a former market, graves, and forts involved in the trade that offer places to pause and contemplate.[13] The trail culminates at a fig tree where Livingstone orchestrated a pact to halt slave trafficking between Nkhotakota and Stanley's Congo, commemorated with a plaque. Rather than adulating Livingstone – unlike the statue at David Livingstone Center in Blantyre, Scotland, where Livingstone is depicted as rescuing a man from a lion– the trail instead offers moments of quiet introspection typical of the UNESCO Slave Routes. It is in this vein that I am interested in linking this lesser-known UNESCO Slave Route to Rivera's equally lesser-known poem as a means of considering the ways in which both text and physical site memorialize a Latin-Africa that challenges understandings of Rivera's place in World Literature.

The rhetorical strategies embedded in the textual memorials of Rivera's poem – like the markers along a Slave Route heritage trail that enable the pilgrim to meditate on the effects of the slave trade – offer an opportunity to pause at and contemplate a Latin-African memory. In other words, reading Rivera's trail through the lens of the UNESCO Slave Route that memorializes the very protagonists of Rivera's poem opens up a path for introspection that rehabilitates or even extends a relation of darkness between Chicanos and Congolese on opposite ends of the Atlantic divide. Like a visitor to the dusty, contemplative roads of Malawi's Slave Route, Rivera revisits his past in the poem. In the lines, "Yet I became lost in my past / I saw myself and became / each one for an instant," Rivera inhabits the bodies of schoolchildren to reroute his own history. As he embodies the children with black hair and dark eyes, he becomes "the student, silent, staring / beyond myself, backwards / to joys so long forgotten of long / roads / dusty roads / that went on forever." Following a path of memory, the poem's speaker arrives at Africa in the dumpster, its exploration both the catalyst of his search and the object of his gaze. It is precisely this path of introspection that connects to the national and global past allegorized by the poem's textual sites, "Livingston," "Henry," and "exploration of Africa," which conjure the scramble for Africa in the Congo and the US's imperial role there.

The enjambments that lead to the sites of Livingstone, Africa, or Stanley – such as "Away from the dump yards / where smoke curled and / with long sticks we turned and turned and / find half-rotten fruit / to be washed and eaten / and books – Livingston's exploration of Africa" – denote pause and

4.2 Textual Routes in Rivera's "Searching at Leal Middle School" 179

are not unlike Malawi's path dotted with graves, markets, or forts that offer places to reflect on the slave trade and delay one's arrival at the Route's culmination. The pauses in the poem offer reflection, too, because like points of interest along a trail, they interrupt the flow of movement to allow deeper connection with the past the trail offers. In fact, this aesthetic move is reminiscent of Yi-Fu Tuan's concept of contemplative space. As he explains, "it is by thoughtful reflection that the elusive moments of the past draw near to us in present reality and gain a measure of permanence" (148). The trail's marked sites and the poem's enjambments offer ways to harness the elusiveness of memory. Similarly, the poem isolates these Atlantic sites with em dashes: "and books – Livingston's exploration of Africa, / the maps, / the blacks, / I became Henry L. in the forest – ." This rhetorical strategy isolates the more specific locators of Central Africa from the more abstract within a single segment to reveal a specific spatiotemporality. The move is not unlike the structure of a "travel story" in which, as Michel de Certeau explains, are "marked by the 'citation' of the places" said journey visits (120). In the poem, Rivera "cites" or "marks out" Stanley's specific locators dotted along his trail, which include terminology such as "the maps / the blacks," but his poem culminates in a resignified blackness: its final lines release blackness from imperialist racialization in the lines, "And now, in the future, / I will search for it also / and for a few / cabezas de pelo negro / de ojos oscuros," where the speaker wants to search for Black features moving forward.

If the poem's speaker constructs a textual path from refuse material in the line, "I searched for words in the dump," the rejected textual memorial of *In Darkest Africa* indeed creates a path for introspection. This relation of exploration recovers subaltern stories precisely because walking the trails of the past disjoints the absolute memorial of History. It is a process similar to what Glissant describes as "a relation of errantry" that "opens up other avenues and soon help[s] to correct whatever simplifying, ethnocentric exclusions may have arisen" (*Poetics* 21). For Rivera, Stanley's textual memorial conveys, rather, the illusion of a nineteenth-century brand of racialization that can only be "corrected" by going "backwards," as the poem suggests. In the poem's localized Congo, a relatable common denominator emerges from the colonial continuities of Atlantic historiography. Disrupting Stanley's logocentrism, Rivera interrogates processes of capitalist exploitation under the guise of social progress. Rather than taking on a syntactical frame, the discursive register of Rivera's relational model in "Searching at Leal Middle School" reconstructs an ethnic origin on both sides of the Atlantic. For Chicanos, as Rivera's text seems to convey, progress is not limited to tracing history back to the kind of ethnopoetry expertly textualized in his summa "The Searchers" ("in our solitude / we found our very being / We moved into each other's / almost carefully, deliberately" 223). Rather, Rivera's Latin-Africa traces African historiographical continuities that remain indelible in the landscape, still noticeable behind the veil of "smoke." If, as Ramón Saldívar once stipulated, Rivera's canonical ...*y no se lo tragó la tierra* served as a "memorial to ... the forgotten history of a peoples' oppression" (*Chicano* 77), I argue that these poetic textual memorials in "Searching at Leal Middle School" also conjure, even unconsciously, a "people's oppression" in solidarity with Stanley's distorted Congo.

I want to make a final point about the World Literature to which Rivera contributes. The Chicano writer has been variously characterized as reconstituting Chicano identity as a whole. As J. Saldívar claims, his work aims at "reconstructing a holistic sense of self and group identity" (*Dialectics* 61). I view this holism as encompassing not only the Latinx experience, but a "Chicanidad" that is far more cosmopolitan, more Atlantic-oriented, than meets the eye. Indeed, this "holistic" frame instead deconstructs an occidentalist transatlantic literary memory. Rivera's poetry can be read as retracing Stanley's Atlantic routes – and their connection to physical memorials across the Atlantic – thus memorializing distortions of Africa and diasporic Africans beyond hemispheric borders. Not only is a racialization that originates in Africa embedded in the poem, destabilizing Eurocentric transatlantic study, but this positioning also has implications for World Literature. Rivera's polemic poem places him in an Atlantic memorialization network that not only locates Chicano literature in relation to the global aims of World Literature, but also challenges World Literature itself. For if Rivera is usually conceived as an ethnopoet within a strictly delimited US Southwest, his poem's retracing of the Congo defiantly stretches the boundaries of a Chicano literary genealogy by transplanting this Central African region to a poetic US Southwest. This move not only redefines Rivera as a beyond-regional writer, but also suggests a re-cartography of the Atlantic and Latin-African connections that World Literature has critically missed.

4.3 Rudolfo Anaya: The US Southwest Plantocracy and *Bless Me, Ultima*'s Maritime Frontier

If Rivera's poem reveals a sociohistorical Latin-African link through the textual site of a nineteenth-century scramble for Africa, I now turn to colonial African continuities embedded in a Chicano classic, Anaya's *Bless*

Me, Ultima. In the novel, not only healing but also witchcraft and the pagan deity of the golden carp are central; I compare such markers with their colonial equivalents in the Congo. Texts by two missionaries engaged in the Congo region, Sandoval but mainly Cavazzi, help me identify the African roots of Anaya's tale. I thus revise previous interpretations of both the novel's healing practices and its pagan magical carp as exclusively indigenous. Mentions of "voodoo," clay dolls, devilish trances, and the golden carp betray an Atlantic haunting embedded in the former plantocracy of the novel's US Southwest. Thus, a previously unidentified African influence permeates a canonical Chicano text, thereby demonstrating a Chicano-African relationality that previous critics have elided along with the naïve ways in which Anaya represents these African influences as "black magic," "witchery," or even "evil" in the novel. In tracing the African roots of the novel through the lens of memorialization, it becomes clear that Anaya borrows from colonial writings about Africa to make room for an Afro-Chicano connection that rehabilitates a Latin-African solidarity. As I will explain, transatlantic markers in Anaya's novel, such as the golden carp, are reiterated not only in colonial texts that distort African golden carp worship but also in both the work of contemporary Congolese writer Sony Labou Tansi and in the oral proverbs of a prominent UNESCO Slave Route. Reading Anaya's golden carp beyond its indigenous formation, and instead through this deity's inscriptions in the Atlantic World, helps rehabilitate the "darkness" the novel confers on paganism. In addition to its revisionist value for Chicano literary genealogy, my interpretation of this novel expands the notion of a Latin-African connection in new directions. While this chapter invites critics to place Chicano writing in a Global South network, this "South"-South framework ultimately challenges readings of an exemplary Chicano representative in World Literature as a regional folklorist whose work neglects the Black Atlantic.

One of the most translated and widely acclaimed novels in the Chicano literary tradition, the bildungsroman *Bless Me, Ultima*, which won the Quinto Sol prize, is set in an isolated town where Antonio Márez Luna's innocent boyhood ends and he struggles with the foundations of his Catholic faith. This struggle begins when the healer Ultima comes to live with his family and takes Antonio under her wing. During this time, not only does Antonio confront the Vodun-like practices of both Ultima and their antagonists – Tenorio Trementino and his alleged daughter witches – but also comes into contact with a pagan belief system that involves worshipping a fish. Antonio's soul-searching journey into manhood after wartime occurs as his village attempts to close in on itself, so that those considered alien face spectacular resistance. For example, the villagers perceive Ultima's remedies as witchcraft. Such rejection is ever more emphatic when it comes to the repressed manifestation of the golden carp deity, which diametrically opposes the Catholicism Antonio's mother wills on him, as she wants him to become a priest. Ultima's cures as well as the myth of the golden carp explicitly question dualities in the Chicano tradition, but implicitly trace an undeniably colonial system of distortion that ignites fear and repression. Most significantly, the marginalized pagan deity's color dialectic – the golden carp and its nemesis, the black bass – calls into question the hemispheric origins of Chicanos' excising of darkness. In the end, as if to prevent further infiltration from an Atlantic World order, the distortions of these spiritual practices drive the narrative to burn its African traces when Antonio heeds Ultima's last wish to destroy her herbs as the story comes to a close. Though the novel seems to deny African memory – echoing Rivera's poem of an Africa seen through smoke – Anaya's novel presents a faint Latin-Africa and moments in which these faint traces can counterdiscursively rehabilitate their colonial distortions.

Born in 1937 in the southwestern desert town of Pastura, Anaya drew inspiration for his stories from New Mexican folklore of his native land. Margarite Fernández Olmos calls this influence a "primal memory" that has been "touched" by the "physical and spiritual landscape" of his environment, which is quite far from the ocean (1, 18–19). Often using the vehicle of the pastoral to underscore the rich etiology and mythmaking traditions of nuevomexicanos, he has often been critiqued as caricaturing Chicanos' "love for fantasy" (Lamadrid *"De vatos y profetas"* 202). For instance, his noteworthy publications – from *Heart of Aztlan* (1976), to *The Man Who Could Fly and Other Stories* (2006), and with his Sonny Baca mystery series and even children's books – all seem to embrace an apolitical and isolationist stance, as opposed to contemporaneous texts featuring fierce Chicano political activism. *Bless Me, Ultima*, for instance, is so embedded in an insular, quasi-fantastical world that the novel has been criticized simultaneously for its extreme local folklore, on the one hand, and magical universalism, on the other.[14] Theresa Delgadillo aptly notes that the novel is anchored "in local history and a context of curanderismo" (159). Yet, perhaps most tellingly, *Bless Me, Ultima* registers a borderland space in between these oppositions – a buried transatlantic space hardly recognizable in the landlocked geography of New Mexico itself.

Recently, Anaya's corpus has been read as quite transatlantic. In a recent anthology on Anaya's corpus, Roberto Cantú interprets *Bless Me, Ultima* as "a long reflection on world empires" that encompass the three continents of Europe, Africa, and Asia (19). Similarly, Monika Kaup emphasizes the novel's "hemispheric continuities of the New World baroque" (153), underscoring the text's notable transatlantic and North African moor influences. Moreover, while Kaup's exegesis locates Anaya's interest in Muslim Iberia, Horst Tonn argues that the novel "seeks to relate [the regional and local] to broader formations of the transnational and the global" (242). Uncannily, both Kaup and Tonn read Anaya into cosmopolitanism, recalling Glissant either directly or indirectly: Kaup explicitly invokes Glissant to dismantle the "single center of Christian theology" (171), while Tonn reads *Bless Me, Ultima* "not [as] foundational, but *relational*" (242, emphasis added). But this worldly reading of Anaya's possible transatlanticism via Caribbean aesthetics is hardly new. J. Saldívar first used Glissant's *relation* specifically to enlarge the global framework of Chicano *costumbrismo* and undo the "sealed" imaginary of the US-Mexico borderland in Bourke's justification for the destruction of New Mexico's Pueblo Indians. Recalling Bourke's relational Congo – this time applied to Anaya's home region – visualizes US imperial culture as "competing mappings of global capital, the multiple discourses of the Black Atlantic and the submarine discourses" (*Border* 165). Indeed, J. Saldívar's "submarine discourses" refer to Glissant, who, in his *Caribbean Discourse*, encapsulates a capitalist system that forces unknown names down in the phrase "history is submarine."[15] To recover these submerged experiences requires understanding both the ubiquitous trans-plantocratic system and faint diasporic discourses in texts.

Precluding such an excavation of Anaya's *Bless Me, Ultima*, however, has been the traditional model of regionalism, which resists claims to the cosmopolitan. As Tonn argues in his explanation of the global references in Anaya's work, "[t]o claim that an 'ethnic text' has universal relevance may weaken the power of that text to articulate cultural difference" (245). But a focus on how Anaya's novel broadens transhemispheric boundaries privileges planetary unity over fearful isolationism. Worldly connections between Anaya and oceanic historiographies, far from diluting the local setting of ethnicity, promote a holistic understanding of subjugated knowledge under a centuries-old capitalistic world system that affects both the regional and the global. After all, even nativist texts such as Bourke's "shows in decidedly spatial terms, how US imperial culture [was] irrevocably local and global" already in the nineteenth century (Saldívar *Border* 165). While this kind of comparative scholarship on Anaya specifically stretches the maritime boundaries of Chicano literary studies, the regional era absent from such global readings of Anaya's dialogic text is precisely the plantocracy of Anaya's "primal memory."

While imperialism is a noted spatiotemporality affecting Chicanos, the slave trade is not usually at the center of the Chicano imaginary, much less graphing Chicanos into a Latin-African Atlantic nexus. In terms of Anaya's southwestern region, this rejection of a Black Atlantic emerges from the fact that, historically, former African slaves "found themselves being swept into an indigenous world . . . and assimilated fully into native communities" (Vinson and Restall *Black Mexico* 10). Historian Martha Menchaca has traced the long history of slavery along the Rio Grande: "[t]he migration of people of African descent to the Southwest began in 1598, when the first colony was established in New Mexico" (22). Informed by chronicles like that of Captain Gaspar Pérez de Villagrá, Menchaca reports that although Black communities lived among and socialized with settlers, these colonial relations often "distorted events by deliberately ignoring the accomplishments of people of color by documenting events in generalities to hide specific information" (84–5). In fact, as Luis Leal mentions, one of New Mexico's famous men of letters was El Negrito Poeta, coincidentally "the son of Congolese parents brought to Mexico as slaves" (Leal and Stavans 330), reinforcing that while the plantocratic dimensions of the US Southwest are manifested in literature, they are also directly tied to the Congo through the transatlantic slave trade. As the aftermath of slavery bled into the imperialist era following Texas's independence, admitting to African ancestry meant losing land entitlements previously ceded to afromestizos by the Mexican government (Menchaca 21). Such spatial repression led to the unrepresentability of blackness in the Southwest, to the point that Anaya lamented literary afrolatinidad's erasure in Chicano perception nearly a century later.[16] Nevertheless, in contemporary analyses of Anaya's corpus, this vector is still significantly overlooked.

In his equally global reading of Anaya's corpus, Cantú has argued that *Bless Me, Ultima* registers primal memory in "maritime metaphors" that derive from Spanish-Mexican connections and "allusions to the Mediterranean and the Gulf of Mexico" (13). While I certainly agree that Anaya's text is filled with dozens of these oceanic allusions, I argue that these textual connections to European maritime prowess also evoke involvement in and relations to Africa and the enslavement of its people. Whether or not Anaya was inspired by myths of Spanish moors and their proximity to Africa[17] or by colonial imposition of Christian theology during the plantocracy, *Bless Me, Ultima*'s curanderismo as a feared praxis and Antonio's belief in a golden carp that is incompatible with Catholicism express colonial distortions rooted in Africa and the Congo specifically. While I have briefly traced the plantocratic genealogy of Anaya's New Mexico, the influences I unearth in the novel emerge from even earlier colonial relations by Spanish missionary Sandoval in West Africa and, significantly, Italian missionary Cavazzi in the Congo during the era of the slave trade. As I have described in Chapter 1, these seventeenth-century narratives represent Vodun trances as monstrous, but particularly demonize the myth of the golden carp and other sea creatures. By revisiting the colonial and African roots of this distortion in language, I disentangle curanderismo's relation with the Atlantic World's slave trade, first in the Caribbean and by extension at its African site of origin. In this vein, I follow a trail of distorted representations of the golden carp from Africa to the Americas to show how the rejection of a Latin-Africa might be both understood and rehabilitated. I end by questioning not only the interminable relationship between a Chicano text and an Atlantic World order, but also the mutually constitutive relations between a slave trade memorial and a borderland text.

4.4 A Trail of Witches and Curanderas

Set against a backdrop of World War II, *Bless Me, Ultima* is more concerned with cultural assimilation and ethnic revival than the contemporaneous 1960s Chicano movement. In fact, even before that movement, Anaya's bildungsroman centered on cultural pressures that lead nuevomexicanos to deny or repress their indigenous roots (Kárai 279) or any spiritual praxis outside an occidentalist system. In the novel, although Ultima's ultimate ethnic origins are unknown, her spiritual duality flirts with paganism. She attends church but does not take communion, and her enigmatic healing practices without a definite origin mystify her to the point that she is later accused of being a witch. As Antonio explains, "because this curandera had this power she was misunderstood and often suspected of practicing witchcraft herself" (4). Even though Antonio's mother's familiarity with Ultima leads her to trust her foreign treatments and bring her into the household, the same cannot be said about the community. Ultima's curanderismo only involves "herbs and remedies of the ancients" to "heal the sick" (4), but the town is so walled in by "cuentos of the people" and enwrapped in "tales of evil done by brujas" (4) that Ultima's healing practices drive Antonio's sister Theresa to ask if "it [is] true [that Ultima] is a witch?" (8). Not only is Ultima's medicinal knowledge rendered frightening, but when Antonio's uncle Lucas grows very ill,

Antonio also regrets that "[t]he church would not allow my grandfather to let [Ultima] use [her] powers" (101), underscoring the fear materialized in the church's prohibition. But in a Southwest where "la Llorona lurked" (81), "dances for el Diablo" abound (87), women cross themselves when "the names of witches" are invoked (89), and people fear being turned into frogs, coyotes, or owls (90, 116), these fears seem projected by colonial distortions. The dread of animal transformation in Anaya's novel can be partly traced to *nahua* traditions of shape-shifting documented in the Inquisition trials in colonial Mexico. This distortion led Francisco Lomelí to conclude that "much of the literature traced back to Mexican literature, through colonial chronicles, memoirs, accounts, and other writings, clearly affected what became the American Southwest" (183). In this vein, it bears considering that, as Mexican anthropologist Gonzalo Aguirre Beltrán has noted, shape-shifting myths were symptomatic of the fears colonial Mexico harbored regarding healers, many of whom were Black (97–100).

Compellingly, while African or indigenous healing practices were demonized in the Inquisition, on the northern side of the Mexican border, they were also related back to the Congo. Bourke, in his infamous "The American Congo," also describes New Mexican healers as "professional 'curanderas,' or female herb doctors" and their trade as "nefarious" or "weird pharmacy," calling their skill that of a "professional 'bruja' or witch" (606). Bourke justified his ensuing destruction of the Pueblo Indians of New Mexico through the very same healing practices and medicinal knowledge he sought to preserve, as he collected "notes, plants, animals, and pictographic artifacts of American Indian and Mexican-American cultures" (Saldívar *Border Matters* 162). Even against this backdrop of apparent admiration, healers' spirituality indirectly threatened civil society. But even earlier, what Ramón Gutiérrez calls "perverse stereotypes" and "racist caricatures" were crafted in southwestern colonial relations where witch trials abounded.[18] This history is reflected in Anaya's novel when people demand Ultima's head one night, screaming "Give us the bruja!" (137). But witchcraft trials in the Southwest, Gutiérrez explains, were just as much a revelation of colonial "anxiety" in the area that is today the Mexico-US borderland as a distortion "through the eyes of Spanish colonial priests and secular officials" (40).

Importantly, Inquisition-led witch hunts also move diasporically. Eerily, the townspeople's gathering to capture Ultima recall the Salem Witch Trials in which Afro-Caribbean slaves like mythical Tituba were accused of sorcery. In their Caribbeanist reading of the novel, Fernández

Olmos and Lizabeth Paravisini-Gebert compare the impediments that keep Ultima from practicing her cures to Antillean populations forced into a colonial religion. Because "Anaya's New World identity responds to [a] religious syncretism," they explain that the novel foregrounds how "the native peoples and others were forced to accept a foreign belief system," for instance Catholicism, "and went underground to avoid persecution" (247). This comparison is not without a colonial Caribbean grounding. In fact, such religious syncretism undergirds novels by two Chicana writers, Alicia Gaspar de Alba's *Calligraphy of the Witch* and Emma Pérez's *Forgetting the Alamo, or, Blood Memory*, where foreign and linguistically differing afromestizas are accused of being "witches" for their spiritual and healing practices in the context of New England and Texas, respectively. The presence of colonially distorted Atlantic curanderas in these contemporary novels not only reiterates the relevance of the Atlantic World's spirituality as a site of racial difference in the Chicano imaginary, but also extends this imaginary's relation with Caribbean literary texts. Literary representations of healers-deemed-witches are a common feature in the work of established authors, such as Martinican Maryse Condé's Salem Trials in *Moi, Tituba sorcière* (1986), or Cuban Mayra Montero's representation of a Vodun priest, Zulé, and her apparent blood sacrifices in *Del rojo de su sombra* (1992). In fact, contemporary Latinx Caribbean novels – such as Dominican-American Ana-Maurine Lara's *Erzulie's Skirt* (2006), Puerto Rican Irete Lazo's *The Accidental Santera* (2008), and Dahlma Llanos-Figueroa's *Daughters of the Stone* – feature such healers as their protagonists. In all of these either French-, Spanish-, or English-language Caribbean examples, a woman who practices trances that originate in Africa pushes back against unrelenting repression.

While such spell-like trances ground many Caribbean novels, they are usually considered less relevant to the Chicano literary tradition. Anaya's novel, however, shares this thematic thread and precedes the contemporary Chicano examples of it by Gaspar de Alba and Pérez. *Bless Me, Ultima* sets up this diasporic trope when it invokes a spell reminiscent of the Vodun-like trances at the center of African slaves' religious praxis during the plantocracy that the US Southwest shared with the Caribbean. Although Ultima's race is never alluded to, a Caribbean-derived trance unexpectedly appears in Anaya's novel when Ultima cures Antonio's uncle Lucas. This happens after the novel's antagonist Tenorio Trementino, a play on the Spanish word for "tremendous," puts a spell on Lucas. While Ultima's cure emphasizes the shortcomings of Western medicine and instead embraces practices condemned during colonial times, Ultima "prepares the herbs and oils she would need to affect her cure" (88–9) by placing Antonio in a trance to aid his uncle. During this time, Antonio reflects on his trance:

> My eyelids grew very heavy ... My gaze fixed on my poor uncle and I could not tear my glance away. I was aware of what happened in the room, but my senses did not seem to respond to commands. Instead I remained in that waking dream. ... his face showed pain, my body too felt pain. I could almost taste the oily hot liquid. I saw his convulsions and my body too was seized with aching cramps. ... our bodies did not seem separated by the distance. *We dissolved into each other, and we shared a common struggle against the evil within.* ... "Dios mío!" were his first words, and with those words the evil was wrenched from his interior. Green bile poured from his mouth, and finally he vomited a huge ball of hair. It fell to the floor, hot and steaming and wiggling like live snakes. (104–7, emphasis added)

First, I would like to stress the Caribbean notion of a *relation* as a curative measure in the term "shared struggle against the evil within" that evokes Glissant's meaning of "Relation."[19] That is, Antonio and his uncle's shared solidarity against the infection is what ultimately cures the uncle, and it helps Antonio understand an alternate spirituality obviously at odds with Catholicism. Most importantly, this relational spell invokes Vodun-like trances that slaves practiced during the plantocracy and that are central to the novels by Condé, Montero, and even Lara mentioned above.

Although Antonio's spellbound relation points to a syncretic integration, Ultima's healing method bears traces of Vodun practice that are not necessarily described as positive. In fact, any elements that resemble Vodun must be expelled, as the novel describes how "bile poured from his mouth" and Lucas spit out a ball of hair "wriggling like live snakes" (107). Although snakes are a sacred deity in Vodun praxis, in the novel they are far from revered; the "snakes" that Lucas ejects from his stomach, along with the "green bile" that he has to exorcise from his body, might even signify the epitome of sin that marks the "evil within" Lucas according to Judeo-Christian faith. I want to consider carefully what this rejection signifies in a novel that portrays Caribbean spirituality as Catholic doctrine's frightful other. In fact, when word gets out that Antonio was under a trance, his friends from school chastise him with "'Do magic" and "Voodoo!" (116). This *cura*, along with the Trementina sisters' "pour[ing] [a beheaded rooster's] blood into a pot" while chanting incantations (90–1) runs parallel to Vodun or Yoruba rituals in Caribbean literary tradition but rather than being represented as restorative, they are linked to black magic.[20] Moreover, the Trementina sisters' hostile performance is viewed as

4.4 A Trail of Witches and Curanderas 189

a "Black Mass in honor of the devil" (90). Subjects repeatedly "rumored to be brujas" (91) are "known to make clay dolls and prick them with needles" (92), recalling Bourke's "nefarious" brujas (606).

However, traditions of Vodun in the Southwest not only relate to the Caribbean through a shared plantational history, but their textual traces also uncannily relate to colonial texts, written in what is today the Congo or at Vodun's birthplace in Benin (as I explained in Chapter 1), that describe Vodun as "black magic." The rhetoric of difference in these colonial texts from West and Central Africa makes manifest the Atlantic origins of distortions of Vodun in the Chicano imaginary, such as those displayed in Anaya's novel. These discourses of racialized religious practice that originate in Africa further cement the indirect ways in which, unlike Díaz's reversal of the dark-light dichotomy in "Monstro," Anaya actually insists upon a maleficent darkness. For example, the novel evokes, "[t]he horror of darkness had never been so complete" (24) and depicts a "dark valley" in which the Trementina sisters become witches dancing "in the forms of balls of fire" (53). But while a kind of racialization first developed in Africa likewise informs the novel's excision of a darkness or "black magic," it also challenges the idea that these rejected practices are exclusively indigenous. Stretching the historiography of Vodun further, the snake evoked in the novel indeed memorializes West African religious praxis, its colonial distortion, and apparent resistance to it in the Americas.

It becomes clear that an African haunting informs Ultima's "voodoo" trance, awakening fears of the demonic, as she too "stuck a pin into each doll" (105) for her enemies. She also has Antonio wear an herbal pouch around his neck (129) identified as "Bolsas de mandinga" traced back to eighteenth-century healers in West and Central Africa (Sweet *Recreating* 180–1). While the markers of the snake, trances, and "witches" are othered, the novel's description of them as palpably evil also invokes the colonial gaze that graphed the African landscape prior to the establishment of a southwestern plantocracy. In Sandoval's relación of the Vodun-practicing Gold Coast in *De instauranda Aethiopum salute* (1627), observations of "the ceremonies of the pagodes, the sacrifices, festivities, and on the end of this many spells, incantations, and a great deal of magic art" convey the formalism of black magic.[21] He attributes these spiritual practices to the "ignorance of the gentile" and categorizes their "sects" as "damned" on various occasions,[22] and even represents them as demonic.[23] The purpose of invoking colonial language here is not to propose the obvious; that racialization took place in Africa as it did in the Americas. Rather, these colonial distortions – etched so neatly into a Chicano text – suggest that the ominous fears of witchcraft in the novel stem from the very specific spatiotemporality of slavery in Africa.

This notion is most clearly demonstrated in Giovanni Antonio Cavazzi's colonial writings, which, when representing African rituals as demonic, remark on macabre adoration of snakes. Traveling on behalf of the Portuguese crown into the Congolese valley in 1659, this Capuchin missionary dwells on colonial Africans' spirituality and portrays practitioners of it as "abhorred" ("aborrecidas") and "abominable" ("as torna abomináveis"), ultimately justifying their enslavement. Mentions of "witchcraft," "ignorance," "damned," and "demonic," which appear occasionally in Sandoval's report, instead dominate Livro 1 of Cavazzi's relación, including in the following example:

> Strange things are to be described by my pain about the *customs* in these three kingdoms, and my religious leaning cannot overcome the *abhorred* issue, either because their *lack of civilization* renders them *abominable*, or because the difference of their customs from our own makes them *incredible*.[24]

Such dichotomies between civilization and the "strange," "abhorred," "abominable," and "incredible" lack of it not only precede the nineteenth-century Manifest Destiny embedded in Bourke's racialized Mexican-American healers, but also demonizes African spirituality from within the continent. To make this paradigm clearer, I turn to the golden carp god that the novel features centrally as an ethnic marker of difference that shares with the snake deity traces of a distortion palpable in these same colonial texts. In what follows, I focus on Sandoval's and Cavazzi's accounts of the golden carp to explain Antonio's supreme anguish when confronted with this belief system that originated in Africa. I seek not only to pinpoint a specific location for the possible origins of a Chicano rejection of Africa, but also to make evident how, through the lens of memorialization, this colonially rooted marker of distortion may be nevertheless rescripted and rehabilitated by the Chicano text.

4.5 The (Atlantic) Golden Carp

At the center of *Bless Me, Ultima* is the repressed myth of the golden carp, whose provenance is most mysterious. An entity relegated to the periphery because it is opposed to the town's avowed Catholic faith, the carp recalls the US Southwest plantocracy; its adoration was prohibited by the Church and the Inquisition during the era of the slave trade on both sides of the Atlantic. In Africa, for instance, treatises against carp worship make

4.5 The (Atlantic) Golden Carp

manifest the original colonial distortions of the golden carp. Anaya's golden carp shares important features with the Atlantic fish worship that appears in both the colonial archive and in an African literary work – a similar carp is found in a text by Labou Tansi. As the similarities between Anaya's golden carp and those of these Atlantic examples become apparent, so too does the dichotomy between light and darkness in golden carp worship that the novel emphasizes. The golden carp can thus help us understand how darkness is distorted and then rejected in the Chicano novel. Anaya's text navigates over and across the Atlantic within an essentially South-South frame. As a connecting vector between the two poles, the golden carp appears first, as an exoticized body in colonial records of Africa, and secondly, as a deterritorialized symbol in the US Southwest that accounts for the "South" within the Global North. In this regard, I turn now to describing how Anaya's carp is continuous with the Congolese carp – both colonial and contemporary – focusing on its singularity as an ethnic marker of difference ubiquitous in the colonial Atlantic World. Yet, as a marker that is supremely racial – and that was constructed in the Atlantic World rather than in an exclusively hemispheric, indigenous context, as previously thought – the golden carp becomes a primordial site of memory for a rehabilitated Latin-African Atlantic.

Bless Me, Ultima initially memorializes the carp in the conflicting intersection of colonial Catholicism and indigenous paganism. Physically situated between the "cliffs where Jason's Indian lived" (81) and a "gigantic railroad" is Aztlán, where the carp dwells amid the juxtaposition of natural and industrialized worlds. When Antonio engages in a conversation with one of his school friends, Samuel, the latter evokes zoolatry:

> A long time ago, when the earth was young and only wandering tribes touched the virgin grasslands and drank from the pure streams, a strange people came to this land. . . . " Were they Indians?" I asked when he paused. "They were *the people*," he answered simply and went on . . . "There was only one thing that was withheld from them, and that was the fish called the carp. This fish made his home in the waters of the river, and he was sacred to the gods." (83–4)

The emergence of the enigmatic golden carp seems symptomatic of the trauma of Indian repression, as numerous scholars have noted.[25] But the carp also serves to question the universality of Catholicism in Chicano tradition, as Antonio's reflections indicate: "[i]f the golden carp was a god, who was the man on the cross?" and "Was my mother praying to the wrong

God?" (85). Explaining that "Ultima's cure and the golden carp occupied my thoughts the rest of the summer," Antonio unearths a repressive spiritual praxis, first through Ultima's healing and then via the appearance of a "pagan god."

Like Rivera's "searching," Antonio's quest to free the golden carp from the depths of distortion reinscribes a transmodern trace in the novel's spatio-temporal memorial.[26] In other words, Antonio seeks out alternative truths in the dark in the same way that Rivera's poetry maps out a Congo through smoke. This "darkness" is akin to what Marta Caminero-Santangelo calls the golden carp's aporia as an "ethnic marker" that has not been deconstructed into its temporal or historiographical levels ("Jason's" 116–17). Mirroring how coloniality dilutes indigeneity, Samuel's ambiguous statement that "they were *the people*" clouds the origin of the golden carp while it enwraps Antonio in "[t]he story of the carp [that] continued to haunt my dreams" (86). Indeed, tracing colonial descriptions of the golden carp confronts the aporia of its constitution and simultaneous repression. After all, Antonio's haunting emerges from a long genealogy of colonial rhetoric that forbade golden carp worship in the first place.

Fish worship was one of the most forbidden aspects of African spirituality in seventeenth-century travelogues of the Congo. According to Sandoval's account, men did not dare eat fish for fear of godly punishment, and the missionary condemned the praxis as superstitious and said "their government" was founded on "the devil."[27] Cavazzi went as far as to violently destroy fish-worship, burning altars for it to the ground:

> Approaching closer once more, I had the certainty that the cottage should serve for some superstition, because inside was a little table with fresh fish. I burst in with zeal and in a moment I threw the fish ... at the waterfall. ... I tried to conceive of them as nothing more than a madness ... and when I was informed that the altars or idols and similar abominations which I had already destroyed were built anew by the obstinacy of those blind, I turned back to destroy them again, two, and many times.[28]

Even though Cavazzi relates that the native communities of the Congo were merely attempting to build altars to increase the fish population, his ire casts into relief their memorialized "idolatry." As a "diabolical" reverence placed over physical "casas de ídolos" ("house of idols"),[29] he gleefully destroys their physical memory. For centuries, his account has implied that the destruction of these altars was justified because their diabolical reverence was so frightening, and has represented the practice of Vodun as "devil-worship" that must be physically razed.

4.5 The (Atlantic) Golden Carp

The golden carp worship in *Bless Me, Ultima* mimics this forbidden and repressed practice; after all, when Samuel tells Antonio the story he "glanced around as if to make sure [they] were alone" (84), and it is only the "magic people [who] all know about the coming day of the golden carp" (114). But what is most peculiar is that the carp's physical features are similar to those of the fish Cavazzi describes. When Antonio finally lays eyes on this strange specimen, he "could not believe its size" and its "bright orange," "huge," and "beautiful" appearance, as the "sunlight glistened off his golden scales" (119). For Antonio, the golden carp's "shiny scales and the light reflected orange and yellow and red" are both magnificent and bewildering. While Antonio's description of the carp is innocent, the scene is reminiscent of a far less benign ethnography. While not in any way an intentional reproduction of the colonial account, Antonio's detailed observations of the god-like fish recall the carp that Cavazzi describes as bewildering, extraordinary, and vile:

> The flying fish, known all over the ocean, can escape the snares of the gold carp, rising above the waters. But after a brief space, he falls miserably into the open mouth of his enemy. These fish abound in the vast ocean, for the benefit of the Fishermen and for distraction of the navigators.[30]

Considering sheer appearance, one cannot help comparing the carp here to Anaya's. Of note is the colossal size of Cavazzi's carp, which ensnares other fish and is both abundant and threatening, setting up a dichotomy by which it provides sustenance for natives ("Fishermen") but "distraction" for colonists ("navigators"). But while Antonio's friend Samuel explains that the golden carp "take[s] care of his people" (84), Cavazzi's distorted carp is menacing, "assaulting a fleet with his enormous walls,"[31] and repeatedly sketched as monstrous, as Figure 4.1 shows.

In both texts, the carp signifies difference, however thematically varied that difference may be. In Anaya's case, this signifier questions Catholic opposition to animistic spirituality. The carp – and its dialectical difference with the Catholic Church – provides "the easiest way into the ethnic content of the text" (Caminero-Santangelo "Jason's" 117), interrogating Chicano religious traditions. Similarly, for the colonial text, the carp not only functions as the extreme opposite of Christianity but also as a means of vilifying a subaltern faith. This vilification occurs through the signifier's particular characteristics, as the description of the carp places it on the far end of a continuum of bewilderment vis-à-vis Anaya's carp, and leads to the repression clearly echoed in Anaya's text.

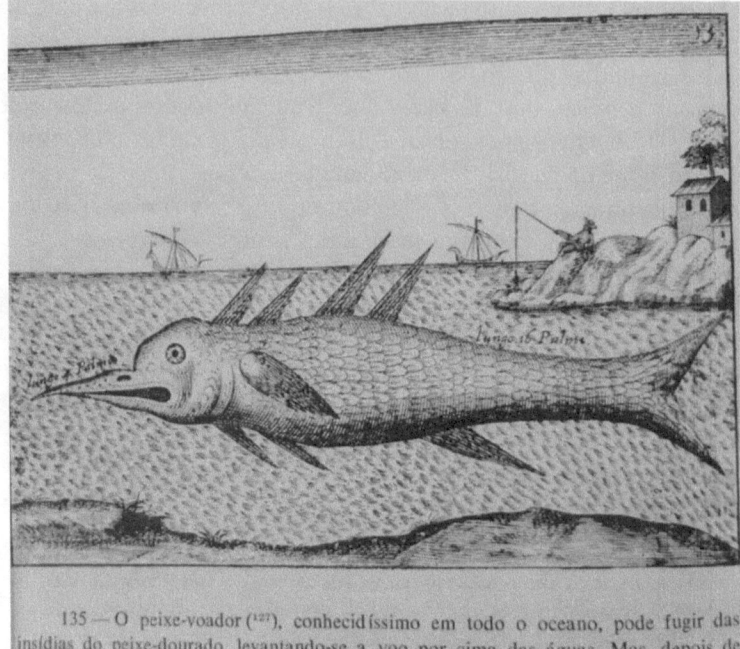

135 — O peixe-voador (¹²⁷), conhecidíssimo em todo o oceano, pode fugir das insídias do peixe-dourado, levantando-se a voo por cima das águas. Mas, depois de um breve espaço, cai miseràvelmente na boca aberta do seu inimigo. Estes peixes abundam no vasto oceano, para proveito dos pescadores e para distracção dos navegantes.

Figure 4.1 "Peixe-dourado" in Giovanni Antonio Cavazzi's *Descrição histórica dos três reinos do Congo, Matamba e Angola*.

Anaya's golden carp descriptions indeed mimic colonial language, not only unearthing transatlantic distortions of African spirituality, but also unlocking connections between regions of the Global South that have real geopolitical relations. I am interested especially in Congolese writer Labou Tansi's *The Seven Solitudes of Lorsa Lopez/Les sept solitudes de Lorsa Lopez* (1985), as it features a synechdochal symbol of the fish that seems to draw from the same colonial records but also borrows from the Boom novel. After all, Tchichellé Tchivéla notes, Labou Tansi's works interpellated recourses of magical realism, especially those of García Márquez (30–1). In fact, the novel rewrites *Chronicle of a Death Foretold*, and in Labou Tansi's work, the town anticipates the death of Estina Benta, a victim of domestic abuse. But the townsfolk do not stop her murder and are later haunted by events that unfold through registers of magical realism. In his saga, Labou Tansi's gendered appropriation of García Márquez's tale recalls the colonial archive when, during a scene in which people gather to gaze upon the battered body of Estina Benta, a magical fish materializes:

> One morning, unprecedented crowds gathered in the Plaza de la Poudra, not to await the arrival of the police, nor to bury Estina Benta's bones … The multitudes jostled *for position to see the fish with the death's head* that the fishermen, Fernando Lambert and Luizo Martinèz Lopèz, had just caught. *It was a winged monster at least seventy feet long and weighing some three tons.* On its hide, covered with scales, feathers and hair gleamed the seven colours of the rainbow … on the top of its forehead, there were what looked like crossed tibias, which emitted a beautiful ray of light. (62, emphasis added)

While Stanley and Bourke project the Congo onto the Americas, Labou Tansi transplants the aesthetics of the Americas to the Congo through a reimagining of a *Macondo*-like town as a critique of coloniality's breakdown in Central Africa. This association is by no means accidental nor unique to *The Seven Solitudes of Lorsa Lopez*. In Labou Tansi's dictatorship novel *L'État honteux* (*The Shameful State*, 1981), Magalí Armillas-Tiseyra evinces the intertextualization of cannibalism in García Márquez's novel *Autumn of the Patriarch*, in which the dictator consumes his assistant at his banquet for foreign dignitaries. But different from García Márquez, Armillas-Tiseyra notes, Labou Tansi's dictator informs his guests of who they are consuming to no avail, thus poignantly critiquing "the complacency of the international community" keeping African authoritarianism alive (138). Like this South-South engagement with García Márquez, Labou Tansi's carp denounces decolonial failure all while also pointing out the colonial roots of this failure. In other words, in Labou Tansi's *The Seven Solitudes of Lorsa Lopez,* the magical realist "winged monster" not only distracts the population from seeking justice for domestic manslaughter, but also exposes a colonially produced neo-imperialism. Written after the Congo's wars of decolonization, Labou Tansi's novel uses the fish metaphor differently than the works of Anaya and Cavazzi: here, the fish is symptomatic of the trauma of Western hegemonic violence following Congolese independence. While the carp is deployed in differing thematic ways, it traces a through line from Cavazzi to Anaya and Labou Tansi.

Of consequence is that both Anaya and Labou Tansi repurpose the colonial language of the carp – which was once used to demonize native Congolese space – for their own ends. Labou Tansi's "death's head" measuring "at least seventy feet long and weighing some three tons" parallels Cavazzi's all-encompassing and "ensnaring" carp. Further, Labou Tansi describes the carp as a "monster" with "feathers and hair"

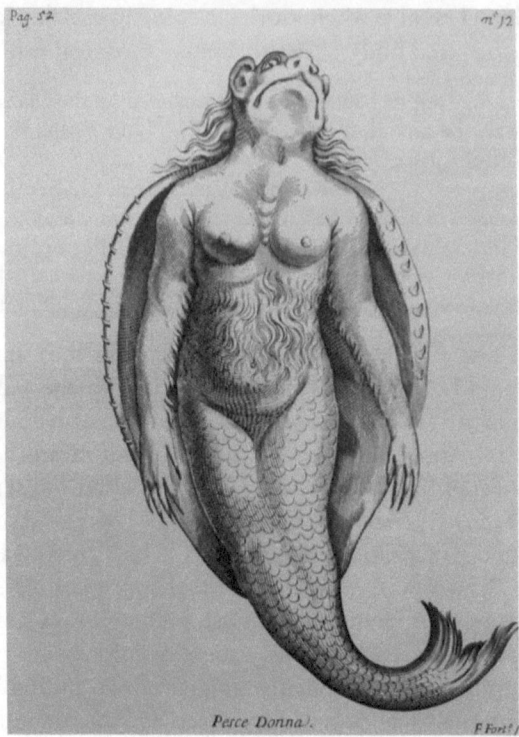

Figure 4.2 "Pesce Donna" in Giovanni Antonio Cavazzi's *Descrição histórica dos três reinos do Congo, Matamba e Angola.*

in a way that echoes Cavazzi's sketch in Figure 4.2. Both Antonio's "shiny scales and the light reflected orange and yellow and red" and Labou Tansi's "scales" that "gleamed the seven colors of the rainbow" use these bewildering othered descriptors, but they do so to unearth a repressed deity that colonial accounts buried. As a signifier that is rehabilitated, Anaya employs the carp as a marker of spiritual difference, while for Labou Tansi, it functions as a metaphoric critique of American neo-imperialism. As a signifier of difference, the repurposing of the carp in these contemporary examples restores its meaning from colonial demonization. But more to the point, Anaya's and Labou Tansi's golden carp both seem to negatively describe their colonial referents to demonstrate the continuity of global capitalism across the Atlantic.

In Anaya's particular case, the golden carp is an entity relegated to the margins as both pagan and prohibited during an era when African slavery was present in the US Southwest. While I have described how Anaya's carp resonates with both the colonial archive (*about* the Congo) and contemporary Congolese literature (*by* the Congo), in all three cases, the carp as a marker of difference emphasizes a textual site at which one should pause and reflect.

Another such site of difference in Anaya's novel is the emergence of the black bass. Dialectically opposed to the golden carp and the most similar to Cavazzi's descriptions, the black bass is introduced in Anaya's novel by another one of Antonio's wise if insubordinate friends. Here, Cico explains to the young narrator that the black bass is a "killer" who eats other fish, as opposed to the golden carp who "does not eat his own kind" (118). Morally charitable, the golden carp has Christ-like attributes while the cannibalistic black bass is relegated to the sons of Ham. Biblical references aside, the bass's "monstrous" physicality deviates greatly from that of its rival: "The evil mouth of the black bass was open and red. Its eyes were glazed with hate ... The huge tail swished and contemptuously flipped it aside. Then the black form dropped into the foaming waters" (114). Here, Antonio's "bewildered" admiration for the carp and its landscape – an Edenic garden of "fruit-laden trees" and "sun-dazzling flowers" – contrasts strongly with the black bass's "darkness of shadows" and "foaming" or murky waters (113–14). In fact, the fear of its darkness aligns perfectly with the town's unrelenting understanding of darkness as macabre, from the Trementina's "Black Book" (145) to descriptions of snow as "dark" and dangerous (167). Cavazzi depicts carp and other kinds of fish like the "Pesce Donna," pictured in Figure 4.2, as both physically and morally monstrous; his representations of fish are thus better aligned with the incivility and monstrosity attributed to the black bass. This doomsday signifier foretells Ultima's demise in the prolepsis of the black bass when Antonio has a haunting nightmare toward the end of the novel. Anaya's eschatological vision produces the nightmare, in which "a valley of flames" claims not only Antonio's parents but also a "beheaded" Ultima whose blood is drunk by Tenorio Trementina and his bewitched daughters. These signifiers of evil bathe in Ultima's blood, driving a "stake through her heart" and burning her, and also "cooked [the carp] in the fires of Ultima's ashes." As they unceremoniously ingest the body of this pagan Christ-like god, the apocalypse announces itself with "a great rift open[ing]." Antonio's nightmare ends with what is traditionally conceived as a zombie apocalypse of "people's skin rotting and falling off," "shrieks of pain and agony," and most tellingly, the "walking-dead" burying their "sleeping dead" (165, 167–8).

The same site that informs Ultima's difference as a healer also registers continuities in Antonio's nightmare. Over the former Vodun-practicing kingdom of Ouidah, Benin, descriptions of fire, blood, and walking dead abound in the colonial relation. African rituals, descriptions of bleedings, the fearful "screams" of those evidently in "trance," "possessed peoples," and "fire" dot the landscape.[32] Anaya's apocalyptic imagery resonates with this colonial V-effekt and suggests an Atlantic haunting. This is because while *Bless Me, Ultima*'s fear-afflicted imagery reflects the archive's misrepresentations and ultimately the "essentializing, or stereotyping" Eurocentric imaginary of what Stanley called "darkest Africa" (MacGaffey 399–400), its transfer to a southwestern plantational system began even prior to the Middle Passage and materializes in an antagonism toward the black bass – an antagonism that reflects Chicano rejections of Africa. Moreover, tracing the colonial distortions in this relation alters the conception – held as much in Latinx studies as in World Literature – of Anaya's narrative as one that is insular or even hemispherically bound to indigenous epistemologies rather than partially informed by a history that originates in Africa, as I have shown. Most importantly, through this transatlantic lens, texts such as *Bless Me, Ultima* can be read as rehabilitating the binaries Antonio perceives through his marginalized "Márez" lineage in Chicano Atlantic memory.

To think about the Latin-African nature of both this imagined apocalypse and the signifiers of good versus evil that are racialized in Anaya's story, it is necessary to dwell on the distorted Atlantic heritage of one of Antonio's last names. If Antonio's mother (Luna) comes from a long line of Catholic agriculturists, his secular father (Márez) urges him to be a mobile conqueror of the sea. But beyond these binaries, it is precisely his father's maritime errancy, embodied in "Márez" that foregrounds the age of the sail in the novel while his Catholic mother relegates this Márez heritage to paganism. Notably, his "Márez" lineage is in fact connected to the paganism of the carp for, as Cico reveals to Antonio, "this whole land was once covered by the sea, a long time ago" – a land that "belonged to the fish before it belonged to us" (123). In spectacularly parallel metaphors, the submerged truth about Antonio's "Márez" lineage seems as elusive as the drained waters in which the golden carp used to dwell. After all, the "Márez" name phonetically recalls "oceans" or "seas" in Spanish, and fishing is also significant in the Atlantic-facing works of Labou Tansi and Cavazzi. Thus, while Antonio's heritage recalls sixteenth-century conquistadores who "tamed the New Mexican wilderness" (Saldívar *Chicano* 106) and gave rise to his mother Luna's "earth-rooted" farmer ancestors, the active symbol of his Márez side is "associated with the sun and the ocean-like plains" to which the father is drawn in the narrative (106). In fact, the narrative suggests as much, stating "Tony Márez arises from the sea" and that his Márez blood "is restless like the sea" (*Bless Me, Ultima* 123). Beyond these symbols hinting at Antonio's repressed maritime past, his Márez and Luna names indicate a tension between sea and land dichotomy that confines Antonio, ontologically and spiritually.

In his spatial reading of *Bless Me, Ultima*, Ramón Saldívar argued that the apocalyptic darkness of the novel – such as the nightmares, Ultima's imagined death, and the atomic bomb of the narrative's 1945 setting – is not only symptomatic of the end of innocence but also a result of endless patriarchal battles between good and evil: "Luna versus Márez; farmer versus vaquero" and even the "Golden Carp versus the black bass" (122). Since the story is told in hindsight, Antonio's critical thinking through these moments of childhood is supposed to reconcile these polarities. But even though Saldívar concludes that this dichotomy does not really hold up in the end, the racial binary his assessment reveals can be organically traced back to coloniality. As the novel seems to hint at Antonio's yearning for "a clean, *undistorted*, hierarchical relationship between dichotomies that order his world" (122, emphasis added), it is also worth considering that the colonial apparatus set up these dichotomies in the first place, and thus that Antonio might decolonially unhinge, rebuild, or collapse them altogether. The descriptors in Antonio's dream – the black bass's evil shrouded in "darkness," "the drinking of blood," the "walking-dead" and "sleeping-dead" – seem symptomatic of colonial sites unconsciously inherited from the likes of Sandoval or Cavazzi.

Having described the relation between Anaya's carp and colonial and contemporary Atlantic carp as well as the novel's subtle diasporic traces, I move to consider the carp that Antonio visualizes as a Latin-African textual memorial. To do so, I turn to the ways in which Anaya's text and African sites of memory mutually constitute these forms of rehabilitation and offer an alternative reading of Anaya's fiction as a textual memorial of this lost heritage. The carp's confinement in the novel – as much mythical as signified – parallels a captivity memorialized deep within the structure of the Atlantic system. In the scene when Antonio discovers the golden carp, he recalls a legend about his people being turned into carp. As the townsfolk continue to consume the sacred fish despite its proverbial "bad luck" (83), Antonio playfully states that "every year the drama [of ingestion] was repeated" (83). The actions of his contemporaries echo those of his Aztlán ancestors, who did not heed the gods' warning and, after a four-year drought, had no choice but to eat the fish; they were turned into carp and "made to live forever in the waters of the river" (84). The Macondo-like confinement of the carp, like that of Labou Tansi's town mirrors Antonio's entrapped subjectivity. But this paradigm of entrapment as well as the carp as a marker of difference is still used contemporarily in one of the most preserved forms of Africa memory: the oral proverb.

At the Slave Route in Benin, fish adoration materializes orally along the heritage trail. As I discussed in Chapter 1, Ouidah's site was the scene of some of the most despicable colonial discourses about Vodun practices, prompting guides to share proverbs invoking the slave trade. One expression that guides recount during the pilgrimage along Ouidah is "the carp fish will never turn into a catfish,"[33] meaning that one cannot change the history of one's people, or you can't change who your ancestors are, textualized in Figure 4.3. The proverb of the carp is articulated over a designated site of memory precisely because of this communal guilt. According to historian Robin Law, the "expression [connotes] the need and desire of the modern inhabitants of Ouidah to come to terms with the town's slave-trading past" (154). In other words, the proverbs are expressions of guilt passed on from the colonial period to contemporary times and used as a means of making peace with the history of enslavement. In fact, as Robert Baum argues, for the coastal peoples of Benin these "memories of selling people – some of them friends and relatives – provoked survivors to create new forms of spirit cults to ease the sense of moral wrongdoing" (397). Proverbs are thus both an expression of

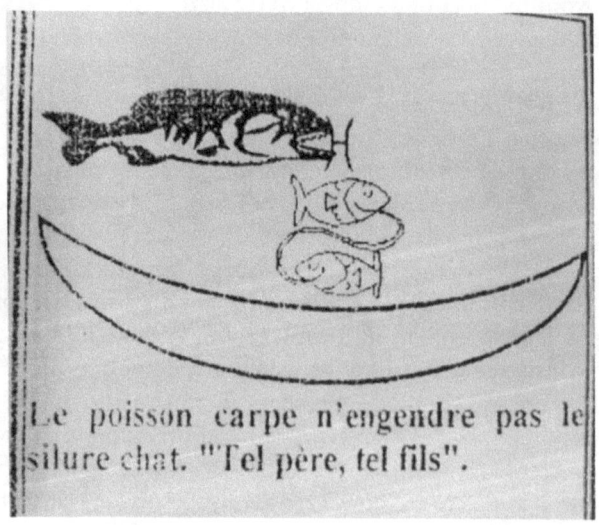

Figure 4.3 Transcribed Proverb of Benin. Courtesy of Director Zphirin Daavo and l'Agence Nationale pour la Promotion des Patrimoines et de développement du tourisme au Bénin. Cotonou, Benin.

culpability and a rehabilitation of the past. One could even argue that the carp proverbs are specifically symptomatic of the Atlantic World order, meant as devices to ease the moral responsibility of Atlantic memory. This proverbial regret on memorial ground is bound to the plantocratic past of Anaya's Southwest.

Parallel to Anaya's story of people being trapped in carp is the fact that Antonio's father resists enclosed spaces and "only the wide expanse of land and sky could feel the freedom" (2). This sentiment is perhaps explained by his "Márez" conquistador ontology, which Antonio chooses over "Luna" at the end of the novel.[34] *Bless Me, Ultima*'s dialectics of enclosure resonate with Anaya's short story "The Man Who Could Fly," in which a landowner places a losing bet against a man who can fly, resulting in the landowner's enslavement (Quesada "The Congo" 112–17). While Anaya's myths could be read as a dialectic of southwestern plantocracy, the epistemology of enclosure finds its ontological roots in the plantation. According to Glissant, the term "enclosure" (*Poetics* 66–7) meditates on the confinability of peoples due to a curse engendered from African slavery. Thus, not only does the black bass represent Chicanidad's guilty acquiescence to colonial racial hierarchies, but the dichotomy between the golden carp and the black bass casts in high relief the opposition of white versus black. Anaya's novel memorializes the relevance of the Atlantic World system to New Mexico's slave-trading past by tracing continuities of entrapment in the golden carp that are barely perceptible. In this vein, R. Saldívar has argued that one of the main drawbacks of this widely read novel is its romantic repression of Mexican-American history: the novel "cancels out 'realism,' attempting to cross it out and lift it up to a realm of truth" (*Chicano* 126). Indeed, capitalist greed and colonial exploitation remain on the margins of the narrative, but through their very marginality function as subtle reminders of a repression Anaya conveys aesthetically. In other words, the novel's traces of not only indigenous but also African history are subtle because the work performs said repression textually. In this way, Anaya's insular myth of origin, inscribed into textual sites that one visits in the novel, are in many ways similar to the proverbs of Ouidah, where trails of memory also reckon with the systematic trauma of oceanic and plantational oppression.

Although the golden carp functions as a memorial site that recovers this Latin-African axis in Anaya's novel, the racialization that the Atlantic World produces is not ultimately rooted out, for the dark-light dichotomies live on in Anaya's fictional world if it is not decolonized through the memorializing lens of my reading here. Put differently, these dichotomies reveal the racial biases of Chicano literary production, which might continue to perpetuate myths of an "evil" darkness if literary criticism does not challenge them. Nevertheless, the novel has one noticeable decolonial moment in which racialized perceptions of darkness are arguably uprooted. Specifically, when Ultima, on her deathbed, beseeches Antonio to "gather [her] medicines and [her] herbs" and "burn everything" (276), the dichotomies embedded in the fish seem somewhat rehabilitated. As Antonio follows her orders, he obliterates any trace of Ultima's curanderismo, but in doing so, Antonio also "ran into the darkness," delivering himself to a "night sky [with] a million stars," like a million answers to his dogged search for truth. This final scene evokes the ways in which we might read Anaya as rescripting the colonial to destabilize its distorted imaginary. The defiant act of burning gestures toward the processes by which the subaltern episteme threatened the core of Western hegemony, resulting in subalternity's obliteration, colonial dread, and the Luna family's fear of otherness. But Antonio's former "horror of darkness" and "terrible, dark, fear" (24–5) dissipates in the novel's anagnorisis. Antonio's embrace of "darkness" is emblematic of a resistance that dislodges the normative Eurocentric conception of darkness as horror, similar to Díaz's recoding of blackness in "Monstro" forty years later. Like the symbols of carp as monstrous or curanderismo as witchcraft, Antonio's decolonial run into darkness effectively suggests the limits of hegemonic dominance. Most importantly, this decolonial turn – reading against the archive, as it were – intimates a deciphering of Chicanos' original rejection of Africanness through colonial navigation and its deep incursion into, as the novel puts it, "*the ocean of the plain*" of Anaya's Southwest (6).

To conclude, we might consider how this reading of Anaya's novel expands the bounds of the Chicano regionalism and local folklore for which it is known in World Literature. Not only is the novel's universalism now localized, as the dichotomies of good versus evil or darkness are framed by locating the distortion of the golden carp, but the novel also underscores the boundless reach of a plantational system in the US Southwest, pointing to African retentions that inform the subtle ways in which the characters in Anaya's novel deviate from dominant concepts of "darkness." Thus, if Caminero-Santangelo argues that "universal" readings of this novel have avoided the origin of the golden carp myth entirely or have "vaguely associated [it] with indigenous beliefs" ("Jason's" 116–17), it is clear that while easy dichotomies of Black versus White originate in various places, the golden carp pinpoints that location in the Atlantic

World. Because this rerouting of the Atlantic within the plains of the Southwest might very well be unintentional, one could conclude that "Anaya has given us perhaps more than he knows or intended" (Hunt 181). But at the very least, *Bless Me, Ultima* unfolds a historiography that is expansive. Ultimately, reading the novel alongside myriad representations of Atlantic history changes the way we read not only this Chicano classic, but also ethnic expectations of Latinx literature in World Literature more broadly.

Reading the foundational figures of Rivera and Anaya as writers who embed the Global South through comparisons with UNESCO Slave Routes indeed sets the stage for thinking of Chicano literary studies specifically, and Latinx literature in general, more expansively and comparatively. In fact, the parallels I have drawn among Anaya, Rivera, and a transatlantic past heed Debra Castillo's comparatist plea that critics envision the "US imaginary ... conceived in its transnational extensions" (177). But as this chapter has demonstrated, such an expansion moves these Chicano writers beyond the transnational. The Latin-African connections presented here, whether via the nineteenth-century imperialist scramble for Africa or the colonial slave trade that their textual memorializations evoke, nuance Chicanos' complex relationship with Africa and with racialization or contemporary representations of "darkness." For as sociologist Agustín Laó-Montes has argued, Africa has long been "imagined" via the aesthetic code Stanley bestowed on it: as a "dark continent" on "the margins of history and outside of civilization" (78). This simple dichotomy of otherness, Laó-Montes argues, materializes as "ethnoracial hierarchies (economic, political, cultural) created in a colonial context," where people aspire to whiteness and darkness becomes subsumed in a racialization complex. Rivera's seeming acceptance of Stanley's racialization of Africa and Anaya's use of darkness to evoke witchcraft and fear, while certainly betraying racial solidarity across the Global South, possess an inherent revisionist quality. As this book has argued, fiction responds to and has the potential to transform the path of world imperialism's symbolic and very real violence which can be traced as far back as the colonial period in Africa. By visiting the UNESCO-like routes and sites in texts to meditate on moments when traces of Africa are excised – the murkiness of the Congo in Rivera and hints of plantation-era in Anaya – the racialization that originated in Africa and haunts Chicano letters provides an access point for revitalizing these transatlantic connections. Despite the insularity that is usually ascribed to them in World Literature, the texts of Rivera and Anaya offer a cosmopolitan engagement through their experience as relational subjects of empire. In this vein, Anaya's novel and Rivera's poem – along with their transatlantic dialogue with the UNESCO Slave Route – have much to offer the concept of the "global" in World Literature, for they challenge perceptions of these Chicano literary canons as regional or exclusively transnational.

Coda

The African Heritage of Latinx and Caribbean Literature is based on the premise that textual memorials in the works of some of the most widely read authors of Latin American descent in the last fifty years are akin to those constituting UNESCO's Slave Route insofar as they memorialize a Latin-African literature neglected in World Literature. The texts I consulted here defiantly stretch the limits of Caribbean, Latinx, or Chicano literary memory, geographically setting the plot in an Atlantic-affected Latin America or a West Africa transplanted to the US Southwest. What emerges in these stories is not only an undeniable rupture from an occidentalist view of "transatlantic" studies, but also a break from the tutelary bounds confining authors to their regional space. In World Literature, Díaz and Obejas are often marketed as representatives of *Dominicanidad* or *Cubanidad*, respectively, overlooking the innovative ways both representative Latinx authors update African memory. By contrast, Rivera and Anaya are often read as rarely leaving the US Southwest, conveying their critics' refusal to engage with Africa. Finally, García Márquez's world appeal has not sufficed to increase attention to the spectacularly underemphasized role of his Angolan enterprise. These transatlantic connections have been either flattened or placed under erasure despite the forceful Black internationalization the narratives convey.

But the African epistemological sites we *visit* in the literature of this book offer opportunities to *read* sites of African historiography throughout the ages. Analogously, the rise of Africa's UNESCO Slave Route offers a similar opportunity: to read the story of African dispersal at their sites of origin while visiting the narratives offered by guides. As mutually constitutive forms, physical and textual memorials interest me not only because of the subtle ways the selected narratives embed a nuanced "Africa" through specific sociohistorical moments of African history, but also because of the ways those sites, inversely, use narrative to convey the African side of the diasporic story. This relationship reconceptualizes the cartography of Atlantic studies generally, and Latin American and American studies specifically, by constructing textual memorials to a Latin-African past. Redirected transatlantic stories focalize, then, on the marked travel of characters, whether fictional or nonfictional. From the unnamed protagonist in Díaz's Haiti to the revolutionary Usnavy in Obejas's Cuba and from García Márquez in Angola to Rivera in the Congo and even Anaya's pseudo-child self in a post-plantocratic New Mexico, these characters circulate along an Atlantic borderland that defies the ethnic expectations placed on both their writing and identity. In moving through an Atlantic circuit, these characters enunciate different points along an African historiography in ways similar to traveling along a heritage trail. If Certeau conceives that "stories of journeys" that "are *marked out by the 'citation' of the places*" are a key feature imbricating movement and text (120, emphasis added), similarly, the stories about these characters' journeys "cite" or "mark out" a Latin-African axis that rewrites the Euro-American historical narrative, capturing the plurality of Latinx and Latin American literary genealogy.

But because Latin-African textual memorials evince a framework that links these sites to a developmentalist agency such as UNESCO, it is necessary to address some additional considerations for our era in World Literature. While I was writing this Coda, Sarah Brouillette published *UNESCO and the Fate of the Literary* (2019), prompting me to circle back to the initial principle of *The African Heritage of Latinx and Caribbean Literature*: the UNESCO-like function of textual memorials in literature. At the base of Brouillette's compelling study is a critique of liberal capitalists' utopic perception that literature alone can improve economic development – and assuage hierarchical rifts between social classes through readership – while ironically embedded in a "developmentalist" or even imperialist ethos (26–7). She reads World Literature in the institution of UNESCO – a hierarchical canon termed a Collection of Representative Works, selected by each nation, translated, and then circulated with an aim of cross-cultural emancipation that does not reach its lofty goal. This is due to the implicit bias of UNESCO ever since its inception: UNESCO's first director, Julian Huxley, advocated the circulation of Western works to raise the enlightenment of the "underdeveloped" in a manner not unlike the inception of the American Studies Association (ASA) based on an attitude of American exceptionalism (Giles 12), or even Goethe's conception of World Literature. The resulting effect is that even the well-intentioned objective of integrating world literatures from the semi-periphery as "well positioned to counter capitalist modernity" (*UNESCO* 3) hinges more on a sense of self-flattery than on equalizing a global playing field through

UNESCO's selected works.¹ A notable example is how World Literature markets an image of a poor Africa, pigeonholing renowned writers such as NoViolet Bulawayo, Chimamanda Ngozi Adichie, or Teju Cole for the benefit of a "Western-facing" audience but also forcing them to rely almost exclusively on an Anglo African literary market, private donors, and prize contests ("African Literary Hustle"). The unfortunate aftereffect of this capitalist consumption of Afropolitanism – what Taiye Selasi terms as the generation that knows "the G8 city or two (or three)" like "the backs of our hands" ("Bye-Bye Babar") – is that it negates the worldwide circulation of African-published works. As James Hodapp argues, in order for an African-born writer to enter World Literature, this work must be ironically "foreign born," translated into a European language, and "appeal to a global audience before it can appeal to an African one" (6). Despite the cosmopolitan nature of Afropolitans, modern and contemporary African authors whose work circulates across the Atlantic, from Nobel laureates like J. M. Coetzee or Nadine Gordimer, to other notable writers like Ben Okri or Chinua Achebe, are chosen by Western institutions. The result of Afropolitanism, as I have argued in this book, is the impossibility of seeing "Africa" in its particularity, as affected by a coloniality occurring in Africa and stubbornly driven on into the twenty-first century.

While I have described these effects mostly in Latinx writing, they are also present in Latin America, as the African referent oscillates between absent to arguably orientalist. Notable Afro-Hispanic contributions such as Panamanian Carlos Guillermo "Cubena" Wilson's *Los nietos de Felicidad Dolores* (1991), which memorializes African slave depots through African proverbs, Peruvian Lucía Charún Illescas's *Malambo* (2001), whose protagonist is a Yoruba *griot* (oral storyteller) in colonial Perú, and even Colombian Manuel Zapata Olivella's African magical realist texts, do not circulate widely in World Literature – in contrast to the work of Zapata Olivella's notable contemporary, García Márquez. On the other hand, in Mexican literature, not only is Africa rarely highlighted in the narrative, in Mexican writer Alberto Ruy Sánchez's *Quinteto de Mogador* (2015), for instance, Morocco has been considered to cast orientalist notions of the continent, even when critics have also read the novel as decentralizing Eurocentricity (Sánchez Prado "África" 61). World Literature, like UNESCO, still perpetuates and strengthens western structures from which this literary field hails, overlooking African epistemologies from both their origins or embedded in lesser-circulated texts from the Americas. This phenomenon translates into the unsuitability of economic development as the driving force behind literature's circulation because not only does this system fail to address a Global South in its particularity, to return to Brouillette's argument, this system also precludes the democratic circulation of literature.

While in agreement with Brouillette, I have argued in this book that democratizing literature entails, first of all, undoing structures that dictate *what* the literary masters write about. From García Márquez to Junot Díaz, I have explained how a Latin-Africa is embedded as a cosmopolitan form both contesting the Eurocentric literary tradition of UNESCO's or World Literature's canon, but also providing the very cross-cultural understanding that UNESCO ultimately fails to deliver. Therefore, while it is true that UNESCO's Slave Route, to which I compare a selection of literatures, emerges from the agency's capitalist structure, the textual memorials of a Latin-African literature function in a global world system to contest western episteme. In other words, if UNESCO made available a certain kind of World Literature that legitimized its existence, my aim has been to use UNESCO's memorialization structure to think of representative worldly authors and the ways they shape world history around us, differently. It is true that literary cultures can be embedded in capitalist structures of development. But literature's "textual memorials" provide sites that contest both UNESCO's neoliberal apparatus and, by extension, World Literature's capitalist tendencies.

Perhaps most importantly, *The African Heritage of Latinx and Caribbean Literature* addresses the memorialization of UNESCO and its Slave Route project in literature for the first time. Even if funded by UNESCO, or even the IMF, I offer that the different Slave Routes and their unscripted performance of history circulate as cosmopolitan points when embedded in the literatures I select here. In a manner of summary, these sites are Benin's Ouidah and its Vodun trail, Badagry's Heritage Site in Nigeria, Senegal's Gorée island and its House of Slaves, Denbigh's Stanley statue in the UK, the Congo's National Institute Museum in Kinshasa, and Malawi's Dr. David Livingstone Trail. These memorial sites, along with their textual counterparts, mutually constitute a revisionist Latin-African memory in a hemispheric literary history. At the same time, these structures of memory are different from the literary texts I have described in this book, and allow visitors to see aspects that texts cannot offer. In what follows, I expand on how these sites individually challenge the occidentalist tendencies that created them in the first place. Briefly revisiting the memorial paradigms that each chapter explored, I offer personal anecdotes from my fieldwork at some of these sites as an elaboration of how their current form, together with the literary, redesigns a memorial of its own and opens the door for future work on the interdisciplinary engagements between heritage tourism and World Literature.

I began this book with Díaz's textual memorial of Ouidah, which I argue is evoked through the short story's zombie figure and its allusions to a discourse that demonizes this zombie at its origin in Benin. Similarly, Ouidah's 3-km "Route de l'Esclave" and the "Porte de non-retour" (the "door of no-return") also invoke fear, this time, of Vodun, the religious praxis from which the zombie is derived. Not only do guides recite proverbs that warn of the reprisals for mistreatment of Vodun deities such as the snake, the fear of Ouidah that my local informants expressed during my fieldwork was perhaps the most surprising. Three local high school students in Cotonou (incidentally, my housemates) noted that "underdevelopment" in "Africa" was connected to a "mauvaise venant" ("the malefic") and "sorcerers" emanating from Ouidah as a source of both slavery and Vodun.[2] From acknowledging the slave trade as the marker of economic demise to attributing that demise to Vodun and its "sorcerers," this contemporary interpretation is not unique to my young informants.[3] While I do not imply that a single sample of urban high school students constitutes the ways in which the Beninese remember Vodun, its zombie, or the slave trade, this anecdote does shed some light on how the Beninese perceive Vodun at the country's most prominent tourist destination. Indeed, this world-renowned site of kidnapping, pillaging, imprisonment, torture, and spiritual distortion even features in Beninese children's fiction. As I mentioned in Chapter 1, Eric Adja's *Les trois héros de Ouidah* features the site as one of violence but also contemplation and African complicity. The guide in the story allows the children to meditate on their "ancestors" and "slaves' atrocious suffering" as their emotional guide admits to African culpability (26–7). Indeed, Ouidah and its ocean-facing arch exist, as Dionne Brand rhetorically states, as a "door [that] induces sentimentality" (90). This is because, to recall Azoulay's term, it exists as a site of "potential history;" it speculatively considers the moment in which calamity could have been avoided had hegemonic violence not prevailed. But although Ouidah conjures the macabre – as my informants prove – death and violence overwhelmingly engulf the zombie site rather than the zombie being a source of salvation in the afterlife. Indeed, Ouidah is textually memorialized by Soyinka as a "Suicide Point" during his pilgrimage or a "Port of Call to hell" in Ivorian poet Bernard Dadié.[4] While the history these writers allude to cannot be refuted, the UNESCO site, on its own, does little to reverse the Eurocentric perception of the zombie's disfigurement nor point that violence away from the zombie figure itself. Díaz's textual memorial of Ouidah, on the other hand, in conversation with these politics of memory, fictionalizes the site and zombie to break down the fear that Vodun has conjured over centuries.

By contrast, Badagry, Nigeria, intertextualized in Obejas's *Ruins*, shores up a critique of neoliberal commodification of an African safari that implicates both sides of the global Latin-African divide. Obejas draws a comparison in the novel between the heritage sites of Badagry and Havana, as the latter reflects the advent of a 1990s tourism industry run amok in Cuba. But as Badagry reminds us, heritage tourism is far from benign. Badagry came to my attention when late Nigerian writer Pius Adesanmi invoked the site in his keynote address for the African Studies Conference, "The Black Atlantic: Colonial and Contemporary Exchanges," at Stanford University in 2011. I came back to Badagry when I read it in Obejas's novel just a few months later. Fast-forwarding nearly a decade, I found his keynote address in a posthumous collection of his essays ("Capitalism and Memory"). In an essay written for a colloquium that borrowed from Gilroy's acclaimed term, Adesanmi laments the commodification of Africa in the concept of the "Black Atlantic": "One obvious problem with a project that traces the roots and routes of these things to the Middle Passage and not to Africa per se is the ease with which we resituate Europe as the History in our histories" (63). Rather than looking to the African continent, African Diaspora studies, he argues, do not look beyond the Middle Passage, rendering Africa an unparticular "space" – "Africa. No name. No localizable people" (65). Profiting from this paradigm, developers exploit heritage tourism, with Badagry as an epitomic victim. Badagry exemplifies how the tourism industry monetizes histories of genocide. Adesanmi referred to the Jackson Five's lavish $3.5 billion-dollar development project that minimized the history of the slave trade at Badagry. The BBC shared the proposed prototype and added derisively that there, "[v]isitors can contemplate the horror of slavery from their luxury rooms."[5] While the project never materialized, this commodification trend of African sites of memory is hardly new. In fact, the neoliberalization of Badagry recalls Ato Quayson's spatial reading of his native Accra in Ghana that, like Badagry, becomes "scaled-down impressionisms of cosmopolitan consumption" (4). As Nigerian writers like Adesanmi and Soyinka bemoan Badagry's neoliberalization, so does Obejas, using this site to critique how the commodification of Africa led to its excision from Cuban and Cuban-American identity. This is because Badagry's heritage sites project a more promotional touristic imaginary of Africa than a revisionist heritage point for comparison to Cuba that writers like Obejas critique. But by tracing the long trajectory of African commodification, Obejas's critique of neoliberalization in *Ruins* releases "Africa" from its frenetic capitalistic and exoticized safari.

Something similar occurs with the disappearance of Africa altogether, as in García Márquez's admittedly forgettable mention of a slaveship sinking in *Crónica de una muerte anunciada*. As I explain in Chapter 3, in joining García Márquez's fictional Senegalese slaves to Fidel Castro's "Latin-African" rhetoric that justified African decolonization, I read these disappeared bodies as García Márquez's symbolic obliteration of the journalistic Angolan solidarity he wrote about – one that was forced to fail by power structures that exist just as much in Cuba as in capitalist hegemonies. Not only did a persistent US foreign policy asphyxiate a Cuban-Angolan alliance that solidified in the 1970s, Castro's Latin-African link was broken as he repressed Cuban racial equality while ironically supporting African political freedom abroad. This irony is also perpetuated at Gorée. While Gorée memorializes slavery – in the same way Castro decries Cuba's plantocracy – the site does not counter systems of oppression. A notable example is that, prior to my arrival on Gorée island, there had been a power outage that lasted over three days, but did not affect the Maison de esclaves, nor any other tourist sectors on the island. Understandably outraged, the locals staged protests and when the ferry arrived to return us to Dakar, the protestors began stoning it, forcing the ferry to retreat. This protest clearly marked local discontent over a site of memory that the state hypocritically used to condemn the capital gains undergirding slavery while neglecting to address capitalism's present-day uneven distribution of resources. Strangely, if UNESCO sites of commemoration attempt to prevent collective amnesia of crimes against humanity, as Renaud Hourcade states, they also feign a "political unity" (137). If in Chapter 3 I read the Senegalese bodies as a point of access to García Márquez's lamented death of a Latin-Africa now forgotten, it is also lamentable that a Latin-Africa – constituted by both text and site – memorializes past oppression but fails to eradicate colonial continuities of that oppression. Through the Angolan-Cuban crucible, I propose to reread García Márquez's post-1970s texts as textual memorials to the ways in which antiblack hegemonic continuities did indeed force a decolonial Latin-Africa to fail although it seems to also resist complete erasure.

The genocidal figure of Henry M. Stanley in Rivera's poem memorialized in Denbigh, Wales evinces how memorialization normalizes White supremacist discourse in the West at the same time as it distorts Africanness. Protests against Denbigh's Stanley celebration in 2011 were renewed in June 2020, when the Black Lives Matter movement demanded the statue's removal in the wake of George Floyd's murder. As with the Stanley statue at Congo's National Institute Museum in Kinshasa, council members at Denbigh explored moving the statue to a museum because its uncritical memorialization fails to acknowledge genocide,[6] leading Denbigh councilwoman Gwyneth Kensler to state that Stanley "loved Africans." In the end, the Denbighshire Council voted 6–5 to keep the statue, agreeing to consult the public after COVID-19 restrictions were lifted but abdicating the responsibility to the townspeople. As of this writing, a final decision in Denbigh has not been reached, but the upholding of imperialist Stanley helps explain how antiblack discourses distorting the African subject become unconsciously internalized even in underrepresented communities, as Rivera's impersonation of Stanley in his poem "Searching at Leal Middle School" shows. But while Rivera's conjuring of both Stanley and Livingstone, the missionary he rescued, reflects an uncritical position regarding Africa, reading Rivera's poem through the lens of memorialization complicates Rivera's poetic trail of memory.

Malawi's Dr. Livingstone Trail, as the mere naming of the trail implies, also upholds the narrative of the "White savior." As geographist Ian Munt has argued, "Dr. Livingstone is frequently invoked to assist in hedonistic discoveries" of African tourist spaces (53). The naming of this trail is perhaps in line with the UNESCO neoliberal tradition, yet a reading of Rivera's poem enables us to turn the neoliberal structure of the trail against itself, relativizing both the trail and the poem. As I mentioned in Chapter 4, even though UNESCO aims to bring attention to a segment of the slave trade that receives far less attention than its west or central African counterparts, UNESCO attempts to emphasize the uniqueness of its preserved spaces along the trail, from colonial forts, to raider's graves, relics, and mosques. UNESCO refers to "the slave routes" in this region as a "rare and unique heritage site in Malawi which records the memories of hardship and inhumanity that the people of Malawi and the entire Central Africa went through in the 19th Century."[7] It is precisely this dotted landscape that calls for pause and meditation along its trail; its stations draw attention to the same mechanisms taking effect in the "long, dusty trail" allegorized in Rivera. To word it differently, Malawi's trail functions as a route on which each site offers a place to pause and reflect.

Anthropologists Simon Coleman and John Eade explain that projects like the Slave Route trail offer a revisionist experience through what they term a "mapping of slave stations of the route" (22). Placing both route and poem together, Rivera's poem not only expresses both sensory and allegorical movement along different "stations"; reading the poem through the framework of this particular trail reveals how Rivera's textual trail pauses at particular sites to reverse Stanley's racialization of "darkness" toward an internationalist racial solidarity instead.

At the end of Chapter 4, I returned to the memory site in the opening chapter of this book. The Slave Route in Ouidah, after all, remains relevant to Anaya's *Bless Me, Ultima* for the ways in which its locale conjures the common proverb of the golden carp. Like Rivera's trail that moves, stops, and meditates on the history of colonial scramble for the Congo, Ouidah for Anaya's novel serves to distinguish historical markers within the story that, once enlarged, bring attention to the plantocratic regime in the US Southwest – a matter usually ignored in Chicano literary studies but that brings Chicano identity closer to the Caribbean's Black Atlantic history. As a result, these archival and oral findings draw attention to the Latin-Africa influences in both the vodun-practicing healers in *Bless me, Ultima* and the golden carp deity itself. In all of these cases, and even if memorial sites may commodify African cultures and histories, reading texts alongside them can change their effects and offer a revisiting of a Latin-Africa previously elided.

At the same time, the exploration of these canonical voices opens the door to examination of the Latin-African axis in the contemporary works not yet anthologized in World Literature. If in the introduction to this book, I mentioned Dahlma Llanos-Figueroa as a Caribbean representative – and indeed, Anne Garland Mahler has traced "a mutual ideological affinity" with a Black global resistance (108) – a Latin-African literature extends into the Chicano tradition as well. Alicia Gaspar de Alba's historical novel *Calligraphy of the Witch* (2007) is set over the memory sites of New England plantations and witch tribunals of Boston. In fact, the author herself recounts her fieldwork at the Salem Witch Museum and the Plymouth Plantation (371–3). Loosely based on this archival work, the story features Sor Juana Inés de la Cruz's afromestiza scribe, Concepción Benavidez, a practicing Catholic in New Spain sold into slavery to northern puritans. Reminiscent of the fear of Vodun in Junot Díaz, her Latina "foreignness" in seventeenth-century Boston will lead her own daughter to denounce her as a witch, for her Spanish, Catholicism, and herbal remedies (166–8). This denunciation leads to the Salem Witch Trials, where

Concepción is imprisoned, tried, and sentenced to death for her alleged seducing "potions or powders" (293) and fertilizers conceived of as "black magic" (199). Undergirding this evidence is the real justification for her arraignment: Concepción is a Spanish speaker, "tawny and foreign" (304), who befriends healer Indian Mawka and diviner Tituba, also women of color who are deemed witches. In the end, it is over the site of the Inquisitional jails – with "stone floors" where prisoners' "ankles were chained to the iron ring in the middle of the floor" (258) – that Concepción writes her story into the foundations of the colonial structure. Here, the jails that house mostly criminalized people of color recall not only West African slave forts, but also inscribe these holding spaces in text. Echoing the Slave Route in West Africa, Gaspar de Alba's memorialization of the "pillory," "back wall," the "iron ring," and "legs chained" (259) writes these spaces against the "jail hill" of Boston's Prison Lane. In this space, captive Concepción is also written into the Tribunal cases that the novel reproduces. In these reproduced inquisitorial cases, her voice revisits the accusations held against her and fictionally provides a counter to the *actual* colonial archive. Moreover, a collection of letters she leaves behind for her daughter after she escapes – cross-dressed and reinvented as a man – traces a textual memorial chiseled into the physical spaces of alleged Black criminalization.

Emma Pérez's picaresque novel *Forgetting the Alamo, or, Blood Memory* (2009), by contrast, tackles the US Southwestern plantation of the nineteenth century. Like Anaya and Rivera before her, she reimagines the transatlantic boundaries of the US Chicano Southwest in the novel's featured Black characters. The story centers on a nineteenth-century queer cowgirl, Micaela Campos, attempting to avenge the murder of her kin in the bloody aftermath of the Battle of the Alamo. In the process, however, she runs into two noteworthy characters: Lucius, a Virginian slave, and Miss Celestine, a mulata fortune-teller. Lucius comes "from a family of warriors. In Africa. Long line of warriors" (101), but in the US Southwest has been reduced to a slave. Miss Celestine, on the other hand, meets Micaela when the cowgirl travels to New Orleans. Miss Celestine is described as "a woman in a head turban, her skin light and dark at once and its darkness was as rich as cinnamon" (127). Her presence only heightens the weight of southern segregation, as Micaela perceives the "strict protocol" that dictates the color line that would survive into the twentieth century (126). Amidst racial inequality, Miss Celestine reveals the devil to Micaela: a man "with horns on his head" following her (130). In the end, the evil that follows Micaela is not a witch or the devil that colonial discourse has propagated throughout the centuries. Rather, Miss Celestine warns her that an iteration of the victors of coloniality, in this case southern White marauders, are once again attempting to deterritorialize people of color and steal Micaela's inherited property. The provisions that Miss Celestine passes on to Micaela through fortune-telling locate the site of subalternity in her racialized (Africanized) spirituality that also writes against the colonial textual memorial to tell an entirely different story.

Although *Calligraphy of the Witch* and *Forgetting the Alamo, or, Blood Memory* do not dwell necessarily on spaces of memory in Africa as do their predecessors or even some of their contemporaries, like Obejas, these non-heteronormative characters expand the racial geographies of their landscape. This transatlantic axis deprovincializes their literary traditions and interpretations of Latinx literature by expanding both narratives' geographical boundaries as well as ethnic expectations. It is as if these literatures lift the burden of representation of Latinx literature by configuring an African epistemology within their spatiotemporality. It is in this vein that Ralph Rodriguez manifests an interest both in the "definitions of Latinx literature" and the "ways the criticism circumscribes what we talk about when we talk about Latinx literature and how we talk about it" (3). Although Rodriguez questions the very taxonomy and aesthetic of "Latinx" as a unifying literary category – to enable Latinx critics to "make more compelling connections to literatures that fall outside of the Latinx parameters" – *The African Heritage of Latinx and Caribbean Literature* has not argued for doing away with the category of "Latinx" literature so much as for stretching its geographical and historical boundaries to settle on what I have termed Latin-Africa. If, as John Morán González has claimed, "Latina/o literature has become increasingly recognized as part of world literature" (xxiii),[8] this trend also allows me to think of the ways the writers in this study produce a world literature of their own. This outlook enables Latinx literature to make these compelling connections to world literatures, but also to those that trace a relational heritage with Latinos. As I have argued, particular sites of Atlantic memory embedded within the texts can both revisit and correct or at least unsettle the ethnic expectations placed on Latinx letters.

While the Latin-African axis begins to emerge in Latinx literary studies, comparative Latin American studies as of late also elucidate the centrality of an African-focused approach. Similar to Jennifer Harford Vargas's exemplary connection between Latin American and Latinx novelistic dictatorship tradition, Magalí Armillas-Tiseyra compellingly finds this genre within a South-South axis. For instance, in the works of two renowned Congolese authors, Henri Lopès's novel *The Laughing Cry* (*Le Pleurer-rire*, 1982) evokes "el Che" Guevara in the dictator's concern about a mysterious "Tché" or "Chez," while Sony Labou Tansi's *L'État honteux* (*The Shameful State*, 1981) intertextualizes García Márquez's *Autumn of the Patriarch* and his dictator's herniated testicle (13, 138). Arguing that this comparative framework "suppl[ies] instructive models and opportunities for solidarity in the future" (13), Latin American and African authors, she argues, have also coincided in their concerns regarding authoritarian regimes in the Global South and their role (or potential complicity) in acquiescing and further perpetuating its regimes in fiction. Similarly, Lanie Millar's transatlantic comparison of post–Cold War Angolan and Cuban narratives following the Angolan decolonization war do not portend a teleological awareness of the other's self-reflection but rather examples of praise and critique within this South-South framework. From the nostalgic focus on humanitarian collaboration in Cuban filmmaker Rogelio París's *Kangamba* (2008), to the failure of that collaboration in Angolan novelist Pepetela's *A Geração da Utopia* (1992), Millar provides another example of a Latin-African axis constituted by texts that are not often, if at all, indexed within the world literary canon. The particularization of Africa also enters in to the Mexican imaginary, albeit minimally. Thea Pitman and Sánchez Prado both identify the examples of Verónica Volkow's poetry in *Diario de Sudáfrica* (1988) which recounts personally witnessing the South African apartheid unfold, or the works of Jorge Ruiz Dueñas in *Las noches de Salé* (1986), María Victoria García's hybrid text *Vi(r)aje a la memoria* (1997), and *Dijo el camaleón* (2016), which all feature Morocco in its particularity ("Postcolonial *Compañeras*" 376–88; "África" 61–79). While these scholarly and literary comparative works ground bridges between Latin American and African literary history they also contest the monolingual and hegemonic structures that have traditionally defined World Literature.

But the Latin-Africa I have offered in this book is part of a two-way engagement. In addition to the examples provided in this book from Ondjaki, Eric Adja, Wole Soyinka, or Sony Labou Tansi, recent African fictions visit sites in the Americas and are the subject of much-needed scholarly elaboration. Tierno Monénembo's *Les coqs cubains chantent à minuit* (*The Cuban Cocks Sing at Midnight*, 2015) is set in Havana, where one of the key protagonists, a Guinean nicknamed "El Palenque" (Spanish for "slave community") returns to Cuba and is haunted by the colonial American legacy of slavery. Sami Tchak's *Hermina* (2003) similarly travels through Mexico, Cuba, and Miami – recognizable sites of memory of the African Diaspora – while his phantasmagorical *Filles de Mexico* (*Girls of Mexico* or *Daughters of Mexico* 2008) looks longingly at the deterioration and lawlessness of Mexico city's Tepito and Colombia's Cartucho neighborhoods. By contrast, Cameroonian Léonora Miano's *La saison de l'ombre* (*Season of the Shadow* 2013), which is set in the West African village of the Mulongo during the height of the Slave Trade, offers the perspective of those who attempt to cope with the imaginary of their family members enslaved in the Americas. In terms of Africanist scholarship, Ato Quayson has been the most representative of an engagement with a contemporary Latin-Africa. Through his insightful analysis of the diasporic reception of salsa, he connects both text and space between "Latin" and "African" poles. In tracing the globalization of "azonte salsa" in Ghana's capital from the late 1990s in his *Oxford Street, Accra* (2014), he states this musical mania is "firmly rooted in a form of Latinidad" (168). Visiting its sites of enunciation, from the nightclub Coconut Grove (and its "Mexican man" instructor) to the Citi 97.3 FM "Salsa Mania" nights, Quayson traces the Ghanaian salsa fever to its diasporic home in Cuba and Venezuela but also Puerto Rico and the US with the advent of the internet. "Many salsa instructors in Accra learned to hone their skills by watching YouTube videos of other salsa instructors" he acknowledges, but "the shared English-language provenance of the YouTube videos and the fact that many of them come from New York or LA means that it is the Puerto Rican version that many of these salsa instructors were first introduced to" (167). While a contemporary Latin-African connection might be clear in this instance, Quayson upstreams its transatlanticism further by not only recalling the primacy of the Cuban plantations for salsa, but underscoring its *actual* African origin. In tracing the music's style and rhythm to colonial West African sites and its eventual dispersal and transformation in the New World, Quayson's fieldwork along contemporary salsa sites in Ghana underscores not only salsa's return to Africa, but the music's Latin-African historiography that is not unlike the literary genealogy traced in this book.[9]

Compellingly, the UNESCO Slave Route intervenes in the memorialization of Quayson's musical Latin-African axis. North of Dakar in the port city of Saint-Louis, graffiti painted on a wall welcomes Afrolatinos in an attempt at Spanish. As Figure 5.1 shows, the spray painted inscription reads "St-Louis veut baila[r]" ("St-Louis wants [to] dance"), referencing the

Figure 5.1 Local store in St-Louis, Senegal. Photo: Sarah M. Quesada, 2012.

famed Jazz festival in St. Louis. This festival, as Senegalese scholar Ibrahima Wane states, serves as "a link between the Americas and Africa,"[10] but specifically the Spanish-speaking Caribbean and its diaspora. This is because the word "baila[r]" indeed references the salsa scene that Quayson has noted. This time in Senegal, during the 1960s and 1970s, Cuban and Puerto Rican music was so admired that popular bands such as *Orchestra Baobab* and its musical base "found themselves [reflected]."[11] Even if in the 1980s Afro-Cuban influence subsided, particularly in Senegal, it reemerged along the Slave Route at the turn of the millennium. This music "continued to flourish in Dakar's many boîtes [clubs]," as witnessed in the popularity of Senegalese James Gadiaga, and even *mbalax* musicians such as Youssou N'Dour and Coumba Gawlo (Shain 186; Wane et al. 3–9). To return to this curious wall graffiti captured just a few days before my departure from Senegal, the Franco-Spanish public writing speaks less to a centralized notion of a French Atlantic space that Casanova surmised for World Literature, and more to a reconception of "transatlanticism" that writers in this study have memorialized. Thus, the graffiti also captures the praxis I have been elaborating all along: one that considers texts as sites to be visited, and sites as texts to be read. Indeed, the marking on a site along the trail of memory in Senegal uses text to speak to the visitor in the same way that the texts I have discussed in this book use sites to welcome their reader-visitor.

Despite these mutually constituting forms of counterdiscursive memory – text and site – that speak back to a colonial archive, this study does not assume that the excising of an African historiography is corrected in twenty-first century Latinx texts, much less canonical Caribbean or Chicano authors. Neither does it assume that studies like this one can bridge the distance between Latin American or US Latinx populations and the African continent. Rather, it sets into motion sites of understanding that propose a revisiting. After all, the Atlantic World looms large in the backdrop of such recognized authors, but has gone unaddressed, ironically due to constructs that the Atlantic World itself has produced. An African-based revisiting of colonial sources – archival, oral, field interviews, and an attention to spatial sites in texts – provides a context within which a Latin-Africa can meaningfully enter into the literary genealogy of Latinx and Latin American letters, and, hopefully, decolonize the various ways in which history, race, ethnicity, and more generally an African sense of identity in the Americas have been indirectly affected by an excision produced in the African continent as well.

The Eurocentric trajectory of American, Latin American, Comparative, and even World Literature has often embraced transatlantic movement between Europe and North America that snubs the more obvious subaltern connections with the slave trade's point of departure. These frameworks occur frequently despite a rise of South-South or transnational blackness that is not unique to Latin American studies. As a result, scholarship on Caribbean authors like Díaz, García Márquez, or Obejas and Mexican-Americans like Rivera and Anaya, who bring the effects of slavery home to roost, can ignore not only the rich archives of colonial Africa and their clear connections to many of the expressions of antiblackness in their fiction, but also the more recent US involvement in Africa, from nineteenth-century resource extraction to the sinister sabotage of democracy that still plagues African nation-states. While this isolationist framework is perhaps unconscious, in our current times, an opening toward other languages, approaches, histories, and social justice movements – which the US government has repeatedly distorted, erased, and muted – is urgent. This is especially true as World Literature, ironically, further circulates these hegemonic and isolationist readings of authors who would be viewed as more "global" if these Latin-African connections were not obscured. The repositioning of Africa over the transnational axis of recognized US Latinx and Latin American writers would not only decolonize much of the western attitudes that govern American literary criticism but would bring World Literature closer to its inclusive and worldly promise.

Notes

Introduction: Textual Memorials of a Latin-African Literature

1. The study of these "remains" or sites of memory, Nora explains, constitutes "the ultimate embodiments of a memorial consciousness" (12).
2. Fela's daughter Mati becomes a healer who takes back the master's house in colonial Puerto Rico, Mati's daughter Concha finds medicinal plants through sensory nodes on her feet, and Concha's daughter Elena finds refuge in the African stories that the stone evokes following her tragic move to New York city.
3. For Anaya, see Marta Caminero-Santangelo's insightful essay "'Jason's Indian': Mexican Americans and the Denial of Indigenous Ethnicity in Anaya's Bless Me, Ultima," and for a discussion on magical realism and the global, see Mariano Siskind's excellent study, *Cosmopolitan Desires: Global Modernity and World Literature in Latin America* (2014).
4. See Sánchez Prado, *Strategic Occidentalism: on Mexican Fiction, the Neoliberal Book Market, and the Question of World Literature* (2018) and Coutinho's *Brazilian Literature as World Literature* (2019).
5. Latinx literature does indeed figure in conversations surrounding World Literature theory. In *The Routledge Companion to World Literature*, Latinx studies is indexed a handful of times, gesturing favorably toward the scholarship of notable critics such as José David Saldívar, Doris Sommer, Richard Perez, or Kirsten Silva Gruesz. The limitations of this indexing are, however, notable, from the misspelling of the names of key Latinx critics and authors to nods toward Latinx theory that treat it only as a possibility fecund in the 1970s and do not actually show *how* Latinx literature is shaping and *has* shaped World Literature.
6. Moreover, scholars such as Marisa Belausteguigoitia played a key role in introducing the work of Chicanas and US Latinas into the Mexican academy through the Programa Universitario de Estudios de Género (PUEG), in which students engaged the feminist writings of Norma Alarcón, Chela Sandoval, Sandra Cisneros, and Gloria Anzaldúa. In 1997, a Latinx studies section was

established in the Latin American Studies Association. Its foundation was not without difficulties, but the establishment of this section within the flagship professional association for Latin American studies was indeed groundbreaking and it has been devoted, in great part, to transnational study. Also critical has been the Tepoztlán Institute for the Transnational History of the Americas in Morelos, México, established in 2004.

7. See Geweck, who notes that the scholarship of Ann-Catherine Geuder's *Chicana/o Literaturbetrieb* (2004), Markus Heide's *Grenzüberschreibungen* (2004), Gabriele Pizar-Ramirez's *MexAmerica* (2005), to name a few, make clear that a rising interest in Chicano writing in Germany can be traced back to the turn of the millennium. Interest in Latinx literature in Britain, however, was complicated by the fact that Latinx literature written primarily in English "had to compete" with the more established "New English" or "Commonwealth literature" in the UK ("Latino/a Literature in Western Europe" 108).

8. Quinto Sol was the first Chicano publisher; its prize in Chicano literature was initiated in 1967 and led by University of California, Berkeley professor Octavio I. Romano, his student Nick C. Vaca, and Herminio Ríos. The first prize was awarded in 1970. For more information, see Héctor Calderón, *Narratives of Greater Mexico*, and "Chicano/a Literature" in the *Routledge Companion to Latino/a Literature*.

9. Obejas has also translated Díaz's *This is How You Lose Her*, as well as selected works of Francisco Gerardo Haghenbeck, Paloma Sánchez-Garnica, and Susana Lopez Rubio.

10. See *The Forked Juniper: Critical Perspectives on Rudolfo Anaya* (2016) for readings that focus on Anaya's Iberian-American axis.

11. Preceding the incorporation of Latinx studies into World Literature was Latin Americanists' critique of World Literature's exclusion of Latin America. Spurred on by Franco Moretti's "Conjectures" and the notion that departments of national literature, such as English departments, might use World Literature as a means to superficially teach regional literatures from other linguistic traditions, such as those of Latin America – Latin Americanists have recurred to revisionism. From establishing that the writings of Latin American authors such as César Vallejo, García Márquez, or Borges have been central to European paradigms and not the other way around, or asserting that Angel Rama's "lettered city" functions as a kind of precedent to Pascale Casanova's "republic of letters," these concerns have not only justified Latin American letters' place in the sovereign "republic" of World Literature, but have also been used to critique the "imperial-colonial" practice of the discipline as a whole (Sánchez Prado "Hijos"; De Ferrari 23).

12. Noteworthy is also Lorgia García-Peña's forthcoming *Translating Blackness*, and Richard T. Rodríguez's *A Kiss across the Ocean*, on European, US, or Caribbean cultural exchanges.
13. Pérez Rosario traces Burgos's appreciation, for example, of Spanish Moor art, promoting "the African cultures brought to this part of the world" (85) and reveals other Global South alignments in poets such as Sandra María Estevez (112).
14. Michael Dowdy has also termed Cruz's synchronization of African roots and a valorization of "Africanness" via "Moorish influence" (*Broken Souths* 54). Similarly, Urayoán Noel has read Nuyorican poet Miguel Piñero's metaphoric "or psychic" interzone of the Lower East Side in New York city as akin to the physical Moroccan interzone of William Burroughs (*In Visible Movement* 51–5).
15. One of these ethical tasks is to be true to a literary work's origin. As Damrosch notes, World Literature's engagement with the global is an ethical pursuit that has "generalists" working conjointly with "specialists": "the generalist should feel the same ethical responsibility toward specialized scholarship that a translator has toward a text's original language: to understand the work effectively in its new cultural and theoretical context while at the same time getting it right in a fundamental way in reference to the source culture" 288). Yet Guillermina De Ferrari also notes that World Literature commits literature to move beyond one's own cultural world ("Utopías" 17).
16. See Isacio Pérez Fernández's *Inventario documentado de los escritos de fray Bartolomé de Las Casas*, Graciela Montaldo's *Ficciones culturales y fábulas de identidad en América Latina* (1999), Maria Gabriela Nouzeilles's *Ficciones somáticas* (2000), and Juliet Hooker's *Theorizing Race in the Americas* (2017). Importantly, as Torres-Saillant notes, Bolívar states with regard to Black soldiers, "[i]s it not proper that the slaves should acquire their rights on the battlefield and that their dangerous numbers should be lessened by a process just and effective?" ("Afrolatinidad" 292).
17. As José David Saldívar has argued, Martí sought to "unify the histories of the Americas" as a counterdistinctive expression to Manifest Destiny (*Dialectics* 5, 9). Laura Lomas argues that Martí's expansive view of equality included the transitory "southern peoples" from the "disdained southern European or Jew" to the "formerly enslaved Africans, and Asian laborers" (35–6). See also José David Saldívar's *Trans-Americanity* (2012).
18. For *Sab*, see Doris Sommer's *Foundational Fictions*. With regard to Zambrana Vasquez, Ivan Schulman has wrongly denoted this genre as "abolitionist." For more on Zambrana, see Estebana Matarrita. For Heredia, see Gruesz (141–2). For Gowen Brooks, or Maria del Occidente, see Gruesz, who also states that Brooks's lyrical output *Zóphiël* and *Idomen* uses the metaphor of slavery for women's liberation through the imaginary of the slave (62–4).

19. See Julie Taylor and George Yúdice. Moreover, as Juan E. de Castro notes in tracing the history of mestizaje, this intermixing of racial elements heightened "miscegenation or cultural mixture as the basis for conceiving a homogenous national identity out of a heterogeneous population" (*Mestizo Nations* 9).
20. See 505–6. Morales defines a "brownologist" as a critic who uses "brown" to "obscure the fact that Latinos come in the full spectrum of racial hues, very much including Black" and "consistently categorize Latinos as distinctively separate from African Americans, a third mestizo wheel in the American race dialogue" (503), while also pointing out the propensity of uncontested racial slurs among Latinos such as "moyeto" or "pelo malo" ("bad hair," 505).
21. Miriam Jiménez Román and Juan Flores note that "the word 'Afro-Latin@'" can be viewed as an expression of long-term transnational relations and of world events that generated and were in turn affected by particular global social movements – not only Pan-Africanism, Negritude, the Harlem Renaissance, and Afrocubanismo, but also "the growth of African liberation movements as part of a global decolonization process, as well as the Civil Rights and Black Panther movements" (1).
22. As Horacio Legrás explains, although "criollo" originally meant Black slaves born in America, it evolved to signify the descendants of Europeans born in the Americas ("Literary *Criollismo*" 222).
23. It is important to point out that although the term "Latinidad" now refers to US Latinos – those of Latin American ancestry living within the political borders of the US and its territories – it was originally used to exclude those living north of the Mexican-American border. Mignolo points out that imperial histories "placed an Anglo America in the north and the Latin America in the south in the new configuration of the Western Hemisphere" (57).
24. Silvio Torres-Saillant notes that the homogenization of US Latinx literature "conceals the tensions, inequities, and injustices in our midst, contributing to a conceptual ambience that legitimizes the absence of Black and Indian faces and voices from Latino fora" ("Problematic Paradigms" 444).
25. Ralph Bauer explained that Latin Americanists viewed Hemispheric studies – housed in American studies departments – as a form of US intellectual expansionism whereby transnationalism was claimed as unprecedented, thus dismissing decades of Latin American research on the subject ("Hemispheric Studies" 236–7).
26. Works that have pointed out this blind spot are Ben Vinson's "Introduction: African (Black) Diaspora History, Latin American History" (2006), Laura Chrisman's "Journeying to Death: Paul Gilroy's The Black Atlantic" (2003), Christine Chivallon and Karen Fields's "Beyond Gilroy's Black Atlantic: The Experience of the African Diaspora" (2002), and Lucy Evans's "The Black Atlantic: Exploring Gilroy's Legacy" (2009).

27. Bauer explains that Hemispheric studies, on the other hand, place more emphasis on the "American" part of the hyphenated cultural self-identifier ("Hemispheric Studies" 238). On Gilroy, Goyal explains that the Black Atlantic model "replicated the problematic exclusion of Africa from modernity" (vi).
28. In my article "An Inclusive 'Black Atlantic': Revisiting Historical Creole Formations," I draw on Africanist historians to show how creole formation was taking place in Africa as much in the New World, before and during the forced migration of African enslaved people to the Americas. A specific example of this paradigm is that fact that colonized Africans well-equipped with European customs were reduced to hybrid terms such as "Euroafricans," "African Christians," or "Atlantic creoles," and thus "seamlessly woven into the narrative of Western democratic triumphalism" (*Domingos* 5).
29. Simon Gikandi was one of the first critics to address this absence of African intellectuals, in "In the Shadow of Hegel: Cultural Theory in an Age of Displacement" (1996). See also Charles Piot's "Atlantic Aporias: Africa and Gilroy's Black Atlantic" (2001), Paul Tiyambe Zeleza's "Rewriting the African Diaspora: Beyond the Black Atlantic" (2005), and Joan Dayan's "Paul Gilroy's Slaves, Ships, and Routes: The Middle Passage as Metaphor" (1996). Moreover, Melville Herskovits, Kwame Nkrumah, Frantz Fanon, Ngũgĩ wa Thiong'o, Mudimbe, Mbembe, Wole Soyinka, and Camara Laye, to name a few Africanist intellectuals featured here, offer a counterdiscourse to archives about "Africa" through a shifted lens from the African continent.
30. Decoloniality implies here not only re-inscribing othered traditions into the logics of Western modernity – as postcolonial studies initially devoted themselves to (Bhambra 16) – but also questioning the very centrality of modernity itself.
31. Right after independence in Africa, Africanist scholars argued for the Africanization of history. Not only did Jan Vansina's research on the Congolese Bantu community argue that oral traditions were African structures of knowledge, he underlined the vital importance of African oral history permeating nearly every facet of African communities. Kenneth Onwuka Dike and Jacob F. A. Ajayi transformed the curriculum to focus on West African studies in Nigeria, Bethwell A. Ogot "rejected the sanitization of colonial history" in Kenya, and several other Africanist historians throughout the continent, and even within the United States, sought to promote an African-centered approach (Bekerie 452–3).
32. Scholars discussing fiction as memorialization are Rita Sakr in *Monumental Space in the Post-Imperial Novel* (2012), Melissa Sodeman in *Sentimental Memorials* (2014), Shelley Fisher Fishkin in *Writing America* (2015), Sylvia

Wynter in "Novel and History, Plot and Plantation" (1971), and Toni Morrison in "The Site of Memory" (1995).

33. Other projects include Sean Heuston's *Modern Poetry and Ethnography*, Renato Rosaldo's *The Day of Shelly's Death*, or Robert Harm's *The Diligent: A Voyage through the Worlds of the Slave Trade*.

34. See Susana Draper's *Afterlives of Confinement*, Avelar's *The Untimely Present*, Judith Butler's *Frames of War: When Is Life Grievable?* and her more personal *Precarious Life: The Powers of Mourning and Violence* (2004).

35. Certeau explains that this happens through a person walking and *appropriating* the "topographical system" around her, *performing* within that space, and finally *relating* to shifting positions of that space (98, emphasis added).

36. Historians have argued that Gorée had long ceased being central to the slave trade when the Maison was built. Some scholars contend it was built in 1776 by Dutch settlers; others state it was built by the French in 1793 (Araujo *Public Memory* 85, footnote 23; *Héritages de l'esclavage*, UNESCO, 83). Emmanuel de Roux, in "Le myth de la Maison des esclaves qui résiste à la réalité," cites research by IFAN (*Institut Fondamental d'Afrique Noire*) that declares that the Maison was not built by the French until 1793, when the slave trade had for the most part ceased in the region. Moreover, as Boubacar Barry states, the abolition of the slave trade in the early eighteenth century contributed to the policing of Gorée, which is why it ceased to be a prominent slave outpost. While it still received a high number of slaves, they were not exported to the Americas and were used to attempt (failed) plantations on the African continent to produce peanuts and oil (130, 137, 144). The site also "served primarily as a private residence for one Anne Pépin," as Michael Ralph explains, who was a merchant who "occasionally held enslaved Africans in the basement of the residence" (102).

37. This argument runs parallel once again to Azoulay, who serves as a chief interlocutor for this theorization since her concept of potential history serves to "historicize the sovereign power of the past and render it potentially reversible" (565). Textual memorials, in contrast, do not serve to "reverse" an imagined course of history but to recall moments of this Latin-African past.

38. See Araujo, *Public Memory*, 9. Benin's neoliberal president Nicéphore Soglo, who had held "various positions in international organizations such as the IMF and World Bank," requested a "Marshall Plan" to renegotiate debt. It is in this 1990s era that "Benin began requesting financial aid from the World Bank and the IMF, and in these circumstances cultural tourist became one of the viable alternatives for promoting the economic developments of the area" (*Public Memory* 131–2).

39. See Sarah Quesada, "Planetary Warning?: The Multilayered Caribbean Zombie in 'Monstro'" in *Junot Díaz and the Decolonial Imagination*, edited by Monica Hanna, Jennifer Harford Vargas, and José David Saldívar.
40. France ruled portions of the north, west, and equatorial Africa; England, vast swaths of the east, south, and west; Belgium what today is the Democratic Republic of the Congo; Portugal the colonies of Mozambique, Angola, and Guinea-Bissau, along with Cape Verde and São Tomé and Príncipe; Spain held onto "Africa occidental española" or the northern portion of Morocco, Equatorial Guinea, and the islands of Ceuta and the Canary islands (which remain Spanish). But in 1958, Prime Ministers Kwame Nkrumah of Ghana and Patrice Lumumba of the Democratic Republic of the Congo created a Union of African States that defied powerful western states and institutions, including the IMF and the United Nations. It also demanded the economic liberation of Mali, Ghana, and Guinea, as well as Belgium's withdrawal from the Congo (interfering with the UN's Security Council resolution, Nkrumah 149).
41. After former French, British, and Belgian colonies began consolidating their independence after 1958, a notable exception were Portugal's former colonies where Cuba intervened. Precisely because of Cuban engagement in the decolonizing wars in Guinea Bissau and Angola indicated Soviet expansion in Africa, the US began considering Cuba a threat. The US's fears had in fact been justified earlier by Cuban involvement in Algeria, Equatorial Guinea, Tanzania, Mali, and the Congo, to name a few. In the Democratic Republic of the Congo, Cuba meaningfully intervened when Ernesto "Che" Guevara's mission began in 1963 to control access to the Indian and Atlantic oceans and to cut off resources to the West.
42. Conflict arose because Portugal decreed that whichever party controlled Angola by November 11, 1975, would establish sovereignty. These political rivalries in Angola were so entrenched, in part because the colonial structure had encouraged "ethnic rivalry" and, in anticipating Portugal's release of Angola, three distinguishable parties vied for control: the anti-communist Jonas Malheiro Savimbi-led UNITA (National Union for the Total Independence of Angola), Agostinho Neto's MPLA (People's Movement for the Liberation of Angola), and Holden Roberto's FNLA (National Liberation Front of Angola). The CIA financed and supported political factions opposed to Cuban-supported MPLA (Gleijeses 259).
43. Critics disagree on why Cuba became such a staunch defender of Angolan liberation specifically or African decolonization in general. One reason offered is that, in the wake of the Bay of Pigs invasion and US failure to eliminate Fidel Castro's triumphant Revolution, the Kennedy and Khrushchev administrations agreed in 1962 that the Soviet Union would remove nuclear warheads from Cuba

if the US promised not to intervene in Cuban affairs (Schmidt 97). As the US heavily policed Cuban revolutionary intervention in Latin America, the first fifteen years since Cuba's overthrow of Batista, "Havana's foreign aid went almost exclusively to Africa" (Gleijeses 228). But other critics argue that it was merely Cuba's socialist agenda to spread a revolution in the Global South, while Afro-Cuban scholars have detailed Cuba's justified allegiance to Africa as a means to overlook racial inequality at home.

1 Fear: Junot Díaz's Zombies and *Les contorsions extraordinaires* in "Monstro"

1. See "Junot Díaz Aims to Fulfill His Dream of Publishing Sci-Fi Novel with 'Monstro'" *Wired*, October 3, 2012.
2. See "Apocalypse: What Disasters Reveal": "Whether it was Haiti's early history as a French colony, which artificially inflated the country's black population beyond what the natural bounty of the land could support and prevented any kind of material progress … and only really allowed to rejoin the world community by paying an indemnity to all whites who had lost their shirts due to the Haitian revolution, an indemnity Haiti had to borrow from French banks in order to pay, which locked the country in a cycle of debt that it never broke free from. … This is what Haiti is both victim and symbol of – this new, rapacious stage of capitalism. A cannibal stage." See also Jennifer Harford Vargas's excellent interpretation of "ruin-reading" ("Dictating a Zafa").
3. Moraña argues further that the use of the zombie was connected "to slavery and colonialism, as well as forms of capitalist production that are considered worse than death insofar as they entail the loss of freedom, the exploitation of the body, the dissolution of consciousness, dehumanization, and alienation" (*The Monster* 168).
4. According to the *Trans-Atlantic Slave Trade Database*, from 1701 to 1800, Jamaica received an estimated 834,681 enslaved people, while Brazil received 1,965,960. (https://slavevoyages.org/).
5. Frantz Fanon calls this color complex a *névrose d'abandon*, or an internalized acceptance of one's inferiority vis-à-vis the color line (*Peau noire, masques blancs* 72).
6. Haiti paid an "indemnity of 150 million francs (roughly $3 billion in today's currency) to compensate slaveholders for their losses" (Dubois *Haiti* 7) and Haiti was "ostracized for the better part of the nineteenth century" while "the country deteriorated economically and politically – in part as a result of this ostracism" (Trouillot *Silencing the Past* 98).
7. When US officers assessed Dominican independence from Haiti in 1845, they sided with Dominicans through a racist logic in which Haitian

Notes to Pages 39–48

blackness was posited as the opposite end of the desired racial spectrum. As Torres-Saillant notes, American commissioner Jonathan E. Green assured the US government that although Dominicans were Black, they were "negro blanco" ("white blacks," "Tribulations" 1087). Dixa Ramírez concludes that "because of this global stance against Haiti, many nineteenth- and twentieth-century Dominican nationalists were eager to suppress Dominican connections to Haiti" (12).

8. See Torres-Saillant, "The Tribulations of Blackness," 1086–90. Lorgia García-Peña also notes that the US was instrumental in shifting Dominican finances to the US mainland to appropriate land on the island for cultivating sugar. During this time, Jim Crow also shaped the US military presence on the island: a color hierarchy of whiteness vis-à-vis blackness that "legitimized the marines' ability to assert masculine authority while justifying criminal actions through the rhetoric of white civility and progress" (60, 75). This military presence facilitated the US-sponsored creation of the Dominican National Guard, "which served as a vehicle for the ruthless dictatorship of Rafael Leonidas Trujillo" (ibid. 60). As Frank Moya Pons explains, Trujillo objected to Haitians living along the border and within Dominican territories (servants, farmers, laborers, or small businessmen) and in October 1937, used this position to commit a genocide against twenty thousand ethnic Haitians but also Afro-Dominicans along the border (Moya Pons *Dominican* 368).

9. See García-Peña for more regarding how *La Sentencia* became a ruling, two decades in the making, based on a term that was initially designated for tourists in "transit," then applied to Haitian laborers, "aimed at disenfranchising ethnic Haitians and divesting them of civil liberties and citizenship rights" (204).

10. See "Author Junot Díaz called unpatriotic" in *The Guardian* (www.theguardian.com/books/2015/oct/25/junot-diaz-author-dominican-republic-haiti-immigration).

11. This phase involves the "brain" of a system's dysfunction in which "the limbs are still moving, and many of the defensive reflexes seem to be working too. The living dead of the free-market revolution continue to walk the earth, though with each resurrection their decidedly uncoordinated gait becomes even more erratic" ("Zombie Neoliberalism and the Ambidextrous State" 7).

12. The quotes from this paragraph are taken from the earlier online version of "Monstro."

13. See Herskovits as he traces the "zombie" to "a Dahomean belief" (*Dahomey* I, 361).

14. See *Police des Noirs* 1777–8: "j'avais promi[s]e Lucille pour le soin de son enfant" and "la negresse ne s'étant point corrigé de ses défauts" (FM_F_1B_1–4), Archives Nationales d'outre-mer, Aix-en-Provence.

15. Ibid. and "colonies 35" in Police des Noirs 1777–8. Archives Nationales d'outre-mer, Aix-en-Provence. In the correspondence, an agent likens Lucille to "le negre Azou" (in "L'affair du negre Azou"), who was also from Ouidah.
16. Vodun's commonplace phrase "nou fet pou n mouri" [we are born to die] "gave 'body' to rebelliousness and hope" (Bellegarde-Smith and Michel *Haitian Vodou* 26).
17. See Dantes Bellegarde, *Histoire du peuple haïtien*, 59.
18. See *Relation du Royaume de Judas en Guinée*,: "le roy de Judas s'étant laissé persuader par ses prestres dépendre à serpent pour un Dieu, s'y triomphou se ses ennemis, il le promit es la guerre ayant été terminé par une bataille qu'il gagna lui le Roy d'ardres il offrit des sacrifices en reconnaissance de sa . . . [/] au serpent et depuis il fut généralement reconnu de ses sujets pour le Dieu tutélaire de la nation" (unaltered transcription 53–4). Another passage that corroborates this claim is the following: "serpent qui à proprement parler est de touttes les divinités celle qu'ils reconnaissent pour la protectrisse de leur nation" ("the serpent that, strictly speaking, is of all divinities, the one they recognize as protector of their nation," 53).
19. For instance, the proverb is "L'écureuil vit sur le sable les traces des pas de panthère et se prosterna en signe de serpent et d'adoration" ("The squirrel saw the footsteps of the panther on the sand and bowed down as a sign of the snake and adoration" conveying its meaning: "All lord, all honor") speaks to the common use of this religious symbol. Common Proverb in Benin.
20. See Lauro, 73. Geoffroy Parrinder has also traced the zombie as emerging from the Ewe in the regions that today compose Ghana and Togo, beyond former Dahomey (166) while others have located the zombie in Congolese tribes of the seventeenth century (Frazer *The Golden Bough* 70).
21. See *Relation du Royaume de Judas en Guinée*, "they enter their house and go into the houses and girls are taken from 7 year-olds to 12 or 14 and lock them in the cages of snakes to see them there. The black deity that is the snake who takes possession of this child and their vaudonnous to better enjoy their game and prevent him from seeing their ridiculous ceremonies have persuaded the negroes that if they allow women to see or run their ceremonies, they will become crazed" ("quelles entrent dans leur maison et quelles entrent dans leur maison et quelles prennent les filles depuis 7 ans jusqu'à 12 ou 14 et les enferment dans les cages des serpents pour les y voir. Le nègre evou que c'est le serpent qui prend possession de cet enfant et leurs vaudonnous pour mieux jouir leur jeu et empêcher que lui ne voye leurs cérémonies ridicules ont persuadé aux nègres qui sils voyaient ces femmes courir ou pratiques leurs cérémonies ils deviendront foux," original transcription 61–2).

22. See Bouche, *Sept ans en Afrique Occidentale. La Côte des Esclaves et le Dahomey*, "'la côte des Esclaves est pour l'Européen un des pays les plus malsains de l'univers'" (9).
23. Ibid. "Les fièvres intermittentes dominent toute la pathologie du pays" (205). See also E. Binet on "les pustules de variole" ("Observations sur les Dahoméens" 250) and Elisée Soumonni, "The prevalence of smallpox was a major problem for European slave traders in Dahomey because of its impact on their human cargo. In the late seventeenth century, many enslaved Africans shipped at Ouidah were found on arrival in the West Indies to be infected with smallpox" ("Disease, Religion, and Medicine: Smallpox in Nineteenth-Century Benin," 38).
24. See Phillips, "finish'd all my business at Whidaw [on the Gold Coast of Africa], I took my leave of the old king. . . . But what the small pox spar'd, the flux swept off, to our great regret, after all our pains and care to give them their messes in due order and season, keeping their lodgings as clean and sweet as possible, and enduring so much misery and stench so long among a parcel of creatures nastier than swine, and after all our expectations to be defeated by their mortality" (85–7).
25. See Julie Minich, "The Decolonizer's Guide to Disability," which reads disease within the poor working or living conditions in Díaz's short stories from *Drown* to *This Is How You Lose Her*, connecting maladies to coloniality. Similarly, Richard Perez has read the face in Díaz's short story "Ysrael" specifically, as a site of enunciation to reveal racial expression ("Racial Spills").
26. By "Americanity" I mean, as J. Saldívar explains, "a crucial geo-social space" that "links up the idea of a coloniality-power couplet with that of ethnicity" (*Trans-Americanity* x–xi). See also J. Saldívar's "Conjectures on 'Americanity'," 120–36.
27. See Sandoval: "*Es monstruo lo que se engendra*, según aquella parte en que se diferencia su principio, y así dice que *las mujeres de alguna manera lo son*, porque no llegan a tener la perfección de su generante . . . Aunque algunos han dicho que suele también suceder *por tener la mujer acto con el demonio*" (30, emphasis added). It is worth noting that in the redacted translation of his text, *Treatise on Slavery*, this particular observation, while alluded to by the editor, is omitted. This editorial decision is confusing: why the deliberate decision to inform the reader of the colonial mindset regarding gender, yet conceal the actual discourse.
28. *Relation du Royaume de Judas*, "Les nègres de Judas sont . . . fins dans leur négoces et abrutis dans leur religion" (43).
29. See Moreau de Saint-Méry, "They turn round and round. And while there are some who tear their clothes in this bacchanal and even bite their own flesh,

others merely lose consciousness and falling down are carried into a neighboring room where in the darkness a disgusting form of prostitution holds hideous sway" (*Description topographique*, ... I, 46–51).

30. Seabrook, "Huddled upon the floor, body to body, some crouching and others prostrate, were a score or more of black men and women, swaying, writhing, moaning. Before the altar of skulls, facing us, stood three human figures, grotesque, yet indescribably sinister. All three who stood there were women. ... Why it was that as simple a thing as smoked goggles seemed horrible, ..." (*Magic* 84).

31. Herskovits in fact explains that, for Vodun practitioners, "the world was created by one god, who is at the same time both male and female" (*Dahomey* 101). Further, Herskovits points out that these women practitioners, far from being Seabrook's "grotesque creatures," are admirable free agents, "dancing" vigorously and "rejoicing because the god had come to her so vehemently" (*Dahomey* 165).

32. Launched February 8–18, 1993, it was a highly successful festival attended by Vodun priestesses and priests, UNESCO representatives, historians and other scholars, and artists spanning the diaspora. In attendance were prominent artists James Brown, Gilberto Gil (then Minister of Culture of Brazil), Haitian-American artist Edouard Duval-Carrié, Afro-Cuban artist Manuel Mendive, who painted the Xevioso/Chango temple. It was also supported by various heads of state in West Africa, as well as prominent literary figures like Léopold Sédar Senghor, Aimé Césaire, Wole Soyinka, Christiane Diop, and René Depestre, among others (Rush, 134, 150–2; Araujo "Welcome" 158–9).

33. Historians note that it was more feasible that slaves were embarked by canoe, through a coastal lagoon that separated the town from the beach (Law 26; Araujo "Welcome" 159).

34. These include the "auction block," the Tree of Forgetfulness the Zomachi Memorial of Repentance, the Zomaï enclosure, the Zoungbodji memorial, and the Tree of Return.

35. See Ciarcia, my translation ("Restaurer le futur" 687).

36. Araujo remarks that locals even appropriate "several monuments representing Vodun deities [along the Slave Route], by placing offerings at the base of the statues as if they were actual Vodun shrines" ("Welcome" 162).

37. The plaque at the Tree of Forgetfulness reads: "The male slaves should run around nine times, the female seven. Once they were finished, the slaves were expected to become amnesic."

38. Law has suggested, based on historical findings in the archive, that rather than slaves circling the tree a number of times, it was the chief who performed this ritual "prior to greeting the Europeans" (153).

39. Collected during fieldwork in Ouidah. The original reads as: "Malheur au qu'il frôle le serpent minute." Transcriptions and meaning are courtesy of Director Zphirin Daavo at l'Agence Nationale pour la Promotion des Patrimoines et de développement du tourisme au Bénin, in Cotonou, Benin. I am particularly thankful to Paulin Hountondji for his mediation during this visit.
40. Quoted in *On the Postcolony*, Mbembe further proposes that "spaces of terror" produce "hysterical masses, faces bereft of humanity, bloated bodies" to "create around the colonized a world of prohibitions and inhibitions far more terrifying than any world of the colonizer" (181–2).
41. See Adja, in which the guide leads the children to the Port of Non-Retour, giving the students an opportunity to meditate on the trade: "Les enfants étaient tout émus. Ils pensaient aux souffrances atroces que les esclaves, leurs lointains et anonymes aïeux, avaient dû subir."
42. See Mintz and Price regarding the gatherings of different ethnic groups of slaves on certain plantations and the subsequent escape of some into maroon communities; termed *palenques*, *quilombos*, or clans. As they explain, these communities were essential for slaves, and planters sought to undo them so as to preclude revolt (26).
43. As Glissant explains, Relation "does not base its principles on itself" and it assumes "change" – in the vein that Spivak understands strategic essentialism – "as rapidly as the elements thus put into play define (embody) new relationships and change them" (*Poetics* 171–2).
44. See Surwillo, 20–1. She also explains the term "Monsters by Trade," the title of her study, in the following way: "Thoroughly brutalized by their experience of brutalizing Africans, reduced to the level of beasts (*fieras*), slave-ship captains ... do not become slaves by nature, but rather monsters by their trade" (21).
45. See *Relation du Royaume de Judas en Guinée*, "faisant le cri des prestres jusqu'à 11 heures ou minuit pour prier leur serpent de leur faire une bonne récolte ("Making the cry of the priests until 11 o'clock or midnight to pray their snake to make them a good harvest") (original transcription 61–2).
46. Ibid. "il est remarqué ue quoy que le Negre soit très enclin au vol pas un n'est assez [hardy] d'aller dépouiller ces cadavres, dans la crainte destre inquiètes après leur mort et déstrépées de sépultures" (original transcription 35).
47. See "All God's Chillen Had Wings" (62–5).
48. While I do refer here to Homi Bhabha's term "mimicry" as a humorous act "in order to be effective" by "continually produc[ing] its slippage, its excess, its difference" (*Location* 86), I also underline precisely its humorous or even subversive quality as a performance that mocks or deconstructs the colonial script. See Eleanor Byrne's *Homi K. Bhabha* (80, 88).

49. See Fernández Retamar, and my translation, "El *caribe*, por su parte, dará el *caníbal*, el antropófago, el hombre bestial situado irremediablemente al margen de la civilización, y a quien es menester combatir a sangre y fuego" (*Todo Caliban* 24).
50. Ibid.; "[e]s característico que el término caníbal lo hayamos aplicado, por antonomasia, no al extinguido aborigen de nuestras islas, sino al negro de África" (25).
51. See Sandoval and Von Germeten, "they arrive here looking like skeletons" (57).
52. In *Essais*, Michel de Montaigne explains in "Des cannibales" (1580) that the term "barbarian" instead meant, vis-à-vis Greek society, "outside of normalcy" (107).
53. Distinct from his later "necropolitics," Mbembe's *Critique of Black Reason* leans on the survivability of blackness. He states that "[t]he term 'Black' was the product of a social and technological machine tightly linked to the emergence and globalization of capitalism. It was invented to signify exclusion, brutalization, and degradation. ... But there is also a manifest dualism to Blackness. In a spectacular reversal, [blackness] becomes a symbol of a conscious *desire for life, a force spring forth, buoyant and plastic, fully engaged in the act of creation and capable of living in the midst of several times and several histories at once*" (6, emphasis added).

2   Commodification: Black Internationalism and the African Safari of Achy Obejas's *Ruins*

1. During her own fieldwork at Cojimar, Obejas states: "I started talking to people in Cojimar about that exodus. And obviously the people of Cojimar who were telling me the stories about what happened and how it had been to have tens of hundreds of thousands of people leaving from this little village, were people who had chosen to stay. So, I wanted to write that story" (Martin "Tell Me More").
2. See Amrita Das who argues that *Ruins* could strengthen comparative ties between Latin Americanists and Latinx studies scholars, and perhaps most importantly, the novel "allows U.S. Latino texts to be introduced in the larger dialogue from which it has been excluded" (21).
3. I borrow this term from Antonio López's *Unbecoming Blackness: The Diaspora Cultures of Afro-Cuban America*, and thank him for introducing me to the various ways in which some Cuban exiles express this attitude in their writing.
4. See Castro, "Cuba, el país latinoamericano que ha ... suprimido la discriminación por motivo de raza o sexo" (Discurso a la Segunda Asamblea Nacional, Plaza de la Revolución, February 4, 1962). His communist party

more forcefully asserted itself to have "eliminated from Cuban life the odious and humiliating spectacle of discrimination because of skin color" (Carneado 54).
5. See Castro, Discurso a la Segunda Asamblea Nacional, Plaza de la Revolución, (February 4, 1962): "Vamos a ponerle fin a la discriminación racial en los centros de trabajo con una nueva consigna: oportunidades de trabajo para todos los cubanos, sin discriminación de raza o de sexo," 1959. Nevertheless, Castro did not think an "antidiscrimination law was necessary," and stated instead that "discrimination could be changed through a campaign condemning public manifestations of racism." Studies on the origins and processes of racial discrimination took place in the media, higher education, and among Cuban intellectuals such as Nicolás Guillén and Salvador García Agüero, in the forms of symposia, conferences, and lectures. Even Ernesto Guevara weighed in, during a committee meeting on April 5, 1959, and a number of governmental organs such as Movement of National Integration, the National Campaign for Racial Integration and Unión Fraternal and Atenas (which emerged from Afro-Cuban clubs) emerged during this time (de la Fuente 263–7).
6. Personal interview with the author. www.youtube.com/watch?v=_zOmO7I MAYo.
7. See Castro (*Cuba and Angola* 31); "La sangre de África corre por nuestras venas. Y de África, como esclavos, vinieron muchos de nuestros antecesores a esta tierra. [...] Somos hermanos de los africanos y por los africanos estamos dispuestos a luchar!" (*Cuba y Angola* 31, emphasis added).
8. For the full text in its context, refer to Castro's speech in *Cuba y Angola*, 31. The full text in its original in Spanish appeared in *Resumen Semanal Granma*, on January 11, 1976.
9. See The World Bank, https://data.worldbank.org/indicator/NY.GDP.PCAP .KD.ZG?end=1995&locations=CU&start=1989.
10. See Olofinlua, "History of Atlantic Slave Trade," https://globalpressjournal .com/africa/nigeria/history-atlantic-slave-trade-chronicled-museums-monu ments-badagry-nigeria/.
11. The proverb's use of water is not fortuitous – it is rather informed by mechanisms of the Atlantic World, a "history of slave trade in Badagry" that "is engraved in the lives of [its] people" and transmitted by "folklores, proverbs, poetry, drama, and wise-saying" (quoted in Harris 21).
12. See Emelike, "Endless Wait for Jackson Park," http://businessday.ng/art-and-travel/article/endless-wait-for-jackson-park.
13. See Moore, in which he includes South African singer Miriam Makeba (incidentally married to the Black Panther's Stokely Carmichael), Angela Davis, and African heads of state such as Amílcar Cabral and Sékou Touré,

to name a few (*Castro* 299, 301, 321). The Black Panther movement had also sought asylum in Cuba (at least until the turn of the millennium, Assata Shakur was still living in Cuba), and as Pedro Pérez-Sarduy and Jean Stubbs note, "the celebration of Cuba's African heritage [was] legitimized by Cuba's involvement in Africa" (20). For a more detailed study on the influence of the so-called "African Decade," see also Pedro Pérez-Sarduy and Jean Stubbs' *Afro-Cuban Voices*.

14. Of interest is that, militarily, Guinea served Cuba as a strategic point to wage a socialist resistance against US forces and their allies; what would culminate in Cuba's first decolonial success in Africa. Also relevant is that Guinea was the first independent African nation-state to send students to Cuba in 1961 through the first foreign scholarship program implemented on the island and between 1972 and 1974, the African state sent 400 university students to Havana alone (Gleijeses 228).

15. Ann Temkin, "Les Demoiselles d'Avignon" *MoMa Learning*. www.moma.org/learn/moma_learning/pablo-picasso-les-demoiselles-davignon-paris-june-july-1907/.

16. Carpentier defines "the marvelous real" ("lo real maravilloso") as "an unexpected alteration of reality (the miracle), of a privileged revelation of reality, an unordinary illumination or singularly favorable to the inadvertent richness of reality" ("una inesparada alteración de la realidad (el milagro), de una revelación privilegiada de la realidad, de una iluminación inhabitual o singularmente favorecedora de las inadvertidas riquezas de la realidad" (3–4). With regard to Lam, he states, "tuvo que ser un pintor de América, el Cubano Wifredo Lam, quien nos enseñara la magia de la vegetación tropical, la desenfrenada Creación de Formas de nuestra naturaleza" ("it had to be a painter from the Americas, the Cuban Wifredo Lam, who taught us the magic of the tropical vegetation, the unstoppable Creation of Forms of our nature," own translation, 3).

17. Nicolás Guillén is lauded both as a pan-Caribbean poet who sought to speak to a diasporic and pan-hemispheric African tradition and as the most representative poet of the Spanish-speaking counterpart of Négritude, Negrismo, most commonly termed Afro-Cubanismo. Moreover, as contemporaries, "Hughes and Guillén met on the American's second trip to Havana, where they struck up a friendship and a long correspondence and eventually began a collaboration that resulted in Hughes's cotranslation of Guillén's poetry" (Leary 134).

18. Translaton is my own. See Guillén, "signo de selva tuyo, . . . nadando en el Zambeze de tus ojos," 19.

19. Fanon's and Soyinka's positions on discourses of color are not unlike those described by Mahler, where "rather than a socialist rhetoric of commonality

based around class, Tricontinentalist discourse sometimes used the term 'color' (such as in 'colored peoples' or 'colored leader') to refer not necessarily to one's race or to one's skin color but to one's alignment with the Tricontinental's anti-imperialist politics" (79).

20. Négritude was a literary movement defined by both its political and esthetic engagement with blackness that included authors such as the Martinican sisters Paulette, Jane, and André Nadal, Aimé Césaire, Guyanese León Damas, and Senegalese Léopold Sedar Senghor, among a few others. Thought to have been initiated in Paris, négritude "posited the idea that people of African descent throughout the world possessed an essence distinguishing them from non-Africans, a difference that was expressed culturally." As Michael Gomez explains, while "négritude maintains that the African-descended seek harmonious rather than exploitative relationship with the environment; that they are warm, sensual, and artistically creative ... not all in Africa or the Diaspora subscribed to such views" (188).

21. San Francisco de Paula was a region that functioned partly as a slave cemetery in Havana directed by the diocese of Díaz de Espada y Landa in the Cuban capital: "En otra disposición de fecha 29 de mayo de 1806, elaborada por Juan José Díaz de Espada y Landa, segundo Obispo de La Habana [1802-1832], ... se regulan los derechos de sepulturas en los tramos del cementerio general de La Habana: la de los párvulos en uno. Y enterrándose todos los dichos párvulos en los cuadros separados, bajo de dicho crucero, y los esclavos adultos en la parte ínfima del cementerio [Sínodo, 1982:201]" (Sarmiento Ramírez 117).

22. Historically, Cojimar, as an entry point for the slave trade, was a crucial fortification for protecting Spanish territory in Cuba. The Gutenberg records document that the fortification at Cojimar built by Governor Viamonte in 1647 protected the capital similar to that of Castillo del Morro.

23. The official name of this restaurant is "La Terraza" but the novel uses "Las Terrazas," as locals also use to refer to the same place.

24. Usnavy's affiliation with the "beautiful beasts" echoes Hemingway's "The Short Happy Life of Francis Macomber," which is told from the point of view of a hunted lion (13).

25. US policy toward Africa shifted radically during the Carter administration. In fact, Carter's ambassador to the United Nations, Andrew Young, supported the Cuban presence in Angola, condemning the US and its allies as "racist" and calling South African apartheid "illegitimate" (Sauldie 72, 73). But when Zaire invaded Angola's Katanga province, US and Cuban relations became complicated again. Carter requested that Cuba relinquish its military presence, but Castro refused on the grounds of his diplomatic promises to

Angola (Gleijenses et al. 16). In the US, the media criticized Cuba for making money off of its intervention, but Gleijenses claims that this myth is based on documents in which Raúl Castro offered to pay Angola's own troops but requested that Angola at least feed them (34–6).

26. Personal interview with the author. www.youtube.com/watch?v=_zOmO7I MAYo.
27. Sweet (*Recreating Africa* 53). See also Stephan Palmié and Luiz de Barros Mott (1988) who examine "a multiracial but still conspicuously Black 'queer Atlantic.'" Both insist that "[a]t least in the Iberian Americas, the contours of such an Atlantic became visible in the record once they were hauled before the Inquisition for charges of 'sodomy'" (quoted in Kummels et al. 68).
28. As he writes to the Assistant Colonial Secretary, he states: "I have the honour to report, for his Excellency's information, that according to instructions received I proceeded to Badagry in the s.s 'Gertrude.' Leaving Lagos at 11.20 a.m. on the 27th instant I reached Badagry at 5.15 p.m., and remained there till 11.30p.m., when having boarded the s.s 'Renner,' and taken the man Astrop prisoner by virtue of a warrant placed in my hands" (324; Assistant Inspector Cuscaden to the Acting Assistant Colonial Secretary, March 29, 1880, *British Parliament Papers: Nigeria*).
29. See Clifford's discussion of his concept of "roots and routes" that are essentially "forms of community consciousness and solidarity that maintain identifications outside the national time/space in order to live inside, with difference" (251).

3 Obliteration: Gabriel García Márquez and His Angolan Chronicles of a "Latin-African" Death Foretold

1. See "Un domingo de delirio" (in *Notas de prensa* 1991, 71). Unless otherwise noted, all translations are my own.
2. See Gene Bell-Villada, who not only underscores Cartagena, as part of Nueva Granada, that was a central port of arrival of slaves from the Congo and Angola, but also mentions that even a township is named "Angola," hosting wooden masks and other African cultural artifacts (*García Márquez: The Man* 37).
3. The Heberto Padilla Affair consisted of the Cuban Revolution's imprisonment of poet Padilla on March 20, 1971, for his outspoken criticism of the Revolution's interference with cultural expression. His imprisonment angered many intellectuals who had initially supported Castro, at least fifty-four Latin American and European writers, including some prominent Boom writers.
4. In 1978, García Márquez stated "cualquiera que haya seguido de cerca los pocos artículos de prensa que escribí, se encontrará con que el más emocional de todos

es el de mi viaje a Angola. Desde entonces he vuelto a tener pesadillas que no tenía desde la niñez ("anybody that has followed closely the few journalistic articles that I wrote, will find that the most emotional of all is my trip to Angola. Since then, I have had nightmares that I did not have since I was a child" (García Márquez and Harguindey "Llegué a creer que Franco" 171).

5. The first story appeared in *Al Día* magazine, which reported that in January 1951, a wealthy twenty-two-year-old student at the Universidad Javeriana de Bogotá, Cayetano Gentile Chimento, was murdered with a machete by Víctor and Joaquín Chica Calas, who believed that Cayetano had been the cause of their sister's inability to marry Miguel Reyes Palencia, who returned her to her family after discovering that she was no longer a virgin. As for the second story, Colombian writer Alvaro Cepeda Samudio actually shared it with García Márquez.

6. García Márquez explains the process by which he researched the story in *Crónica de una muerte anunciada*, somewhat echoing the narrator's words in the novel, "Después volví dos veces, siempre en relación con el proyecto del libro. La primera fue unos 15 años más tarde, tratando de *rescatar de la memoria* de la gente *las numerosas piezas desperdigadas del rompecabezas del crimen*" ("I came back twice, always in relation to the project of the book. The first time, it was 15 years later *trying to rescue from* people's *memory, the numerous shattered pieces of the puzzle of the crime*," "El cuento del cuento," *Notas* 1991, 150, emphasis added).

7. See Jaramillo Agudelo, "notas de corte poético-filosófico-humorístico-literario" (12).

8. Quoted in Jaramillo Agudelo, "reconstrucción literaria de sucesos o figuras, género donde el empeño formal domina sobre las urgencias informativas" (13).

9. See Rotker, "dos escrituras aparentemente diversas – la del periodismo, la de la ficción – ... están conectadas por el cordon umbilical de la crónica."

10. *Prensa Latina's* successful propagation of news around the world was in part due to its opening about ten bureaus or news satellites across Latin America, and offices in New York, Washington, Paris, Geneva, Prague, and London (Walsh 105–7).

11. See García Márquez, "El drama de las dos Cubas," in which he relates menacing threats from exiled Cubans in a phone call at the Rockefeller Center: "Prepárense, ñángaras, que les llegó su hora. Vamos para allá" ("Get ready, bastards, your time has come, we are headed over to get you" 33).

12. See Franco Altamar "una organización global 'esquemática'" ... "exposición, desarrollo, resolución, caloración y epílogo" (25 6).

13. See Hugo Méndez Ramírez, "llamado crónica y no novela para prestar la *realidad histórica* a los sucesos que narra" (936, emphasis added).

14. "Por un lado, se encuentran aquellos que interpretan la novela en términos de la fatalidad tan *persistente* en la obra de García Márquez ... por el otro, están los que la explican en función de la violencia (culpa) colectiva" (Ibid 934–5, emphasis added).
15. For more on the 2016 adaptation, see Instituto Cervantes, Nueva Delhi https://nuevadelhi.cervantes.es/en/default.shtm. Dieter Zimmer, "Autopsie an Frau Ananke" Hamburg, Germany: *Die Zeit*, 43 (October 16, 1981), 11: "the opening line of Chronicle of a Death Foretold already denotes it as a classical story of world literature." Moreover, see Charles Ramirez Berg, "Chronicle of a Death Foretold by Gabriel García Márquez." New York, NY: Nuestro 7.4 (May 1983) p. 62: the novel "gives us the chance all great literature give: a chance to make sense of the world."
16. See N. Gonzalez's *Bibliographical Guide to Gabriel García Márquez 1986–1992* : "for the first time in history of the publication of works by Latin American writers, *Crónica* was published simultaneously by four important publishing houses from four different countries." These were: Oveja Negra, Editorial Diana, Editorial Sudamericana, Bruguera (in Colombia, Peru, Argentina, and Spain, respectively, 350).
17. This period of journalism was also one in which García Márquez denounced the war in Vietnam and US intervention in Nicaragua, and uplifted France's socialist François Mitterrand, Chile's Salvador Allende, and other revolutions taking place in Central and Latin America (*García Márquez: The Man* 58).
18. "Operation Carlota" (in *Cuba and Angola* 124). See also Castro, "que lo sepan los racistas de África del Sur y que lo sepan los imperialistas yanquis ... en esa lucha contra los racistas y frente a los imperialistas, sin vacilación alguna, estaremos junto a los pueblos de África" ("Let the South African racists and the Yankee imperialists be warned. [...] in Africa's struggle against racists and imperialists, we'll stand, ... side by side with the peoples of Africa" (*Cuba and Angola/Cuba y Angola* 31).
19. Because *Crónica de una muerte anunciada* had taken him so long to write, García Márquez reported that the story "le faltaba una pata" ("was missing a leg"). Bell-Villada details that it was actually Cepeda Samudio who verbalized that the story was "missing a leg" (*García Márquez: The Man* 207). But García Márquez noted this himself in *Notas de prensa* (1991, 148).
20. Kutzinski, comparing García Márquez to Alejo Carpentier, states that the former "never wrote *about* blacks" (133), although, in her essay, she makes the case that "black" traditions *are* subtly present in García Márquez's "Un señor muy viejo con unas alas enormes"/"A Very Old Man with Enormous Wings." See also Hunsaker.
21. See Megenney, "el autor nunca se daba cuenta de que en su mundo de platanales y palos de matarratón hubiese elementos vivos de una vieja tradición subsahárica" (215).

22. See Callen King, "Santiago Tyrannos"; Palencia-Roth, "La primera novela"; Penuel, *Intertextuality;* Rama "La caza literaria"; Kercher, "García Márquez's Chronicle"; Gustavo Pellón "Myth, Tragedy"; Méndez Ramírez "La reinterpretación paródica"; Juan Goytisolo "Intelectuales," 152.
23. García Márquez admits that "El libro policial genial es el Edipo Rey de Sófocles, porque ahí el investigador descubre que él mismo es el asesino" ("The genius crime fiction is that of the *Oedipus Rex*, because there the detective discovers that he is the assassin" ("La Revolución cubana" 1979, 209)), referencing his own sense of guilt for Santiago's murder. García Márquez mentions *Oedipus Rex* at least four times in the collection of his interviews from 1967 to 1979, *García Márquez habla de García Márquez*, but these mentions are not surpassed by his mentions of Angola either.
24. García Márquez has spoken about his admiration of particularly Greek tragedy in "Intelectuales" (152), but also the realm of World Literature. See his interviews, "García Márquez se confiesa" (156) and "Es un crimen" (137).
25. See "poco café" (182), "Intelectuales," (1977, 152), and "El periodismo" (196). Paraphrasing from García Márquez, he also states that a novel is a poetic projection reality (138) and that literature will intervene in the politics of nations, particularly socialism, which he fully supported as an admitted communist ("Conversaciones" 1968, 33, 138).
26. See García Márquez, "poco café," "En mi viaje a Angola encontré que en muchas formas populares del arte africano se encuentran manifestaciones estéticas muy similares a las que tenemos en toda la zona del Caribe" (182).
27. See García Márquez and Apuleyo, "el viaje que hice por Angola en 1978, es una de las experiencias más fascinantes que he tenido ... desde el momento mismo que olí el aire, me encontré de pronto en el mundo de mi infancia" ("the trip I did in Angola in 1978 is one of the most fascinating experiences that I've had ... from the very moment I smelled the air, I found myself all of a sudden in the world of my infancy") (*El olor* 54).
28. Ibid., García Márquez states, "en el Caribe, al que pertenezco, se mezcló la imaginación desbordada de los esclavos negros africanos con la de los nativos pre-colombinos ... esa aptitud para mirar la realidad de cierta manera mágica es propia del Caribe y también del Brasil" ("In the Caribbean, to which I belong, the unbound imagination of the black slaves from Africa was mixed with that of the pre-Colombian natives ... that ability to look at reality in a magical way is Caribbean and also Brazilian" *El olor* 54).
29. Most translations in this chapter are my own, other instances are from Rabassa.
30. "Au sieur Marin au sujet des efforts qu'il déploie pour récupérer une partie des effets embarqués sur l'Hermione naufragée près de Carthagène (3 août 1707)" FR ANOM COL B 28 F 577.

31. The King of Spain from 1700 to 1748 was Bourbon Phillip V, born in Versailles and second son of Louis of France, who of course would maintain the alliance between France and Castille.
32. See "Au sieur Marin...," FR ANOM COL B 28 F° 577, Archives nationales de département d'outre mer, Aix-en-Provence, France.
33. To stop the spread of communism but not bestow too much power on Portugal, Kennedy courted "moderate" nationalists who would side with Western conceptions of government "while mollifying African discontent" and thus supported a rival to the Cuban-aligned People's Movement for the Liberation of Angola (MPLA), Roberto Holden's National Liberation Front of Angola (FNLA), a party that Kennedy's administration considered less radical and non-communist (Schmidt 83–4). As the US supported the FNLA through the CIA, it also "assisted 150,000 Angolan refuges in the Congo and provided scholarships to Portuguese African students living in exile – but rebuffed MPLA requests for assistance" (85). In 1986, with staunch support from and lobbying by Cuban-Americans, the US Congress allowed for the restoration of aid to Angola's UNITA (the National Union for the Total Independence of Angola party) which would support the rebel factions "with some of the most sophisticated American weapons on the market" (126). In 1987, the US spent $30 million and guaranteed the continued presence of the Cuban military, when they were hoping to exit.
34. See *Angola: Hearings before the Subcommittee on African Affairs of the Committee on Foreign Relations*, before the Subcommittee on African Affairs, where Houser states that the MPLA party is not communist (135). The US thought that the Soviets were involved in Angola because Cuba, considered a Soviet proxy, was involved. But in fact, Castro decided to intervene in Angola independently of the Soviets. See also Gliejenses, *Africa y Cuba*, who states that Kissinger waged war because he thought it would be an easy one that would give the US much-needed prestige after the failed Vietnam war, especially since other western nations supported the FNLA and UNITA and, he thought, opposing the spread of communism. But in fact, the Soviet Union was wary of the MPLA, and limited its support because it did not want to jeopardize an accord with the US (5).
35. See *Angola: Hearings before the Subcommittee on African Affairs of the Committee on Foreign Relations* (135). See also "Cold War in Africa: Stage II" in *Africa 72*, where reporter Madan Sauldie states specifically that "[f]or years these two minority White regimes [South Africa and Rhodesia] have capitalized on raising Communist bogey, and thereby eliciting the support of the West and some circles in the United States" (71).
36. See "Paper Prepared by the National Security Council Interdepartmental Group for Africa, 17," AF/NSC–IG 69–8 Rev. A, Washington, December 9,

Notes to Pages 137–44

1969, Vol. xxviii, in *Office of the Historian*. https://history.state.gov/historicaldocuments/frus1969-76v28/d17.

37. See Anadeli Bencomo's "Crónicas and New Journalism" in *The Routledge Handbook to the Culture and Media of the Americas*.

38. García Márquez and Walsh played a role in consolidating the testimonio genre that these two publications initiated, and also participated in discussions about its norms and classification in Cuba's Casa de las Américas – Latin America's intellectual institute par excellence. Moreover, Walsh's *Quién mató a Rosendo* (1969) and *Caso Satanowsky* (1973) helped establish the genres of literary journalism and testimonio as central to Latin American literary tradition. He later served as the judge for the Casa de las Américas' prize in the nonfiction category in 1968 and for testimonio in 1970.

39. See Finch 146, who also consults the following archive: ANC, CM 30–3; ANC, María Regla f. 120–22; Adriano Gangá f. 25–27/23–25v. La Habana, Cuba.

40. Considering Cuba's shortcomings regarding racial equality, political scientist Jacques Lévesque notes that "sending a contingent to an African country to fight against South Africa's goals could strengthen Cuba's feelings of Black national belonging and help the country's social cohesion. It is no coincidence that the Cuban expeditionary force was named "Operación Carlota" ("l'envoi d'un contingent dans un pays africain, pour lutter contre les objectifs de l'Afrique du sud, pouvait renforcer les sentiments d'appartenance nationale des noirs cubains et aider à la cohésion sociale du pays. Ce n'est pas par hasard que l'envoie du corps expéditionnaire cubain a été baptisé 'Opération Carlotta,'" 297–8).

41. These traces of pessimism about socialist democracies are most perceptible in "Cuba de cabo a rabo" ("Cuba from cape to tail" 1975), "El Kissinger de Reagan" (1981), and "EEUU: política de suposiciones" ("The US: politics of assumptions" 1982).

42. "Cuba de cabo a rabo" (1975) is a resounding ode to the Cuban revolution vis-à-vis a pre-revolutionary island "entregado a los gringos" ("given up to the gringos" 64). It was written around the time of Angolan victory; although some hope remains, a worrisome US victory lurks. For instance, García Márquez attests that the Cuban revolution provides education, nourishment, affordable living, and free medical insurance despite a "criminal" US embargo that was not only a "corte del cordón umbilical" ("cut to the umbilical cord") with empire, but also "una feroz tentativa de genocidio promovida por un poder casi sin límites cuyos tentáculos aparecían en cualquier parte del mundo" ("a ferocious genocidal attempt promoted by an almost limitless power, whose tentacles would emerge anywhere in the world" 64–5). Employing metaphors – tentacles and even umbilical cord – to imply empire's "limitless" reach, the term "genocide"

noticeably informs the effects of US imperial (over)reach that García Márquez invokes in much of his journalism.

43. See García Márquez, "Pez rojo," "genio creador," and "dinero estéril" (*Notas de prensa* 1996, 322).

44. Ibid., and in "Angola, un año después," García Márquez states: "Desde diciembre de 1975, la compañía norteamericana Gulf Oil, que explota los yacimientos de Cabinda, había interrumpido sus operaciones por intrigas políticas de los Estados Unidos" and "Angola perdió regalías por un millón y medio de dólares diarios durante más de un año" ("Since December 1975, the American company Gulf Oil, that exploits the oil reserves of Cabinda, had interrupted its operations due to US political intrigues" and "Angola lost benefits totaling $1.5 million dollars daily for over a year," *Por la libre* 171).

45. These anti-imperialist US interventions he conjures are contained in "El Salvador está en llamas" (80), "Nicaragua no ha vuelto a dormir tranquila" (81), "Cuba, por su parte, está otra vez en pie de guerra," and ever-sarcastically, in "Panamá es el primero que ha reconocido . . . la vocación imperial y el estilo rupestre del general [of Reagan]," to name a few (*Notas de prensa* 1996).

46. This is a criticism that emerges more than anything else out of the US's defeat in Vietnam, as he states that the empire's policy is "empantanado" ("swamped"). See "EEUU" in *Notas de prensa* 1996 (304–5).

47. In the Angolan capital, Ndalu and his friends remark on the "revolutionary spirit" that renders their foreign presence oddly natural and heroic. When one of the pupils reprimands another for teasing their teacher, she states, "she was Cuban and she was in Angola to help us" (12).

48. See Ann Talbot, "The Angolan Civil War and US Foreign Policy" (*Global Policy Forum*), who notes sarcastically, "the US government and the CIA were the innocent parties, embroiled in a war of others making." www.globalpolicy.org/component/content/article/155/25956.html.

49. García Márquez "Caribe mágico" (1981), where he writes a brief ode to the continental Caribbean, around the same time he published *Crónica de una muerte anunciada*, and memorialized Suriname due to his interest in Cayenne (and Suriname's proximity to the French colony). Cayenne, in turn, becomes significant for Bayardo, since many townspeople believe he hails from there. He states of Cayenne: "los pocos que lograron fugarse de aquel infierno, . . . se dispersaban por las islas numerosas de las Antillas" ("the few that succeeded in escaping that hell, ...would disperse into the numerous Antillean islands," in *Notas de prensa* 1991, 44).

50. This text made an impression on García Márquez, who in an interview mocked a critic who read Carpentier's Victor Hughes in *Cien años* (Durán "Conversaciones" 32). In *Crónica de una muerte anunciada*, he seems to further play with this illusion.

51. While Rabassa translates this as "farmhouse" as this is the Iberian definition of the term "casa de campo," the term also has colonial roots. Such houses were called quinta because their colonist-owners paid a fifth part of their earnings as rent to the King (*Real Academia Española*). And yet, in Colombian and Mexican Spanish, quinta is also referred to as "Casa con antejardín, o rodeaeda de jardines" ("house with an ante-garden or surrounded by gardens"), which would underscore the wealth of said "house."
52. See Galina Bakhtiarova, who establishes colonial connections between the Catalan presence in the Spanish colonies and their wealth acquisition by way of the slave trade or Maluquer de Motes's "La burgesia catalana i l'esclavitud colonial"/ "The Catalan Bourgeoisie and Colonial Slavery" on Catalan intervention in the slave trade during Spanish colonization. Ilan Stavans also mentions in *El grupo de Barraquilla*, that the Catalan Xius was inspired by the bookkeeper and intellectual Luis Vicens (*Gabriel García Márquez* 66–70).
53. Rabassa uses the Peruvian version of the word "tambo," which refers to small establishment ("tienda rural pequeña") rather than the Mexican term – which García Márquez would have been more familiar with, given his years residing in Mexico – which means "tonel de lámina," long barrels or aluminum cylinders. See *La Real Academia Española*.
54. As Elizabeth DeLoughrey states, "there is probably no other region in the world that has been more radically altered in terms of human and botanic migration, transplantation, and settlement than the Caribbean" (1).
55. See *Crónica de una muerte anunciada*, "cada vez econtrábamos menos cosas de valor en los aposentos abandonados ... la quinta empezó a desmigajarse" ("each time we found fewer things of value in the abandoned rooms ... The house began to crumble," 98–9, 86–7).
56. As Hartman states, "if you look at the sea enough, scenes from the past come back to life" (*Lose* 136). Moreover, as Araujo notes, the Door of No Return and its "opening to the sea helped to construct a fantasist narrative on slavery and the Atlantic slave trade" (*Public Memory* 62).
57. The current *Maison des esclaves* pamphlet states that "15 to 20 million black people from all of West Africa left Gorée for the Americas, of which 6 million died from privation or bad treatment" ("La Maison des Esclaves de Gorée" in *Dakar Port Authority* 18).
58. The novel specifies a slave market and the abolition of the slave trade in the Spanish colonies, and a direct reference to the slave quarters (11, 13, 14). Also telling of an insistence on slave trade memory is that Sierva María renames herself María Mandinga (31), learns slaves' language and sings in Yoruba (42), and troublingly performs slaves' customs in blackface (14).
59. Bell-Villada justifies this outcome given that many topics broached by the novel, such as slavery, African folklore, and especially a Jesuit cleric's

obsessions with a twelve-year-old, were not topics that critics inside or outside of Latin America would readily want to confront (*García Márquez: The Man* 436).

4 Archival Distortion: The Chicano Congo of Tomás Rivera and Rudolfo Anaya

1. Luis Leal states that the invisibility of blackness in Mexican-American culture can be traced to colonial Mexico – parts of which are today the US Southwest – where Black people's "presence is numerically much less than it is in regions like the Caribbean" (Leal and Stavans 328).
2. It should be noted that Rivera distorts both Stanley's name in "Henry L." (as opposed to the correct version, "Henry *M.* Stanley") and the spelling of "Livingston" (as opposed to the correct spelling, "Livingstone"). Whether this was playful or intentional remains unknown.
3. In his transformative work, John Alba Cutler explains that Rivera's canonical ...*y no se lo tragó la tierra* had been criticized as failing to read as "literature" because it was "too documentary" (97). Although his argument seeks to contest this notion of literature as narrowly defined, the documentary essence of Rivera's work that "asserted the right to folklore, testimonio..." (97) also sheds light on the ways in which Rivera's work is conceived as reproducing a Chicanx culture of ethnography.
4. See *Stanley and African Exhibition: Catalogue of the Exhibits* (London, 1890), where an 1890 exhibition on Stanley's exploration fetishized routes of discovery that displayed the "heart of savage Africa" while casually juxtaposing "huts," "forests," and "slave boys" in the announcement.
5. For more on antiblack US foreign policy in the Congo, see Tillery 505; Namikas 5–7.
6. As Sarah Brouillette has argued, African literary festivals and prizes are funded by interest groups such as petrol industries in Nigeria and mineral and diamond mining in the Congo. Prestigious African works cherry-picked by Western organizations have had little choice but to unintentionally yet unabatedly perpetuate literary representations of "darkest Africa" ("African Literary Hustle").
7. See Brouillette, "On the African Literary Hustle"; Sánchez Prado, "África en la imaginación," 78; and Irr, 121–9.
8. Consider the following: "near each settlement was a waste," "wastes unpeopled by ivory hunters" (207, 216); "this may end in smoke," "and out it came smoke and sparks of fire" (33, 379); "driving us out with sticks" (317); "Even the rotten fruit was not rejected" (231).
9. Stanley often uses the term "limit" to extend colonial rule over equatorial or central African territories (253–4, 328, 415).

10. See Erika Doss, *Memorial Mania* (313–16; 358–376). In Rivera's Texas, the Oñate statue also attracted protests.
11. Leopold inaugurated Tervuren Museum in Belgium as a means of exhibiting his colonial treasures and has been criticized for failing to clearly state the brutal impact of Leopold's imperialism, while celebrating the grandeur of his rule. The museum now houses over 140,000 artifacts from Central Africa. Although the Congo (DRP) has recalled many of them, only about 200 have been repatriated. With regard to Stanley, Viviane Baeke, a curator at Tervuren, states, "Clearly it wouldn't be right to restore Stanley and put him in the streets of Kinshasa, but he belongs here in a museum of Congo's history." See www.independent.co.uk/news/world/africa/the-disfigured-statue-of-henry-morton-stanley-we-presume-1923812.html.
12. See "Malawi Slave Routes and Dr. David Livingstone Trail." This UNESCO website explains that British Commissioner in Malawi, Sir Harry Johnston, defeated Livingstone's nemesis, a Swahili-Arab slave trader, Salim-bin Abdullah ("Jumbe") when Livingstone himself could not: "One of the policies of his administration stipulated was to bring slave trade to an end. Sir Harry Johnston with a force of Sikh soldiers attacked Jumbe in 1894. He was tried and banished to Zanzibar." https://whc.unesco.org/en/tentative lists/5603/.
13. Further, Livingstone's native Scotland and its National Library has built Livingstone's textual memorialization around slavery. See the National Library of Scotland's "Picturing Africa: Illustrating Livingstone's Travels," where "Slavery" features as one of the headers in the virtual and physical exhibit, which also includes Livingstone's various sketches of the ills of slavery (www.nls.uk/exhibitions/david-livingstone). Rivera's memorialization manifests most prominently in the Rivera Library at UC Riverside, which coincidentally has hosted, since 2017, one of the most important exhibits on slavery on the West coast.
14. Genaro Padilla is one of the first scholars to criticize the absence of the 1960s–1970s Chicano movement in Anaya's novel (128). Enrique Lamadrid has explained that the novel's "mythic dimensions" did not contain the "usual cast of characters found in Chicano poetry and murals" such as pre-Hispanic representations, and that the golden carp seemed "naïve and idiosyncratic, proof of what they [critics] perceived as the apolitical qualities of Anaya's writing" (*"De vatos y profetas"* 202). Tonn has argued that the ethnic insistence of the narrative renders it universal (241–52) and Rosaura Sánchez has read ancient genealogies in Anaya's other works as "simulacra of the past" (226).
15. See Saldívar, 66. Moreover, Caminero-Santangelo has pointed out that the novel's conclusion finds Antonio still seeking to find connections with a broader "Chicanidad." Although referencing the indigeneity that is

diluted in the story, Caminero-Santangelo notes that at the end of the novel, Antonio seems to "feel less lost in and threatened by the 'labyrinth of a time and history [he] did not know,'" stating that Antonio has yet to make a "connection" with the population of his town and that "at least he is now watching for their 'traces'" (*On Latinidad* 50).

16. In Bruce-Novoa, Anaya reflects on his disappointment that few people – especially Chicanos – have read or recognize US Puerto Rican poet Víctor Hernández Cruz, author of the widely anthologized poem "African Things" (193–4).

17. Not only does Anaya reveal these influences in *Bless Me, Ultima* when Antonio realizes that "common herbs" also hail from "even of those in the old, old country, the Moors" (39, 45), but the Spanish Atlantic is also revealed in his Sonny Baca novels where, in *Shaman Winter*, Spanish forces sweep "the Moors south, out of Granada, and finally back to Africa" (260).

18. Ramón Gutiérrez argues that the Inquisition in the colonial Southwest conceived that "[w]itches were attackers and deceivers using what was impure and demonic to pollute the pure and holy" and prosecuted several deemed-witches in the early and mid-sixteenth century. From María Domínguez in 1734 to Josepha de la Encarnación of El Paso in 1719, and Beatriz de los Angeles, who in 1731 was accused of flying or magically transporting herself two hundred miles away in New Mexico (30–1), all of these women also happened to be both mistresses *and* indigenous (33).

19. Glissant terms in his theory of Relation the experience that both "diversifies forms of humanity" and also "br[ings] [them] into contact" (*Poetics* 160).

20. For instance, Antonio's trance even mirrors that of Cristina García's protagonist in *Dreaming in Cuban*, who, following the sacrifice of a goat, "grew sleepy and felt as though she were drifting through the heavens." In the novel, Felicia also "tasted the goat's blood ... then she sampled the blood of many more creatures" (187).

21. See Sandoval, "las ceremonias de los pagodes, los sacrificios, las fiestas, y a vueltas de estos muchas hechicerías, encantamientos, y gran parte de arte mágica" (36).

22. *Ibid.*, "Es tanta la ignorancia de estos gentiles" (71); "de estas malditas sectas" or "su maldita secta" (71–4).

23. *Ibid.*, "en cada reino hay algún lugar dedicado al demonio, donde van a hacer los sacrificios más solemnes.... En estas partes tiene el demonio muchos ministros que con hechizos y brebajes acaban cuanto quieren." He also states that their religion is false, or in its exact terms, "Y de su falsa religión" (74).

24. See Cavazzi, "Coisas *estranhas* tem de descrever a minha pena acerca dos costumes desses três reinos, e a minha qualidade de religioso não deixa de ficar *aborrecida* por este assunto, quer porque a *falta de civilização* as torna

abomináveis, quer porque a sua diference dos nossos costumes as torna *incríveis*" (81, emphasis added). In this first book, he reports on what he views as gendered superstition, and states that women's belief in feiticeiros renders their offspring "monstrous" ("quando prometem [dos feiticeiros] um parto feliz, pois, às vezes, a mesma Naturaliza, para não derrogar as prerrogativas da África, parece produzir verdadeiras monstruosidades," 121). At other times, he generally notes the moral "monstrosity" practiced by those who are pagans ("são as monstruosidades morais de muitos habitantes destes reinos"). He also faults the feiticeiros for gaining favor by curing people of diseases by "superstitious" means ("conseguirem a cura das doenças por meio de remédios supersticiosos" 87).

25. See R. Saldívar, *Chicano Narrative*, 126; Caminero-Santangelo, "Jason's Indian," 115–23; Kárai, "The Postmodern Use of Mythopoeia," 279.
26. J. Saldívar explains the neologism as an "alternative to the Eurocentric formulation of postmodernity" that oversaw not only structures of "capitalism," "liberalism," "machismo," White supremacy, and ecological devastation ("Conjectures" ft. 7, 135).
27. See Sandoval, "La mesma adoración y reverencia hacen a los peces de un gran río que pasa por su ciudad, y no comerán ninguno si por ellos los mataren o se viesen morir de hambre"; "su gobierno y religión se fundaban en tradición y en uso antiguo introducido del mismo demonio," 51, or "en cada reino hay algún lugar dedicado al demonio" (Libro 1, 71, 82).
28. See Cavazzi, "Aproximando-me ainda mais, tive a certeza de que a casita devia server para alguma superstição, porque dentro havia uma mesita com peixe fresco. Ardi de zelo e num momento fiz lançar o peixe . . . na cachoeira. . . . Procurei concebê-los de que tudo aquilo não passava duma loucura . . . e quando eu era informado de que os altares ou ídolos e semelhantes" (129–30).
29. *Ibid.*, He states that these "houses" are "ministers of Satan" representing "beasts, monsters, and demons" ("com autoridades de ministro de Satanás, recebe as estátuas dos ídolos. Muitas destas estátuas têm feições de homens ou de mulheres; outras de animais, feras, monstróes e demónios" 88).
30. *Ibid.*, "O peixe voador, conhecidíssimo em todo o oceano, pode fugir das insídias do peixe-dourado, levantando-se a voo por cima das águas. Mas, depois de um breve espaço, cai miseravelmente na boca aberta do seu inimigo. Estes peixes abundam no vasto oceano, para proveito dos pescadores e para distração dos navegantes" (72).
31. *Ibid.*, "tinha assaltado o navio" and "grossíssimas paredes" (72).
32. See *Judas*, "ils se servent aussi de la saignée" (59); "qui prend possession" (61); "lors que le feu prend dans ce temps personne ne donnent secours" (62). See also Cavazzi, in "hurlent," "faisant le cri des prêtres" (61).

33. Common oral proverb from Ouidah, Benin, "le poisson carpe n'engendre pas le silure chat."
34. When one of his uncles on his mother's side states that he is proud that there is finally an "educated Luna, a man of the people" in the family, Antonio brusquely responds, "I am a Márez" (265).

Coda

1. Brouillette explains that the Warwick Research Collective (WReC) held this assumption and "quite convincingly use[s] the theory of combined and uneven development to explain formal developments in world literature" (*UNESCO* 3).
2. I reproduce the conversation here, which took place when I asked them what Ouidah represented for them, and they responded that it was "a mauvaise venant": -Quel mauvaise venant? (What bad luck?).
 -Sister 1: Ce qui s'est passé en Afrique. L'Afrique n'était pas civilisé comme il l'est maintenant ; ils avaient des royaumes et des rois qui avaient des esclaves. Les blancs français nous ont vendu des armes quand nous n'avions pas (That which happened in Africa. Africa was not civilized like it is now; there were kingdoms and kings who had slaves. The whites sold us (their) weapons when we didn't have any). -Sister 2: Les esclaves sont allées en France pendant le trafic triangulaire (Slaves went to France during the triangular trade). . . . C'est triste parler de ça (It is sad to speak of that). -Sister 1: C'est pour ça que l'Afrique est sous-développé (That is why Africa is underdeveloped). -Me: Parce que vous n'aviez pas des armes? (Because you didn't have arms?). -Sister 1: Non, parce que . . . sorcières, ils te tuent si tu les croises. (No, because of . . . sorcerers, they kill you if you cross paths with them). -Me: Qui a dit ça? (Who has said that?). -Sister 1: Les gens (People).
3. See Jung Ran Forte in "Marketing Vodun: Cultural Tourism and Dreams of Success in Contemporary Benin" and Jeffrey Kahn's "Policing 'Evil': State-sponsored Witch-Hunting in the People's Republic of Bénin."
4. See Soyinka, "of all the landmarks of slavery that I had ever traversed, none, not even the grim tunnels of Gorée or Cape Coast, worn smooth by the yet echoing slaps of feet on the passage to hell, could match the eerie evocation of the walk toward Embarkation Point on the coast Ouidah, in the Republic of Benin, then known as the Kingdom of Dahomey." Moreover, Soyinka recalls his "travers[ing] the actual route taken by the slaves on their way to embarkation" and how his group "stood on the spot from which to cast a last look on homeland," which he calls "Suicide Point" (*Burden* 65–8). See also Bernard Dadié, "Black Star."
5. See http://news.bbc.co.uk/2/hi/africa/7858010.stm.
6. See www.bbc.com/news/uk-wales-53156106.

7. See Malawi Slave Routes and Dr. David Livingstone Trail," https://whc.unesco.org/en/tentativelists/5603/.
8. With his edited volume for Cambridge University Press on "Latina/o American Literature," Morán González is one of the trailblazers for thinking of Latinx studies in these comparative terms.
9. See Quayson, "The irony in this scenario is that while salsa may have originated in the Cuban slave plantations and subsequently become a means for people from Latin America to express their cultural dance preferences in New York and Los Angeles, its return to Africa has been via the circuits of the middle classes and their transnational cohorts" (174).
10. Personal interview with scholar Ibrahima Wane on July 12, 2012, "lien entre les Amériques et l'Afrique." Wane also states that the percussion in salsa was made Senegalese, resulting in a modern percussion now found in the very popular genre of Senegalese *mbalax*. I thank Elisabeth Boyi for mediating this conversation. I also thank Fatoumata Seck for her input regarding this wall writing in St-Louis.
11. Ibid. See also Aleysia Whitmore's "Cuban Music in African Music," 113. In this article, she discusses specifically the influence of the *Orchestra Baobab*, a highly popular band that was one of the first to mix Senegalese and Cuban music, marking their musical craft as "modern and cosmopolitan."

Bibliography

Archival Manuscripts and Informant Interviews

AIX-EN-PROVENCE, FRANCE

Les Archives Nationales d'Outre-Mer
Correspondance adressée aux colonies, FR ANOM COL B 28–24
    Au sieur Marin au sujet des efforts qu'il déploie pour récupérer une partie des effets embarqués sur l'Hermione naufragée près de Carthagène, 1707
    A monsieur de Charritte, . . . Carthagène et la Compagnie de l'Assiento, de la manière illégale dont il s'est ampère d'une partie de la cargaison d'un navire anglais perdu près du Cap., 1710

Mémoire concernant le comptoir de Judas (ouidah) 1691–1791 dont 15: memoire concernant le commerce de noirs qui se fait à la côte de Guinée, 7 mars 1715, 16 DFC/75
    Carton #3, "Relation du Royaume de Judas en Guinée, de son Gouvernement, des mœurs de ses habitants, de leur religion, et du négoce qui sy fait" (anonymous and undated [ca. 1714] ms, in Archives d Outre-Mer, Aix-en-Provence: Dépôt des Fortifications des Colonies, Côtes d'Afrique,"104

Miscellaneous, FR ANOM COL B 28 F° 577/ 127 MIOM/15
    E. Binet Papers, "Observations sur les Dahoméens"
    M. de Chauillars Papers, "Correspondance"
    Brazza Papers_1879, 127 MIOM/15, 2, 9

Police des Noirs 1777–1778 (FM_F_1B_1–4)
    Mme. Paquet : Correspondence concerning slave Lucille

AUSTIN, TEXAS

Harry Ransom Center Collection, University of Texas
MSS, García Márquez, Scrapbook, osb_9B_120

"Cuba en Angola: Operación Carlota" in *Proceso*
"El drama de las dos Cubas" in *Areito*
"Vietnam, el país que destruyó Estados Unidos" in *Proceso*

COTONOU, BENIN

Interviews: Housemates, community members, students from Université d'Abomey-Calavi.
Proverbs," l'Agence Nationale pour la Promotion des Patrimoines et de développement du tourisme au Bénin, in Cotonou, Benin

GOREE, SENEGAL

Interview: Mr. Coly, *Maison des esclaves/House of Slaves*
Pamphlet, "La Maison des Esclaves de Gorée," Printed by *Dakar Port Authority*

HAVANA, CUBA

Archivo Nacional de Cuba
Biblioteca Nacional José Martí
Personal interview with Roberto Fernández Retamar, 2011. Casa de las Américas.

OUIDAH, BENIN

Interviews: Guides at Slave Trade Route; Tree of Forgetfulness, the Zomachi Memorial of Repentance, the Zomaï enclosure, the Zoungbodji memorial, the Tree of Return, and the Door of No Return
"Tableau Statistique de l'année 2011/2010," Ouidah, Port Portugais

PARIS, FRANCE

Les Archives Nationales
Moreau de Saint-Méry, *Description topographique, physique, civile, politique et historique de la partie française de l'isle Saint-Domingue.*
"Nouveau plan de Cartagène, Colombie, avec les dernières attaques des forts par l'amiral Vernon," 1741
Relation De Divers Voyages Faits Dans L'Afrique, Dans L'Amérique, & Aux Indes Occidentales. La Description Du Royaume De Juda, & Quelques Particularités Touchant La Vie Du Roy Régnant. Paris: C. Jombert, 1718.

URBANA-CHAMPAIGN, ILLINOIS

British Parliament Papers, Nigeria
Correspondence, "The Trial of Certain Persons at Sierra Leone for the Murder of a Slave Girl at Onitsha on the River Niger," London, 1882
Illinois University Library, University of Illinois, Urbana-Champaign
Missione evangelica al regno de Congo, 1665–1668, Giovanni Antonio Cavazzi.

Works Cited

"Jacksons Star in Nigeria Resort Row." BBC, February 16, 2009. http://news.bbc.co.uk/2/hi/africa/7858010.stm.
"Héritages de L'esclavage: Un Guide pour les Gestionnaires de Sites et Itinéraires de Mémoire." *UNESCO*, 2017. www.unesco.org/new/fr/social-and-human-sciences/themes/slave-route/right-box/publications/legacies-of-slavery/.
"La Maison des esclaves." *Le Monde*, August 8, 1991. www.lemonde.fr/archives/article/1991/08/08/9-la-maison-des-esclaves_4000001_1819218.html.
"Maison des esclaves de l'île de Gorée" / "The Slave House of Gorée Island." *Dakar Port Authority*, Dakar, pp. 3–41.
"Picturing Africa: Illustrating Livingstone's Travels." National Library of Scotland. www.nls.uk/exhibitions/david-livingstone.
Ackermann, Hans W., and Jeanine Gauthier. "The Ways and Nature of the Zombi." *The Journal of American Folklore* 104, no. 114, 1991, pp. 466–94.
Adesanmi, Pius. "Capitalism and Memory: Of Golf Courses and Massage Parlors in Badagry, Nigeria." Annual conference of the Stanford Forum for African Studies, October 29, 2011, Stanford University, The Stanford Humanities Center, Palo Alto, California. Keynote Address, http://saharareporters.com/2011/10/31/capitalism-and-memory-golf-courses-and-massage-parlors-badagry-nigeria-pius-adesanmi.
Who Owns the Problem? Africa and the Struggle for Agency. Michigan State University Press, 2020.
Adja, Eric. *Les trois héros de Ouidah*. Éditeurs de la République Biblique, 1990.
Aguirre Beltrán, Gonzálo. *Medicina y magia: el proceso de aculturación en la estructura colonial*. Instituto Nacional Indigenista, 1963.
Alaimo, Stacy, Sarah Wald, David J. Vázquez, Priscilla S. Ybarra, Sarah J. Ray, Laura Pulido, *Latinx Environmentalisms: Place, Justice, and the Decolonial*. Temple University Press, 2019.
Alberto, Eliseo. *Caracol Beach*. Alfaguara, 1998.
Alvarez, Julia. *How the García Girls Lost Their Accents*. Algonquin Books of Chapel Hill, 2010.
Almaguer, Tomás. "At the Crossroads of Race Latino/a Studies and Race Making in the United States." *Critical Latin American and Latino*

Studies, edited by Juan Poblete, University of Minnesota Press, 2003, pp. 206–22.

Alvarez-Borland, Isabel. "From Mystery to Parody: (Re)readings of GM's *Crónica de una muerte anunciada*." *Symposium*, vol. 38, no. 4, 1984, pp. 278–286.

Álvarez-Tabio Albo, Emma. "The City in Midair," *Havana Beyond the Ruins: Cultural Mappings after 1989*, edited by Anke Birkenmaier and Esther Whitfield, Duke University Press, 2011, pp. 149–72.

Amodeo, Christian. "Man with a Mission." *Geographical*, 2004, pp. 34–40.

Anaya, Rudolfo. *A Chicano in China*. University of New Mexico Press, 1986.

Bless Me, Ultima. Grand Central Publishing, 1999.

Heart of Aztlan: A Novel. University of New Mexico Press, 1988.

Shaman Winter. University of New Mexico Press, 2009.

The Man Who Could Fly and Other Stories. University of Oklahoma Press, 2006.

Angola: Hearings before the Subcommittee on African Affairs of the Committee on Foreign Relations, United States Senate, Ninety-fourth Congress, Second Session, on U.S. Involvement in Civil War in Angola. United States. Congress. Senate. Committee on Foreign Relations. Subcommittee on African Affairs, 1976.

Anstee, Margaret, "Forgotten Tragedy." *African Research Bulletin*, vol. 30, no. 4, 1993, pp. 1–30.

Aparicio, Frances and Susana Chávez-Silverman. *Tropicalizations: Transcultural Representations of Latinidad*. Dartmouth College Press, 1997.

Apter, Emily S. *Against World Literature: On the Politics of Untranslatability*. Verso, 2013.

Araujo, Ana Lucia. *Politics of Memory: Making Slavery Visible in the Public Space*. Routledge, 2012.

Public Memory of Slavery: Victims and Perpetrators in the South Atlantic. Cambria Press, 2010.

"Welcome the Diaspora: Slave Trade Heritage Tourism and the Public Memory of Slavery." *Ethnologies* 32.2, 2010, pp. 145–78.

Arbino, Daniel and Núria Sabaté. "El monstruo en 'Monstro': Una perspectiva neobarroca." *Label Me Latina/o*, vol. 7, 2017, pp. 1–22.

Armillas-Tiseyra, Magalí *The Dictator Novel: Writers and Politics in the Global South*. Northwestern University Press, 2019.

Avelar, Idelber. *The Untimely Present: Postdictatorial Latin American Fiction and the Task of Mourning*. Duke University Press, 1999.

Azoulay, Ariella A. *Potential History: Unlearning Imperialism*. Verso Books, 2019.

"Potential History: Thinking through Violence." *Critical Inquiry* 39.3 (2013): 548–74.

Bakhtiarova, Galina. "Americanos, indianos, mulatas y otros: Cataluña y Cuba entre el deseo colonial y la nostalgia imperial." *Memoria colonial e inmigración: la negritude en la España posfranquista*, edited by Rosalía Cornejo Parriego, Ediciones Bellatierra, 2007, pp. 39–52.

Barcia Paz, Manuel. *West African Warfare in Bahia and Cuba: Soldier Slaves in the Atlantic World, 1807–1844*. Oxford University Press, 2014.
Barry, Boubacar. *Senegambia and the Atlantic Trade*. Cambridge University Press, 1998.
Bauer, Ralph. "Hemispheric Studies." *PMLA* 124. 1, 2009, pp. 234–50.
Baum, Robert M. "Religions, African." *The Princeton Companion to Atlantic History*, edited by Joseph C. Miller et al., Princeton University Press, pp. 395–98.
Bekerie, Ayele. "The Ancient African Past and the Field of Africana Studies."*Journal of Black Studies*, vol. 37, no. 3, 2007, pp. 445–60.
Bell-Villada, Gene H. *García Márquez: The Man and His Work*. University of North Carolina Press, 2010.
Bellegarde-Smith, Patrick and Claudine Michel, editors. *Haitian Vodou: Spirit, Myth, and Reality*. Indiana University Press, 2006.
Bencomo, Anadeli, "Crónicas and New Journalism." *The Routledge Handbook to the Culture and Media of the Americas*, edited by Wilfried Raussert et al., Routledge, 2020.
Berenson, Edward. *Heroes of Empire: Five Charismatic Men and the Conquest of Africa*. University of California Press, 2011.
Bhabha, Homi K. *The Location of Culture*. New York: Routledge, 1994.
Bhambra, Gurminder K. "Postcolonial and Decolonial Dialogues." *Postcolonial Studies* vol. 17, no. 2, 2014, pp. 115–21.
Binet, E. "Observations sur le Dahoméens." *Bulletins et Mémoires de la Société d'Anthropologie de Paris*, vol. 1, no. 1, 1900, pp. 244–53.
Birkenmaier, Anke and Esther Whitfield, editors. *Havana Beyond the Ruins: Cultural Mappings after 1989*. Duke University Press, 2011.
Bobes, Velia Cecilia. "Visits to a Non-Place: Havana and Its Representation(s)." *Havana Beyond the Ruins: Cultural Mappings After 1989*, edited by Anke Birkenmaier and Esther Katheryn Whitfield, Duke University Press, 2011, pp. 15–30.
Bouche, Pierre. *Sept ans en Afrique Occidentale: la côte des esclaves et le Dahomey*. Hachette Livre – BNF, 2018.
Bourdieu, Pierre. "The Essence of Neoliberalism." Trans. Jeremy J. Shapiro. *Le Monde diplomatique*, December 1998. https://mondediplo.com/1998/12/08bourdieu.
Bost, Suzanne and Frances R. Aparicio. *Routledge Companion to Latino/a Literature*. Routledge, 2013.
Bourke, John Gregory. "The American Congo." *Scribners' Magazine*, vol. 15, 1894, pp. 590–610.
Brady, Mary P. *Extinct Lands, Temporal Geographies: Chicana Literature and the Reinvention of Space*. Duke University Press, 1997.
Brand, Dionne. *A Map to the Door of No Return: Notes to Belonging*. Vintage Canada, 2001.
Brantlinger, Patrick. "Victorians And Africans: The Genealogy of the Myth of the Dark Continent." *Critical Inquiry*, vol. 12, no. 1, 1985, pp. 166–203.

Brouillette, Sarah. *UNESCO and the Fate of the Literary*. Stanford University Press, 2019.
"On the African Literary Hustle." *Blind Field: A Journal of Literary Inquiry*, August 2017. https://blindfieldjournal.com/2017/08/14/on-the-african-literary-hustle.
Bruce-Novoa, Juan. *Chicano Authors: Inquiry by Interview*. University of Texas Press, 1980.
Butler, Judith. *Frames of War: When Is Life Grievable?* Verso, 2009.
Precarious Life: The Powers of Mourning and Violence. Verso, 2004.
Byrne, Eleanor. *Homi K. Bhabha*. Palgrave, 2009.
Calderón, Héctor. "Chicano/a Literature." *The Routledge Companion to Latino/a Literature*, edited by Suzanne Bost and Frances Aparicio, Routledge, 2013, pp. 396–405.
Narratives of Greater Mexico: Essays on Chicano Literary History, Genre, and Borders. 1st ed., University of Texas Press, 2004.
Calderón, Camilo and Julio Roca, *Al Día*, April 28, 1981, pp. 51–60.
Callen King, Katherine. "Santiago Tyrannos: Dialogic Voices in García Márquez's *Crónica de una muerte anunciada*." *Comparative Literature*, vol. 43, no. 4, 1991, pp. 305–25.
Calvi, Pablo. "Latin America's Own 'New Journalism.'" *Literary Journalism Studies*, vol. 2, no. 2, 2010, pp. 63–84.
Caminero-Santangelo, Marta. "'Jason's Indian': Mexican Americans and the Denial of Indigenous Ethnicity in Anaya's *Bless Me, Ultima*." *Critique: Studies in Contemporary Fiction*, vol. 45, no. 2, 2004, pp. 115–28.
On Latinidad: U.S. Latino Literature and the Construction of Ethnicity. University Press of Florida, 2007.
Candelario, Ginetta E. B. *Black Behind the Ears: Dominican Racial Identity from Museums to Beauty Shops*. Duke University Press, 2007.
Cantú, Roberto, editor. *The Forked Juniper: Critical Perspectives on Rudolfo Anaya*. Oklahoma University Press, 2016.
Cardoso, Boaventura. *Maio, mês de Maria*. Campo das Letras, 1997.
Carneado, José Felipe. "La discriminación racial en Cuba no volverá jamás." *Cuba Socialista*, vol. 2, no. 5, 1962, pp. 54–67.
Carpentier, Alejo. *El reino de este mundo*. HarperCollins, 2009.
The Kingdom of This World. Translated by Pablo Medina. Farrar, Straus and Giroux, 1949.
Casamayor-Cisneros, Odette. *Utopía, distopía e ingravidez: reconfiguraciones cosmológicas en la narrativa postsoviética cubana*. Iberoamericana; Vervuert, 2013.
Casanova, Pascale, and M. B. DeBevoise. *The World Republic of Letters*. Harvard University Press, 2004.
Castillo, Debra A. "Te has desmaterializado ya? González Viaña, Los sueños de América." *The Other Latinos: Central and South Americans in the United States*, edited by José Luis Falconi and José Antonio Mazzotti, Harvard University Press, 2007, pp. 177–94.

Castillo, Debra A. and Shalini A. Puri. *Theorizing Fieldwork in the Humanities: Methods, Reflections, and Approaches to the Global South.* Palgrave Macmillan, 2016.

Castro, Fidel. "Discurso en el Estadio '28 de Septiembre,' 3 de mayo." El Futuro es el Intercionalismo: Recorrido del Comandante Fidel Castro por Países de Africa y Europa Socialista, 3 de Mayo–5 de Julio de 1972. Havana, Instituto Cubano del Libro, 1972, p. 17.

Cuba y Angola: Luchando por la libertad de África y la nuestra. Pathfinder Press, 2013.

Castro, Fidel, et al. *Cuba & Angola: Fighting for Africa's Freedom and Our Own.* Pathfinder Press, 2013.

Castro, Juan E. de. *Mestizo Nations: Culture, Race, and Conformity in Latin American Literature.* University of Arizona Press, 2002.

Cavazzi, Joao Antonio Cavazzi de. *Descrição Histórica Dos Três Reinos do Congo, Matamba e Angola.* Junta de Investigacoes do Ultramar, 1965.

Certeau, de Michel. *The Practice of Everyday Life.* 1984. Translated by Steven Rendall, University of California Press, 1988.

Certeau, de Michel et al. *The Practice of Everyday Life.* University of Minnesota Press, 1998.

Césaire, Aimé. *Discourse on Colonialism.* Monthly Review Press, 1972.

Charún-Illescas, Lucía. *Malambo.* Universidad Nacional Federico Villarreal, Editorial Universitaria, 2001.

Chancy, Myriam J. A. *From Sugar to Revolution: Women's Visions of Haiti, Cuba, and the Dominican Republic.* Wilfrid Laurier University Press, 2013.

Ciarcia, Gaetano. "Restaurer le futur. Sur la Route de l'Esclave à Ouidah (Bénin)." *Cahiers d'études africaines*, vol. 4, no. 192, 2008, pp. 687–706.

Cisneros, Sandra. Trans. by Elena Poniatowska. *La casa en Mango Street.* Vintage Books, 1994.

Clifford, James. *Routes: Travel and Translation in the Late Twentieth Century.* Harvard University Press, 1997.

Coleman, Simon, and Eade, John. *Reframing Pilgrimage: Cultures in Motion.* Routledge, 2004.

Comaroff, Jean, Mbembe, Achille, and Shipley, Jesse Weaver. "Africa in Theory: A Conversation Between Jean Comaroff and Achille Mbembe." *Anthropological Quarterly*, vol. 83, no. 3, 2010, pp. 653–78.

Comaroff, Jean, and Comaroff, John. "Alien-Nation: Zombies, Immigrants, and the Millennial Capitalism." *The South Atlantic Quarterly*, vol. 101, no. 4, 2002, pp. 779–805.

Condé, Maryse. *Moi, Tituba, Sorcière: Noire de Salem: Roman.* Mercure de France, 1986.

Conrad, Joseph. *Heart of Darkness.* Broadview Press, 1999.

Cooper, Frederick. *Africa since 1940: The Past of the Present.* Cambridge University Press, 2002.

Cornejo Polar, Antonio. "Crónica de una muerte anunciada (Book Review)." *Revista de Crítica Literaria Latinoamericana*, vol. 7, no. 13, 1981, pp. 140–2.

Cornejo Parriego, Rosalía. editor. *Memoria colonial e inmigración: la negritud en la España posfranquista*. Edicions Bellaterra, 2007.

Cotera, Maria Eugenia. "Refiguring 'The American Congo': Jovita González, John Gregory Bourke, and the Battle over Ethno-Historical Representations of the Texas Mexican Border." *Western American Literature*, vol. 35, no. 1, 2000, pp. 75–94.

Cutler, John Alba. *Ends of Assimilation: The Formation of Chicanx Literature*. Oxford University Press, 2014.

Dadié, Bernard Binlin. *Hommes de tous les continents: poèmes*. Présence africaine, 1985.

Dalleo, Raphael, and Elena Machado Sáez. *The Latino/a Canon and the Emergence of Post-Sixties Literature*. Palgrave Macmillan, 2007.

Damrosch, David. *What Is World Literature?* Princeton University Press, 2003.

Darrigrandi, Claudia. "Crónica latinoamericana: Algunos apuntes sobre su estudio." *Cuadernos de literatura*, vol. 17, No. 34, 2013, pp. 122–43.

Das, Amrita. "Negotiating a New Identity for U.S. Latino Literature in Achy Obejas's *Ruins*." *Label Me Latina/o* Special Edition, Latina Authors: Asserting Female Agency no. 2, 2012, pp. 1–23.

Dayan, Joan. *Haiti, History and the Gods*. University of California Press, 1995.

de Grand-Pierre, Dralsé. *Relation De Divers Voyages Faits Dans L'Afrique, Dans L'Amerique, & Aux Indes Occidentales. La Description Du Royaume De Juda, & Quelques Particularitez Touchant La Vie Du Roy Regnant*. C. Jombert, 1718.

Delgadillo, Theresa. *Spiritual Mestizaje: Religion, Gender, Race, and Nation in Contemporary Chicana Narrative*. Duke University Press, 2011.

DeLoughrey, Elizabeth M. et al., editors. *Caribbean Literature and the Environment: Between Nature and Culture*. University of Virginia Press, 2005.

Diagne, Souleymane Bachir, et al. "Artwork Taken from Africa, Returning to a Home Transformed." *The New York Times* www.nytimes.com/2019/01/03/arts/design/african-art-france-museums-restitution.html.

Díaz, Junot. *American Voces*, Johns Hopkins University, September 16, 2013.

  "Apocalypse: What Disasters Reveal." *Boston Review*, 1 May 2011. www.bostonreview.net/junot-diaz-apocalypse-haiti-earthquake.

  The Brief Wondrous Life of Oscar Wao. Riverhead Books, 2007.

  "Junot Díaz Aims to Fulfill His Dream of Publishing Sci-Fi Novel with Monstro." *Wired*, October 3, 2012. www.wired.com/2012/10/geeks-guide-junot-diaz/.

  "Monstro." *The New Yorker*. June 4, 2012. www.newyorker.com/magazine/2012/06/04/monstro.

Díaz, Junot, Leo Espinosa, and Teresa Mlawer. *Lola*. Dial Books for Young Readers, 2018.

Díaz, Junot and Leyshon, Cressida. "This Week in Fiction: Junot Díaz." *The New Yorker*, May 27, 2012. www.newyorker.com/books/page-turner/this-week-in-fiction-junot-daz-2.

Dimock, Wai Chee, and Lawrence Buell. *Shades of the Planet: American Literature as World Literature*. Princeton University Press, 2007.

Di Iorio, Lyn. "The Latino Scapegoat: Knowledge through Death in Short Stories by Joyce Carol Oates and Junot Díaz." *Contemporary U.S. Latino/a Literary*

Criticism. Edited by Lyn Di Iorio Sandín and Richard Perez. Palgrave Macmillan, 2007, pp. 15–33.
Doss, Erika. *Memorial Mania: Public Feeling in America*. University of Chicago Press, 2010.
Dowdy, Michael. *Broken Souths Latina/o Poetic Responses to Neoliberalism and Globalization*. University of Arizona Press, 2013.
Draper, Susana. *Afterlives of Confinement: Spatial Transitions in Postdictatorship Latin America*. University of Pittsburgh Press, 2012.
Driver, Felix. "Henry Morton Stanley and His Critics: Geography, Exploration, and Empire." *Past and Present* vol. 133, 1991, pp. 134–166.
Dubois, Laurent. *Haiti: The Aftershocks of History*. Metropolitan, 2012.
Duneer, Anita. "The Old Man and the City: Literary Naturalism and the Postcolonial Subject in Achy Obejas's Ruins." *Studies in American Naturalism*, vol. 10, no. 2, 2015, pp. 150–71.
Durán, Armando. "Conversaciones con Gabriel García Márquez." *Sobre García Márquez*, edited by Pedro Simón Martínez, Biblioteca de Marca, 1971, pp. 34.
Dzidzienyo, Anani and Suzanne Oboler. *Neither Enemies nor Friends: Latinos, Blacks, Afro-Latinos*. Palgrave Macmillan, 2005.
Eco, Umberto. *The Aesthetics of Thomas Aquinas*. Harvard University Press, 1988.
Edgerton, Robert B. *The Troubled Heart of Africa: A History of the Congo*. 1st ed., St. Martin's, 2002.
Edwards, Brent Hayes. *The Practice of Diaspora: Literature, Translation, and the Rise of Black Internationalism*. Harvard University Press, 2003.
Emelike, Obinna. "Endless Wait for Jackson Park." *Business Day: Nigeria*, May 3, 2013. http://businessday.ng/art-and-travel/article/endless-wait-for-jackson-park.
Falola, Toyin, and Matt D Childs. *The Yoruba Diaspora in the Atlantic World*. Indiana University Press, 2004.
Fanon, Frantz. *Black Skin, White Masks*. Grove Press, 1967.
Peau Noire, Masques Blancs. Éditions du Seuil, 1971.
The Wretched of the Earth. Grove Press, 1963.
Toward the African Revolution. Translated by Haakon Chevalier, Grove Press, 1994.
Fara, Patricia and Karalyn Patterson, editors. *Memory*. Cambridge University Press, 1998.
Feather, A. G. *Daring Deeds in the Tropics. A Thrilling Narrative of Remarkable Adventures, Terrible Experiences, Amazing Achievements and Important Discoveries of Great Travelers in Southern Climes*. J. E. Potter, 1894. https://hdl.handle.net/2027/loc.ark:/13960/t4bp0z34 r.
Ferguson, James. *Global Shadows: Africa in the Neoliberal World Order*. Duke University Press, 2006.
Ferguson, Stephen C. *Philosophy of African American Studies: Nothing Left of Blackness*. Palgrave Macmillan, 2015.
Fernández Olmos, Margarite. *Rudolfo A. Anaya: A Critical Companion*. Greenwood Press, 1999.

Fernández Olmos, Margarite and Lizabeth Paravisini-Gebert, *Creole Religions of the Caribbean: An Introduction from Vodou and Santería to Obeah and Espiritismo*. New York University Press, 2003.
Fernández Retamar, Roberto and Fredric Jameson. *Todo Caliban*. Ediciones Callejón, 2003.
Fernández Retamar, R. *Calibán: Apuntes sobre la cultura en nuestra América*. Editorial la Pleyade, 1973.
Fernández Retamar, R., Edward Baker, and Fredric Jameson. *Caliban and Other Essays*. University of Minnesota Press, 1989.
Ferrari, Guillermina De. "Utopías críticas: la literatura mundial según América latina." *1616: Anuario de la Sociedad Española de Literatura General y Comparada* 2, 2012, pp. 15–32.
Figueroa-Vázquez, Yomaira C. *Decolonizing Diasporas Radical Mappings of Afro-Atlantic Literature*. Northwestern University Press, 2021.
Finch, Aisha K. *Rethinking Slave Rebellion in Cuba La Escalera and the Insurgencies of 1841–1844*. 1st ed. University of North Carolina Press, 2015.
Fisher Fishkin, Shelley. *Writing America: Literary Landmarks from Walden Pond to Wounded Knee, a Reader's Companion*. Rutgers University Press, 2015.
Forte, Jung Ran. "Marketing Vodun. Cultural Tourism and Dreams of Success in Contemporary Benin." *Cahiers D'études Africaines*, vol. 49, no. 1–2, Éditions de l'EHESS, 2009, pp. 429–51.
Foucault, Michel. *The Order of Things: An Archaeology of the Human Sciences*. Pantheon Books, 1971.
The Archeology of Knowledge. Harper & Row, 1972.
Franco Altamar, Javier. *El camino de la crónica*. Universidad del Norte, 2017.
Franco, José Luciano. *La gesta heróica del Triumvirato*. Editoriales de ciencias sociales, 2012.
Franqui, Carlos. *Retrato de familia con Fidel*. Seix Barral, 1981.
Frazer, James George. *The Golden Bough; A Study in Magic and Religion. Part II. Taboo and the Perils of the Soul*. Macmillan, 1927.
Fuente, Alejandro de la. *A Nation for All Race, Inequality, and Politics in Twentieth-century Cuba*. University of North Carolina Press, 2001.
García, Cristina. *Dreaming in Cuban: A Novel*. Alfred Knopf Press, 1992.
The Agüero Sisters. Domestic Fiction, 1997.
García, María Victoria. *Vi(r)aje a la memoria. Benemérita Universidad Autónoma de Puebla* Dirección General de Fomento Editorial, 1997.
Dijo el camaleón. Universidad Veracruzana, Dirección Editorial, 2016.
García Márquez, Gabriel. *Chronicle of a Death Foretold*. Vintage, 2003.
Crónica de una muerte anunciada. Diana, 2007.
Del amor y otros demonios. Mondadori, 1994.
El amor en los tiempos del cólera. Debolsillo, 2005.
"El drama de las dos Cubas." *Areito*, vol. 6, no. 21, 1979, pp. 31–3.
El otoño del Patriarca. Vintage Español, 2010.
"Es un crimen no tener participación política." *García Márquez habla de García Márquez*. Bogotá, Rentería Editores, 1979.

"Marcel Proust interroga a García Márquez." *García Márquez habla de García Márquez*. Bogotá, Rentería Editores, 1979.
Notas de prensa, 1980–1984. Mondadori, 1991.
Notas de prensa, 1980–1984. 2nd ed., Grupo Editorial Norma, 1996.
Of Love and Other Demons. Translated by Edith Grossman, Penguin Books, 1995.
"Operación Carlota." *Por La Libre: (1974–1995)*. 2nd ed., Editorial Sudamericana, 2000.
Por La Libre: (1974–1995). 2nd ed., Editorial Sudamericana, 2000.
Relato de un náufrago. Tusquets, 1970.
The Autumn of the Patriarch. Harper, 2006.
"Vietnam, el país que destruyó a Estados Unidos." *Proceso*, no. 164, 1979, pp. 6–10.
Vivir Para Contarla. 1st ed. Barcelona: Mondadori, 2002.
García Márquez, Gabriel and Armando Durán. "Conversaciones con Gabriel García Márquez." *García Márquez habla de García Márquez*. Bogotá, Rentería Editores, 1979.
García Márquez, Gabriel and Ernesto González Bermejo. "Ahora doscientos años de soledad." *García Márquez habla de García Márquez*. Bogotá, Rentería Editores, 1979.
García Márquez, Gabriel and Eva Norvind. "Intelectuales interrogan a Gabriel García Márquez." *García Márquez habla de García Márquez*. Bogotá, Rentería Editores, 1979.
García Márquez, Gabriel and Gabriel Angel Harguindey. "Llegué a creer que Franco no se moriría nunca." *García Márquez habla de García Márquez*. Bogotá, Rentería Editores, 1979.
García Márquez, Gabriel, John Sturrock and Frank Mac Shane. "García Márquez Analizado por el New York Times." *García Márquez habla de García Márquez*. Bogotá, Rentería Editores, 1979.
García Márquez, Gabriel and Josep Sarret. "Estoy tan Metido en la Política que Siento Nostalgia de la Literatura." *García Márquez habla de García Márquez*. Bogotá, Rentería Editores, 1979.
García Márquez, Gabriel and Juan Gossaín. "El regreso a Macondo." *García Márquez habla de García Márquez*. Bogotá, Rentería Editores, 1979.
García Márquez, Gabriel and Plinio Apuleyo Mendoza. "El encuentro entre dos camaradas." *García Márquez habla de García Márquez*. Bogotá, Rentería Editores, 1979.
García Márquez, Gabriel and Luis Suárez. "El Periodismo me Dió Conciencia Política." *García Márquez habla de García Márquez*. Bogotá, Rentería Editores, 1979.
García Márquez, Gabriel and Manuel Osorio. "García Márquez en México: Poco café y mucha política." *García Márquez habla de García Márquez*. Bogotá, Rentería Editores, 1979.
García Márquez, Gabriel And Manuel Pereiro. "La Revolución Cubana me Libró de Todos los Honores Detestables de este Mundo." *García Márquez habla de García Márquez*. Bogotá, Rentería Editores, 1979.

García Márquez, Gabriel and Plinio Apuleyo Mendoza. *El olor de la guayaba: Conversaciones con Plinio Apuleyo Mendoza*. Bruguera, 1982.
García Márquez, Gabriel and Rita Guibert. "Algún día Estados Unidos hará su revolución socialista." *García Márquez habla de García Márquez*. Bogotá, Rentería Editores, 1979.
García Márquez, Gabriel and Vicente Romero. "García Márquez habla sobre Cuba." *García Márquez habla de García Márquez*. Bogotá, Rentería Editores, 1979.
García-Peña, Lorgia. *The Borders of Dominicanidad: Race, Nation, and Archives of Contradiction*. Duke University Press, 2016.
Gaspar de Alba, Alicia. *Calligraphy of the Witch*. Arte Público Press, 2007.
Geary, William Newill M. *Nigeria under British Rule*. Methuen, 1927.
Gehman, Richard J. *African Traditional Religion in Biblical Perspective*. East African Educational, 1993.
Gewecke, Frauke. "Latino/a Literature in Western Europe." *Routledge Companion to Latino/a Literature*, edited by Suzanne Bost and Frances R. Aparicio, Routledge, 2013, pp. 107–15.
Gikandi, Simon. "In the Shadow of Hegel: Cultural Theory in an Age of Displacement." *Research in African Literatures*, vol. 27, no. 2, 1996, pp. 139–50.
Giles, Paul. *The Global Remapping of American Literature*. Princeton University Press, 2011.
Gilroy, Paul. *The Black Atlantic: Modernity and Double Consciousness*. Harvard University Press, 1993.
Ginzburg, Carlo. *Clues, Myths, and the Historical Method*. Trans. John and Anne Tedeschi. Johns Hopkins University Press, 1989.
Glissant, Édouard. *Poetics of Relation*. University of Michigan Press, 2009.
Glissant, Édouard and Dash, J. M. *Caribbean Discourse: Selected Essays*. Virginia University Press, 1989.
Gleijeses, Piero. *Conflicting Missions: Havana, Washington, and Africa, 1959–1976*. University of North Carolina Press, 2002.
Gleijeses, Piero et al. *Cuba y África: Historia común de lucha y sangre*. Editorial De Ciencias Sociales, 2007.
Goffman, Ethan. *Imagining Each Other: Blacks and Jews in Contemporary American Literature*. State University of New York Press, 2000.
Gomez, Michael A. *Reversing Sail: A History of the African Diaspora*. Cambridge University Press, 2005.
González, Aníbal. "The Ends of the Text: Journalism in the Fiction of Gabriel García Márquez." *Gabriel García Márquez and the Powers of Fiction*, edited by Julio Ortega and Claudia Elliott, University of Texas Press, 1988, pp. 61–73.
  "Modernist Prose." *The Cambridge History of Latin American Literature* II, edited by Enrique Pulpo-Walker and Roberto González Echevarría, Cambridge University Press, 1996, pp. 69–113.
González, John Morán. *The Cambridge Companion to Latina/o American Literature*. Cambridge University Press, 2016.
Gonzalez, Nelly S. *Bibliographic Guide to Gabriel García Márquez, 1986–1992*. Greenwood Press, 1994.

Goyal, Yogita. *Romance, Diaspora, and Black Atlantic Literature*. Cambridge University Press, 2010.

Grant, Caesar. "All God's Chillen Had Wings." *The Book of Negro Folklore*, edited by Langston Hughes and Arna Wendell Bontemps, Dodd, Mead, 1958, pp. 62–65.

Green, Toby. "A Fistful of Shells: West Africa from the Rise of the Slave Trade to the Age of Revolution" in *New Books in African Studies*, May 2019. http://ppaa.player.fm/series/new-books-in-african-studies-2421479/toby-green-a-fistful-of-shells-west-africa-from-the-rise-of-the-slave-trade-to-the-age-of-revolution-u-chicago-press-2019.

—"'Dubbing' Precolonial Africa and the Atlantic Diaspora: Historical Knowledge and the Global South." *Atlantic Studies Global Currents*, 2019, pp. 1-15.

Grohs, G. K. "Frantz Fanon and the African Revolution." *The Journal of Modern African Studies*, vol. 6, no. 4, 1968, pp. 543–56.

Gruesz, Kirsten Silva. *Ambassadors of Culture: The Transamerican Origins of Latino Writing*. Princeton University Press, 2002.

Guillén, Nicolás. *Sóngoro Cosongo, Motivos de son, West Indies Ltd.: España, poema en cuatro angustias y una esperanza*. Buenos Aires, Losada, 1952.

Guridy, Frank Andre. *Forging Diaspora: Afro-Cubans and African Americans in a World of Empire and Jim Crow*. University of North Carolina Press, 2010.

Gutiérrez Azopardo, Ildefonso. "El Comercio y mercado de negros esclavos en Cartagena de Indias (1533-1850)." *Quinto Centenario*, vol. 12, 1987, pp. 187–210.

Gutiérrez, Ramón A. "The Spell of New Mexico: The Witches and Sorcerers of Colonial New Mexico" *The Forked Juniper: Critical Perspectives on Rudolfo Anaya*, edited by Roberto Cantú, University of Oklahoma Press, 2016, pp. 27–43.

Haen, Theo d'. et al. *The Routledge Companion to World Literature*. Routledge, 2012.

Hagen, Ryan. "Exhibit at UC Riverside Brings the Reality of Slavery Home." *The Press Enterprise*, February 19, 2018. www.pe.com/2018/02/19/uc-riverside-exhibit-takes-deep-dive-into-slavery/.

Halbwachs, Maurice. Translated by Lewis A. Coser. *On Collective Memory*. University of Chicago Press, 1992.

Harford Vargas, Jennifer. *Forms of Dictatorship: Power, Narrative, and Authoritarianism in the Latina/o Novel*. Oxford University Press, 2017.

—"Dictating a Zafa: The Power of Narrative Form as Ruin-Reading." *Junot Díaz and the Decolonial Imagination*. Edited by Monica Hanna, Jennifer Harford Vargas, and José David Saldívar. Duke University Press, 2016, pp. 201–30.

Harris, Lynn. *Sea Ports and Sea Power: African Maritime Cultural Landscapes*. Springer International, 2017.

Hartman, Saidiya V. *Lose Your Mother: A Journey Along the Atlantic Slave Route*. Farrar, Straus and Giroux, 2007.

"Venus in Two Acts." *Small Axe: A Caribbean Journal of Criticism*, vol. 26, 2008, pp. 1–14.

Harunah, Hakeem B. *Nigeria's Defunct Slave Ports: Their Cultural Legacies and Touristic Value*. First Academic Pub, 2000.

Hatzky, Christine. *Cubans in Angola South-South Cooperation and Transfer of Knowledge, 1976–1991*. The University of Wisconsin Press, 2015.

Headley, Joel Tyler. *Stanley's Adventures in the Wilds of Africa. A Full Account of the Two Famous Expeditions of Henry M. Stanley, the Fearless and Peerless Explorer of the Dark Continent . . . Including Stanley's Final Journey Down the Congo, from Its Headwaters to the Ocean*. Hubbard Brothers, 1882.

The Achievements of Stanley and Other African Explorers. Comprising All the Late and Really Great Achievements Won in the Exploration of the Vast Unknown Region of Equatorial Africa. Hubbard Brothers, 1878.

Helg, Aline. "Introduction to Part III." *Breaking the Chains, Forging the Nation: The Afro-Cuban Fight for Freedom and Equality, 1812–1912*, edited by Aisha Finch and Fannie Rushing, Louisiana State University Press, 2019, pp. 213–22.

Hemingway, Ernest. *Green Hills of Africa*. New York: Permabooks, 1935.

Herskovits, Melville J. *Dahomey: An Ancient West African Kingdom*. Northwestern University Press, 1967.

Hirsch, Marianne. *The Generation of Postmemory: Writing and Visual Culture After the Holocaust*. Columbia University Press, 2012.

Hodapp, James, ed. *Afropolitan Literature as World Literature*. Bloomsbury Academic, 2020.

Hooker, Juliet. *Theorizing Race in the Americas: Douglass, Sarmiento, Du Bois, and Vasconcelos*. Oxford University Press, 2017.

Hourcade, Renaud. "Commemorating a Guilty Past: The Politics of Memory in the French Former Slave Trade Cities." *Politics of Memory: Making Slavery Visible in the Public Space*, edited by Ana Lucia Araujo, Routledge Press, 2013, pp. 124–40.

Howard, David John. *Coloring the Nation: Race and Ethnicity in the Dominican Republic*. Signal Books, 2001.

Hoyos Ayala, Héctor. *Beyond Bolaño: The Global Latin American Novel*. Columbia University Press, 2015.

Hughes, Langston. "The Negro Speaks of Rivers." *The Crisis: A Record of the Darker Races*, vol. 22, no. 2, 1921, pp. 71.

Hughes, Langston, edited by Arnold Rampersad. *The Collected Works of Langston Hughes*: Volume 1. The Poems: 1921–1940. University of Missouri Press, 2001.

Hughes, Langston and Arna Bontemps. *The Book of Negro Folklore*. Dodd, Mead, 1958.

Hulme, Peter. *Colonial Encounters: Europe and the Native Caribbean, 1492–1797*. Routledge, 1992.

Hunsaker, Steven V. "Representing the mulata: El amor en los tiempos del cólera and Tenda dos milagres." *Hispania*, vol. 77, no. 2, 1994, pp. 225–34.

Hunt, Alex. "In Search of Anaya's Carp: Mapping Ecological Consciousness and Chicano Myth." *Interdisciplinary Studies in Literature and Environment*, vol. 12, no. 2, 2005, pp. 179–206.

Hyde, Alexander. *Stanley in Africa: the Story of His Wonderful Marches across the Continent, Voyages on the Great Equatorial Lakes, Perilous Descent of the Congo, and Desperate Encounters with Cataracts and Cannibals, Told Chiefly in His Own Words, Together with a Narrative of the Exploits of Sir Samuel W. Baker and Commander V. L. Cameron*. Columbian Book Co., 1878.

Inda, Jonathan Xavier. "Foreign Bodies: Migrants, Parasites, and the Pathological Body Politic." *Discourse: Journal for Theoretical Studies in Media and Culture*, vol. 22, no. 3, 2000, pp. 46–62.

Irizarry, Ylce. *Chicana/o and Latina/o Fiction: The New Memory of Latinidad*. University of Illinois Press, 2016.

Irr, Caren. *Toward the Geopolitical Novel: US Fiction in the Twenty-First Century*. Columbia University Press, 2014.

Jaffe, Sarah. "Zombie Neoliberalism: How 'There Is No Alternative' gave us Donald Trump." *Dissent Magazine*, 2017.

Jaramillo Agudelo, Darío, editor. *Antología de crónica latinoamericana actual*. Alfaguara, 2012.

Jeal, Tim. *Stanley: The Impossible Life of Africa's Greatest Explorer*. Yale University Press, 2007.

Jiménez Román, Miriam, and Juan Flores. *The Afro-Latin@ Reader: History and Culture in the United States*. Duke University Press, 2010.

Johnson, Sarah E. *The Fear of French Negroes: Transcolonial Collaboration in the Revolutionary Americas*. University of California Press, 2012.

Kahn, Jeffrey. "Policing 'Evil': State-Sponsored Witch-Hunting in the People's Republic of Bénin." *Journal of Religion in Africa*, vol. 41, no. 1, 2011, pp. 4–34.

Kalman, Harold. "Destruction, Mitigation, and Reconciliation of Cultural Heritage." *International Journal of Heritage Studies*, vol. 23, no. 6, 2017, pp. 538–55.

Kaplan, Amy, and Donald E. Pease. *Cultures of United States Imperialism*. Duke University Press, 1993.

Kárai, Attila. "The Postmodern Use of Mythopoeia in the Narrative Temporality of Rudolfo Anaya's *Bless Me, Ultima*." *Hungarian Journal of English and American Studies*, vol. 14, no. 2, 2008, pp. 265–85.

Kaun, Alexandra. "When the Displaced Return: Challenges to Reintegration in Angola." *UN High Commissioner for Refugees (UNHCR)*, vol. 152, 2008, pp. 1–46.

Kaup, Monika. "Rudolfo Anaya's *Bless Me, Ultima*: A Nuevomexicano Contribution to the Hemispheric Genealogy of the New World Baroque" *The Forked Juniper: Critical Perspectives on Rudolfo Anaya*, edited by Roberto Cantú, University of Oklahoma Press, 2016, pp. 153–78.

Kazanjian, David. *The Brink of Freedom: Improvising Life in the Nineteenth-Century Atlantic World*. Duke University Press, 2016.

——. "Two Paths Through Slavery's Archives." *History of the Present*, vol. 6, no. 2, 2016, pp. 133–45.

Kerasote, Ted. "Untouchable Wild." *Audubon*, vol. 101, no. 5, 1999, pp. 82–6.

Kercher, Dona M. "Garcia Marquez's 'Crónica de una muerte anunciada' ('Chronicle of a Death Foretold'): Notes on Parody and the Artist." *Latin American Literary Review*, vol. 13, no. 25, 1985, pp. 90–103.

Konrad, Walecia. "Going Abroad to Find Affordable Health Care." *The New York Times*, March 20, 2009. www.nytimes.com/2009/03/21/health/21patient.

Koselleck, Reinhart. *Futures Past: On the Semantics of Historical Time*. Trans. Keith Tribe. Columbia University Press, 2004.

Sediments of Time: On Possible Histories. Trans. Sean Franzel and Stefan-Ludwig Hoffmann. Stanford University Press, 2018.

Kun, Josh. *Audiotopia: Music, Race, and America*. Berkeley: University of California Press, 2005.

Kutzinski, Vera. "The Logic of Wings: Gabriel García Márquez and Afro-American Literature." *Latin American Literary Review*, vol. 13, no. 25, 1985, pp. 133–46.

Labou Tansi, Sony. *Les septs solitudes de Lorsa Lopez*. Points, 2009.

Seven Solitudes of Lorsa Lopez. Heinemann Educational Publishers, 1995.

L'état honteux: Roman. Paris: Editions du Seuil, 1981.

Lam, Wifredo and Max-Pol Fouchet. *Wifredo Lam*. Ediciones Poligrafa, 1976, pp. 188–9.

Lamadrid, Enrique. "*De vatos y profetas*: Cultural Authority and Literary Performance in the Writing of Rudolfo Anaya." *The Forked Juniper: Critical Perspectives on Rudolfo Anaya*, edited by Roberto Cantú, University of Oklahoma Press, 2016, pp. 197–209.

Lane, Jill. *Blackface Cuba, 1840–1895*. University of Pennsylvania Press, 2005.

Laó-Montes, Agustín. "Afro-Latin@ Difference and the Politics of Decolonization." *Latin@s in the World-System: Decolonization Struggles in the Twenty-First Century U.S. Empire*, edited by Ramón Grosfoguel et al., Paradigm Publishers, 2005, pp. 75–88.

Lara, Ana-Maurine. *Erzulie's Skirt*. RedBone Press, 2006.

Lauro, Sarah Juliet. *The Transatlantic Zombie: Slavery, Rebellion, and Living Death*. Rutgers University Press, 2015.

Law, Robin. *Ouidah: The Social History of a West African Slaving "Port", 1727–1892*. Ohio University Press, 2004.

Laye, Camara. *L'enfant noir*. Paris: Plôn: Presses Pocket, [1976] c1953 (*The African Child*. Collins, 1965).

Lazo, Irete. *The Accidental Santera: A Novel*. St-Martin's Press, 2008.

Leal, Luis and edited by Ilan Stavans. *A Luis Leal Reader*. Northwestern University Press, 2007.

Leary, John Patrick. "Havana Reads the Harlem Renaissance: Langston Hughes, Nicolás Guillén, and the Dialectics of Transnational American Literature." *Comparative Literature Studies* 47.2 (2010): 133–58.

Lefebvre, Henri. *Critique of Everyday Life*. Verso, 1991.

The Production of Space. Blackwell, 1991.

Lefort, Rebecca. "Row over Statue of 'Cruel' Explorer Henry Morton Stanley." *The Telegraph*. July 25, 2010. www.telegraph.co.uk/news/worldnews/africaan dindianocean/congo/7908247/Row-over-statue-of-cruel-explorer-Henry-Morton-Stanley.html.

Legrás, Horacio "Literary Criollismo and Indigenism." *Literary Cultures of Latin America: A Comparative History,* vol. 3, edited by Mario J. Valdés and Djelal Kadir, Oxford University Press, 2004, pp. 222–31.

Lévesque, Jacques. "L'URSS et l'activité de ses alies dans le Tiers-Monde: des années 70 aux annés 80." *International Journal*, vol. 37, no. 2, 1982, pp. 285–306.

Lipsitz, George. *The Possessive Investment in Whiteness: How White People Profit from Identity Politics.* Temple University Press, 1998.

Llanos-Figueroa, Dahlma. *Daughters of the Stone.* St Martin's Press, 2009.

Lomas, Laura. *Translating Empire: José Martí, Migrant Latino Subjects, and American Modernities.* Duke University Press, 2008.

Lomelí, Francisco. "Chican@ Literary Imagination: Trajectory and Evolution of Canon Building from the Margins." *The Forked Juniper: Critical Perspectives on Rudolfo Anaya*, edited by Roberto Cantú, University of Oklahoma Press, 2016, pp. 179–97.

López, Antonio, *Unbecoming Blackness: The Diaspora Cultures of Afro-Cuban Americans.* New York University Press, 2012.

López, Marissa K. *Chicano Nations: The Hemispheric Origins of Mexican American Literature.* New York University Press, 2011.

Lugones, María. "Toward a Decolonial Feminism." *Hypatía*, vol. 25, no. 4, 2010, pp. 742–59.

Los días del agua. Directed by Manuel Octavio Gómez. Instituto Cubano del Arte e Industrias Cinematográficos, 1971.

Luis-Brown, David. *Waves of Decolonization: Discourses of Race and Hemispheric Citizenship in Cuba, Mexico, and the United States.* Duke University Press, 2008.

MacGaffey, Wyatt. "Religions, African, Historiography of." *The Princeton Companion to Atlantic History*, edited by Joseph C. Miller et al, Princeton University Press, 2015, pp. 398–401.

Maguire, Emily. *Racial Experiments in Cuban Literature and Ethnography.* University Press of Florida, 2011.

"The Heart of a Zombie: Dominican Literature's Sentient Undead." *Alambique: Revista académica de ciencia ficción y fantasía* 6.1 (2018): 1–20.

Mahler, Anne Garland. *From the Tricontinental to the Global South: Race, Radicalism, and Transnational Solidarity.* Duke University Press, 2018.

Malaquias, Assis. *Rebels and Robbers: Violence in Post-colonial Angola.* Nordiska Afrikainstitutet, 2007.

Maluquer de Motes, Jordi. "La Burgesia Catalana i L'esclavitud Colonial: Modes de Producció i Pràctica Política." *Recerques: Història, Economia, Cultura*, no. 3, 1974, pp. 83–136.

Manson, Katrina. "The Disfigured Statue of Henry Morton Stanley, We Presume." *Independent*. March 19, 2010. www.independent.co.uk/news/world/africa/the-disfigured-statue-of-henry-morton-stanley-we-presume-1923812.html.
Marcum, John. *The Angolan Revolution: The Anatomy of an Explosion (1950–1962)*. MIT Press, 1969.
Mariscal, George. *Brown-Eyed Children of the Sun: Lessons from the Chicano Movement, 1965–1975*. University of New Mexico Press, 2005.
Martí, José. "Nuestra América." *La Revista Ilustrada* January 10, 1981.
Martin, Gerald. "The General and his Labyrinth." *The Cambridge Companion to Gabriel García Márquez*, edited by Philip Swanson, Cambridge University Press, 2010.
Martínez-Ruiz, Bárbaro. "The Impossible Reflection: A New Approach to African Themes in Wifredo Lam's Art." *Miami Art Museum*, 2008, pp. 23–31.
Matarrita, Esteban. "La relevancia de la excusa en El negro Francisco. *LETRAS*, vol. 34, no. 1 2002, pp. 155–68.
Matibag, Eugenio. *Afro-Cuban Religious Experience: Cultural Reflections in Narrative*. University Press of Florida, 1996.
Mbembe, Achille. *Critique of Black Reason*. Duke University Press, 2017.
  On the Postcolony. University of California Press, 2001.
  "The Subject of the World," *Facing Up to the Past: Perspectives on the Commemoration of Slavery from Africa, the Americas and Europe*, edited by Gert Oostindie, Ian Randle Publishers, 2001.
McLynn, Frank. "Sorcerer's Apprentice." *Stanley: Dark Genius of African Exploration*, vol. 2, Random House, 2016.
Medina, Pablo. *Exiled Memories: A Cuban Childhood*. University of Texas Press, 1990.
Megenney, William. "Gabriel García Márquez y el Caribe afronegroide." *Centro Virtual Cervantes*, vol. 41, no. 13, 1986, pp. 211–24.
Melas, Natalie. "Losing Césaire." *Nka: Journal of Contemporary African Art*, vol. 24, 2009, pp. 102–7.
Menchaca, Martha. *Recovering History, Constructing Race: The Indian, Black and White Roots of Mexican Americans*. University of Texas Press, 2006.
Méndez Ramírez, Hugo. "La reinterpretación paródica del código de honor en Crónica de una muerte anunciada." *Hispania*, vol. 73, no. 4, 1990, pp. 934–42.
Métraux, Alfred. *Voodoo in Haiti*. Oxford University Press, 1959.
Miano, Léonora. *La saison de l'ombre: roman*. Grasset, 2013.
Mignolo, Walter *The Idea of Latin America*. Blackwell Publishing, 2005.
Milian, Claudia. *Latining America Black-Brown Passages and the Coloring of Latino/a Studies*. University of Georgia Press, 2013.
Millar, Lanie. *Forms of Disappointment: Cuban and Angolan Narrative after the Cold War*. State University of New York Press, 2019.
Minich, Julie A. "The Decolonizer's Guide to Disability." *Junot Díaz and the Decolonial Imagination*. Edited by Monica Hanna, Jennifer Harford Vargas, and José David Saldívar. Duke University Press, 2016, pp. 49–68.
Minter, William. "The US and War in Angola." *Review of African Political Economy*, vol. 18, no. 50, 1991, pp. 135–44.

Mintz, Sidney Wilfred and Richard Price. *The Birth of African-American Culture: An Anthropological Perspective*. Beacon Press, 1992.
Monénembo, Tierno. *Les coqs cubains chantent à minuit: roman*. Editions Seuil, 2015.
Montaigne, Michel de. *Essais de Montaigne, avec les notes de M. Coste*. Jean Nourse & Vaillant, 1771.
Montaldo, Graciela R. *Ficciones culturales y fábulas de identidad en América Latina*. 1st ed., B. Viterbo Editora, 1999.
Montero, Mayra. *Del rojo de su sombra*. Tusquets, 1992.
   In the Palm of Darkness. HarperCollins Publishers, 1997.
Moore, Carlos. *Castro, the Blacks, and Africa*. Center for Afro-American Studies, University of California Press, 1988.
   El Caribe y la política exterior de la revolución cubana, 1959–1963. San Germán, Universidad Interamericana de Puerto Rico, Centro de Investigaciones del Caribe y América Latina, 1986.
Morales, Ed. "Brown Like Me?" *The Afro-Latin@ Reader: History and Culture in the United States*, edited by Miriam Jiménez Román and Juan Flores, Duke University Press, 2010, 499–507.
Morán González, John. "Introduction." *The Cambridge Companion to Latina/o American Literature*, edited by John Morán González, Cambridge University Press, 2016, xxiii–xxxv.
Moraña, Mabel. "The Boom of the Subaltern." *The Latin American Cultural Studies Reader*, edited by Ana del Sarto et al., Duke University Press, 2004, pp. 643–54.
   The Monster as War Machine. Cambria Press, 2018.
Moreno, Marisel C. "Debunking Myths, Destabilizing Identities: A Reading of Junot Díaz's 'How to Date a Browngirl, Blackgirl, Whitegirl, or Halfie'." *Afro-Hispanic Review* 26.2 (2007): 9–23.
   "'Swimming in Olive Oil': North Africa and the Hispanic Caribbean in the Poetry of Víctor Hernández Cruz." *Hispanic Review* 83 no.3 (2015): 299–316.
Morris, Andrea E. *Afro-Cuban Identity in Postrevolutionary Novel and Film: Inclusion, Loss, and Cultural Resistance*. Bucknell University Press, 2012.
Morrison, Toni. *Playing in the Dark: Whiteness and the Literary Imagination*. Vintage, 1993.
   "Sites of Memory." *Inventing the Truth: The Art and Craft of Memoir*, edited by William Zinsser, Houghton Mifflin, 1995, pp. 83–102.
Moya Pons, Frank. *Historia Colonial de Santo Domingo*. Universidad Católica Madre y Maestra, 1977.
   The Dominican Republic: A National History. Markus Wiener, 1998.
Mudimbe, V. Y. *The Invention of Africa: Gnosis, Philosophy, and the Order of Knowledge*. University of Indiana Press, 1988.
Munt, Ian. "Eco-Tourism or Ego-Tourism." *Race & Class*, vol. 36, 1994, pp. 49–60.
Murphy, James E. "The New Journalism: A Critical Perspective." *Journalism Monographs*, vol. 34, 1974, pp. 1–44.
Mutua, Makau. "(Book Review) Stanley: The Impossible Life of Africa's Greatest Explorer by Tim Jeal." *South African Journal of International Affairs*, vol. 14, no. 2, 2007, pp. 172–6.

Namikas, Lise A. *Battleground Africa: Cold War in the Congo, 1960–1965*. Stanford University Press, 2013.
Ngũgĩ Wa Thiong'o. *Decolonising the Mind: The Politics of Language in African Literature*. J. Currey; Heinemann, 1986.
Nicholls, David. "African Americans in Dakar's Liminal Spaces." *Monuments of the Black Atlantic: Slavery and Memory*, edited by Joanne Braxton, Edwin Cummings, and Maria Diedrich. Lit Verlag, 2004, pp. 141–50.
Nkrumah, Kwame. *Revolutionary Path*. Panaf Books, 1973.
Noel, Urayoán. *In Visible Movement: Nuyorican Poetry from the Sixties to Slam*. University of Iowa Press, 2014.
Nora, Pierre. "Between Memory and History: Les Lieux de Mémoire." *Representations*, vol. 26, 1989, pp. 7–24.
Obejas, Achy, "Author Tells of a 90s Cuba." Interview by Michael Martin. *Tell Me More*, National Public Radio, July 23, 2009. www.npr.org/templates/story/story.php?storyId=106917751.
Days of Awe. Bellatine, 2001.
Havana Noir. New York: Akashic Books, 2007.
Ruins. Akashic Books, 2009.
We Came All the Way from Cuba so You Could Dress Like This?: Stories. Cleis, 1994.
Obejas, Achy, and Sarah M. Quesada. "Achy Obejas' *The Tower of the Antilles* and a Literary Life in Retrospect." *Latino Studies* vol. 18, 2019, pp. 129–36.
Obisakin, Lawrence O. *Proverbs in Communication: A Conflict Resolution Perspective*. Triumph Publishing, 2010.
Ondjaki. *Good Morning Comrades: A Novel*. Trans. Stephen Henighan. Biblioasis, 2008.
Olivares, Jorge. "García Márquez's *Crónica de una muerte anunciada* as Metafiction." *Contemporary Literature*, vol. 28, no. 4, 1987, pp. 483–92.
Olofinlua, Temitayo, "History of Atlantic Slave Trade Chronicled by Museums, Monuments in Badagry, Nigeria" *Global Press Journal*, December 1, 2017. https://globalpressjournal.com/africa/nigeria/history-atlantic-slave-trade-chronicled-museums-monuments-badagry-nigeria/.
Oropeza, Lorena. *Raza Sí!, Guerra No!: Chicano Protest and Patriotism During the Viet Nam War Era*. University of California Press, 2005.
Ortiz, Fernando. *Contrapunteo Cubano Del Tabaco Y El Azúcar*. Biblioteca Ayacucho, 1978.
Padilla, Genaro M. "Myth and Comparative Cultural Nationalism: The Ideological Uses of Aztlán." *Aztlán: Essays on the Chicano Homeland*, edited by Rudolfo A. Anaya and Francisco A. Lomelí, University of New Mexico Press, 1989, pp. 111–31.
Palacios Preciado, Jorge. *La Trata de Negros por Cartagena de Indias*. Universidad Pedagógica y Tecnológica de Colombia, 1973.
Palencia-Roth, Michael. "La primera novela de García Márquez después del Premio Nobel." *Boletín Cultural y Bibliográfico*, vol. 24, no. 12, 1987, pp. 3–17.

Palmié, Stephan. "On Talking Past Each Other, Productively: Anthropology and the Black Atlantic, Twenty Years On." *Transatlantic Caribbean: Dialogues of People, Practices, Ideas*, edited by Ingrid Kummels et al., Transcript, 2014.

Paredes, Américo. *With His Pistol in His Hand: A Border Ballad and Its Hero*. University of Texas Press, 2004.

Paredes, Raymund A. "Contemporary Mexican American Literature, 1960-Present." *A Literary History of the American West*, edited by the Western Literature Association, Texas Christian University Press, 1987, pp. 1101–17.

Parrinder, Geoffroy. *West African Psychology*. Lutterworth Press, 1951.

Peck, Jaime. "Zombie Neoliberalism and the Ambidextrous State." *Theoretical Criminology*, vol. 14, no. 1, 2010, pp. 104–10.

Pellón, Gustavo. "Myth, Tragedy and the Scapegoat Ritual in Crónica de una muerte anunciada." *Revista Canadiense de Estudios Hispánicos*, vol. 12, no. 3, 1988, pp. 397–413.

Penuel, Arnold M. *Intertextuality in García Márquez*. Spanish Literature Publications, 1994.

"The Sleep of Vital Reason in García Márquez's *Crónica de una muerte anunciada*." *Critical Essays on Gabriel García Márquez*, edited by George R. McMurray, G. K. Hall, 1987, pp. 168–87.

Perez, Richard. "Racial Spills and Disfigured Faces in Piri Thomas's *Down These Mean Streets* and Junot Díaz's Ysrael." *Contemporary U.S. Latino/a Literary Criticism*. Edited by Lyn Di Iorio Sandín and Richard Perez, 93–114. Palgrave Macmillan, 2007.

Pepetela. *A Geração da Utopia*: Romance. Leya, 2013.

Pérez Fernández, Isacio, and Parish, Helen Rand. *Inventario documentado de los escritos de fray Bartolomé de las Casas*. 1st ed., Centro de Estudios de los Dominicos del Caribe, 1981.

Pérez Firmat, Gustavo. *Next Year in Cuba: A Cubano's Coming of Age in America*. Anchor, 1995.

Pérez Sarduy, Pedro and Jean Stubbs. *Afro-Cuban Voices: On Race and Identity in Contemporary Cuba*. University of Florida Press, 2000.

Pérez, Emma. *Forgetting the Alamo, or, Blood Memory: A Novel*. University of Texas Press, 2009.

Pérez Rosario, Vanessa. *Becoming Julia de Burgos: The Making of a Puerto Rican Icon*. University of Illinois Press, 2014.

Peterson, Matt. "How an American Lobbyist Stoked War Halfway Across the World: Paul Manafort Pulled Strings in Washington to Keep Angola's War going." *The Atlantic*, February 20, 2018.

Phillips, Thomas. "Journal." *Black Voyage: Eyewitness Accounts of the Atlantic Slave Trade*. Edited by Thomas Howard, Little, Brown and Company, 1971, pp. 85–7.

Pitman, Thea. "Postcolonial *compañeras*? The Desire for a Reciprocal Gaze in Two Mexican Women's Accounts of Africa." *Journal of Transatlantic Studies*, vol. 7, 2009, pp. 376–88.

Ponte, Antonio José. "La Habana: City and Archive." *Havana Beyond the Ruins: Cultural Mappings after 1989.* edited by Anke Birkenmaier and Esther Whitfield. Duke University Press, 2011, pp. 249–69.
Pope, Randolph D. "The Spanish American Novel from 1950 to 1975." *The Cambridge History of Latin American Literature,.* edited by Roberto González Echeverría and Enrique Pupo-Walker. Cambridge University Press, 1996, pp. 226–278.
Puga, María Luisa. *De cuerpo entero.* Coordinación de Difución Cultural, Dirección de Literatura, Universidad Nacional Autónoma de México, 1990. *Las posibilidades del odio.* 2nd ed. Siglo Veintiuno, 1978.
Pratt, Mary L. *Imperial Eyes: Travel Writing and Transculturation.* Routledge, 1992.
Prunier, Gérard. *Africa's World War: Congo, the Rwanda Genocide, and the Making of a Continental Catastrophe.* Oxford University Press, 2009.
Quayson, Ato. *Oxford Street, Accra: City Life and the Itineraries of Transnationalism.* Duke University Press, 2014.
Quesada, Sarah M. "Atlantic Continuities in Tomás Rivera and Rudolfo Anaya." *The Oxford Handbook of Latino Studies,* edited by Ilan Stavans, Oxford University Press, 2019, pp. 104–24.
"An Inclusive 'Black Atlantic': Revisiting Historical Creole Formations." *Latin American and Caribbean Ethnic Studies* (LACES), vol. 10, no. 2, 2015, pp. 226–46.
"A Planetary Warning?: The Multilayered Zombie in Junot Díaz's 'Monstro'." *Junot Díaz and the Decolonial Imagination,* edited by José David Saldívar, Jennifer Harford Vargas, Monica Hanna, Duke University Press, 2016, pp. 291–318.
Quijano, Aníbal. "Coloniality of Power, Eurocentrism, and Latin America." *Nepantla: Views from the South,* vol. 1, no. 3, 2000, pp. 533–80.
Quiroga, José. *Cuban Palimpsests.* University of Minnesota Press, 2005.
Radović, Stanka. *Locating the Destitute Space and Identity in Caribbean Fiction.* University of Virginia Press, 2014.
Ralph, Michael. *Forensics of Capital.* University of Chicago Press, 2015.
Rama, Ángel. "García Márquez Entre la Tragedia y la Policial, ó la Crónica y Pesquisa de una Muerte Anunciada." *Sin Nombre,* vol. 13, no. 1, 1982, pp. 7–27.
"La caza literaria es una altanera fatalidad." *Crónica de una Muerte Anunciada,* Círculo de Lectores, 1983.
La ciudad letrada. Ediciones del Norte, 1984.
Ramírez, Dixa. *Colonial Phantoms: Belonging and Refusal in the Dominican Americas, from the 19th Century to the Present.* New York University Press, 2018.
Reid-Vazquez, Michele. "Formidable Rebels: Enslaved and Free Women of Color in Cuba's Conspiracy of La Escalera, 1843–1844." *Breaking the Chains, Forging the Nation: The Afro-Cuban Fight for Freedom and Equality, 1812–1912,* edited by Aisha Finch and Fannie Rushing, Louisiana State University Press, 2019, pp. 158–77.

Ricœur, Paul. *Memory, History, Forgetting.* University of Chicago Press, 2004.
  Time and Narrative. 3 vols. University of Chicago Press, 1984.
Rivera, Tomás. *...y no se lo tragó la tierra*, edited by Gustavo Buenrostro and Julio Ramos, Ediciones Corregidor, 1971, 2012.
Rivera, Tomás, edited by Julián Olivares. *The Complete Works.* Arte Público Press, 1992.
Rodó, José Enrique. *Ariel.* Librería Cervantes, 1911.
Rodriguez, Ralph E. *Latinx Literature Unbound: Undoing Ethnic Expectation.* Fordham University Press, 2018.
Román, Elda María. *Race and Upward Mobility: Seeking, Gatekeeping, and Other Class Strategies in Postwar America.* Stanford University Press, 2018.
Rosaldo, Renato. *Culture & Truth: The Remaking of Social Analysis: with a New Introduction.* Beacon Press, 1993.
Rosenthal, Elisabeth. "The Growing Popularity of Having Surgery Overseas." *The New York Times.* August 6, 2013. www.nytimes.com/2013/08/07/us/the-growing-popularity-of-having-surgery-overseas.html.
Rotker, Susana. *La invención de la Crónica.* Ediciones Letra Buena, 1992.
Roux, Emmanuel de. "Le mythe de la Maison des esclaves qui résiste à la réalité." *Le Monde*, vol. 72, 1996, p. 23.
Ruíz Dueñas, Jorge. *Las noches de Salé.* Biblioteca del Issste, 1998
Rush, Dana. *Vodun in Coastal Benin: Unfinished, Open-ended, Global.* Vanderbilt University Press, 2013
Russ, Elizabeth Christine. *The Plantation in the Postslavery Imagination.* Oxford University Press, 2009.
Ruy, Sánchez A. *Quinteto De Mogador.* Alfaguara, 2014.
Said, Edward W. *Culture and Imperialism.* Knopf, 1993.
Sakr, Rita. *Monumental Space in the Post-Imperial Novel: An Interdisciplinary Study.* Continuum International, 2012.
Saldaña-Portillo, María Josefina. "From the Borderlands to the Transnational? Critiquing Empire in the Twenty-First Century." *A Companion to Latina/o Studies*, edited by Juan Flores and Renato Rosaldo, Blackwell Publishing, 2007, pp. 502–12.
  Indian Given: Racial Geographies Across Mexico and the United States. Duke University Press, 2016.
Saldívar, José David. *Border Matters: Remapping American Cultural Studies.* University of California Press, 1997.
  "Conjectures on 'Americanity' and Junot Díaz's 'Fukú Americanus' in *The Brief Wondrous Life of Oscar Wao*." *The Global South*, vol. 5, no. 1, 2011, pp. 120–36.
  The Dialectics of Our America: Genealogy, Cultural Critique, and Literary History. Duke University Press, 1991.
  Trans-Americanity: Subaltern Modernities, Global Coloniality and the Cultures of Greater Mexico. Duke University Press, 2012.
Saldívar, Ramón. *Chicano Narrative: The Dialectics of Difference.* University of Wisconsin Press, 1990.

Sánchez, Rosaura. "Rudolfo Anaya's Historical Memory." *The Forked Juniper: Critical Perspectives on Rudolfo Anaya*, edited by Roberto Cantú, University of Oklahoma Press, 2016, pp. 221–40.
Sánchez Prado, Ignacio M. "África en la imaginación literaria mexicana. Exotismo, desconexión y los límites materiales de la 'epistemología del Sur'." *Re-Mapping World Literature. Writing, Book Markets and Epistemologies Between Latin America and the Global South / Escrituras, Mercados y Epistemologías Entre América Latina y El Sur Global*, edited by Jorge J. Locane et al., De Gruyter, 2018, pp. 61–79.
"Los Hijos de Metapa: un recorrido conceptual de la literature mundial." *América Latina en la "Literatura Mundial"*, edited by Ignacio Sánchez-Prado, Instituto Internacional de Literatura Iberoamericana, 2006, pp. 7–46.
Strategic Occidentalism: On Mexican Fiction, the Neoliberal Book Market, and the Question of World Literature. Northwestern University Press, 2018.
Sandoval, Alonso de. *De instauranda Aethiopum salute; El mundo de la esclavitud negra en América*. Empresa nacional de publicaciones, 1956.
Sandoval, Alonso de and Nicole Von Germeten. *Treatise on Slavery: Selections from De Instauranda Aethiopum salute*. Hackett Publishing, 2008.
Sarmiento Ramírez, Israel. "Los negros en la Cuba colonial: Un grupo forzado a la marginalidad social que sufre desprecio, prejuicio y discriminación." *Anales del Museo de América*, vol. 17, 2009, pp. 112–29.
Sarto, Ana del et al. *The Latin American Cultural Studies Reader*. Duke University Press, 2004.
Sauldie, Madan. "Cold War in Africa: Stage II." *Africa*, vol. 72, 1977, pp. 65–73.
Savage, Kirk. "The Past in the Present: The Life of Memorials." *Harvard Design Magazine* 9 (1999): 1–5.
Sawyer, Mark Q. "Racial Politics in Multiethnic America: Black and Latina/o Identities and Coalitions." *Neither Enemies nor Friends: Latinos, Blacks, Afro-Latinos*, edited by Anani Dzidzienyo and Suzanne Oboler, Palgrave Macmillan, 2005, pp. 265–79.
Racial Politics in Post-Revolutionary Cuba. Cambridge University Press, 2006.
Schmidt, Elizabeth. *Foreign Intervention in Africa: From the Cold War to the War on Terror*. Cambridge University Press, 2013.
Seabrook, William B. *The Magic Island*. Paragon House, 1989.
Seck, Ibrahima. "Senegal." *The Palgrave Handbook of Conflict and History Education in the Post-Cold War Era*, edited by Luigi Cajani, Simone Lässig, and Maria Repoussi, Routledge, 2019, pp. 541–52.
Selasi, Taiye. "Bye-Bye Babar." The Lip 5 Africa, 2005. http://thelip.robertsharp.co.uk/?p=76.
Serna, Enrique. *El orgasmógrafo*. Seix Barral, 2014.
Shain, Richard. "The Republic of Salsa: Afro-Cuban Music in Fin-de-Siècle Dakar." *Africa*, vol. 79, no. 2, 2011, pp. 186–206.
Sharpe, Christina Elizabeth. *In the Wake: On Blackness and Being*. Duke University Press, 2016.

Sims, Robert. "García Márquez's Non-Fiction Works." *The Cambridge Companion to Gabriel García Márquez*, edited by Philip Swanson, Cambridge University Press, 2010, pp. 144–59.
"Sir Henry Morton Stanley, G.C.B., D.C.L., LL.D. 1840–1904." *Scottish Geographical Magazine*, 20:6: (1904): 281–84.
Siskind, Mariano. *Cosmopolitan Desires Global Modernity and World Literature in Latin America*. Northwestern University Press, 2014.
Slaughter, Joseph R. *Human Rights, Inc: The World Novel, Narrative Form, and International Law*. New York: Fordham University Press, 2007.
Sodeman, Melissa. *Sentimental Memorials: Women and the Novel in Literary History*. Stanford University Press, 2015.
Soja, Edward. *Thirdspace: Journeys to Los Angeles and Other Real-and-Imagined Places*. Blackwell, 1996.
Somerville, Keith. *Angola: Politics, Economics and Society*. Frances Pinter, 1986.
Soumonni, Elisée. "Disease, Religion and Medicine: Smallpox in Nineteenth-Century Benin." *História, Ciências, Saúde* 19 Suppl 1:35–45, December 2012.
Soyinka, Wole. *Myth, Literature, and the African World*. Cambridge University Press, 1976.
  Of Africa. Yale University Press, 2012.
  The Burden of Memory, the Muse of Forgiveness. Oxford University Press, 1999.
Stanley, Henry M. *In Darkest Africa*. S. Low and Marston, Searle and Rivington, 1890.
  Through the Dark Continent or the Sources of the Nile around the Great Lake of Equatorial Africa and Down the Livingstone River to the Atlantic Ocean, vol. 1. George Newnes, 1899.
Stavans, Ilan. *Gabriel García Márquez: The Early Years*. Palgrave Macmillan, 2010.
Stavans, Ilan, Edna Acosta-Belén et al. *The Norton Anthology of Latino Literature*. 1st ed., W. W. Norton, 2011.
Strandsbjerg, Camilla. "Kérékou, God and the Ancestors: Religion and the Conception of Political Power in Benin." *African Affairs*, vol. 99, no. 396, 2000, pp. 395–414.
Sundquist, Eric J. *To Wake the Nations: Race in the Making of American Literature*. Belknap Press of Harvard University Press, 1993.
  Strangers in the Land: Blacks, Jews, Post-Holocaust America. Belknap Press of Harvard University Press, 2008.
Surwillo, Lisa. *Monsters by Trade: Slave Traffickers in Modern Spanish Culture*. Stanford University Press, 2014.
Sweet, James H. *Domingos Álvares, African Healing, and the Intellectual History of the Atlantic World*. University of North Carolina Press, 2011.
  Recreating Africa: Culture, Kinship, and Religion in the African-Portuguese World, 1441–1770. University of North Carolina Press, 2003.
Tafel, Boericke H. A. *Roosevelt in Africa: Containing Also a Complete History and Study of Wild Animals of the World, with Thrilling and Exciting Experiences of Hunters of Big Game*. Forgotten Books, 2012.

Talbot, Ann. "The Angolan Civil War and US Foreign Policy." *Global Policy Forum*, 13 April 2002. www.globalpolicy.org/component/content/article/155/25956.html.
Taylor, Julie and George Yúdice. "Mestizaje and the Inversion of Social Darwinism in Spanish American Fiction." Literary Cultures of Latin America: A Comparative History, *vol.* 3, edited by Mario J. Valdés and Djelal Kadir, Oxford University Press, 2004, pp. 310–19.
Tchak, Sami. *Hermina: Roman*. Gallimard, 2003.
Les filles de Mexico. Mercure de France, 2008.
Tchivéla, Tchichellé. "Un parenté outre-atlantique." *Notre Librarie*, vol. 92, 1988, pp. 30–4.
Testa, Daniel. "Extensive/Intensive Dimensionality in Anaya's Bless Me, Ultima." *Latin American Literary Review*, vol. 5, no. 10, 1977, pp. 70–8.
Theroux, Paul. "Stanley, I Presume." *Sunday Book Review, The New York Times*, September 30, 2007. www.nytimes.com/2007/09/30/books/review/Theroux-t.html.
Tillery, Alvin B. "Black Americans and the Creation of America's African Policies: The De-Racialization of Pan-African Politics." *The African Diaspora: African Origins and New World Identities*, edited by Isidore Okpewho et al., Indiana University Press, 1999, pp. 504–4.
Tonn, Horst. "Imagining the Local and the Global in the Work of Rudolfo Anaya." *The Forked Juniper: Critical Perspectives on Rudolfo Anaya*, edited by Roberto Cantú, University of Oklahoma Press, 2016, pp. 241–52.
Torres-Saillant, Silvio. "Afrolatinidad: Phoenix Rising from a Hemisphere's Racist Flames." *The Cambridge History of Latina/o American Literature*, edited by John Morán González and Laura Lomas, Cambridge University Press, 2018, pp. 276–308.
"Inventing Race: Latinos and the Ethnoracial Pentagon." *Latino Studies*, vol. 1, no. 1, 2003, pp. 123–51.
"Problematic Paradigms. Racial Diversity and Corporate Identity in the Latino Community." *Latinos. Remaking America*, edited by Marcelo M. Suárez-Orozco and Mariela Páez University of California Press, 2002, pp. 435–55.
"The Tribulations of Blackness Stages in Dominican Racial Identity." *Callaloo*, vol. 23, no. 3, 2000, pp. 1086–111.
Tracy, Francis. *The Wizard of Africa: Henry M. Stanley's Last Expedition through the Dark Continent: the Rescue of Emin Pasha*. Barclay & Co., 1890.
Trouillot, Michel-Rolph. *Silencing the Past: Power and the Production of History*. Beacon, 2015.
Troyano, Alina. "Milk of Amnesia / Leche de amnesia." *The Drama Review*. 39.3 (Fall 1995): 94.
Tuan, Yi-Fu. *Space and Place: The Perspective of Experience*. University of Minnesota Press, 2003.

Vansina, Jan. *Oral Tradition as History*. University of Wisconsin Press, 1985.
Vasconcelos, José. *La raza cósmica*. Porrúa, 2007.
Vidal Ortega, Antonio and Jorge Enrique Elias Caro. "La desmemoria impuesta a los hombres que trajeron. Cartagena de India en el siglo XVI y XVII. Un depósito de esclavos." *Cuadernos de Historia*, vol. 37, 2012, pp. 7–31.
Vigil, Ariana E. *Echoes of War: Gender and Militarization in U.S. Latina/o Cultural Production*. Rutgers University Press, 2014.
  Public Negotiations: Gender and Journalism in Contemporary US Latina/o Literature. Columbus: The Ohio State University Press, 2019.
Vinson, Ben. "Introduction: African (Black) Diaspora History, Latin American History." *The Americas*, vol. 63, no. 1, 2006, pp. 1–18.
Vinson, Ben and Matthew Restall. *Black Mexico: Race and Society from Colonial to Modern Times*. University of New Mexico Press, 2009.
Verónica Volkow. *Diario de Sudáfrica*. Siglo XXI, 1988.
Walcott, Derek. *Selected Poems*, edited by Edward Baugh. Farrar, Straus and Giroux, 2007.
Walsh, Rodolfo J. *Caso Satanowsky*. Buenos Aires: Ediciones de la Flor, 1973.
  Ese hombre y otros papeles, edited by Daniel Link. Seix Barral, 1996.
  Operación Masacre. Libros del Asteroide, 2018.
  Quién Mató a Rosendo? Editorial Tiempo Contemporáneo, 1969.
Wane, Ibrahima et al. "Editorial: Across Media: Mobility and Transformation of Cultural Materials in the Digital Age." *Journal of African Media Studies*, vol. 7, no. 1, 2015, pp. 3–9.
Weber, Ronald. *The Literature of Fact*. Ohio University Press, 1980.
Wheat, David. "The First Great Waves: African Provenance Zones for the Transatlantic Slave Trade to Cartagena de las Indias, 1570–1640." *Journal of African History*, vol. 52, no. 1, 2011, pp. 1–22.
Williams, Raymond L. *A Companion to Gabriel García Márquez*. Tamesis, 2010.
  The Columbia Guide to the Latin American Novel since 1945. Columbia University Press, 2007.
Wilson, Carlos Guillermo "Cubena". *Los nietos de Felicidad Dolores*. Ediciones Universal, 1991.
Wolfe, Thomas. *The Electric Kool-Aid Acid Test*. Farrar, Straus and Giroux, 1968.
  "Why They Aren't Writing the Great American Novel Anymore." *Esquire*, 1972. www.esquire.com/lifestyle/money/a20703846/tom-wolfe-new-jounalism-american-novel-essay/.
Woodruff, Nan Elizabeth. *American Congo the African American Freedom Struggle in the Delta*. Harvard University Press, 2003.

World Bank. "GDP per Capita Growth: Cuba." World Development Indicators, *The World Bank Group*. https://data.worldbank.org/indicator/NY.GDP.PCAP.KD.ZG?end=1995&locations=CU&start=1989.

"Haiti." World Development Indicators, *The World Bank Group*. http://data.worldbank.org/country/Haiti.

Wynter, Sylvia. "Novel and History, Plot and Plantation." *Savacou*, vol. 5, 1971, pp. 95–102.

Y... temenos sabor. Directed by Sara Gómez. Instituto Cubano del Arte e Industrias Cinematográficos, 1967.

Index

Accra, 8, 210
Achebe, Chinua, 170
Adesanmi, Pius, 29, 89, 210
Adja, Eric, 62, 209
Africa
    appropriation of, 100
    artwork about, 90, 95
    as point of origin, 10
    attribution of disease to, 153
    capitalist systems in, 46
    civil unrest in, 2
    colonial discourses about, 1, 3, 6, 13, 52, 53
    connections to, 7
    continent of, 6, 15
    Cuban defiance of US in, 106
    engagement with, 5
    essentialization of, 84, 90, 112
    fear of otherness in, 46
    idealization of, 96, 102, 111
    nostalgia for in *Ruins*, 92
    perception of, 1
    racialization and exploitation of, 160
    rejection of, 17, 18, 35, 88
    relationship with Latin American and Latino culture, 13, 15, 27, 79
    representations of, 104, 163, 164, 171
    Soviet influence in, 133
    spatiotemporality of, 5
    traditions of, 4
African ancestry, 35
African archive, 1–6, 10, 19, 47, 50, 54, 68
African diaspora, 21, 61, 86
African epistemology, 17, 19, 21, 35, 77, 88, 90, 110, 112
African heritage, 4, 21, 30, 36, 37, 46, 121
African historiography, 2, 5, 6, 17, 27, 205, 206
    exclusion of, 12, 219
    in Chicano literature, 163, 173
    memorialization of, 166
African history, 6, 18, 19, 27, 50, 109, 201, 205
African imaginary, 77, 78, 79, 87, 104

African literature, 19, 62
African memorialization and memory, 5, 62, 74, 90, 97, 107, 164
African oral history, 49, 59
African origins, 1, 46, 63, 64, 96
African safari, 85, 93, 97, 99, 100, 105, 112, 115
African spirituality, 4, 19, 31, 160, 187, 190, 192
African utopia, 78, 99, 104
Afro-Cubans, 29, 77, 79, 81, 83, 99, 109, 115, 143
Afro-Dominicans, 39
Afrolatinidad, 3, 7, 12, 15, 46
    activism in, 40
    and Latin-Africa, 78
    erasure of in Chicano perception, 184
    in the US, 14
Afropolitanism, 12
Age of Reason, 4
Aguirre Beltrán, Gonzalo, 186
Alberto, Eliseo, 110, 111
    Caracol Beach, 110, 111
Allende, Salvador, 132, 139
Alvarez, Julia, 40
American studies, 6, 8, 165, 206
American Studies Association (ASA), 206
Anaya, Rudolfo, 2–10, 30–2, 160, 162, 182, 205 *See also Bless Me, Ultima*
    A Chicano in China, 8
    comparative scholarship on, 183
    plantocracy in, 184
    reception and critique of, 9, 183
    representation of Africa in, 160, 162, 181
Angola, 5, 6, 11, 29, 30, 84
    after independence, 106, 133, 144
    civil war in, 84, 107
    Cuban interests in, 76, 103
    Cuban narrative of, 109
    Cuban teachers in, 146
    destabilization of, 146
    García Márquez's travels in, 10, 119, 121, 124, 128, 132
    Portuguese presence in, 133

Index

postcolonial scramble for, 133
social inequality in, 112
subsidizing of colonial enterprise in, 133
US involvement in, 107, 133
War of Independence, 111, 133
Anti-Haitianism, 40, 46, 54
Aparicio, Frances, 9
apartheid, 2, 84, 103, 132, 135
Apocalypse: What Disasters Reveal (Díaz), 5, 34, 35, 41–5, 70
Aponte, Antonio, 79
Apter, Emily, 7, 8
Araujo, Ana Lucia, 22, 157
archives, 19, 20, 46, 49, 50 *See also* African archive
  Atlantic, 4, 34
  British, 112, 113
  colonial, 112, 191, 195, 197, 214, 219
  French, 20, 22, 34, 53, 119
Archives nationales d'outre-mer, 19, 119
Armillas-Tiseyra, Magalí, 195, 216
Atlantic borderland, 6, 114, 147, 206
Atlantic heritage, 21, 198
Atlantic World, 4, 12, 27, 31, 73
  and Cuban historiography, 92
  and US Southwest, 163, 201
  cannibals in, 70
  carp proverbs and, 201
  Chicano identity in, 164
  scholarship on, 19
  signifier of disease in, 40, 52
  slavery in, 37, 117
Azoulay, Ariella, 25, 61, 209

Badagry, 21, 76, 77, 86, 89, 90, 208
  and murder of young slave Amé, 113
  as slave port, 86
  colonial history of, 112
  heritage trail at, 87, 112
  lessons from, 88, 114
  rehabilitation of, 85, 86, 89
  relevance to Cuba of, 29, 86
  slavery in, 86
Bahía de las ánimas, 117–21, 129, 130, 131, 151, 155, 156
balseros, 76–82, 93, 96, 105, 106, 108, 112, 113
Bay of Pigs, 119, 126, 132, 139, 143
Bay of Souls. *See* Bahía de las ánimas
Belgium, 31, 170, 177
Benin, 2, 6, 34–6, 53–8, 69, 94, 200
Black Atlantic, 18, 100, 115, 184
  framework of, 2
  heritage of, 85, 118
  history of, 82
  in Cuba, 151

memorialization of, 176
studies of, 18, 19
Black internationalism, 79, 81, 92, 205
  chronicles of, 132
  fall of, 111, 126, 145
  in Alberto, 111
  in Cuba, 84, 96, 100, 103, 119, 121, 139
  in *Ruins*, 101
Black Lives Matter, 23
blanqueamiento, 37, 38, 40, 74
Bless Me, Ultima (Rivera), 5, 32, 160, 162, 181
  accolades and summary of, 181
  and African religious practice, 187
  and Ouidah, 213
  and The Man Who Could Fly," 201
  colonial sites in, 199
  criticism of, 182
  curanderismo in, 184
  misrepresentations in, 198
  references to the Atlantic in, 184
Borges, Jorge Luis, 166
Bourke, John Gregory, 31, 163–9, 183–6, 189, 190
Brady, Mary Pat, 21, 23, 26
Brouillette, Sarah, 206, 208, 246 n. 6

Cabral, Amílcar, 92, 133, 144
Caliban, 29, 34, 64, 72, 73
Caminero-Santangelo, Marta, 16, 192, 202, 247 n. 15
cannibals and cannibalism, 36, 64, 69–71, 195
Caribbean, 6, 10, 31, 37, 43, 151
  authors from, 5, 6, 7, 40, 165
  cannibals in, 70
  etymology of, 70
  history of in *Crónica*, 153
  identity and culture of, 3, 13, 64, 188
  US Southwest in, 165
Carlota. *See* Lukumí, Carlota
Carpentier, Alejo, 35, 48–50, 62, 98, 123, 149
Cartagena, 117, 129, 148, 153
  and Columbus, 117, 121
  and Latin-Africa, 119
  in García Márquez, 121, 150
  lack of Black Atlantic memorialization in, 155
  slave trade in, 121, 131, 152, 153, 155, 157, 158
Casanova, Pascale, 7
Castillo, Debra A., 203
Castro, Fidel, 30, 77, 78
  and African decolonization, 78, 79, 84, 92, 101, 107, 140, 142
  and Operación Carlota, 119
  and the Mariel Boatlift crisis, 80
  and the UN General Assembly, 92
  and US antiblack policy, 142
  celebration of Africanness, 84

Castro, Fidel (cont.)
    rhetoric of black solidarity, 78, 81, 102, 103, 126, 142
    statement to Second National Assembly, 82
Cavazzi, Antonio, 31, 162, 164, 181, 185, 190
    golden carp in, 192, 193, 197
Certeau, Michel de, 3, 24, 62, 179, 206
Césaire, Aimé, 71
Chancy, Myriam J.A., 40
Chicano awakening, 170
Chicano identity, 7, 164, 185, 191, 198, 203, 213
Chicano imaginary, 160, 164, 176, 184, 187, 189
Chicano literary studies, 183, 213
Chicano literature, 8, 21, 160, 163, 202, 203
Christophe, Henri, 48, 49, 50
Chronicle of a Death Foretold (García Márquez). See *Crónica de una meurte anunciada* (García Márquez)
Cien años de soledad (García Márquez), 123, 126, 149, 158
Cisneros, Sandra, 8, 9
Clifford, James, 114, 168
Coetzee, J.M., 170, 207
Cold War, 2, 10, 27–30, 76, 107, 158
    Angola and Cuba in, 85, 110
    in Africa, 127, 132
    US imperialism and, 115, 121, 135
colonialism, 6, 12, 18, 23, 34, 40
Columbus, Christopher, 117, 119, 121, 129, 131, 148
commodification, 76
    and sites of memory, 99
    in *Crónica*, 150
    in *Ruins*, 76, 78, 83, 104, 108, 115
    of Africa, 29, 77, 85, 87, 97, 107, 114, 115, 210
    of African safari, 210
    of Badagry, 77, 88, 89, 90, 112, 115
    of Kwele Gon masks, 94
Condé, Maryse, 187, 188
Congo, 6, 31, 32, 172
    belief systems in, 162, 186
    imperialism in, 166, 170, 174
    in Chicano culture, 165, 169
    in Rivera and Anaya, 160
    memorialization of, 163, 164, 166
    National Institute Museum of, 21
    plundering of by Belgium, 162
    slavery in, 168
    Stanley in, 163, 177
    ties to US Southwest via the slave trade, 184
Conrad, Joseph, 52, 167
    Heart of Darkness, 52
cosmopolitanism, 7, 10, 158, 208
    and Anaya, 165, 183
    and Díaz, 37
    and García Márquez, 122

and Llanos-Figueroa, 5
and Rivera, 165
Crónica de una muerte anunciada (García Márquez), 5, 30, 117–24
    and García Márquez's Angolan journalism, 119, 148
    and Latin American chronicles, 122, 123
    connection between Gorée and Cartagena in, 157
    literary criticism of, 121, 125
    memorialization of a failed Latin-Africa in, 155
    slave ship in, 128, 129, 131, 140, 148, 211
Cuba, 14, 29, 30, 76, 80 *See also* Bay of Pigs; Havana; special period
    and Afro-Cuban traditions, 81
    and Angolan decolonization, 76, 77, 85, 100, 107, 108, 132, 143, 227 n. 41
    and the 1966 Tricontinental Conference, 92
    as Latin-African nation, 78, 84, 106
    Black internationalism in, 10, 29, 30, 78, 140, 142, 147
    caribs in, 70
    Hemingway in, 104, 105
    Matanzas slave rebellion in, 140
    Museo de la Ruta del Esclavo in, 141
    on opposite side from US in Angola, 141
    opening to tourism of, 79
    race in, 82, 103, 115
    relationship with Africa of, 79, 84
    shift toward capitalism in, 83
    slavery in, 86, 107
    Soviet Union subsidies to, 107
    support of MPLA in Angola, 133
    US embargo in, 139
Cuban Adjustment Act of 1966, 80
Cuban American identity, 29, 210
Cuban Americans, 77, 79, 80, 81
Cuban Revolution, 80–3, 101, 124, 132
    African-American supporters of, 103
    and African American political engagement, 103
    and anticapitalism, 83
    and racial equality, 83
    Boom writers and, 119
Cuban-Angolan alliance, 78, 107
curanderismo, 162, 185, 187, 202
Cutler, John Alba, 9, 11, 246 n. 3

Dahomey, 28, 34, 47–53, 57, 68
Dakar, 211, 217
Damrosch, David, 7, 223 n. 15
Danticat, Edwidge, 40
Davis, Angela Y., 170
de la Fuente, Alejandro, 84, 142

decolonization, 23
  in Angola, 81, 106
  in Latin-Africa, 94, 144
  movement for, 2, 15, 29, 30
  of Africa, 10, 77, 100, 103, 141
Díaz, Junot, 5–10, 28, 33–41, 44–7, 52, 57, 59, 69, 205 *See also* "Apocalypse: What Disasters Reveal"; "Monstro"
  and monster, 36, 54, 72, 73
  apocalypse in, 69
  decolonial shift in, 74
  environmental critique in, 44
  Haiti as memorial in, 35
  heritage trail in, 35
  in World Literature, 37
  journalism of, 34, 42
  memorialization in, 59
  race in, 33, 41, 46, 72
  The Brief Wondrous Life of Oscar Wao, 9, 33, 40, 52, 71
  zombies in, 34–6, 41, 45, 46, 59, 63, 64, 71–4
Dimock, Wai Chee, 8
distortion
  colonial, 185, 189
  colonial system of, 182
  of Africa, 22, 163, 164, 167, 172, 173, 176, 180
  of African historiography, 166
  of African spirituality, 164
  of indigenous healing practices, 186
  of non-occidental religious customs, 186
  of Stanley, 168
  of the Congo, 169, 176, 180
  of the golden carp, 191, 202
  of Vodun, 189
Dominican Americans, 36
Dominican Republic, 33, 34, 37–48
  diaspora from, 40
  literature from, 40
  nationalism in, 39
  race in, 34, 43, 46
Dominicans, 36, 38, 41, 62
  and Haiti, 34, 42
  identity of, 35, 37, 40
  White nationalism among, 38
Door of No Return (Gorée), 24, 156, 157
Door of No Return (Ouidah), 26, 53, 57
Dr. David Livingstone Trail, 21

Edwards, Brent Hayes, 99
El amor en los tiempos del cólera (García Márquez), 122, 157
el mal de Luanda (yellow fever), 153

Fanon, Frantz, 62, 78, 100, 103
  and Marxism, 103
  and support of decolonization in Algeria, 100, 103
  in *Ruins*, 114
fear, 36, 42, 52, 55, 59, 64, 70
  and the colonial imagination, 62
  cause of, 71
  colonial, 63
  concealed with sarcasm, 65
  destabilization of through storytelling, 59
  discourse of, 57, 61, 62, 73
  in "Monstro," 65, 69
  in *Relation*, 55
  of Africa's blackness, 74
  of otherness, 46
  of slave rebellion, 28
  of the black bass, 197
  of Vodun, 29, 35, 54, 59
  of witchcraft, 32
  of zombies, 29, 47, 62, 68
  site of, 57, 74
Ferguson, James, 90
Fernández Olmos, Margarite, 182
Fernández Retamar, Roberto, 36, 70, 72
  and criollo identity, 73
  Calibán, 36, 72
  rehabilitation of mambí in, 73
Finch, Aisha, 140, 141
Floyd, George, 23
Foucault, Michel, 22, 36, 63, 72
Frente Nacional de Libertação de Angola (FNLA), 134

Gamboa, Zézé, 110, 111
  O herói, 110
García Márquez, Gabriel, 2, 5, 7, 9, 10, 30, 205 *See also Crónica de una muerte anunciada; Cien años de soledad; El amor en los tiempos del cólera;* "Operación Carlota"
  admiration for Cuba, 149
  admiration for Global South authors, 128
  African trope of tambos (drums) in, 152
  and Bay of Pigs invasion, 124, 132
  and magical realism, 158
  and Operación Carlota, 30
  and *Prensa Latina*, 124
  Angolan chronicles of, 10, 30, 119–21, 132–9, 155
  Black internationalist chronicles of, 144
  Caribbean identity in, 7, 128
  condemnation of colonialism in, 138
  El drama de las dos Cubas, 124, 125, 139
  friendship with Castro, 119, 124, 142
  influence on Tansi of, 194
  influence on testimonio of, 137
  Latin American chronicles of, 123
  Latin-Africa in, 30, 120, 121, 126, 132, 146

García Márquez, Gabriel (cont.)
  memorialization in, 128, 131, 156, 158
  on Cuba-Angola alliance, 126, 133
  on Kissinger, 145
  on US foreign policy, 127, 144, 145, 146, 147
  racialized shipwrecks in, 141
  Senegalese slaves in, 211
  testimonio and New Journalism in, 137
  the literary as a vessel for tragedy in, 155
García-Peña, Lorgia, 39, 47, 229 n. 8, 229 n. 9
Gaspar de Alba, Alicia, 187, 213, 214
  Calligraphy of the Witch, 187, 213, 215
Ghana, 4, 89, 217 *See also* Accra
Gilroy, Paul, 18, 210
Glissant, Édouard, 6, 66, 155, 179, 183, 188, 201
Global South, 2, 6, 7, 11, 15, 19, 27, 30, 31, 172, 194, 208
  African independence and anti-capitalism in, 92
  and Atlantic history, 143
  and Rivera and Anaya, 203
  Chicano writing in, 181
  Congo and US Southwest in, 170
  Cuban alliances in, 90, 127
  decolonization in, 27, 84
  imperialism in, 177
  Manifest Destiny in, 145
  socialist hope in, 144
  solidarity in, 115, 116, 143, 203
  US destabilization of, 145
Goethe, Johann Wolfgang von, 7, 206
golden carp, 32, 162, 181, 190, 213
  and Atlantic World origin, 202
  as critique of American neo-imperialism, 196
  as marker of difference, 196, 197
  as site of memory, 191, 201
  as transatlantic marker, 181
  colonial description of, 192, 194
  dichotomy with black bass, 201
  memorialization of in *Bless Me*, 191
  Sandoval and Cavazzi on, 190
Gorée, 21, 25, 26, 121, 156, 157, 208, 211 *See also* Maison des esclaves
  in the slave trade, 156, 157
  memorial of slavery at, 24, 159
Goyal, Yogita, 18
Gruesz, Kirsten Silva, 17
Guevara, Ernesto "Che," 124, 139, 144, 216
Guillén, Nicolás, 78, 81, 100–4
Guinea, 4, 94, 143, 216
Guinea Bissau, 144

Haiti, 2, 28, 33–41, 45–56, 69
  2010 earthquake in, 34, 41, 44, 63, 69
  Atlantic racial history of, 67
  Black historical spaces in, 49
  Dominican antipathy toward, 37
  in "Monstro," 52, 69, 73
  occupation of the Dominican Republic by, 39
  relationship to the Dominican Republic of, 38, 46
  repatriation of Dominican citizens to, 39
  slavery in, 46
  US occupation of, 47
  Vodun in, 48, 56, 68
  zombies in, 36, 69
Haitian Revolution, 35, 38, 48, 49
Haitians, 38–45, 62
  and Dominicans, 40, 48
  as outcasts, 41, 52
  blackness and, 39, 41, 52, 61
  genocide against, 39
  in the Dominican Republic, 45
Hartman, Saidiya, 20, 52, 89, 114
Havana, 29, 76, 77, 85, 91, 93, 100, 216
  and Badagry in *Ruins*, 115
  and nostalgia, 83, 99
  Black heritage of, 79
  Casa de las Américas in, 123
  Military Units to Aid Production (UMAP) camps, 109, 110
  Old Havana, 89
  ruins in, 93
  Tiffany glass in, 100
  tourism industry in, 76, 83
Hemingway, Ernest, 76, 82, 100
  African safari in, 76, 78, 104
  Green Hills of Africa, 105
  in Cuba, Kenya and Tanzania, 104
  in *Ruins*, 101, 105, 106
  representations of Africa in, 104
  signifiers of race in, 103
  The Old Man and the Sea, 82, 105
  trophy hunting by, 105
heritage sites, 6, 34, 35, 90
heritage tourism, 1, 21, 23, 34, 35, 57–62, 77
  and capitalism, 2, 28, 53, 58, 76, 210
  at Badagry, 210
  in Carpentier, 48, 49, 62
  in *Ruins*, 29, 77
  in "Searching at Leal Middle School," 173
  in West Africa, 85
  of memory, 24
Herskovits, Melville, 47, 56, 232 n. 30
Hirsch, Marianne, 26, 61, 93
Hispaniola, 35, 37, 48, 67, 68, 73
Hotel Theresa, 92, 103
House of Slaves. *See La Maison des esclaves*
Hughes, Langston, 78, 100, 101, 102

Hughes, Victor, 149
Hugo, Victor, 38

imperialism, 31, 104, 106, 146, 160, 184, 203
  by Belgium, 170
  by Britain, 170
  by the US, 6, 30, 91, 99, 115, 127, 135, 142, 144, 148
  in Africa, 31, 132, 141, 142, 143, 170
  in Rivera, 172
  in the Americas, 18, 132
  in the Congo, 166, 169, 170
In Darkest Africa (Stanley), 52, 161, 164, 167, 170
  as distortion of Africa, 167
  civilization versus darkness in, 174
  depictions of the Congo in, 174
  othering of blackness in, 173
International Monetary Fund (IMF), 28, 57, 77, 89, 208

Jim Crow (laws), 14, 19, 39, 47
Johnson, Sarah E., 38

Kaplan, Amy, 164
Kaup, Monika, 183
Kazanjian, David, 18, 19
Kenya, 100, 104, 171, 172
Kinshasa, 208, 212
Kissinger, Henry, 145
Kwele Gon mask, 93, 94, 96

Lam, Wilfredo, 76, 78, 97, 98, 99
Laó-Montes, Agustín, 203
Latin America, 6, 10, 31, 48, 62, 174
  antiblack attitudes in, 14, 72
  colonial trauma in, 14
  comparativism in, 17
  dictatorship in, 128
  essence of, 49, 50, 158
  ideal of whiteness in, 13
  identity in, 3, 12, 13, 16, 17, 121
  literary criticism in, 4, 10, 158
  literature from, 5–7, 11, 20, 30, 135, 206
  representations of, 99, 158
Latin American studies, 6, 7, 206, 215
Latin-Africa, 2–7, 17, 19, 21, 29, 30, 63, 115, 139, 208, 211
  allegories of, 67
  alliance, 14, 30, 135
  and "marvelous real," 48
  and Cuba, 73, 127, 142
  and Latinx literature, 215
  and Operación Carlota, 119, 142
  borderland of, 12, 97, 143
  consciousness of, 108

  construct of, 5, 75, 81
  failure of, 119, 155, 156
  framework of, 36
  heritage of, 1, 6, 21, 36, 50, 81, 87
  in Anaya, 160, 182
  in García Márquez, 10, 30, 119–27, 139, 146, 148, 158
  in Obejas, 78, 96, 97, 108, 115
  in Rivera, 160, 180
  in World Literature, 11
  narrative of, 61
  rehabilitation of, 63
  rejection of, 15, 185
  reversal of, 62
  utopia in, 120
Latin-African axis, 5–12, 59, 75, 206, 216
Latin-African connection, 10, 20, 49, 61, 107, 163, 164
  and Castro, 84, 92, 211
  and Ouidah, 61
  in Anaya, 181, 203
  in García Márquez, 128, 137
  in Obejas, 110
  in Rivera, 166, 203
  memory of, 172
  rehabilitation of, 114
Latin-African history, 49, 77, 78, 107, 112, 120
Latin-African imaginary, 116, 126
Latin-African literature, 11, 27
Latin-African memorial, 75, 114, 147, 206
Latin-African memorialization, 10, 157, 178
Latin-African memory, 20, 59
  formation of, 173
  in García Márquez, 126
  in Obejas, 99, 106, 115
  in Rivera, 166, 178
  reclamation of, 88
Latin-African victory, 107, 139
Latinidad, 12, 15, 16, 17, 224 n. 23
Latinx
  activism among, 2
  and NAACP opposition, 15
  and race, 14, 15
  rejection of Africa by, 13
Latinx authors, 5, 6, 165
Latinx identity, 1, 3, 12, 13, 16, 17, 180
Latinx literary studies, 4, 10, 215
Latinx literature, 4–12, 116, 206, 207, 215, 221 n. 5
  distortions of Africa in, 172
  ethnic expectations of, 203
Latinx studies, 7, 10, 16, 17, 18
  Anaya in, 198
  physical memorials and fiction in, 21
Laurent-Perrault, Evelyne, 61
Law, Robin, 200

Laye, Camara, 50
Lefebvre, Henri, 96, 153
Lezo, Don Blas de, 129, 130, 131
lieux de mémoire. See sites of memory
Livingstone, David, 161, 167, 168
   as abolitionist, 168, 178
   memorial in Malawi of, 163, 177
   Stanley's affiliation with, 162
   statue in Scotland of, 178
Llanos-Figueroa, Dahlma, 1, 12, 13, 14, 187, 213
   Daughters of the Stone, 1, 3
López, Antonio, 14, 80
Lugones, Maria, 56, 67
Lukumí, Carlota, 30, 133, 140, 141, 148
   and naming of Cuban intervention in Angola, 141
   as leader of slave rebellion, 140
   homage to, 140
   in Cuban military history, 141
   memorial statue of, 141
   obliterated archival memory of, 141
Lumumba, Patrice, 92, 170

magical realism, 7, 121, 126, 158, 194
Maguire, Emily, 45, 67
Mahler, Anne Garland, 11, 19, 84, 143, 213, 237 n. 19
Maison des esclaves, 24, 30, 121, 149, 156, 157, 226 n. 36
Malawi, 21, 163, 177, 208
   Livingstone trail in, 178, 212
   Slave route in, 178, 179
mandinga, 3, 189
Manifest Destiny, 165, 190
Mariel Boatlift crisis, 80
Martí, José, 157, 82, 123, 146
Martínez-Ruiz, Bárbaro, 99
marvelous real, 48, 49, 50, 99
Mbembe, Achille, 4, 27, 46, 69, 74, 89, 97, 115, 131, 175
Melas, Natalie, 99
memorialization. *See subheadings under main headings for places, authors, and works (e.g. García Márquez)*
Menchaca, Martha, 184
Menchú, Rigoberta, 25
Méndez Ramírez, Hugo, 125
mestizaje, 13, 14, 31
Métraux, Alfred, 56
Mexican-American border, 14, 16, 17
Mexican-American imaginary, 172
Mexico, 43, 171, 172, 186, 217
   and NAFTA aftermath, 43
   Rivera and, 165, 166
Middle Passage, 13, 47
Mignolo, Walter, 15

Millar, Lanie, 18, 85, 143, 146, 216
Mobutu, Joseph, 170, 177
modernism, 93, 96, 102
   and *La Jungla* (Lam), 97
   and primitivism, 93
   in Cuba, 97
   representations of Africa in, 94, 97
"Monstro," 5, 28–36, 40–6, 62, 70, 72
   allegory in, 65
   and Foucault, 63
   as ecoparable, 43
   as textual memorial, 59
   bewitchment in, 69
   blackness in, 34, 37, 52, 64, 71, 74
   colonialism in, 45, 66, 69
   decolonization in, 69, 71
   metamorphosis in, 44, 65
   monstrosity in, 63, 64, 67
   sites of difference in, 66
Montero, Mayra, 40, 187, 188
Moraña, Mabel, 36, 42
Moreno, Marisel, 10, 12
Morocco, 207, 216
Movimento Popular de Libertação de Angola (MPLA), 107, 133, 134
   support by Cuban troops, 135
   victory, 135, 139
Mudimbe, V.Y., 31, 71
Mutua, Makau, 167

N'Diaye, Joseph, 156, 157
National Liberation Front of Angola. *See Frente Nacional de Libertação de Angola (FNLA)*
National Union for the Total Independence of Angola. *See União Nacional para a Independência Total de Angola (UNITA)*
Négritude, 104
neoliberal era, 2, 6, 23, 28, 29, 34, 35, 41, 63, 71, 74
neoliberalism, 44, 57, 159, 170, 172
   and Badagry, 29, 89, 112, 115, 210
   and Cuba, 79
   policies of, 44, 45, 89
   system of, 43, 45
Neto, Agostinho, 134
New Journalism, 123, 124, 132, 135, 137, 139
   and testimonio, 137
   in García Márquez, 137, 138
Ngũgĩ wa Thiong'o, 65, 170
Nigeria, 1, 6, 86, 113
Nixon, Richard, 135
Nkrumah, Kwame, 145
Non-Aligned Movement, 77, 92
Nora, Pierre, 3, 19

Obama, Barack, 24, 162
Obejas, Achy, 2, 5–10, 28, 29, 76–82, 205 *See also* *Ruins*
   and Cuban identity, 79, 80, 90
   and World Literature, 78
   critique of neoliberalism in, 105, 110, 115, 116, 210, 211
   Havana Noir, 9
   on Cuban tourism, 83
   on the Cuban Revolution, 92
Ondjaki, 146, 147
"Operación Carlota" (García Márquez), 30, 119, 121, 126, 132–41, 147
   as memorial to Carlota, 141
   as site of memory, 121
   Latin-African lens on, 142
Operación Carlota (mission), 30, 119, 133, 134, 135
   as memorial to Cuban internationalism, 142
   García Márquez's memorialization of, 127
   South African retreat, 139
oral histories, 19, 20, 87, 88
oral proverbs, 87, 181, 200 *See also* proverbs
oral traditions, 3, 20, 87
Organization for Economic Cooperation and Development (OECD), 28
Ouidah, 21–36, 46–61, 66, 89, 198, 208
   and Dahomey kingdom, 50, 57
   and politics of memory, 61
   as site of difference, 66
   as site of memory, 59, 62
   as source of disease, 53, 55
   emotional potency of, 61
   fish adoration in, 200
   heritage tourism in, 58, 59, 62
   in Díaz, 209, 210
   in memoires, 63
   memorial site in, 57, 61, 62, 67
   place des enchères, 59
   port of departure, 67
   Porte de non-retour, 209
   rehabilitation of Vodun in, 58
   Route de l'Esclave, 57, 58, 59, 60, 75, 209
   Slave Route Museum, 62
   spiritual power of, 63
   zombie in, 75

Paris, 7, 48, 94
Paz, Octavio, 166
People's Movement for the Liberation of Angola. *See* Movimento Popular de Libertação de Angola (MPLA)
Pérez, Emma, 187, 214
   Forgetting the Alamo, or, Blood Memory, 187, 214, 215
Phillips, Thomas, 34, 54, 66, 67

physical memorials, 1, 2, 20, 24–30, 35, 47, 61, 180
   and memorialization, 59
   fictionality of, 59
   in literature, 172
   in Senegal, 156
   of Stanley, 163
Picasso, Pablo, 76, 78, 94, 95, 96, 97, 98
plantocracy, 32, 35, 38, 41–7, 69, 74
   history of, 31, 46
   in Cuba, 78, 93, 110, 113, 211
   in Haiti, 66, 68
   in Latin America, 148
   in the Caribbean, 37
   in US Southwest, 162, 165, 187, 190, 202
   life under, 45, 47
Poniatowska, Elena, 8
Port-au-Prince, 37, 44
Portugal, 29, 30, 31, 119, 133, 144
   African colonies of, 133, 135
   and Angolan independence, 127, 133, 134, 227 n. 42
   Angolan exiles in, 147
   exploitation of Angola, 133
   García Márquez on, 138
   US support of in Africa, 145
Pratt, Mary Louise, 31, 167
Prensa Latina, 10, 119, 124
proverbs, 19, 20, 50, 60, 61, 209 *See also* oral proverbs
Puerto Rico, 1, 4, 12
Puga, Maria Luisa, 171, 172

Quayson, Ato, 8, 210, 217, 218
Quijano, Aníbal, 13

rafters. *See* balseros
Ramírez, Dixa, 40, 229 n. 7
Relation du Royaume de Judas en Guinée, 34, 55, 68, 69
Rivera, Tomás, 5–9, 30, 31, 32, 160, 180, 205 *See also* "Searching at Leal Middle School"
   and Chicano awakening, 165
   and García Márquez, 165
   and Latin America, 166
   and Stanley, 160, 162, 164, 166
   influence of *In Darkest Africa* on, 171
   interrogation of capitalism in, 179
   on US Mexico borderland, 171
Rodriguez, Ralph, 9, 215
Ruins (Obejas), 5, 10, 29, 76, 77, 81, 88, 90, 210
   and Angolan and Cuban narratives, 110, 112
   Badagry in, 29, 77, 85, 86, 90
   memory of Africa in, 106
   race in, 79
   the special period in, 79

safari, 102, 105, 106, 111 *See also* African safari
Saint Thomas Aquinas, 100, 101
Saint-Domingue, 38, 47, 48, 53, 70, 131
Saldaña-Portillo, María Josefina, 11, 17, 71
Saldívar, José David, 11, 16, 74, 169, 170, 180, 183, 223 n. 17
Saldívar, Ramón, 180, 199, 201
Sánchez Prado, Ignacio, 8, 171, 216
Sandoval, Alonso de, 31, 34, 50–6, 71, 164, 181, 185, 189, 192
Sans Souci citadel, 48, 49, 62
Santería, 109
Santo Domingo (Dominican Republic), 33
Sarr, Felwine, 94
Savimbi, Jonas Malheiro, 134, 138
Savoy, Bénédicte, 94
scramble for Africa, 6, 30, 31, 166, 178, 203
 and Manifest Destiny, 165
 and Rivera, 160, 170
 and Stanley, 170
 moral justification for, 168
Seabrook, William, 56, 62, 68
"Searching at Leal Middle School" (Rivera), 5, 32, 160, 172, 212
 and Mexican literature, 171
 and Stanley, 166, 169, 172
 as literary memorial of Africa and Congo, 172
 biases in, 172
 textual memorial in, 180
Sékou Touré, Ahmed, 143
Senegal, 1, 6, 86, 121, 156 *See also* Gorée
 Cuban and Puerto Rican music in, 218
 in *Crónica*, 129, 131
 Saint-Louis, 217
 slave ship from, 119, 121, 131, 156
 slaves from, 140, 148, 155, 156, 157
serpent, 46, 50, 52, 60, 61, 68, 188, 189
 as deity, 50, 190, 209
 in *Bless Me, Ultima*, 189
Shaka Zulu, 109, 110
Sharpe, Christina, 14, 26, 128, 129, 131
Siskind, Mariano, 121, 122, 158
sites of memory, 2, 3, 19–26, 35, 57, 62, 115
 African memory, 2, 21, 164
 and capitalism, 24, 35, 211
 and oral history, 3, 21, 59
 emotion and, 26
 in Gorée, 156
 in Ouidah, 59
 in *Ruins*, 92, 99, 107
 in "Searching," 176
 texts as, 19, 23, 158
Slaughter, Joseph, 18
slave trade, 1, 27, 28, 35, 37, 46, 52, 55, 58, 61, 88, 150, 177, 210, 217

and Chicano imaginary, 160, 184
and curanderismo, 185
and Stanley, 168
and the Atlantic Ocean, 88
and the slave ship, 128
archive of, 114
carp worship during, 190
diaspora of, 113
erasure of Black bodies in, 131
in *Crónica*, 119
in East Africa, 177
in *Ruins*, 105, 108
in the Caribbean, 121, 155
memorialization of, 58, 89
textual memorial of, 121
snake. *See* serpent
South Africa, 6, 11, 15, 30, 84, 135 *See also* apartheid
 and threat to Cuban interests in Angola, 103
 attack on Angola by, 107, 135
 US pressure on, 135
South-South alliances, 75, 102
South-South framework, 2, 7–12, 18, 116, 191, 216
South-South history, 27
Soviet Union, 76, 90, 107
Soyinka, Wole, 24, 29, 78, 87, 100, 104
 and Marxism, 103
 and support of decolonization in Nigeria, 100
 critique of discourses about Africa, 104
 critique of neocolonialism, 116, 170
 in *Ruins*, 101, 114
 on Badagry, 89, 210
 on Ouidah, 209, 250 n. 4
Spain, 31, 90, 217
special period (in Cuba), 11, 29, 76, 77, 84, 85, 106, 111, 114
 collective memory during, 90
 dependency during, 78, 108
 in *Ruins*, 81, 84
 ruins of, 91
 tourist reaction to, 80
Stanley, Henry Morton, 6, 22, 31, 32, 52, 160, 167 *See also In Darkest Africa*
 and Africa as a "dark continent," 203
 and Livingstone, 168
 and slave trade, 168
 and the Congo, 162, 168, 172
 as imperialist, 168, 170
 in Rivera, 161
 memorialization of, 166, 168
 statues of in Kinshasa and Denbigh, 176
Surwillo, Lisa, 67, 150, 151
Sweet, James, 110

Tansi, Sony Labou, 181, 194, 195, 199
 and García Márquez, 194

golden carp in, 191, 195, 196
L'État honteux, 195, 216
Les sept solitudes de Lorsa Lopez, 126, 194, 195
Tanzania, 100, 104, 167
Tchivéla, Tchichellé, 194
Tepoztlán Institute, 8
testimonio (literary genre), 132, 135, 137, 139, 156
textual memorials, 1–4, 20–30, 61, 121
  and memorialization, 59
  and moral justification of slavery, 71
  golden carp as, 199
  in Anaya, 163, 199
  in *Crónica*, 121, 126, 149
  in Fanon, 103
  in García Márquez, 120, 121, 139, 156, 211
  in Hemingway, 105
  in literature, 172, 206
  in "Monstro," 59, 62, 74
  in Rivera, 163, 167, 179
  in *Ruins*, 90, 100, 115
  in "Searching," 176, 178, 179, 180
  of Badagry, 90
  of Latin-Africa, 59, 206, 208
  relationship with physical memorials of, 156
Tonn, Horst, 183
Torres-Saillant, Silvio, 38, 223 n. 16
transatlantic connection, 1, 17, 46, 58
transatlantic studies, 1, 5, 10, 11, 18, 20
Tree of Forgetfulness, 59
Tripartite Agreement, 107
Trouillot, Michel-Rolph, 49, 50
Trujillo Molina, Rafael Leónidas and the *Trujillato*, 39, 40
Tuan, Yi-Fu, 179

UN General Assembly, 92
UNESCO, 28, 85, 86, 89, 141, 157, 206, 208
  Collection of Representative Works, 206
  neoliberalism and, 212
  World Literature in, 206
UNESCO Slave Route Project, 1, 2, 6, 19–28, 35, 46–9, 57, 61, 76, 77, 163, 178, 205, 217
  advent of, 28, 77, 90
  and memorialization, 3, 158, 208
  and Vodun, 35
  in Haiti, 48
  in Hartman, 89
  in Malawi, 177
  in Rivera and Anaya, 204
  in *Ruins*, 86
  in Senegal, 121, 156
União Nacional para a Independência Total de Angola (UNITA), 107, 134
  US aid to, 146

Vansina, Jan, 19, 225 n. 31
visiting texts while reading sites, 1, 2, 3, 23
Vodun, 28–35, 46–56, 58, 60, 61, 68, 69
  African practitioners of, 63, 64, 69
  and bewitchment, 68
  and disease, 56
  and fear, 57, 59, 209, 210, 213
  and festival Ouidah 92, 57
  and grave robbery, 69
  and healing, 56
  as devil worship, 192
  as source of rebellion, 48
  demonization of, 57
  discourse regarding, 62
  distortion of, 56, 57, 68
  ethnographic accounts of, 54
  female leaders of, 54, 55
  gender-nonconformity in, 55, 56
  historiography of, 189
  history of, 57
  in Alvarez, 40
  in Benin, 36, 58, 59, 209
  in *Bless me, Ultima*, 162, 181, 187, 188
  in Carpentier, 48, 49
  in Haiti, 46, 47
  in Montero, 40
  in Ouidah, 36, 69
  in Seabrook, 56, 62
  in US Southwest, 189
  in West Africa, 57
  proverbs from, 60
  rituals in Caribbean literature, 189
  sacred sites of, 57
  slave practitioners of, 47, 59, 66, 68
  trances in, 50, 68, 188
  transferal to the New World, 69
  voodoo, 162, 164
  zombies in, 28, 61, 63

Walsh, Rodolfo, 124, 125, 137
Well of Attenuation, 87, 88
West Africa, 4, 20, 31–5, 46, 52, 54, 61, 67, 70
  colonial rule in, 55
  epistemology of, 75
  ethnographies of, 56, 73
  IMF and the World Bank in, 89
  mambí in, 73
  religious praxis, 189
  spirituality in, 32
  trade route from, 131
Wolfe, Tom, 123, 137, 138
World Bank, 78, 57, 89
World Literature, 5–12, 19, 222 n. 11
  Africa in, 79, 170, 207
  African writers in, 207

World Literature (cont.)
  and Anaya, 165, 198, 202, 203
  and *Crónica*, 125, 126
  and Díaz, 8, 37, 75, 205
  and García Márquez, 7, 156
  and Obejas, 9, 78, 205
  and Rivera, 165, 166, 178, 180, 203
  and transnational dimensions, 10
  Chicano and Mexican literature in, 171, 181
  eurocentrism in, 7, 207, 219
  Latin-Africa in, 158, 164
  magical realism in, 122, 158
  marketing of Latinx literature in, 9, 165
  reception of Chicano and Latinx authors in, 8
  South Atlantic studies in, 116
  the "global" in, 204

zombie apocalypse, 35, 36, 60, 63, 197
zombies, 6, 17, 28–37, 42, 44–52, 62, 63, 64, 68, 209
  and capitalism, 41
  and grave robbery, 69
  and Vodun, 47, 55, 57, 61, 62
  as allegory, 64
  as demon, 68
  as deracinated slave, 52
  as signifier of difference, 59
  as signifier of sin, 50
  as textual memorial, 75
  decolonization of, 69, 73
  discourse of, 74
  distortion of, 47
  economics of, 42
  Eurocentric perception of, 57, 209
  evolution of, 36, 37, 63
  fear of, 29, 46
  in Africa, 47
  in "Monstro," 34, 35, 59, 63, 65, 73, 75
  in pop culture, 56
  monstrosity of, 63
  new zombies, 42, 43, 44, 45, 72
  rehabilitation of, 75
  rejection of, 65
  reproduction of in America, 52
  transformation of, 64, 66, 71

For EU product safety concerns, contact us at Calle de José Abascal, 56–1°,
28003 Madrid, Spain or eugpsr@cambridge.org.

www.ingramcontent.com/pod-product-compliance
Lightning Source LLC
LaVergne TN
LVHW041622060526
838200LV00040B/1389